T0074173

Quantum-Safe Cryptography Algorithms and Approaches

Quantum Computing

Edited by
Pethuru Raj and Abhishek Kumar

Quantum-Safe Cryptography Algorithms and Approaches

Impacts of Quantum Computing on Cybersecurity

Edited by
Satya Prakash Yadav, Raghuraj Singh, Vibhash Yadav,
Fadi Al-Turjman and Swarn Avinash Kumar

DE GRUYTER

Editors

Dr. Satya Prakash Yadav
G.L. Bajaj Institute of Technology
and Management
Department of Computer Science
and Engineering
Kalam Road, Plot No. 2
Greater Noida 201306
Uttar Pradesh
India
prakashyadav.satya@gmail.com

Federal Institute of Education, Science,
and Technology of Ceará (IFCE)
Graduate Program in
Telecommunications Engineering (PPGET)
Fortaleza-CE
Brazil

Prof. Dr. Raghuraj Singh
Professor, School of Engineering
Computer Science and Engineering Department
&
Dean, Harcourt Butler Technical University
Planning and Resource Generation
Kanpur 208002
Uttar Pradesh, India

&
Ex. Director
Kamla Nehru Institute of Technology
Sultanpur, Uttar Pradesh, India
rscse@rediffmail.com

Dr. Vibhash Yadav
Rajkiya Engineering College
Department of Information Technology
Banda 210201
Uttar Pradesh
India
vibhashds10@gmail.com

Prof. Dr. Fadi Al-Turjman
Near East University
Research Center for AI and IoT,
AI and Robotics Institute
Mersin 10
Turkey
fadi.alturjman@neu.edu.tr

Swarn Avinash Kumar
Indian Institute of Information Technology,
Allahabad
Department of Information Technology
Priya Shringar Kendra, 4, IIIT Rd
Jhalwa, Prayagraj 211012
Uttar Pradesh
India
swarnavinashkumar@ieee.org

ISBN 978-3-11-079800-5
e-ISBN (PDF) 978-3-11-079815-9
e-ISBN (EPUB) 978-3-11-079836-4
ISSN 2940-0112

Library of Congress Control Number: 2023935789

Bibliographic information published by the Deutsche Nationalbibliothek
The Deutsche Nationalbibliothek lists this publication in the Deutsche Nationalbibliografie;
detailed bibliographic data are available on the internet at http://dnb.dnb.de.

© 2023 Walter de Gruyter GmbH, Berlin/Boston
Cover image: Vitalii Gulenok/iStock/Getty Images Plus
Typesetting: Integra Software Services Pvt. Ltd.
Printing and binding: CPI books GmbH, Leck

www.degruyter.com

MIX
Papier | Fördert
gute Waldnutzung
FSC
www.fsc.org   FSC® C083411

Preface

Quantum computers from various established technology giants have demonstrated that they have the inherent potential to outperform classical computers in many areas. Especially in real-time analytics of big data, quantum computing (QC) has strongly established its superiority. Worldwide researchers in the past decade have built and deployed quantum computers for multiple use cases including homeland security, drug discovery, genome engineering, etc. Some researchers pursue quantum computing's potential to unlock the secrets of physics and to facilitate the development of new chemicals to aid the welfare of the humanity. Quantum computing is being increasingly used for artificial intelligence (AI) applications. With clouds being proclaimed as the one-stop IT solution for business automation needs, there is a rush of deploying quantum computers in cloud environments. Quantum computing as a service (QCaaS) is the latest service offering of cloud service providers.

The goal of this book is to facilitate and stimulate cross-disciplinary research initiatives and implementations in the cybersecurity domain due to the continuous advancements in the paradigm of quantum computing. Today, there are small-scale quantum computers getting produced and installed in hyperscale cloud environments in order to deliver quantum computing as a service. Industry professionals and academic researchers are able to access the distinct capabilities of quantum computing today without any hitch or hurdle. However, the rise of quantum computing has brought in a series of positive and negative implications. One of the major impacts is that the currently available cryptography algorithms are bound to be broken when a powerful quantum computer get built and released. Quantum computers can process big data easily. They can do computation thousands of times faster than the classical computers. Such a tremendous speed is being seen as a huge problem for traditional cryptographic algorithms. This book is to dig deep and dwell at length on the various impacts of quantum computing and how the impending challenges and concerns can be surmounted through quantum-resistant cryptography algorithms.

The main focus of this book is to bring all the related technologies, novel findings, and managerial applications of Quantum Information Science on a single platform to provide great readability, easy understanding, and smooth adaptability of various basic and advanced concepts to undergraduate and postgraduate students, researchers, managers, designers, academicians, and practitioners doing work in this domain.

https://doi.org/10.1515/9783110798159-202

Contents

Biographies

Dr. Satya Prakash Yadav is Associate Professor at the Department of Computer Science and Engineering, GL Bajaj Institute of Technology and Management (GLBITM), Greater Noida (India). He has awarded his Ph.D. degree entitled "Fusion of Medical Images in Wavelet Domain" to Dr. A. P. J. Abdul Kalam Technical University (AKTU) (formerly UPTU). A seasoned academician having more than 14 years of experience, he has published four books (*Programming in C, Programming in C++,* and *Blockchain and Cryptocurrency*) with I.K. International Publishing House Pvt. Ltd., including *Distributed Artificial Intelligence: A Modern Approach,* published in 2020 by CRC Press. He has undergone industrial training programs during which he was involved in live projects with companies in the areas of SAP, Railway Traffic Management Systems, and Visual Vehicles Counter and Classification (used in the metro rail network design). He is an alumnus of Netaji Subhas Institute of Technology (NSIT) at Delhi University. A prolific writer, Dr. Yadav has published two patents and authored many research papers in web of science indexed journals. Additionally, he has presented research papers at many conferences in the areas of Image Processing, Information retrieval, Features extraction and Programming, Digital Image Processing, Feature Extraction, Information Retrieval, C, C++, C#, Data Structure, and Java. Also, he is a lead editor at CRC Press, Taylor and Francis Group Publisher (USA), Tech Science Press (Computer Systems Science and Engineering), International Springer Publisher, Science Publishing Group (USA), and Eureka Journals, Pune (India).

Dr. Raghuraj Singh is a B.Tech. (CSE), M.S. (Software Systems) and Ph.D. (Computer Science and Engineering) from U.P. Technical University. He has about 23 years of experience in teaching. Currently, he is Head of Department of CSE in HBTU Kanpur. He has guided 7 Ph.D. and 17 M.Tech., and several B.E./B.Tech. projects. He is the Chairman, Kanpur Chapter, CSI, Life Member of ISTE; Member of the Institution of Engineers (India); Fellow Member of IETE; professional member of ACM; and Senior Member of International Association of IACSIT. He has more than 80 papers in national/international conferences and journals to his credit. Currently, four students are working for Ph.D. and four are pursuing M.Tech. under his guidance.

Dr. Vibhash Yadav holds B.Tech. (CSE) from C.S.J.M University; Kanpur, M.Tech. (CSE) from Maharshi Dayanand University, Rohtak; and Ph.D. (CSE) from Uttrakhand Technical University, Dehradun, India. He has about 14 years of experience in teaching. Currently, he is Associate Professor and Head of IT Department at Rajkiya Engineering College, Banda. He is also a member of CSI, IEEE, etc. Dr. Yadav is also a reviewer of number of reputed journals/conferences and has more than 40 papers in national/international conferences and journals to his credit. Additionally, Prof. Yadav is supervising number of Ph.D./M.Tech. students.

Prof. Dr. Fadi Al-Turjman received his Ph.D. in computer science from Queen's University, Canada, in 2011. He is the Associate Dean for Research and the Founding Director of the International Research Center for AI and IoT at Near East University, Nicosia, Cyprus. Prof. Al-Turjman is the head of Artificial Intelligence Engineering Department, and a leading authority in the areas of smart/intelligent IoT systems, wireless, and mobile networks' architectures, protocols, deployments, and performance evaluation in Artificial Intelligence of Things (AIoT). His publication history spans over 400 SCI/E publications, in addition to numerous keynotes and plenary talks at flagship venues. He has authored and edited more than 40 books about cognition, security, and wireless sensor networks' deployments in smart IoT environments, which have been published by well-reputed publishers such as Taylor and Francis, Elsevier, IET, and Springer. He has received several recognitions and best paper awards at top international conferences. He also received the prestigious Best Research Paper Award from Elsevier's *Computer Communications* journal for the period 2015–2018, in addition to the Top Researcher Award for 2018 at Antalya Bilim University, Turkey. Prof. Al-Turjman has led a number of international symposia and

https://doi.org/10.1515/9783110798159-204

workshops in flagship communication society conferences. Currently, he serves as book series editor and the lead guest/associate editor for several top tier journals, including the *IEEE Communications Surveys and Tutorials* (IF 23.9) and Elsevier's *Sustainable Cities and Society* (IF 7.8), in addition to organizing international conferences and symposiums on the most up to date research topics in AI and IoT.

Mr. Swarn Avinash Kumar is an applied research scientist at Meta Platforms, Inc. (previously Facebook), USA. He has previously worked at AI divisions of Lyft, Google, and Amazon as well. He has a total professional research experience of 9 years with more than 20 publications with reputed, peer-reviewed national and international journals, books, and conferences. His research area includes Artificial Intelligence (AI), computer vision, robotics, data mining, and machine learning. He has filed multiple patents in the field of AI. He has been a reviewer for Springer, IEEE, Hindawi, and IET conferences. He has co-authored two books (published by Institution of Engineering and Technology and Eureka Publications) and edited two books (published and ongoing with Institution of Engineering and Technology and Eureka Publications).

List of contributors

Chapter 1
Dr. J. Albert Mayan
Associate Professor, Department of CSE
Sathyabama Institute of Science and Technology
Chennai, Tamil Nadu, India
albert.cse@sathyabama.ac.in

Dr. G. Swamy Reddy
Associate Professor, Department of Mathematics
S. R. University, Warangal, Telangana, India
swamyreddy.g@gmail.com

Dr. G. Madhava Rao
Professor, Department of Mathematics
Malla Reddy University, Hyderabad, Telangana,
India
rao.gmr.madhav@gmail.com

Chapter 2
Dr. Thippeswamy G. R.
Professor, Department of CSE
Don Bosco Institute of Technology, Bangalore,
Karnataka, India
thippeswamygowda9@gmail.com

Ms. Preethi M. P.
Software Engineer, Sonata Software Company
Bangalore, Karnataka, India
preethi.papanna@gmail.com

Dr. Buli Yohannis Tasisa
Associate Professor, Dambi Dollo University
Dambi Dollo, Ethiopia
buliyohannis99@gmail.com

Chapter 3
Dr. R. Menaka
Associate Professor, Department of ECE
Chennai Institute of Technology, Chennai,
Tamil Nadu, India
menaka.govindaraj@gmail.com

Dr. S. Thenmalar
Associate Professor, Department of Networking
and Communications
SRM Institute of Science and Technology
Kattankulathur, Chennai, Tamil Nadu, India
thenmals@srmist.edu.in

Dr. V. Saravanan
Associate Professor, Department of Computer
Science
Dambi Dollo University, Ethiopia
reachvsaravanan@gmail.com

Chapter 4
Dr. M. Sunil Kumar
Professor and Head of Department,
Department of CSE
School of Computing, Mohan Babu University
(erstwhile Sree Vidyanikethan Engineering
College), Tirupathi, Andhra Pradesh, India
sunilmalchi1@gmail.com

Dr. Harsha B. K.
Assistant Professor, Department of ECE
CMR Institute of Technology, Bengaluru,
Karnataka, India
harsha405@gmail.com

Dr. Leta Tesfaye Jule
Physics Department, Dambi Dollo University
Dambi Dollo, Oromia Region, Ethiopia
laterajule@gmail.com

Chapter 5
Dr. N. Karthikeyan
Professor, Department of Computer Science and
Engineering
SNS College of Technology, Coimbatore,
Tamil Nadu, India
profkarthikeyann@gmail.com

https://doi.org/10.1515/9783110798159-205

Mr. P. Sivaprakash
Assistant Professor, Department of Computer
Science and Engineering
PPG Institute of Technology, Coimbatore,
Tamil Nadu, India
sivaprakashcse0402@gmail.com

Dr. K. Periyakaruppan
Professor, Department of Computer Science
and Engineering
SNS College of Engineering, Coimbatore,
Tamil Nadu, India
kperiyakaruppan@gmail.com

Dr. M. Shobana
Assistant Professor, Department of Computer
Science and Engineering
SNS College of Technology, Coimbatore,
Tamil Nadu, India
shobanavsm@gmail.com

Chapter 6
Dr. Deepali Virmani
Professor and Head of Department, B.Tech.
Programmes
Vivekananda Institute of Professional Studies
Technical Campus, School of Engineering and
Technology, Delhi, India
deepalivirmani@gmail.com

Dr. T. Nadana Ravishankar
Assistant Professor, Department of Data Science
and Business Systems
SRM Institute of Science and Technology,
Chennai, Tamil Nadu, India
nadanart@srmist.edu.in

Mr. Mihretab Tesfayohanis
Department of IT, Dambi Dollo University, Dambi
Dollo, Ethiopia
miremsc2011@gmail.com

Chapter 7
Dr. S. Karthik
Professor and Dean, Department of Computer
Science and Engineering
SNS College of Technology, Coimbatore,
Tamil Nadu, India
profskarthik@gmail.com

Ms. Thenmozhi
Research Scholar, Department of Computer
Science and Engineering
SNS College of Technology, Coimbatore,
Tamil Nadu, India
then.shan.in@gmail.com

Dr. R. M. Bhavadharini
Associate Professor, Department of Computer
Science and Engineering
VIT Deemed University Chennai 600037,
Tamil Nadu, India
rmbhavadharini@gmail.com

Dr. T. Sumathi
Assistant Professor, Department of Information
Technology
Government College of Engineering
Erode 641032, Tamil Nadu, India
sumathiirtt@gmail.com

Chapter 8
Mrs. Kumari Manisha
Assistant Professor, Department of ECE
Gokaraju Rangaraju Institute of Engineering
and Technology, Hyderabad, Telangana, India
manisha.kx@gmail.com

Dr. V. Dhanunjana Chari
Professor and Dean of School of Sciences
Department of Physics
Malla Reddy University, Maisammaguda,
Dulapally, Hyderabad, Telangana, India
dhanunjay@mallareddyuniversity.ac.in

Dr. Leta Tesfaye Jule
Physics Department, Dambi Dollo University
Dambi Dollo, Oromia Region, Ethiopia
laterajule@gmail.com

Chapter 9
Ms. Swati Tiwari
Assistant Professor, Department of Computer
Science
Kalinga University, Chhattisgarh, India
swati.tiwari@kalingauniversity.ac.in

Mr. Kamlesh Kumar Yadav
Assistant Professor, Department of IT
Kalinga University, Chhattisgarh, India
kamleshkuyadav05@gmail.com

Dr. D. Palanikkumar
Professor, Department of CSE, Dr. NGP Institute
of Technology
Coimbatore, Tamil Nadu, India
palanikkumard@gmail.com

Chapter 10
Dr. Kaushal Kishor
Professor, IT Department, ABES Institute of
Technology
Ghaziabad, Uttar Pradesh, India
kaushal.kishor@abesit.in
kaushal.rastogi07@gmail.com

Chapter 11
Dr. B. Aruna Devi
Professor, Department of Electronics and
Communication Engineering
Dr. NGP Institute of Technology, Coimbatore,
Tamil Nadu, India
arunadevi@drngpit.ac.in

Dr. N. Alangudi Balaji
Professor, Department of CSE
Koneru Lakshmaiah Education Foundation,
Vaddeswaram, Vijayawada, Andhra Pradesh,
India
alangudibalaji@gmail.com

Dr. Mulugeta Tesema
Department of Chemistry (Analytical)
Dambi Dollo University, Dambi Dollo, Ethiopia
efa.ntust@gmail.com

Chapter 12
Dr. Kaushal Kishor
Professor, IT Department, ABES Institute of
Technology
Ghaziabad, Uttar Pradesh, India
kaushal.kishor@abesit.in

Chapter 13
Dr. Shally Nagpal
Assistant Professor, Panipat Institute of
Engineering and Technology
Samalkha, Panipat, Haryana, India
shally.ngpl@gmail.com

Dr. Puneet Garg
Assistant Professor, ABES Engineering College
Ghaziabad, Uttar Pradesh, India
puneetgarg.er@gmail.com

Ms. Shivani Gaba
Assistant Professor, Panipat Institute of
Engineering and Technology
Samalkha, Panipat, Haryana, India
sgsgknl@gmail.com

Ms. Alankrita Aggarwal
Associate Professor, Panipat Institute of
Engineering and Technology
Samalkha, Panipat, Haryana, India
alankrita.agg@gmail.com

Chapter 14
Ms. Swati Gupta
Assistant Professor, Vaish College of Engineering
Rohtak, Haryana, India
swati.mangla.555@gmail.com

Dr. Puneet Garg
Assistant Professor, ABES Engineering College
Ghaziabad, Uttar Pradesh, India
puneetgarg.er@gmail.com

Chapter 15
Dr. Annapantula Sudhakar
Associate Professor, Department of ECE, GMR
Institute of Technology
Rajam, Andhra Pradesh, India
sudhakar.a@gmrit.edu.in

Dr. G. R. S. Murthy
Professor, Department of CSE, GVPCDPGC(A),
E & T Program
Rushikonda Campus, Visakhapatnam, Andhra
Pradesh, India
murthy.grs@gmail.com

Dr. Thirukumaran S.
Associate Professor, Data Science Department
SoS.B2
Jain University, Bangalore, Karnataka, India
s.thirukumaran@jainuniversity.ac.in

Chapter 16
Dr. Sreelatha P.
Professor, Department of Biomedical
Engineering
KPR Institute of Engineering and Technology
Arasur, Tamil Nadu, India
sreelathaselvaraj@gmail.com

Dr. Nitin Purohit
Associate Professor, Department of Computer
Science
Kebri Dehar University, Kebri Dehar, Somali
Region, Ethiopia
nitinpurohit111@kdu.edu.et

Dr. S. Chandra Sekaran
Professor, Department of CSE, PSV College of
Engineering and Technology
Krishnagiri, Tamil Nadu, India
chandrudpi@gmail.com

Chapter 17
Dr. Kaushal Kishor
Professor, IT Department, ABES Institute of
Technology
Ghaziabad, Uttar Pradesh, India
kaushal.kishor@abesit.in
kaushal.rastogi07@gmail.com

Chapter 18
Dr. Ayushi Prakash
Department of Computer Science and
Engineering
ABES Engineering College, Ghaziabad,
Uttar Pradesh, India
ayushi5edu@gmail.com

Ms. Sandhya Avasthi
Department of Computer Science and
Engineering
ABES Engineering College, Ghaziabad,
Uttar Pradesh, India
sandhya_avasthi@yahoo.com

Dr. Pushpa Kumari
Chemistry Department, Lok Maha Vidyalaya
Chapra, Bihar, India
drpushpakumari5@gmail.com

Dr. Mukesh Rawat
Department of Computer Science and
Engineering
Meerut Institute of Engineering and Technology
Meerut, Uttar Pradesh, India
mukesh.rawat@miet.ac.in

Dr. Puneet Garg
Department of Computer Science and
Engineering
ABES Engineering College, Ghaziabad,
Uttar Pradesh, India
puneetgarg.er@gmail.com

Chapter 19
Dr. S. Karthik
Professor and Dean, Department of Computer
Science and Engineering
SNS College of Technology, Coimbatore,
Tamil Nadu, India
profskarthik@gmail.com

Ms. H. Summia Parveen
Research Scholar, Department of Computer
Science and Engineering
SNS College of Technology, Coimbatore,
Tamil Nadu, India
summiaparveen@yahoo.in

Dr. R. Sabitha
Professor, Department of Computer Science and
Engineering
SNS College of Technology, Coimbatore,
Tamil Nadu, India
dr.r.sabitha@gmail.com

Dr. B. Anuradha
Professor, Department of Computer Science and
Design
SNS College of Engineering, Coimbatore,
Tamil Nadu, India
pskanu80@gmail.com

Chapter 20
Dr. M. S. Kavitha
Associate Professor, Department of Computer
Science and Engineering
SNS College of Technology, Coimbatore,
Tamil Nadu, India
drmskavitha@yahoo.com

Mr. Ramachandra Rao G.
Research Scholar, Department of Computer
Science and Engineering
SNS College of Technology, Coimbatore,
Tamil Nadu, India
grrsoft30@gmail.com

Dr. K. Sangeetha
Professor and Head, Department of Computer
Science and Engineering
SNS College of Technology, Coimbatore,
Tamil Nadu, India
sangithaprakash@gmail.com

Dr. A. Kowshika
Assistant Professor, Department of Information
Technology
SNS College of Engineering, Coimbatore,
Tamil Nadu, India
shika2906@gmail.com

Chapter 21
Dr. J. Shanthini
Professor, Department of Computer Science and
Engineering
Dr. NGP Institute of Technology, Coimbatore,
Tamil Nadu, India
drjshanthini@gmail.com

Ms. R. Sathya
Research Scholar, Department of Computer
Science and Engineering
Dr. NGP Institute of Technology, Coimbatore,
Tamil Nadu, India
sathyagbsri@gmail.com

Dr. K. Sri Hari
Professor, Department of Computer Science and
Engineering
SNS College of Technology, Coimbatore,
Tamil Nadu, India
harionto@gmail.com

Dr. A. Christopher Paul
Associate Professor, Department of Information
Technology
Karpagam Institute of Technology, Coimbatore,
Tamil Nadu, India
profachristo@gmail.com

J. Albert Mayan*, G. Swamy Reddy, G. Madhava Rao

1 Optimizing the traffic flow in VANETs using deep quantum annealing

Abstract: We have developed an optimization for the traffic flow in VANETs using deep quantum annealing. Deep quantum annealing is designed to maintain an optimal traffic flow without congestion in smart cities. Careful considerations are made to improve the flow in a manner that is better than the conventional methods. Simulation is carried out to test the efficacy of deep quantum annealing in VANETs. The results show that the proposed method achieves higher rate of accuracy in maintaining the traffic flow than expected.

1.1 Introduction

In order to reduce traffic accidents and save more lives, it is crucial that more modern vehicles be built with computing and wireless communication facilities that allow them to connect to the internet and other vehicles. Due to these, we can hope to see fewer traffic fatalities. VANETs [1, 2] are a special case of mobile ad hoc networks in which a collection of automobiles collaborates to build a network. VANETs are multi-hop wireless networks with a dynamic topology, caused by the mobility of its nodes. This occurs because of the nonstop motion of the mobile node.

Vehicle-to-vehicle (V2V) [3, 4] and vehicle-to-infrastructure (V2I) [5, 6] communication, in which motor vehicles exchange data with one another and with roadside infrastructure units (RSUs), are made possible by VANETs. Each RSU acts as a gateway by collecting data packets from the connected vehicles and uploads them to the network. The radio source units (RSUs) are the backbone of VANET communications, together with other devices like the application unit (AU) and the onboard unit (OBU) [6].

The OBU in the cars handles wireless communications; the AU is linked to the OBU via wireless or cable connections to provide in-car communication services. The OBU is a key part of VANETs that permits a wide range of user actions, such as managing traffic flow, enforcing security measures, and re-routing information [7].

*Corresponding author: J. Albert Mayan, Department of CSE, Sathyabama Institute of Science and Technology, Chennai, Tamil Nadu, India, e-mail: albert.cse@sathyabama.ac.in

G. Swamy Reddy, Department of Mathematics, S. R. University, Warangal, Telangana, India, e-mail: swamyreddy.g@gmail.com

G. Madhava Rao, Department of Mathematics, Malla Reddy University, Hyderabad, Telangana, India, e-mail: rao.gmr.madhav@gmail.com

https://doi.org/10.1515/9783110798159-001

Because of these features, VANET can use multi-hop communication between cars or with RSUs to send information on traffic conditions, such as accidents and congestion [8]. There are still a number of challenges that need to be resolved, despite the fact that VANETs provide a lot of advantages like predictable mobility, infinite power constraints, variable density, dynamic architecture, and high computation capabilities. The most serious difficulties faced by VANETs include connectivity problems, signal attenuation, insufficient capacity, unsuitable routing, and, finally, insufficient security.

In this work, we develop an optimizing solution for the traffic flow in VANETs using deep quantum annealing. Deep quantum annealing is designed to maintain an optimal traffic flow without congestion in smart cities. Careful considerations are made to improve the flow in a manner that is better than the conventional methods.

1.2 Related works

Drivers can usually choose from a number of different routes in a road network to get where going. This estimation could be enhanced and negative traffic effects mitigated if we made better use of the information at our disposal [8]. Several different routing systems have been built and discussed in the existing literature, and they all make use of IoT, big data, and AI.

In [9], we provide an urban traffic routing system with powerful adaptive learning capabilities. The goal of this system is to provide help to motorists in congested city centers. Multi-agent reinforcement learning, a branch of AI, is used in this strategy to reduce auto traffic. It pairs algorithms and estimates travel expenses by factoring in the unique and changing features of various traffic conditions.

Responsible for creating a smart city traffic management system, the author [10] emphasized the importance of big data throughout their work (travel distance). The New York Traffic Map is used extensively during the whole traffic data collection process. Based on these values, the ARIMA method is applied to compare and analyze data from the previous year to predict traffic congestion. In order to make these estimates, we looked back at information from the previous year. The shortest path between two points in a graph can be found with an enhanced version of the Dijkstra algorithm by selecting the path with the lowest total weight. The shortest path between two points on a graph is calculated in this manner. Next, the proposed system for traffic management is evaluated and optimized with the use of a modern time-forecasting algorithm. Finally, a process flowchart for identifying traffic in a map analysis context has been made public. It is performed with the help of Apache Spark and the R statistical computation, and map analysis tools. The use of both of these methods makes this a reality.

The Internet of Vehicles (IoV), a subset of IoT technology, relies heavily on Vehicular Ad-Hoc Networks (VANET). In order to address traffic issues, VANET is used in a centralized dynamic multi-objective optimization approach, as described by [11].

Each RSU makes an effort to learn about the condition of the road system segment for which it is responsible, and shares that data with others [12–16]. A centralized new approach called SA-VIKOR combines elements of both the VIkOR and Simulated Annealing (SA) methods for finding solutions to complex problems (CSA-VIKOR). Using a cost function in the VIKOR range, the best routes can be chosen for directing cars to their destinations. By considering characteristics such as road traffic signals and road width, the CSA-VIKOR algorithm finds the least congested routes possible. This is accomplished through the MADM approach. Because of this, the algorithm is able to direct traffic along the most direct paths.

1.3 Methods

In this section, with the help of a number of different deep quantum annealing sampling strategies, we evaluate the performance of VANETs, which involves following their L1-norms as they acquire knowledge of a stochastically binarized subset. Both the Inception Score and the Functional Independence Measure were utilized to assign a grade to their overall performance, as in Figure 1.1.

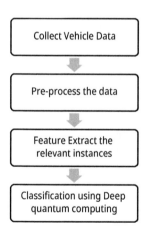

Figure 1.1: Proposed routing model.

It is not as yet clear how to detect the benefits of raising the complexity of the latent space when it comes to deep learning frameworks like the quantum-assisted Helmholtz machine and those that aim to exploit quantum models. While it is easy to demonstrate that more connections lead to a better model, it not so clear how to recognize the advantages of a more intricate latent space.

We found no evidence that the complexity of a latent space model affected the robustness of the resulting latent variable generative model. To get the most out of this application, deep learning frameworks that employ quantum hardware for training in latent spaces should not smooth over any enhancements made feasible by the application via backpropagation. The inclusion of a quantum model in a deep learning system, like the one discussed here, raises questions about whether or not the performance improvement gained from using the model on a brief test task would be noticed. This is due to the fact that it is not known whether the model can tell the difference between a long- and a short-test task.

Given the goals of the presentation and the need to prevent chaining, we have decided to employ a sparse connection model in this specific case. Larger models can be implemented on the upcoming quantum hardware without the need for chaining. Future applications of sampling by quantum annealing are predicted to make use of simpler graphical models due to the requirement of O(n2) more qubits than logical variables for a complete logical graph, the reason being that more qubits are needed for a full logical graph. According to the Moore law, the density of computing resources should double every two years.

Given these constraints, we had to utilize a special kind of neural network called an inception network, which is trained to classify images with 95% accuracy using the MNIST dataset. We came up with a metric we call the Inception Score to measure how convincing a model results appear to be (eq. 1.1). The probability that an image is typical of its category is typically demonstrated by the dominance of a single value of y in the probability distribution $p(y|x)$. Second, there needs to be a fairly balanced distribution of classes across the entire collection, reflecting the diversity in distribution.

$$IS = exp(\mathrm{E}_{x \sim \rho} \mathrm{KL}(p(y|x)||\mathrm{p}(y))). \tag{1.1}$$

To meet the first condition, it is necessary to stipulate that the entropy of the distributions of classes across individual images be low. The first condition will be met if and only if this happens. The second requirement is that there has to be a substantial quantity of entropy spread across the system. The KL distance is calculated to evaluate the dissimilarities between the two distributions: In this case, a high value of y suggests a $p(y)$ distribution with multiple classes and a $p(y|x)$ distribution with a single class. When this score is averaged over all data, it paints a clear picture of the network performance.

1.3.1 Deep quantum computing

Quantum bits, sometimes called qubits, are the smallest data unit that can be handled by quantum computers. A qubit is a two-dimensional quantum mechanical system that can be in one of two fundamental states: 0 or 1. Classical bits of information are encoded in these states (0 and 1, respectively). The system is capable of superposing or existing in both the 0 and 1 states at once. One of the most fundamental characteristics of quantum systems is their ability to exist in every possible state at once. This characteristic is what makes it possible for quantum computers to perform massively parallel computations.

In a two-qubit system, it is feasible that the two qubit states cannot be characterized in isolation from one another. From a mathematical perspective, the state cannot be represented by the product of two unrelated tensors. To describe this effect, we use the term entanglement of the states. However, classical computers may have trouble effectively modeling certain sorts of highly entangled systems, making more modern approaches necessary.

Tensor networks, for example, are well-suited to characterizing systems with only low levels of entanglement. In order for a quantum algorithm to outperform the most advanced classical method, it will need to make heavy use of entanglement. Quantum cryptography, quantum teleportation, and quantum sensing are just three of the many non-computing applications that make use of entanglement.

The more basic set of operations is another feature that sets conventional computing apart from quantum computing. The most elementary components of a computer are binary operations like NOT and AND gates. NOT and AND are the only two Boolean operators that are required to perform any other Boolean operation. However, the Schrödinger equation demonstrates that quantum evolution can be reversed. Quantum behavior is lost whenever measurements or other procedures that impair reversibility are performed. To achieve a quantum gain, use only reversible and unitary gates [17]. Several of these gates have been shown to be universal.

Algorithm 1: Deep quantum computing

In most cases, these five steps are incorporated while developing a quantum algorithm as in Figure 1.2:

Step 1: Encoding the input data into the state of individual qubits is the initial step.

Step 2: The second step is to superpose the qubits over several others (i.e., use quantum superposition).

Step 3: Third, take advantage of quantum entanglement among the qubits simultaneously.

Step 4: Make use of quantum interference.

Step 5: Count the number of qubits or calculate the length of a single qubit (5th step).

Step 6: The outcome of a measurement in quantum physics is sometimes seen as arbitrary.

We define this category and explain the significance of portfolio optimization in this section. Choosing the optimal portfolio is NP-hard, making it difficult, if not impossible, for conventional computers to do. Quantum annealing is the most well-known of the various quantum optimization algorithms.

This article will provide an explanation of adiabatic quantum computation, the mechanism that lies at the core of quantum optimization strategies. The optimization

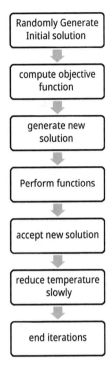

Figure 1.2: Proposed deep quantum algorithm.

problem can be translated into the physical challenge of finding the ground state of the Hamiltonian HP.

Starting with the ground state of an initial Hamiltonian H0, we prepare the system for operation. Because its ground state is readily accessible and well-defined, this initial Hamiltonian was selected. Following this, we subject H0 to a longer adiabatic transition to produce HP. If the lowest energy levels of a system are non-degenerate and the development is slow, then the system will always be in a state remarkably close to the one in which it was initially created, as stated by the adiabatic theorem.

When evolution is fast, the system always returns to a state relatively close to its initial condition. In most cases, the option with the smallest energy difference between the immediate ground and the initial state into which the particle has exited is the one we choose. Once the system has reached the end of its evolutionary phase, it is possible that the HP ground state will be measured. Given how widely used this model is, it should be able to execute any quantum algorithm that is thrown at it.

Quantum annealing is a physical process that can be used to perform an adiabatic quantum computation. As the temperature drops, the solution is unlikely to undergo changes that would make it more troublesome to work with. These bounds are pushed by quantum tunneling phenomena during the annealing phase. In cases where the energy barriers are high and modest, this method explores the terrain of local minima more efficiently than thermal noise does.

Quantum annealing is an approach to quantum computing, although it can be challenging to obtain the conditions necessary for adiabatic computation. Making sure the system evolves adiabatically and chooses the right ground state for the initial Hamiltonian are two instances of this issue. Because of this, quantum annealing can be thought of as a method that comes very near to adiabatic computing. Approximation adiabatic computing was shown by Zagoskin to be able to tackle a problem that was previously regarded to be NP-hard by finding a solution that was almost perfect, in just a polynomial period of time.

1.4 Evaluation

This section assesses the efficiency of the proposed approach to classify the traffic routes. In order to simulate the proposed Deep quantum computing, the values of the parameters were used, the experimental setups that utilized the SUMO traffic generator, and the NS2 network simulator. Its versatility as an object-oriented and event-driven simulator with TCL/OTCL and C++ support makes NS2 a go-to model for researchers and practitioners alike when testing out new network configurations – that is because of how well these elements work together. AODV is used as the routing protocol to send and receive packets of data during this 500-second test.

In addition, 70 vehicles were used in the urban environment and 200 vehicles were used in the rural environment on a testing site spanning 700 m by 700 m. The posted speed limit for motorists in urban areas is typically between 10 and 50 km/h, whereas the rural speed limit is typically between 50 and 100 km/h. In these simulations, cars exchange packets of data with one another in a wireless network environment that is compliant with the IEEE 802.11P standard.

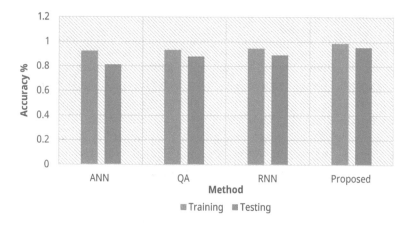

Figure 1.3: Accuracy of traffic flow prediction.

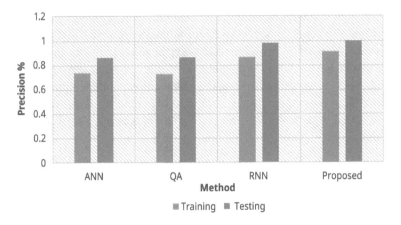

Figure 1.4: Precision of traffic flow prediction.

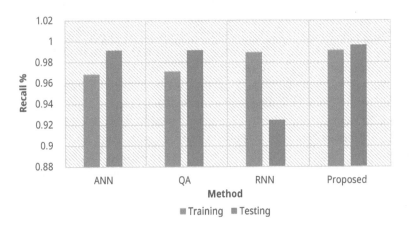

Figure 1.5: Recall of traffic flow prediction.

In these results (Figures 1.3–1.7), UDP serves as the underlying transport protocol, and the packet size of the vehicles is 512 bytes, more so, the traffic uses a constant data rate and the wireless communication between vehicles has a 300-meter range. In addition, we run each of these tests twenty times and average the results. In addition, ten RSUs were utilized throughout the course of these studies in an effort to identify the Sybil attack using the stated and tested techniques. Both the vehicle density in the VANET and the driving patterns of the vehicles are crucial to the success of the strategy, which uses a voting system to verify the positions of the vehicles.

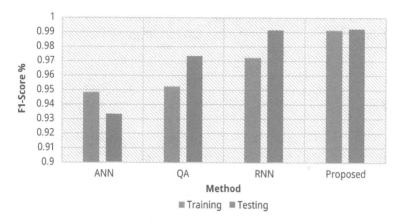

Figure 1.6: F-Measure of traffic flow prediction.

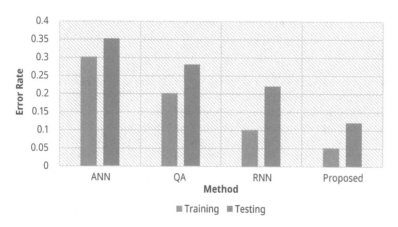

Figure 1.7: Error rate of traffic flow prediction.

1.5 Conclusion

In this work, a deep quantum annealing method is employed to optimize the flow of traffic in VANETs. With the help of deep quantum annealing, smart cities can ensure a steady flow of traffic without backups. In order to improve the flow more effectively than with more conventional methods, careful considerations are made.

Inefficient traffic management is a common cause of traffic congestion, but this issue can be remedied with the help of AI-based technologies that have shown promising results in other areas of transportation. It is possible to reduce emissions, fuel consumption, and environmental impact by prioritizing emergency vehicles like ambulances, firetrucks, and police cars, taking into account the need to prioritize these vehicles. Road traffic management systems can benefit from cloud computing's lower cost and increased efficiency.

References

[1]   Tsai, C. W., Hsia, C. H., Yang, S. J., Liu, S. J., & Fang, Z. Y. (2020). Optimizing hyperparameters of deep learning in predicting bus passengers based on simulated annealing. *Applied Soft Computing*, *88*, 106068.

[2]   Vista, F., Musa, V., Piro, G., Grieco, L. A., & Boggia, G. (2022). Boosting Machine Learning Mechanisms in Wireless Mesh Networks Through Quantum Computing. *Wireless Mesh Networks for IoT and Smart Cities: Technologies and Applications*, *101*, 225.

[3]   Zhang, C., Zhu, C., Li, Y., Nie, M., & Zhu, Y. (2021). Path Integral Monte Carlo Quantum Annealing-based Clustering and Routes Optimization of Clustered UAV Network. In: 2021 12th International Symposium on Parallel Architectures, Algorithms and Programming (PAAP) pp. (92–96). IEEE.

[4]   Yadav, S. P., Bhati, B. S., Mahato, D. P., & Kumar, S. (eds). Federated Learning for IoT Applications. EAI/Springer Innovations in Communication and Computing. Springer, Cham, https://doi.org/10.1007/978-3-030-85559-8.

[5]   Kumar, A., Rajalakshmi, K., Jain, S., Nayyar, A., & Abouhawwash, M. (2020). A novel heuristic simulation-optimization method for critical infrastructure in smart transportation systems. *International Journal of Communication Systems*, *33*(11), e4397.

[6]   Zhang, S., Shi, Y., Zhang, R., & Shen, L. (2018). Roadside units non-full coverage optimization deployment based on simulated annealing particle swarm optimization algorithm. In: 2018 IEEE 4th International Conference on Computer and Communications (ICCC), pp. (544–549). IEEE.

[7]   Kannan, S., Dhiman, G., Natarajan, Y., Sharma, A., Mohanty, S. N., Soni, M., & . . . Gheisari, M. (2021). Ubiquitous vehicular ad-hoc network computing using deep neural network with iot-based bat agents for traffic management. *Electronics*, *10*(7), 785.

[8]   Zhang, D. G., Du, J. Y., Zhang, T., & Fan, H. R. (2020). New method of traffic flow forecasting based on QPSO strategy for Internet of Vehicles. In: 2020 IEEE International Conference on Smart Internet of Things (Smartiot) (pp. 102–108).

[9]   Yadav, S. P. (2022). Blockchain Security. In: Baalamurugan, K., Kumar, S. R., Kumar, A., Kumar, V., Padmanaban, S. (eds). Blockchain Security in Cloud Computing. EAI/Springer Innovations in Communication and Computing, Springer, Cham. https://doi.org/10.1007/978-3-030-70501-5_1.

[10]   Zeynivand, A., Javadpour, A., Bolouki, S., Sangaiah, A. K., Ja'fari, F., Pinto, P., & Zhang, W. (2022). Traffic flow control using multi-agent reinforcement learning. *Journal of Network and Computer Applications*, *207*, 103497.

[11]   Sekaran, S. C., Saravanan, V., RudraKalyanNayak, R., & Shankar, S. S. Human health and velocity aware network selection scheme for WLAN/WiMAX integrated networks with QoS. *International Journal of Innovative Technology and Exploring Engineering*, ISSN, 2278–3075.

[12]   Nama, M., Nath, A., Bechra, N., Bhatia, J., Tanwar, S., Chaturvedi, M., & Sadoun, B. (2021). Machine learning-based traffic scheduling techniques for intelligent transportation system: Opportunities and challenges. *International Journal of Communication Systems*, *34*(9), e4814.

[13] Ouallane, A. A., Bahnasse, A., Bakali, A., & Talea, M. (2022). Overview of Road Traffic Management Solutions based on IoT and AI. *Procedia Computer Science*, *198*, 518–523.

[14] Sepasgozar, S. S., & Pierre, S. (2022). Fed-NTP: A Federated Learning Algorithm for Network Traffic Prediction in VANET. *IEEE Access*.

[15] Hu, X., Li, D., Yu, Z., Yan, Z., Luo, W., & Yuan, L. (2022). Quantum harmonic oscillator model for fine-grained expressway traffic volume simulation considering individual heterogeneity. *Physica A: Statistical Mechanics and Its Applications*, *605*, 128020.

[16] Kannan, S., Dhiman, G., Natarajan, Y., Sharma, A., Mohanty, S. N., Soni, M., & . . . Gheisari, M. (2021). Ubiquitous vehicular ad-hoc network computing using deep neural network with iot-based bat agents for traffic management. *Electronics*, *10*(7), 785.

[17] Maleknasab Ardakani, M., Tabarzad, M. A., & Shayegan, M. A. (2022). Detecting sybil attacks in vehicular ad hoc networks using fuzzy logic and arithmetic optimization algorithm. *The Journal of Supercomputing*, 1–33.

Thippeswamy G. R.*, Preethi M. P., Buli Yohannis Tasisa

2 Quantum annealing-based routing in UAV network

Abstract: The unmanned aerial vehicle, commonly known as a UAV, offers a number of distinct advantages when compared to traditional aircraft, particularly in the event of operations that are boring, unclean, or dangerous. Having access to a large number of UAVs in the event of an emergency can be of aid in the process of decision-making, regardless of whether the support being provided is by the government or by rescue teams. Within the scope of this discussion, unmanned aerial vehicles, also known as UAVs, are frequently utilized in order to capture images of disaster zones in order to immediately update information. UAVs are also used regularly to transport essentials to persons who are stranded in hazardous conditions where traditional vehicles cannot reach. In this work, a quantum annealing-based routing in UAV network is discussed. The simulation shows that the proposed method has higher packet delivery rate than other methods.

2.1 Introduction

Internet of Things (IoT) networks on the ground have made extensive use of unmanned aerial vehicles (UAVs) in information coverage and relay services [1]. This is due to the fact that UAVs have the capability of functioning as well as the quality of the user experience (QoE) for users. UAVs have a significant advantage over conventional vehicles due to the fact that they are not constrained by roads and typically engage in more straightforward obstacle avoidance scenarios [2]. This gives UAVs a distinct advantage over conventional vehicles. As a consequence, UAVs are ideally suited for use in operations during natural catastrophes [3].

For UAVs, the two most important considerations are the assignment of jobs and the planning of flight paths within the context of the application scenarios described previously. The subject of UAV path planning can be broken down into its component parts and analyzed as an optimization problem, subject to a number of constraints [4]. The shortest possible flight distance, the shortest possible flight length, and the highest possible energy efficiency are all elements that contribute to the issue.

*Corresponding author: Thippeswamy G. R.,** Department of CSE, Don Bosco Institute of Technology, Bangalore, India, e-mail: thippeswamygowda9@gmail.com
Preethi M. P., Software Engineer, Sonata Saftwar Company Bangalore, Karnataka, India, e-mail: preethi.papanna@gmail.com.
Buli Yohannis Tasisa, Dambi Dollo University, Dambi Dollo, Ethiopia, e-mail: buliyohannis99@gmail.com.

https://doi.org/10.1515/9783110798159-002

The problem that occurs when trying to allocate tasks to a group of (UAVs) has been solved by employing a wide variety of different strategies and methods. The evolutionary algorithm can be put to a number of uses, one of which is to allocate a large number of agents to a range of tasks that are spread across a number of distinct objectives [5–6]. The planning of cooperative reconnaissance missions using UAVs by employing a genetic algorithm (GA) allowed them to successfully carry out the missions. A model [7] for work planning with the assistance of the modified K-means clustering approach made available by simulated annealing takes into account the many responsibilities that are placed on each UAV.

The authors present a method for hierarchical work assignment that uses mixed-integer programming and the ant colony algorithm to tackle the problem by first deconstructing it into smaller, more manageable assignments. In order to do this, the authors provide a hierarchical work assignment technique. This methodology may be located in [8], and the authors are responsible for its creation. An iterative method was devised in the article [9], which was produced in order to improve the efficiency of work allocation and path planning in distributed applications involving a large number of UAVs. The article was written with the goal of increasing the effectiveness of these processes. A quantum evolutionary-inspired technique is offered in [10] as a means of enhancing the dependability of UAV coalitions in the face of issues associated with job distribution when operating in a dynamic environment. This method seeks to make the most efficient use of available resources while simultaneously reducing the amount of waste produced.

2.2 Related works

A trust evaluation scheme for the IoT that makes use of mobile edge nodes was developed [11]. The problems of congestion and severe energy dissipation are explored in [12]. This system is intended to solve these problems. According to the architecture that has been suggested, it is the responsibility of the source nodes to calculate the adaptive direct trust value, while it is the responsibility of the sink nodes to figure out the indirect trust value. The rapid identification of untrustworthy nodes that is carried out by edge nodes in this scenario helps lower the risk of attacks, as a result of which the threat of assaults is reduced.

With reference to [13], we would like to suggest the implementation of a tactic that is known as virtual force data collection (VFDC). In this strategy, a mobile edge node makes its way to all of the trustworthy nodes in the system and collects data from each of them in order to guarantee that the system is efficient as well as secure. Intelligent Trust Cloud [14] management (ITCM) is an alternative method that is used to evaluate which components of the Internet of Medical Things (IoMT) are unreliable. The first step is the creation of the trust clouds, the second step is establishing them with the help of the fuzzy inference system, and the third step is looking for untrustworthy nodes deep within the structure itself.

According to the author suggestions in [15], the data is gathered from trustworthy nodes by exploiting edge nodes or edge intelligence – a system that makes use of deep reinforcement learning in order to accurately track targets. This strategy is efficient in achieving its objectives, but only at the expense of a significant amount of time and effort invested in computation as well as the consumption of physical resources. When it comes to the IoT in industry, reliability is a crucial component in ensuring that activities are carried out safely. When it comes to a sensor network that is enabled by the cloud, the trustworthiness of each individual node in the network is just as crucial as the routing of the individual nodes in the network. In order to ensure that the node routing process is carried out in an efficient manner, researchers have created a wide variety of optimization methods.

In sensor networks that are based on the IoT, effective pathways for the nodes can be designed with the assistance of optimization. The K-means with Ant Lion Optimization (ALO-K) technique and the K-means with Modified Bee Colony Optimization method are two examples of hybrid clustering methods that were proposed in [16]. Both of these methods are based on the K-means algorithm.

The authors [17] apply a parallelized form to identify and guarantee proper environments. As a preventative measure against cyberattacks, this measure is taken. The authors of [18] discuss the problem of trust in agricultural IoT applications and propose a solution based on blockchain technology as a way to overcome the problem. Despite the fact that it is difficult to implement from a computing standpoint, this technique has a low cost associated with each unit of output that it produces.

According to the reference [19–20], the technology of blockchain was also employed to solve the issue of trustworthiness in digital twins. This was accomplished by using a consensus mechanism. This network is described in this research work. Due to this mechanism, the network is able to supply data that is routed effectively.

The issues of energy consumption and safety are addressed by the aforementioned approaches in a variety of unique and effective ways. Some potential solutions to these issues include trust-based data collecting, optimal routing, and edge node-enabled safe data transfer, to name just a few examples. On the other hand, it has been noted that the level of efficiency and security given by the algorithms suffers at the cost of one another. This is because the algorithms compete with one another for resources. This is due to the fact that some researchers advocate the use of edge nodes for secure and prosperous transmission based on node trust values, while others favor the use of optimum routing to improve the system quality of service characteristics.

Clustered UAV networks call for the execution of a hybrid approach that includes the incorporation of edge node computing in addition to the creation of efficient pathways for the transmission of data. This is necessary in order to meet the requirements of the network. It enables rapid convergence without the normal issues that are connected with finding optimal solutions at a local level. In a similar fashion, it selects dependable nodes by using a technique for determining trustworthiness at each node. The mobile edge node is in a position to efficiently acquire data from all dependable nodes as a result of the route path that was constructed with the assistance of an artificial bee colony optimizer. This is possible because the route path connects all of the nodes.

We are looking into different ways to plan routes for (UAVs) as the problem falls into the NP-Complete class in the vast majority of instances, applied to an enormous degree in order to get the findings that have been sought. The research described in the aforementioned publication resulted in the development of an offline path planner for UAVs, which made use of a differential evolution-based architecture (DE). This planner had the capability of generating 2D routes through a set of waypoints while simultaneously taking into consideration certain coordination restrictions. In addition, researchers have used DE in conjunction with quantum-behaved particle swarm optimization (PSO) with the aim of designing flight routes for UAVs in aquatic environments.

The multi-objective DE offers a potential solution to the challenge of planning the route that synthetic aperture radar UAVs will take. Additionally, DE has been applied to the fields of trajectory tracking and UAV formation, both of which have seen advancements as a result of DE implementation. Popular examples of population-based evolutionary algorithms include the GA and PSO, as well as various variations on both of these algorithms. The researchers then compared the two algorithms and discovered that the GA generated better trajectories than the PSO. In addition to this, GA has been used in multi-objective mission planning for a fleet of UAVs working in conjunction with a number of base stations.

Even though it is not a population-based strategy like DE or GA, the meta-heuristic method known as simulated annealing (SA) is widely used for the goal of finding solutions to problems requiring task and path planning. One example of a scenario in which SA and GA can be used to successfully complete the task at hand is the process of designing a path that comprises three dimensions.

In a different scenario, a number of (UAVs) were programmed with a mixture of the K-means algorithm and the SA algorithm, so that they could do a range of jobs.

2.3 Methods

In this section, we take a look at the issue of how to schedule UAVs when doing so is confined by either a particular time resolution or a maximum allowable flying distance. Both of these factors can make scheduling UAVs difficult. This leads to the design of a universal distance matrix, which is then followed by the development of a model that adds time-balanced restrictions. Ultimately, this leads to the conclusion that the universe is infinite. A discussion is also held regarding the strategy that will be used in order to characterize the issue and produce workable answers as in Figure 2.1.

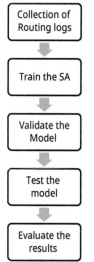

Figure 2.1: Proposed UAV.

We take into account the UAV application scenario, in which a fleet of UAVs will be programmed to leave the depot and fly to a set of predetermined target nodes within a set amount of time and, of course, within the maximum flying distance of each UAV. The target nodes will be predetermined before the fleet of UAVs leaves the depot. This will be completed without exceeding the maximum flying distance of any of the UAVs that are being used. When UAVs are sent out on periodic sensing missions, situations quite similar to these can develop. During these missions, a fleet of UAVs must traverse the ground between predetermined nodes and report back to base with data that has been time-stamped in order to ensure that accurate map updates are supplied on time.

Figure 2.1 is a display of the application scenario model that was created for the purpose of making assignments to UAVs and organizing the flight paths the vehicles will take.

This allows us to generate a single trip that meets all of the requirements. It changes the nature of the problem from one that demands the creation of several different routes to one that if the objective is to travel the shortest possible path between two sites, as illustrated in Figure 2.2, then the process of assigning jobs to many UAVs and designing routes for them is equivalent to the Traveling Salesman Problem (TSP). The constraints that apply to this scenario, on the other hand, are more difficult to comprehend than the restrictions that apply to the TSP, which is a member of the NP-Complete family of problems.

It is imperative that the fact that the target nodes in this scenario are not the same as the job locations be taken into mind. As a result of the fact that UAVs do not have to conduct their work by flying directly over the target nodes, the actual task sites are free to be located anywhere within the vicinity of the target nodes. Images taken from specific job locations by UAVs, such as building sites or disaster zones, can be used as part of the periodic sensing missions that are used to update map data. These missions are carried out by aircraft that are flown by remote control.

However, before making any preparations, it is essential to define the areas that UAVs are required to fly over or remain in. This must be done before any other arrangements can be made. These particular nodes are known as the target nodes in the network. UAVs, which operate in a manner analogous to that of drones, do not necessarily stick to a set path. Despite this, a collection of straight lines can be used to illustrate the fundamental flight order as well as the distances between all of the target nodes. This information can therefore be used for taking into consideration the actual flight distance before it is planned.

2.3.1 Solution

It is possible to express as an array a solution that is practicable for a fleet of UAVs to traverse the target nodes, if the components of the array are positioned in an optimal manner. By employing an array that is analogous to the one used by the TSP, we are able to articulate a method for solving the issue of target scheduling and path planning that can be put into practice. This array contains every target node as well as every virtual depot node; the only difference is that the pathways between the virtual depot nodes are less than ideal.

This objective can be accomplished in one of two ways: first, we can increase the number of virtual depot nodes included in the array of target nodes; second, we can eliminate any distance that exists between any virtual depot nodes.

(UAVs) will be present in a total number of three, and there will be a total of seven nodes that need to be targeted. The number 0 refers to the storage facility, which is the node in question. As the first of four steps, add depot nodes 0 to the beginning and end of the array. After that, as the second step, add depot nodes 1 to the middle of the array. Add depot nodes 0 to the beginning and end of the array, and then add depot nodes 1 to the middle of the array. The first step is to randomly order the array of target nodes; the second step is to randomly select M1 positions from N1 of all; the third step is to add depot nodes 0 to the beginning and end of the array; and the fourth step is to add depot nodes 1 to the middle of the array.

It is vital to keep in mind that the multiple UAVs will really begin their flights at the same moment, despite the fact that the final array of potential solutions looks to be in sequence. This is because the UAVs are designed to take off simultaneously. According to the most recent visiting order, UAV1 is currently in seventh place, UAV2 is in first place, and UAV3 is in fifth place. It is necessary that all three UAVs leave the depot at the same time and return there once they have made a single stop at each of their designated nodes. It is also imperative that they return there once they have completed the mission.

The following are some of the qualities of a solution that are visible in Figure 2.3, which show that it is feasible: the length of the array is $N + M + 1$, it will never have two consecutively appearing virtual depot nodes, and it will always have a leading 0 and a trailing 0 as its first and last values. The length of the array is always $N + M + 1$. It is a function that will return the value "true" if the input array has a solution, but it will return the value "false" if the array does not contain a solution. The first algorithm presents a standard method for determining whether or not a solution that is the result of random permutation is sensible. This technique is presented in the form of an algorithm. In this particular instance, in order to make the operation more time-efficient, we decided not to check the constraints.

By using a technique that is based on an average allocation, we are frequently in a position to provide an estimation of the maximum lengths that a single UAV is capable of covering prior to the execution of an assignment. This will occur because of the fundamental properties of the model. This demonstrates that, in essence, constraints can be validated at the end of each program.

The algorithm was one of the earliest examples of its kind. In the process of dealing with mixed-continuous optimization issues, this step is taken. DE has been shown to be capable of solving generalized combinatorial optimization problems, as can be seen in the previous paragraph.

When utilizing canonical DE, each parameter is constrained by its lowest and maximum bounds, and the process begins with a randomly generated population of NP-D-dimensional vectors (individuals) that encode the potential solutions to the issue. Canonical DE is a type of differential evolution. Due to the UAV scheduling model that was proposed is a combinatorial optimization problem, we were required to modify a standard DE algorithm in order to represent a workable solution as an array that is composed of target nodes and virtual depot nodes in a specific order. This was done in order to ensure that the proposed model could be implemented. Thus, we were able to discover a solution to the problem that would actually work. In order to perform the modification, instead of adding the difference between two vectors, we follow the same line of reasoning as we do when adding the difference between two arrays.

During this stage of the process, the four methods of mutation that are most frequently referenced in scholarly research are put into practice. Due to the similarities in the makeup of the people, the crossover operation of the conventional DE method may be carried out easily. Be aware that in order to guarantee that this is the case, you may need to perform extra operations on top of the ones that were directly generated in the results.

Both the trial array that is formed during the crossover stage and the donor array that is generated during the mutation stage need to have feasible solutions in order for the process to be successful. In just a moment, we are going to go over the process with a great deal more specificity. The selection phase operates in a manner that is akin to that of traditional DE in that it applies the greedy principle to pick the individuals who will constitute the core of the upcoming generation. This phase also functions in a manner that is analogous to that of traditional DE.

Another example of a meta-heuristic approach that has been shown to be successful in combinatorial optimization. The SA algorithm is based on a technique that is known as simulated annealing, and it uses this technique as its starting point. Both the TSP problem and the UAV path planning problem are common applications for SA, and its use to find solutions to these problems is common. This is because combinatorial optimization may be applied to solve both of these problems.

It is necessary to have a representation of the solution, a method for computing the internal energy of the solution, a starting temperature of T0 and an ending temperature of T', as well as a cooling factor, in order to put into practice the traditional SA algorithm. In addition to these things, it is also necessary to have a cooling factor. SA functions in a manner that is akin to the way that minimization occurs naturally by minimizing the difference in value that exists between the value of the function and the energy. It is always permissible to experience a decrease in energy, but it is only appropriate to experience an increase in energy under particular situations. The following are the conditions that must be met: a number that is evenly distributed between the intervals $[0, 1]$ must be smaller than an exponential term, and the probability of accepting solutions that are less optimal decreases as the temperature decreases.

The determination of an acceptable rule to produce a neighboring solution X' from the already existing solution X is the single most critical activity for SA. This proves that SA is not a population-based method and differentiates it from the other two meta-heuristic algorithms. We are of the opinion that the most productive way to produce locally feasible ideas in a timely manner is to use a strategy known as exchange and judge.

The Swap-and-Judge approach was designed with the goal of increasing productivity in terms of the generation of workable solutions, without losing the adaptability with which the solution space can be probed. We are currently able to accomplish this by explicitly selecting the target nodes as well as the virtual nodes for the swap operation.

In the same manner that the mutation and crossover operations in the previously mentioned algorithms might create erroneous swaps, but the risk of it happening here is significantly lower. The swap operation is carried out on the current solution following the judge function, which, in the event that it returns false, causes the random picking operation to be carried out once more until the result is true. This is done in order to guarantee that the surrounding solution is workable. After that, the swap operation is carried out on the existing solution in order to produce the solution immediately adjacent to it.

One alternate strategy that can be used to enhance SA is called the delete-and-replace method. The SA algorithm is produced by substituting the adjacent solution generation approach with the Delete-and-Insert (D&I) method. This transforms the algorithm into an SA process. Before performing the swap operation, this approach requires that all of the virtual nodes in the already implemented solution be removed. Afterwards, the virtual nodes are reintroduced.

2.4 Evaluation

In this section, the performance of a high-end computer with 8 gigabytes of RAM, an i7 CPU core, and Windows 10 is measured using the MATLAB software in order to determine how effective the proposed SA is. Before running the simulation, there are a few parameters that need to be configured first.

The degree to which the system is able to recognize nodes that are not to be trusted is one way in which one may quantify how precise the trust evaluation process is; this is a crucial metric to consider. The graph makes it abundantly clear that the lifetime of the network, which is denoted by the total number of rounds, is determined at three different points: upon the loss of the first node, upon the loss of the second half of the network nodes, and upon the loss of the final node in the network. These three points are distinguished from one another by the fact that the lifetime of the network is determined by the total number of rounds. These three facets can be identified from one another in a straightforward manner.

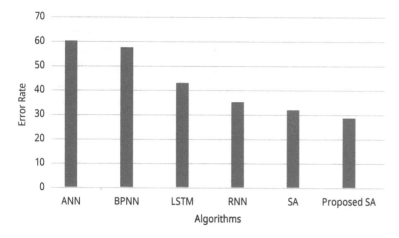

Figure 2.2: Packet error rate.

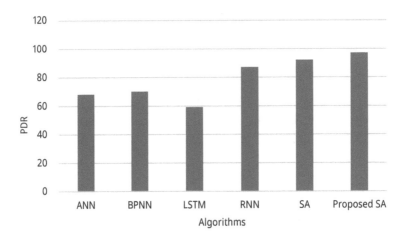

Figure 2.3: F-measure of traffic flow prediction.

The results (Figures 2.2 and 2.3) model that was presented offers the longest net-work life for each of the three scenarios, which ensures that the system will continue to be efficient and reliable over a more extended period of time. It has been estab-lished that the scenario with a high number of UAV devices has a shorter predicted lifetime than the scenario with a small number of UAVs for a given size of network. This was found to be the case when comparing the two scenarios with the same amount of network space.

A strategy has been proposed in which the scale of the network is kept the same while an increase in the number of nodes is made. It has been proved that the scenario with 50 nodes is highly equivalent to the case with 200 nodes in terms of the amount of work that needs to be done. On the other hand, when it comes to ITCM, this very same characteristic is what explains why the lifespan of the network is so limited.

It has been demonstrated that the suggested strategy outperforms the second scenario in terms of energy efficiency and that this outperformance is maintained even after a greater number of rounds. In this regard, the suggested strategy outperforms the second scenario. This illustrates how the functionality of the network will start to decline as the proportion of malicious nodes continues to rise. This objective can be accomplished through the use of trusted nodes in the sensor network to establish trust routes and recog-nize faulty or untrustworthy nodes. The method that has been proposed does this.

2.5 Conclusion

In this work, we evaluate several different meta-heuristic algorithms and propose Swap and Judge Simulated Annealing (SJSA) as a solution to the issue of task assignment and path planning for multiple UAVs participating in real-world missions. This is an immensely helpful addition to the model since it makes it possible to generate solutions that can be processed by heuristic algorithms. In order to reduce the amount of computational complexity that is associated with the process of delegating duties to many UAVs, it has been recommended that the concept of a universal distance matrix be utilized. This would allow for a reduction in the amount of time spent on delegating tasks.

The model for the assignment of tasks and the planning of routes is developed after taking a variety of different constraints into consideration. These steps were taken in order to locate the optimal solution. Studies show that the proposed SA is competitive when compared to other proposed meta-heuristic algorithms and is effective in finding near-optimal solutions when compared to the existing algorithm. Despite the fact that population-based algorithms might not be the best fit for the discrete combinatorial optimization problem at hand, this is still the case.

References

[1]   Sim, G. P. (2020). *Embracing Disruption: Urban Streets and Infrastructure of the 21 st Century* (Doctoral dissertation, University of Maryland, College Park).

[2]   Prasad, S. K., Sharma, T., Sharma, V., & Chauhan, S. (2022). RSETR: Route Stability Based Energy and Traffic Aware Reactive Routing Protocol for Mobile Ad Hoc Network. In: 2022 IEEE Delhi Section Conference (DELCON) (pp. 1–9). IEEE.

[3]   Veerappan Kousik, N. G., Natarajan, Y., Suresh, K., Patan, R., & Gandomi, A. H. (2020). Improving power and resource management in heterogeneous downlink OFDMA networks. *Information, 11*(4), 203.

[4]   Liu, B., & Zhou, X. (2020). Topology optimization of interactive visual communication networks based on the non-line-of-sight congestion control algorithm. *Complexity, 2020*.

[5]   Das, R., & Dash, D. (2022). A comprehensive survey on mobile sink-based data gathering schemes in WSNs. *Adhoc & Sensor Wireless Networks, 52*.

[6]   Li, J., Liang, W., Xu, Z., Jia, X., & Zhou, W. (2021). Service provisioning for multi-source IoT applications in mobile edge computing. *ACM Transactions on Sensor Networks (TOSN), 18*(2), 1–25.

[7]   Yuvaraj, N., Praghash, K., Raja, R. A., & Karthikeyan, T. (2022). An investigation of garbage disposal electric vehicles (GDEVs) integrated with deep neural networking (DNN) and intelligent transportation system (ITS) in smart city management system (SCMS). *Wireless Personal Communications, 123*(2), 1733–1752.

[8]   Srivastava, A., Pillai, A., Punj, D., Solanki, A., & Nayyar, A. (2021). TINB: A topical interaction network builder from WWW. *Wireless Networks, 27*(1), 589–608.

[9]   Kumar, C. D. N., & Saravanan, V. (2018). Weighted multi-objective cluster based honey bee foraging load balanced routing in mobile Ad Hoc network. *International Journal of Applied Engineering Research, 13*(12), 10394–10405.

[10] AlAqad, K. F., Burhanuddin, M. A., & Harum, N. B. (2020). A Comprehensive Survey on Routing Protocols for Cognitive Radio-Based Disaster Response Networks. In: 2020 International Conference on Promising Electronic Technologies (ICPET) (pp. 133–139). IEEE.

[11] Saravanan, V., & Sumathi, A. (2013). Location and Priority based vertical handoff approach for seamless mobility. *International Journal of Computer Applications, 975*, 8887.

[12] Verma, J., & Kesswani, N. (2019). AMIGM: Animal migration inspired group mobility model for mobile Ad hoc networks. *Scalable Computing: Practice and Experience*, *20*(3), 577–590.

[13] Saha, S., & Chaki, R. (2021). QoS-based congestion evasion clustering framework of wireless sensor networks. *Kuwait Journal of Science*.

[14] Yadav, S. P., & Yadav, S. (2019). Fusion of medical images using a wavelet methodology: A survey. *IEIE Transactions on Smart Processing & Computing*, *8*(4), 265–271.

[15] Carpentier, M., Giguere, P., & Gaudreault, J. (2018, October). Tree species identification from bark images using convolutional neural networks. In: 2018 IEEE/RSJ International Conference on Intelligent Robots and Systems (IROS) (pp. 1075–1081). IEEE.

[16] Yadav, S. P., Bhati, B. S., Mahato, D. P., & Kumar, S. (eds). Federated Learning for IoT Applications. EAI/Springer Innovations in Communication and Computing. Springer, Cham. https://doi.org/10. 1007/978-3-030-85559-8.

[17] Abbas, R., Amran, G. A., Alsanad, A., Ma, S., Almisned, F. A., Huang, J., & . . . Alzahrani, A. I. (2022). Recommending reforming trip to a group of users. *Electronics*, *11*(7), 1037.

[18] Kurdi, M. M., & Elzein, I. A. (2022). Implementing a TSP Path Controller for Autonomous Robot. In: 2022 International Conference on Decision Aid Sciences and Applications (DASA) (pp. 1435–1440). IEEE.

[19] Saravanan, V., Sumathi, A., Shanthana, S., & Rizvana, M. (2013). Dual mode mpeg steganography scheme for mobile and fixed devices. *International Journal of Scientific Research and Engineering Development*, *6*, 23–27.

[20] Xu, C., Zhang, T., Kuang, X., Zhou, Z., & Yu, S. (2021). Context-aware adaptive route mutation scheme: A reinforcement learning approach. *IEEE Internet of Things Journal*, *8*(17), 13528–13541.

R. Menaka*, S. Thenmalar, V. Saravanan

3 Cyberbullying detection of social network tweets using quantum machine learning

Abstract: Cyberbullying refers to bullying that takes place via the Internet or other technological means of communication. Cyberbullying comes from a wide variety of new places, thanks to developments in technology. The prevalence and public discussion of cyberbullying have both grown steadily over the past few years. As comparable contents from many sources may represent diverse perspectives and interpretations, the concept of cyberbullying is currently vague. The chapter discusses cyberbullying detection of social network tweets using quantum machine learning. Quantum machine learning enables detection of instances through a series of processing stages. Simulation shows improved accuracy of detecting the instances than other methods.

3.1 Introduction

The vast majority of information is saved digitally as there have been advances in technology. The expansion of multimedia content, such as text, photographs, musical compositions, and videos, can mostly be credited to the widespread availability and accessibility of the Internet [1]. Multimedia content includes text, image, musical compositions, and videos [2].

There has been an increase in research pertaining to this topic, which, in conjunction with advancements in Machine Learning (ML and DL, has resulted in the creation of cutting-edge intelligent systems that are intended to identify and interpret emotional information that is concealed within multimedia and multi-modal sources [3–4]. These cutting-edge intelligent systems are designed to identify and interpret emotional information that is concealed within multimedia and multi-modal sources.

Existing analysis issues in this field are exemplified by the incredibly huge size and high dimensionality characteristics of multimedia data. Finding means to extract inferences from such a massive amount of data that is both multi-modal and noisy is something that needs to be done in a research field that is both fascinating and

*Corresponding author: **R. Menaka**, Department of ECE, Chennai Institute of Technology, Chennai, Tamil Nadu, India, e-mail: menaka.govindaraj@gmail.com

S. Thenmalar, Department of Networking and Communications, SRM Institute of Science and Technology, Kattankulathur, Chennai, Tamil Nadu, India, e-mail: thenmals@srmist.edu.in

V. Saravanan, Department of Computer Science, Dambi Dollo University, Ethiopia, e-mail: reachvsaravanan@gmail.com

https://doi.org/10.1515/9783110798159-003

demanding [5]. To extract in-depth characteristics from multimedia files, the recommended strategy involves the use of hundreds of layers of nodes that are fully connected to each other [6–10].

The fully connected layer features are the ones that are taken into account by the model rather than the convolution layer features. This is because the fully connected layer features are more discriminatory than the convolution layer features. As it is able to generate low-dimensional deep features, the model that was proposed gets superior results than state-of-the-art methods for the categorization of images [11]. This is mostly due to the fact that it can generate low-dimensional deep features.

Recent research [12–15] has shown that using neural networks to learn lexical and contextual properties can replace the necessity for handcrafted features. The development of quantum-based machine learning has made this a practical possibility. Word embeddings are put to use in the training of quantum machine learning. These three types of neural networks have all been shown to outperform state-of-the-art methods on a variety of large-scale datasets, as demonstrated in these publications. Even though the performance of approaches based on quantum machine learning is unparalleled, it may be difficult to describe how these methods actually function.

The chapter discuses cyberbullying detection of social network tweets using quantum machine learning. The quantum machine learning enables detection of instances through a series of processing stages.

3.2 Related works

Cyberbullying is described in [16] as the purposeful and repeated infliction of damage via electronic means. Intention, repetition, and injury are also essential components of the core definition of bullying. Therefore, cyberbullying is the practice of sending threatening words or photos to other people through the Internet with the intent to do them harm.

Cyberbullying is [17] the harmful and repetitive dissemination of information about others via electronic means by individuals or groups. The victim of cyberbullying is subjected to communications that are either threatening or sexually provocative. The fields of natural language processing (NLP) and ML have made increasing emphasis on developing automatic methods for detecting cyberbullying. Whether or if the text contains cyberbullying content is the primary subject of automatic cyberbullying detection activities.

Cyberbullying is an important issue that deserves more study. The negative effects of cyberbullying can range from mild to severe. The seriousness of cyberbullying incidents may vary depending on variables such as the incident context and the people involved. That is why it is helpful to have a way to detect and categorize the severity of cyberbullying in real time; it can aid in the management of actual cyberbullying incidents [18].

In NLP, text classification is routine. Sentiment analysis, spam categorization, and topic classification have all been the subject of many academic investigations [19].

Artificial intelligence programs can use these characteristics to identify instances of cyberbullying and other forms of hostile speech. For supervised learning, most strategies rely on labeled training data.

Most cyberbullying detection studies have overlooked user demographics and instead concentrated on comment content. As a result, information about the age of the commenter and previous comment history should be used to identify the bullying nature of a post. Cyberbullying identification has been enhanced by incorporating other variables such as the frequency of assault terms [20].

A Twitter dataset [21] automatically detects cyberbullying content using keywords as characteristics. By taking into account user relationships and undertaking social network analysis, they were able to increase the detection accuracy.

Cyberbullying occurrences with areas under the curve greater than 90% [22] use a random forest classifier to differentiate between general, offensive, and cyberbullying users.

Images, personal profiles, timestamps, and geographical coordinates are just some of the forms of data [23] deemed to be part of a social network overall informational landscape. Information of this sort is useful for developing heterogeneous networks of multi-modal information-based detection models for cyberbullying.

3.3 Methods

The term cyberbullying refers to any form of bullying that takes place through the use of digital media, such as the internet or other forms of online communication. Due to developments in information and communication technologies, the persons and locations that can be the perpetrators of cyberbullying have grown to include a much wider range of options. Over the course of the past few years, there has been a consistent rise in the number of instances of cyberbullying that have been documented. As identical content can originate from a variety of sources, it is now difficult to obtain a clear image of what constitutes cyberbullying. This is because each of these sources may present a unique perspective or interpretation of what constitutes cyberbullying, shown in Figure 3.1.

Figure 3.1: Proposed UAV.

3.3.1 Data collection

The act of sending threatening or harassing messages to another Internet user is one type of cyberbullying that is quite common. For instance, one bully may post cyberbullying content on a post, and then additional bullies may contribute to the first post by generating comments that are also intended for the victim. These remarks may also be directed toward the victim.

It is possible that comments like these were made on the initial post. Visual inspection alone is insufficient to uncover cases of cyberbullying. Given that the definition of cyberbullying requires the participation of at least two individuals, the primary focus of data collection ought to be on conversations that center on a single topic, a single focal point, and multiple remarks from each participant.

3.3.2 Cyberbullying annotation

It is clear as a consequence of the data collection that was carried out with the assistance of the data crawler that some forms of material, such as emoticons and hyperlinks, should not be included in the classification of incidents of cyberbullying. The following is a recap of everything that took place during the phase in which the processing took place:

- **Filtration**: Cyberbullying can be distinguished from traditional bullying in a number of ways, one of which is the demand for screening in order to remove content that has been posted repeatedly by a number of different people. A chain was created as a result of the series of conversations that took place, with each link containing its own distinct set of observations and responses. In the vast majority of the cases, a minimum of twenty comments contributed to each and every chat was required.
- **Samples filtration**: The severity of cyberbullying is the focus of this article. The samples were put through a human filtering procedure to remove any remarks that were not pertinent to the issue that was being discussed.

- **Feature scoring**: Following the application of the labeling criteria to each and every one of the encounters concerning cyberbullying, points were allotted to each and every annotation that was made by one of five subject-matter experts who were working independently. The regularity with which it occurred, the level of hatred that was expressed, as well as who or what was the target, all contributed to the overall seriousness of the cyberbullying that was taking place. For each criterion, responses ranged from a score of 1 (which indicated a severe disagreement) to a score of 3 (which indicated agreement) (strongly agree). Due to this, it is possible to assign one of the three levels of seriousness that follow to each and every one of the conversations that take place.
- **Severity labeling**: The intensity of the cyberbullying that was being discussed in a conversation was used to characterize the conversation according to the following sentence: The value in the middle was picked to represent the rating whenever more than three distinct experts supplied the same rating. We also collected the scores that were supplied by the five experts and averaged them in order to rule out the possibility of any findings that were particularly extreme. Finally, the talks that were scored 3, 4, or 5 were considered to have a light level of intensity, those that were scored 6 or 7 were considered to have a mid level of intensity, and those that were scored 8 or 9 were considered to have a serious level of intensity.

3.3.3 Data pre-processing

There is a wide variety of word embeddings, some of which group words together based on their immediate surroundings, while others take into account the relationship that a word has with each and every other word in a text. Some word embeddings group words together based on their immediate surroundings, while others take into account this relationship.

The most well-known of them is called Continuous Bag of Words, or CBOW for short. The meaning of this text shifts depending on where in the world you are. Others take into consideration the connection that a word has with each and every other word that is found in a sentence.

The meaning of this text shifts depending on the setting in which it is spoken. The global vectors for word representation are yet another sort of prediction model that is capable of accurately capturing global context (GloVe). We use a technique of word embedding that takes into account the overall context in order to detect sarcasm. This is due to the fact that we are of the opinion that this is necessary for accurate sarcasm detection.

To obtain embeddings for each word in the sentence in dimension D, we must first tokenize the S using a normal tokenizer and then apply some pre-trained models. This will allow us to obtain embeddings for each word in the sentence. Our model receives its input in the form of a variety of embeddings, which are denoted by the equation:

$$S = \{e_1, e_2, \ldots, e_N\}, \, S \in R^{N \times D}$$

Sentence S needs to be broken down in order to locate the key terms that have sarcastic meanings and negative emotional overtones. This is necessary in order to determine whether or not sarcasm is being used in the sentence. As the contexts in which these cue words are employed is what determines the relevance of these words, there are a number of different variables that can be considered. The model that we built makes use of a method that is referred to as multi-head self-attention in order to extract these cue words from the text that is provided as input.

The study of the challenges that arise when attempting to manipulate data in quantum mechanical systems, such as storing, processing, and sending information, is the primary emphasis of the discipline of quantum computing. Specifically, these challenges include: The transmission of quantum information refers to the specific method of transmitting data using quantum states. Models of quantum computing entail the existence of a probabilistic sort of time-reversible computation. A time-reversible computation is a type of computation that can be described as a type of computation in which the outcome precisely replicates the data that was input.

Using density matrices allows for the quantitative expression of physical states to be achieved in quantum theory. This is an important step in the development of quantum mechanics. The concept of probability distributions is expanded upon through the use of density matrices, which are positive, trace-one, semidefinite matrices. The logical states of a quantum computational model are converted into the appropriate physical states of the quantum system that is in charge of operating the model. This process is referred to as state translation.

It is possible to carry out a computation in a manner that is compatible with previous iterations by first initializing a state and then proceeding to apply a sequence of unitary matrices to that state. This will result in the calculation being backward-compatible. The probabilistic output that is generated is based on the distribution that was encoded using the final density matrix, and the distribution that was encoded using the final density matrix is used to construct the probabilistic output.

3.3.4 Classification

In Figure 3.2, the standard logical values of 0 and 1 correlate with the states of quantum systems that have two degrees of freedom that can be seen by an observer.

In other words, 0 and 1 are the values that are used to represent zero and one, states respectively. To put it another way, the only values that may take on the states

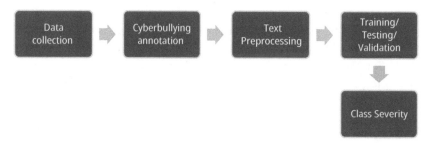

Figure 3.2: Proposed classificaiton model.

of zero or one are one and zero. In the context of this conversation, a qubit is a vector of the form $\psi = a_0 e_0 + a_1 e_1$, in which 0 and 1 are both unsigned small constants, a_0, $a_1 \in C$, and e_i is the ith standard basis vector. In other words, a qubit is a vector with the form:

$$|a_0|^2 + |a_1|^2 = 1$$

It is possible to express the values of distributions based on 0 and 1 using the notation $|\{|a_1|^2, |a_2|^2\}$, respectively. It is a well-established fact that a single qubit is capable of storing the same quantity of data as a single bit. A tensor product is used whenever it is necessary to build registers that include a large number of qubits. On the other hand, logic gates can be viewed as extensions of unitary matrices that operate on a finite number of qubits. These gates are used to process information.

Interference is a necessary component of quantum processing, and it is brought about as a result of the dynamics that are produced within the system. Quantum computers make use of the interference effects in order to carry out simultaneous evaluations of a function at every location across the domain in which it is being used.

This is done in spite of the fact that the result of this computation is inaccessible to a classical observer. The quantum computer will have an advantage over classical computers and other devices in its capacity to address these problems. Structure, particular symmetries, and non-classical correlations are thought to play a significant role in the reported increases, despite the fact that the real roots and extents of quantum speedups are still a mystery.

We are able to concisely illustrate exponentially huge probability distributions by combining conventional methods of data analysis with quantum encoding, which is a method for encoding information in a way that is only accessible to subatomic particles. An example of a state that may be represented by any arbitrary number of qubits, such as n, is the n-dimensional probability vector $v = (v_1, \ldots v_{2n})$, which has $2n$ dimensions:

$$\psi = \sum_{i=1}^{n} v_i - \sqrt{e_i}$$

These things cannot be improved in any way. In point of fact, quantum states are known for their fragility, and as a consequence, significant error correction is required in order to shield against the noise that is introduced by the environment around them. The theory of error correction provides a guarantee that the system will be able to be efficiently fixed if the magnitude of the physical defects is low enough to meet the requirements.

3.4 Evaluation

With the use of Twitter dataset, human annotators detect and classify sarcastic tweets simply based on the content of the tweets themselves. This method relies on human intervention to be completed. It is not necessary to have any background information or past experience with the topic being discussed in order to comprehend these tweets.

Tweets that are clear and do not contain sarcasm or require further context to be understood properly belong to this category. Before tweets are broadcast into the world, they go through an initial step of processing where they are cleaned up and formatted. During this phase, any mentions of users are converted to the format @user, and any URLs that were present are eliminated.

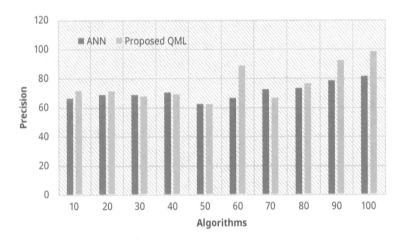

Figure 3.3: Precision.

We present the detection of sarcasm (Figures 3.3–3.6) as a classification problem for the goal of determining whether or not the models that have been developed are beneficial. As assessment metrics, we employ precision, recall, F1-score, and accuracy. The percentage of sarcastic sentences that were anticipated but did not materialize expressed as a percentage of the total number of sarcastic statements that were anticipated.

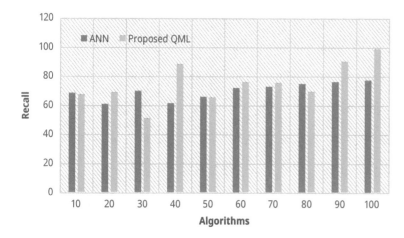

Figure 3.4: Recall.

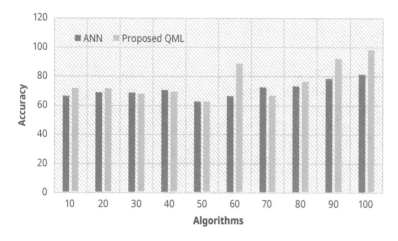

Figure 3.5: Accuracy.

Divide the total number of sarcastic sentences that were found in the ground truth by the number of sarcastic sentences that were accurately expected. Count how many sarcastic sentences there are in the straightforward truth. The harmonic mean of the recall and accuracy scores is also referred to as the F-score. In order to calculate these scores, we begin by giving the model predictions a threshold value of 0.5.

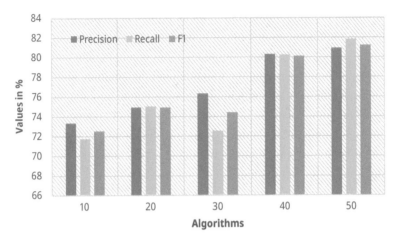

Figure 3.6: Performance analysis of testing.

3.5 Conclusion

The chapter presents a quantum deep learning architecture in this body of work that is capable of determining whether or not a given passage of text contains sarcasm. Data preprocessing, multi-head self-attention, gated recurrent units, classification, and interpretability are the five pillars that make up the methodology that we have suggested. By employing a method known as multi-head self-attention, we might be able to zero in on the essential markers of sarcasm that are included within a sentence.

The output from this layer is fed into a fully connected classification layer so that a final classification score can be obtained. This layer is fully connected when it has all of its connections made. This procedure must be followed in order to acquire the score.

Experiments were run on a large number of datasets derived from a variety of different sources, and the results show that a clear improvement over the state-of-the-art models in terms of evaluation measures across the board.

To highlight the importance of different components of our model, we conducted ablation studies and analyzed the trained model. We interpreted the model by examining its attention weights and found that it can identify the textual cues that indicate sarcasm.

References

[1] Jain, V., Saxena, A. K., Senthil, A., Jain, A., & Jain, A. (2021). Cyber-Bullying Detection in Social Media Platform using Machine Learning. In: 2021 10th International Conference on System Modeling & Advancement in Research Trends (SMART) (pp. 401–405). IEEE.

[2] Wu, J. L., & Tang, C. Y. (2022). Classifying the severity of cyberbullying incidents by using a hierarchical squashing-attention network. *Applied Sciences*, *12*(7), 3502

[3] Toapanta, S. M. T., & Gallegos, L. E. M. (2020). Parameters to Determine Cyberbullying in Social Networks in the Ecuador. In: Proceedings of the 2020 the 4th International Conference on Information System and Data Mining (pp. 144–151).

[4] Koley, S., & Kar, A. Changing our modern society in different levels using quantum computing device. *Computer*, *3*, 4.

[5] Achuthan, K., Nair, V. K., Kowalski, R., Ramanathan, S., & Raman, R. (2022). Cyberbullying research – Alignment to sustainable development and impact of COVID-19: Bibliometrics and science mapping analysis. *Computers in Human Behavior*, 107566.

[6] Singh, J., & Dhiman, G. (2021). A survey on machine-learning approaches: Theory and their concepts. *Materials Today: Proceedings*.

[7] Kumar, S., Mahanti, P., & Wang, S. J. (2019). Intelligent computational techniques for multimodal data. *Multimedia Tools and Applications*, *78*(17), 23809–23814

[8] Shi, W., Goodchild, M., Batty, M., Li, Q., Liu, X., & Zhang, A. (2022). Prospective for urban informatics. *Urban Informatics*, *1*(1), 1–14

[9] Chauhan, S., Mittal, M., Woźniak, M., Gupta, S., & Pérez de Prado, R. (2021). A technology acceptance model-based analytics for online mobile games using machine learning techniques. *Symmetry*, *13*(8), 1545

[10] Yuvaraj, N., Chang, V., Gobinathan, B., Pinagapani, A., Kannan, S., Dhiman, G., & Rajan, A. R. (2021). Automatic detection of cyberbullying using multi-feature based artificial intelligence with deep decision tree classification. *Computers & Electrical Engineering*, *92*, 107186.

[11] Sahana, B. S., Sandhya, G., Tanuja, R. S., Ellur, S., & Ajina, A. (2020). Towards a Safer Conversation Space: Detection of Toxic Content in Social Media (Student Consortium). In: 2020 IEEE Sixth International Conference on Multimedia Big Data (BigMM) (pp. 297–301). IEEE.

[12] Rani, P., Verma, S., Yadav, S. P., Rai, B. K., Naruka, M. S., & Kumar, D. (2022). Simulation of the lightweight blockchain technique based on privacy and security for healthcare data for the cloud system. *International Journal of E-Health and Medical Communications (IJEHMC)*, *13*(4), 1–15. http://doi.org/10.4018/IJEHMC.309436.

[13] Kadam, S. R., Pawar, S. N., Hamza, N. M., Ouf, S., El-Henawy, I. M., Aathira, M., & . . . Upadhya, S. 4th International conference on computing methodologies and communication [ICCMC 2020]. *Machine Learning*, *56*, 11.

[14] Vashisht, V., Kumar Pandey, A., & Prakash, S. (2021). Speech recognition using machine learning. *IEIE Transactions on Smart Processing and Computing, SCOPUS*, *10*(3), 233–239, ISSN: 2287–5255, https://doi.org/10.5573/IEIESPC.2021.10.3.233.

[15] Sando, S. (2019). Digital ethical building as a proactive educational approach against cyberbullying, with Aristotle, Løgstrup and barad as sources for a philosophical framework. *Nordidactica: Journal of Humanities and Social Science Education*, *2019*, (4), 54–75.

[16] Saravanan, V., & Neeraja, A. (2013). Security issues in computer networks and stegnography. In: 2013 7th International Conference on Intelligent Systems and Control (ISCO) (pp. 363–366). IEEE.

[17] Yuvaraj, N., Srihari, K., Dhiman, G., Somasundaram, K., Sharma, A., Rajeskannan, S. M. G. S. M. A., & . . . Masud, M. (2021). Nature-inspired-based approach for automated cyberbullying classification on multimedia social networking. *Mathematical Problems in Engineering*, 2021.

[18] A, I. T. S. (2019). The educational intelligent economy: Big data, artificial intelligence, machine learning and the internet of things in education. *Governance, 5,* 226.

[19] Mahlknecht, B., & Bork-Hüffer, T. (2022). 'She felt incredibly ashamed': Gendered (cyber-) bullying and the hypersexualized female body. *Gender, Place & Culture,* 1–23.

[20] Arabnia, H. R., Deligiannidis, L., Grimaila, M. R., Hodson, D. D., Joe, K., Sekijima, M., & Tinetti, F. G. (eds.). (2021). Advances in Parallel & Distributed Processing, and Applications: Proceedings from PDPTA'20, CSC'20, MSV'20, and GCC'20. Springer International Publishing.

[21] Patel, K., Agrahari, S., & Srivastava, S. (2020). Survey on fake profile detection on social sites by using machine learning algorithm. In: 2020 8th International Conference on Reliability, Infocom Technologies and Optimization (Trends and Future Directions)(ICRITO) (pp. 1236–1240). IEEE.

[22] Parikh, P., Abburi, H., Chhaya, N., Gupta, M., & Varma, V. (2021). Categorizing sexism and misogyny through neural approaches. *ACM Transactions on the Web (TWEB), 15*(4), 1–31

[23] Joshi, C., Bhole, C., & Vaswani, N. (2022). A Scrutiny Review of CPS 4.0-Based Blockchain with Quantum Resistance. In: Advancements in Quantum Blockchain with Real-Time Applications (pp. 131–157). IGI Global.

M. Sunil Kumar*, Harsha B. K., Leta Tesfaye Jule

4 AI-driven cybersecurity modeling using quantum computing for mitigation of attacks in IOT-SDN network

Abstract: The implementation of quantum learning strategies is turning out to be increasingly crucial. When it comes to cybersecurity, one of the key benefits of using machine learning is that it makes the detection of malware more effective, scalable, and actionable than traditional human approaches. This is one of the primary advantages of employing machine learning. The cybersecurity risks posed by quantum learning must be effectively managed on a logical and theoretical level in order to be mitigated. It is necessary to prevail over these obstacles. Deep learning, support vector quantums, and Bayesian classification are just a few examples of the quantum learning and statistical technologies that have showed promise in the area of reducing the consequences of cyberattacks. When designing intelligent security systems, it is essential to unearth previously unknown patterns and insights hidden within network data, as well as to develop a data-driven quantum learning model to counteract the threats posed by these attacks. Additionally, it is essential to uncover previously unknown patterns and insights hidden within network data. The chapter develops AI-based modeling to improve the detection of cybersecurity attacks in Internet of Things--Software-Defined Network (IoT-SDN). The collection of network logs, preprocessing, and classification of instances enables the model to classify the attacks from the network. The simulation is conducted in Python to test the effectiveness of the AI-driven model. The results show that the proposed method achieves higher rate of accuracy in detecting the instances than other methods.

---

*Corresponding author: **M. Sunil Kumar**, Department of CSE, School of Computing, Mohan Babu University (erstwhile Sree Vidyanikethan Engineering College), Tirupathi, Andhra Pradesh, India, e-mail: sunilmalchi1@gmail.com

Harsha B. K., Department of ECE, CMR Institute of Technology, Bengaluru, Karnataka, India, e-mail: harsha405@gmail.com

Leta Tesfaye Jule, Physics Department, Dambi Dollo University, Dambi Dollo, Oromia Region, Ethiopia, e-mail: laterajule@gmail.com

https://doi.org/10.1515/9783110798159-004

4.1 Introduction

Unauthorized access [1, 2], denial of service [2], malware attack [3, 4], zero-day attack [4, 5], data breach [5, 6], social engineering or phishing [7, 8], and other forms of cybercrime have all skyrocketed over the course of the past decade as a direct result of the growing significance of information technology. Fewer than 50 million distinct executable forms of malicious software were documented by the global security community in 2010.

It has been established that both people and corporations can incur considerable financial losses as a result of cybercrime and network assaults [7, 8]. These losses can range anywhere from tens of thousands to hundreds of millions of dollars. According to the thoughts of security specialists [9, 10], it is projected that the volume of records that are cracked would virtually quadruple during the course of the coming five years. As a direct result of this, it is absolutely vital for companies to create and implement an all-encompassing cybersecurity plan in order to forestall additional monetary losses. This is done for the purpose of protecting the company from cyberattacks.

Recent socioeconomic research [11] indicates that it is of the utmost importance for the government to promptly find a solution to the problem of identifying different cyber occurrences, including those that have been seen before and those that have not, and to appropriately protect essential systems from being attacked by cybercriminals.

The term cybersecurity refers to the collection of precautions that are taken to protect data, computer networks, and other digital assets [12]. The term cybersecurity is an umbrella term that encompasses a wide variety of specialized subfields, the most prominent of which are corporate computing and mobile computing.

These include (i) network security, which is concerned with preventing hackers from accessing a network; (ii) application security, which is concerned with ensuring that applications and hardware are safe from cyber threats; (iii) information security, which is concerned with protecting sensitive information; and (iv) operational security, which is concerned with the methods by which data assets are handled and protected. Among these, network security is the most important. Using firewalls, antivirus software, and intrusion detection systems are the traditional ways for protecting a computer network and the data contained within it.

Discovering previously unknown patterns is one of the primary goals of data science, and quantum computing, an essential component of the subfield of study known as artificial intelligence, has the potential to play a vital role in this endeavor. Data science is currently at the vanguard of a new scientific paradigm, and the arrival of quantum computing has had far-reaching implications on the field of cybersecurity [13, 14]. Both of these developments have occurred in recent years. The increase in the number of devices that are capable of communicating with one another has led to an increase in the level of sophistication of cyberattacks, as discussed in [15].

We have come to the conclusion that the most fruitful approach for our investigation will be to focus on quantum computing as it relates to the field of cybersecurity.

This is due to the fact that we believe that security and effective methods for processing data are all essential components of a successful investigation [16].

The security of data is the primary emphasis of this research, and the techniques of quantum computing are applied in order to both anticipate the occurrence of future cyberattacks and improve upon the precautions that are already in place. This effort can be beneficial to researchers working in academic institutions as well as those working in enterprises, if they are interested in exploring and building data-driven, intelligent cybersecurity models using technology related to quantum computing [17].

In this section, we developed a Quantum Intelligence (QI)-based model in order to increase the network ability to detect and respond to cybersecurity threats posed by IoT-SDN environments. These threats are posed by the combination of the two technologies. The ability of the model to categorize attacks on a network is made possible by the collecting, pre-processing, and subsequent categorization of network logs. In order to evaluate how well the AI-driven model works, a simulation has been developed that is written in Python. When it comes to accurately spotting the instances, the findings make it plainly clear that the suggested technique performs significantly better than the alternatives.

4.2 Related works

It is likely that this will result in the memory of the relaying nodes becoming corrupted over time. This is due to the fact that IoT nodes have a finite amount of resources. It is now possible to develop applications that can detect and mitigate distributed denial of service (DDoS) attacks with a greater degree of ease than was previously possible with traditional hardware as a result of the introduction of SDN, which has made it possible to develop applications that can detect and mitigate DDoS attacks [18]. A significant number of new methods that further augment the network level of security has been established.

In order to detect and stop malicious traffic, data samples are taken from the network and then analyzed. This process begins with the collection of data samples from the network. Numerous statistical methodologies have been developed, each of which makes use of a distinct metric [19]. These methodologies have been used to study a wide range of phenomena, from population genetics to disease transmission. These strategies have been devised, so that it may be determined whether or not a specific flow constitutes an attack. The policy of the switch is the core of the protection, and it is responsible for defining the flows that are forwardable while identifying all other flows as malicious [20].

Let think about the quantums that are driven by quantum learning. In recent years, traditional quantum learning methods that were applied to the problem of analyzing and classifying diverse flows to acquire harmful information have shown promising results, drawing the attention of the scientific community [21]. This was because these methods were applied to the problem of evaluating and classifying various flows in order to gain an attack [22].

In [23], software tools that are able to identify and stop distributed denial of service attacks are discussed. Honeypots are also being developed in order to leverage the network in order to detect and mitigate DDoS attacks. Additionally, Network Functions Virtualization (NFV) is being used in order to install services that increase the functioning of the attacks.

4.3 Methods

An intrusion detection system, commonly referred to as an IDS, is software, hardware, or a system, according to one definition of the term. This is merely one of several definitions that might be used for an IDS, which is shown in Figure 4.1.

Figure 4.1: Proposed UAV.

In order to handle any potential security issues, an IDS will collect data from a number of crucial nodes that are spread out over a network or system and then analyze that data. The use of an IDS makes it possible to recognize both external and internal threats simultaneously. Depending on the principal function that they are designed to protect, IDS can be placed into one of several different categories. IDS can, for all intents and purposes, be split into two separate categories based on factors to be considered. When choosing an IDS, the deployment or data source is one of the most significant elements to think about, and the other is the IDS that will be used to identify potential risks. Both of these factors should be considered carefully before making a decision.

When classifying the many different possibilities for deployment, one can draw from many different academic fields for inspiration. Both of these systems monitor the computer they are installed on for any indications of potentially malicious behavior.

4.3.1 Monitoring

The initial stage in the process is to begin monitoring the network in order to collect data regarding it. In the second step of the process, a detection algorithm that is based on an entropy calculation is trained using the data that was previously gathered. The

Internet Protocol (IP) addresses of the sender and the recipient, as well as the ports that were used and specifics regarding the protocol that was used are included among the pieces of information that were evaluated for this article. In SDN, the development of an algorithm for tracking the activity of a network can be done in any one of a number of different ways.

OpenFlow specifies the messages that must be used in the communication that takes place between controllers and switches in order to incorporate native monitoring into its architecture. This communication takes place throughout the design phase of OpenFlow. Even though the controller has access to the flow tables of the switches, the data that can be obtained from these tables is insufficient to retrieve. This is the case despite the fact that the controller has access to the flow tables of the switches. The IP addresses of the origin and destination of the traffic are included among these attributes.

The monitoring of alternative methods is the responsibility of the government. This monitoring is carried out entirely by the switch, which also does its own analysis of the data independently of the controller and without the participation of the latter in the process. In order to accomplish this goal, the switch consults both of its flow tables and its state tables. This strategy not only makes the algorithm more accurate but also makes it possible to identify an attack that is designed to deny service to several users simultaneously.

4.3.2 Detection

The monitoring phase of the entropy algorithm collects data, which is then analyzed in the detecting phase of the algorithm. The monitoring phase job is to collect data so that the detecting phase task, which is to identify detrimental flows, can be accomplished. Statistical procedures, such as the computation of entropy, do not call for a substantial amount of memory or storage space, in contrast to tools that are based on patterns. When this is accomplished, the methodologies in issue are transformed into a solution that is not only operational but also has the potential to be incorporated into the SDN network components.

The following equation, which takes into consideration the probabilities of occurrence $(p(x_i))$, can be used to compute the entropy of the detection system. This equation takes into account the total number of events (n).

$$H(X) = - \sum_{i=1}^{n} p(x_i)\log_2 p(x_i)\log_2 n$$

A distribution with a high degree of concentration will have a low entropy number because of the high degree of concentration. On the other hand, the behavior that is projected to identify attacks in networks is characterized by a lowly concentrated distribution, which implies a bigger entropy value. This behavior can be identified as having a higher entropy value. This conduct stands in stark contrast to that discussed in the preceding paragraph. The accuracy of the method used in the determination of the entropy values at the minimum and maximum ranges is a crucial factor in determining whether or not the detection procedure will be successful.

A preliminary training phase is necessary, during which the algorithm must be provided with the traffic data in order for the entropy and distribution bounds to be calculated using the equation. This phase can only begin after the initial training phase has been completed. Repeated entropy analysis of all relevant parameters, such as source and destination IP addresses and source and destination ports, is performed at regular intervals in order to detect attacks. The attack has been recognized if the entropy calculation is either excessively high or excessively low in accordance with the settings that you set:

$$Limits = \mu \pm \theta\sigma,$$

where θ is category, μ is mean, and σ is standard deviation.

4.3.3 Quantum convolutional neural network

The study proposes that classical logs be substituted at the input of neurons by quantum states that are encoded with amplitude and phase. This would be done in place of the current system, which uses classical logs. The terminal of the neuron also generates a quantum state, and this state is dependent on the linear superposition of the states that are fed into the neuron.

Each of the quantum states that are inputted receives a one-of-a-kind amplitude and phase-weighting that is determined on the basis of the complex weights. Incorporating the signal phase into a model of a neural network is linked to a generalization of the error back-propagation method, which is used for training conventional perceptrons. Incorporating the signal phase into a model of a neural network is linked to a generalization of the method.

It is clear from this that, with the exception of the effects caused by nonlinear processes, quantum neural networks and optical neural networks are essentially the same. Significant progress has been made in recent years in the field of optical quantum neural networks. In the common models of quantum neural networks, the phase of setting up the network begins with a series of classical operations being carried out. This is necessary in order to get the process started. Measurement and the establishment of states are both included in these procedures.

It has been shown that the convolutional neural network, often known as a CNN, is a good illustration of a quantum neural network. The quantum advantage can be seen in action in the identification of complicated objects thanks to this network. The data from one layer of Quantum Convolution Neural Network (QCNN) is used by successive layers of the QCNN to build a new intermediate two-dimensional array of pixels known as a feature map. This map is used to assist in the classification of images. This creation is the collective responsibility of each layer.

These layers are referred to as the convolutional layers, the subsampling layers, and the conventional perceptron layers. In a multi-layer perceptron, the first two layers are the ones that are used to provide an input feature vector for the network. These layers are arranged in an alternating fashion.

QCNNs typically have a detection accuracy that is 10–15% greater than that of ordinary neural networks. This is due to the fact that QCNN makes use of more complicated algorithms. The QCNN rapid learning is made feasible by purely parallelizing the convolution procedure for each map and by applying reverse convolution as the error spreads across the network.

4.4 Evaluation

In this section, we use a real IoT data set named Bot-IoT, which has been completed by us in order to demonstrate that the solution is effective when applied in an IoT setting. The design of Bot-IoT was modified so that it could be used for the purpose of collecting data on traffic, and thus allowed the system to become available for use. This data collection is suited for the research since it contains both benign and malicious traffic. The findings may also be applicable to other IoT use cases as well, which is another advantage of using this data collection.

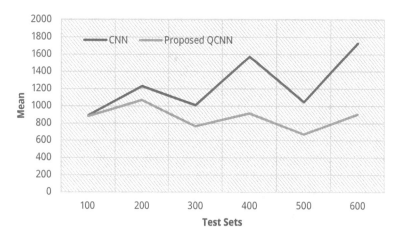

Figure 4.2: Mean.

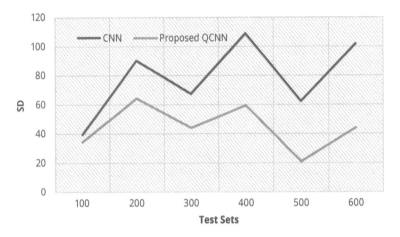

Figure 4.3: SD.

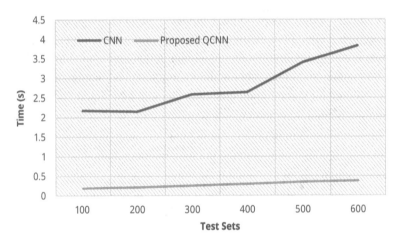

Figure 4.4: Run times (s).

The size of the dataset has an impact on the number of false positives that it generates; the size of the window and the size of the dataset have to be updated in accordance with the volume of traffic that the system encounters. The proposed method with existing comparison is shown in Figures 4.2 to 4.5.

The algorithm needs a substantially longer learning period in order to accurately fine-tune the distributional bounds when these conditions are present. This arises as a result of the considerable fluctuation in entropy that takes place after an attack has been found and countered, which makes false positive detection conceivable. This takes place after an attack has been uncovered and fought back against. After an attack has been

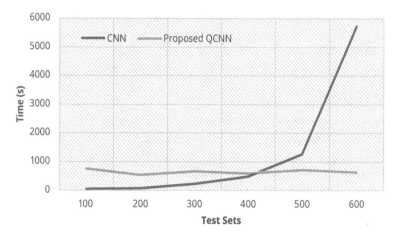

Figure 4.5: Computational times (s).

thwarted, the rate of false positives remains reasonably stable at about 20% throughout the investigation process.

Due to the fact that there was not even a single instance of a false positive being detected, the false positive ratio in this scenario is accurate. It is essential to emphasize the fact that expanding the size of the window resulted in an increase not just in the standard deviation but also in the mean amount of time that needed to be spent mitigating the risk. This is because whenever the window size is expanded, the algorithm is compelled to process a bigger number of states that are obtained from the data plane. As a result, the amount of time required to compute the entropy will grow as a direct consequence of this.

Following the discovery of an attack, revised flow rules are transmitted to the appropriate switches in order to block the passage of malicious traffic, while preserving the integrity of the flow of regular traffic. The entirety of the traffic includes both legitimate and illegitimate packets, the overall number of packets, as well as the number of User Datagram Protocol (UDP) packets. As a consequence of this, it is possible, even after the attack has been halted, to check to determine whether or not the host that was the target of the attack is still getting valid traffic. This can be done either during or after the attack depending on your preference.

4.5 Conclusion

With the assistance of a quantum approach, it is possible to detect and mitigate DDoS attacks in networks that are connected to the IoT. The specifics of this method are discussed in greater detail in the following chapter. It has been shown that an increase in capabilities is a candidate that might be used as a viable approach for network monitoring.

This improvement eliminates the necessity of sending packets to the controller, which was previously a pre-requisite. In order to determine the relevance of this statistic in relation to a wide range of conditions, we carried out the efficiency test on the application in three distinct settings.

The findings of the experiments demonstrated that it is beneficial to exploit the correlation of the entropy values of various attributes in order to detect the attack and that SDN may simply eliminate the threat by adding entries to the flow tables of the switches. This was shown by the results of the experiments. The findings of the experiments provided evidence for this assertion.

References

[1]   Porambage, P., Gür, G., Osorio, D. P. M., Livanage, M., & Ylianttila, M. (2021). 6G Security Challenges and Potential Solutions. In: 2021 Joint European Conference on Networks and Communications & 6G Summit (Eucnc/6G Summit) pp. (622–627). IEEE.

[2]   Tao, F., Akhtar, M. S., & Jiayuan, Z. (2021). The future of artificial intelligence in cybersecurity: A comprehensive survey. *EAI Endorsed Transactions on Creative Technologies, 8*(28), e3–e3.

[3]   Gill, S. S., Tuli, S., Xu, M., Singh, I., Singh, K. V., Lindsay, D., & . . . Garraghan, P. (2019). Transformative effects of IoT, Blockchain and artificial Intelligence on cloud computing: Evolution, vision, trends and open challenges. *Internet of Things, 8*, 100118.

[4]   Siriwardhana, Y., Porambage, P., Liyanage, M., & Ylianttila, M. (2021). AI and 6G security: Opportunities and challenges. In: 2021 Joint European Conference on Networks and Communications & 6G Summit (EuCNC/6G Summit) (pp. 616–621). IEEE.

[5]   Catak, F. O., Kuzlu, M., Catak, E., Cali, U., & Unal, D. (2022). Security concerns on machine learning solutions for 6G networks in mmWave beam prediction. *Physical Communication, 52*, 101626.

[6]   Çağlayan, M. U. (2022). AI and Quality of Service Driven Attack Detection, Mitigation and Energy Optimization: A Review of Some EU Project Results. In: International ISCIS Security Workshop pp. (1–12). Springer, Cham.

[7]   Al-Hawawreh, M., Moustafa, N., Garg, S., & Hossain, M. S. (2020). Deep learning-enabled threat intelligence scheme in the internet of things networks. *IEEE Transactions on Network Science and Engineering, 8*(4), 2968–2981.

[8]   Clim, A. (2019). Cyber security beyond the Industry 4.0 era. A short review on a few technological promises. *Informatica Economica, 23*(2), 34–44.

[9]   Gill, S. S., Xu, M., Ottaviani, C., Patros, P., Bahsoon, R., Shaghaghi, A., & . . . Uhlig, S. (2022). AI for next generation computing: Emerging trends and future directions. *Internet of Things, 19*, 100514.

[10]   Williams, P., Dutta, I. K., Daoud, H., & Bayoumi, M. (2022). A survey on security in internet of things with a focus on the impact of emerging technologies. *Internet of Things, 19*, 100564.

[11]   Yadav, S. P., Bhati, B. S., Mahato, D. P., & Kumar, S. (eds.). Federated Learning for IoT Applications. EAI/Springer Innovations in Communication and Computing. Springer, Cham. https://doi.org/10.1007/978-3-030-85559-8.

[12]   Mangla, C., Rani, S., Qureshi, N. M. F. & Singh, A. (2022). Mitigating 5G security challenges for next-gen industry using quantum computing. *Journal of King Saud University-Computer and Information Sciences.*

[13] Saravanan, V., & Raj, V. M. (2016). A seamless mobile learning and tension free lifestyle by QoS oriented mobile handoff. *Asian Journal of Research in Social Sciences and Humanities*, 6(7), 374–389.

[14] Nguyen, V. L., Lin, P. C., Cheng, B. C., Hwang, R. H., & Lin, Y. D. (2021). Security and privacy for 6G: A survey on prospective technologies and challenges. *IEEE Communications Surveys & Tutorials*, 23(4), 2384–2428.

[15] Yadav, S. P. (2022). Blockchain Security. In: Baalamurugan, K., Kumar, S. R., Kumar, A., Kumar, V., Padmanaban, S. (eds.) Blockchain Security in Cloud Computing. EAI/Springer Innovations in Communication and Computing. Springer, Cham. https://doi.org/10.1007/978-3-030-70501-5_1.

[16] Ghiasi, M., Niknam, T., Wang, Z., Mehrandezh, M., Dehghani, M., & Ghadimi, N. (2023). A comprehensive review of cyber-attacks and defense mechanisms for improving security in smart grid energy systems: Past, present and future. *Electric Power Systems Research*, 215, 108975.

[17] Natarajan, Y., Raja, R. A., Kousik, N. V., & Saravanan, M. (2021). A review of various reversible embedding mechanisms. *International Journal of Intelligence and Sustainable Computing*, 1(3), 233–266.

[18] Zeadally, S., Adi, E., Baig, Z., & Khan, I. A. (2020). Harnessing artificial intelligence capabilities to improve cybersecurity. *Ieee Access*, 8, 23817–23837.

[19] Gobinathan, B., Mukunthan, M. A., Surendran, S., Somasundaram, K., Moeed, S. A., Niranjan, P., & . . . Sundramurthy, V. P. (2021). A novel method to solve real time security issues in software industry using advanced cryptographic techniques. *Scientific Programming*, 2021.

[20] Yamin, M. M., Ullah, M., Ullah, H., & Katt, B. (2021). Weaponized AI for cyber attacks. *Journal of Information Security and Applications*, 57, 102722.

[21] Saravanan, V., Rajeshwari, S., & Jayashree, P. (2013). Security issues in protecting computers and maintenance. *Journal of Global Research in Computer Science*, 4(1), 55–58.

[22] Geluvaraj, B., Satwik, P. M., & Ashok Kumar, T. A. (2019). The Future of Cybersecurity: Major Role of Artificial Intelligence, Machine Learning, and Deep Learning in Cyberspace. In: International Conference on Computer Networks and Communication Technologies pp. (739–747). Springer, Singapore.

[23] Gupta, C., Johri, I., Srinivasan, K., Hu, Y. C., Qaisar, S. M., & Huang, K. Y. (2022). A systematic review on machine learning and deep learning models for electronic information security in mobile networks. *Sensors*, 22(5), 2017.

N. Karthikeyan*, P. Sivaprakash, K. Periyakaruppan, M. Shobana

5 Machine learning-based quantum modeling to classify the traffic flow in smart cities

Abstract: The intelligent transportation system (ITS) includes a number of highly effective research applications, one of which is the vehicle ad hoc network. It provides information that can be used to either prevent or lessen the occurrence of traffic bottlenecks. By using the V2V and V2I protocols, a vehicular ad hoc network is able to facilitate communication not just between the vehicles themselves but also between the vehicles and the infrastructure that connects them. In this chapter, machine learning-based quantum modeling to classify the traffic flow in smart cities is proposed and validated.

5.1 Introduction

The management of traffic in smart cities involves a number of difficult challenges, including problems of pollution, energy consumption, congestion, and delays in traffic [1]. It takes a variety of various kinds of systems to effectively manage traffic, such as an intelligent parking management system, a vehicle routing management system, and a traffic prediction system [2].

If we want to be effective in saving lives, we have to address the biggest public concerns, which is the constantly increasing death toll from road accidents. This is the case if we want to be successful in saving lives. User behavior, road infrastructure, ambient circumstances, and mechanical faults are among the key elements that contribute to automotive collisions [3–4]. One of the most significant problems that is now being faced by the nation transportation system that has to be solved is congestion [5].

Inadequate management of traffic flow, insufficient law enforcement, infrastructure that is either outdated or nonexistent, and faulty signals are all potential

*Corresponding author: **N. Karthikeyan**, Department of Computer Science and Engineering, SNS College of Technology, Coimbatore, Tamil Nadu, India, e-mail: profkarthikeyann@gmail.com
P. Sivaprakash, Department of Computer Science and Engineering, PPG Institute of Technology, Coimbatore, Tamil Nadu, India, e-mail: sivaprakashcse0402@gmail.com
K. Periyakaruppan, Department of Computer Science and Engineering, SNS College of Engineering, Coimbatore, Tamil Nadu, India, e-mail: kperiyakaruppan@gmail.com
M. Shobana, Department of Computer Science and Engineering, SNS College of Technology, Coimbatore, Tamil Nadu, India, e-mail: shobanavsm@gmail.com

https://doi.org/10.1515/9783110798159-005

contributors to accidents that occur on the road. There is no doubt that preventative transportation safety measures will lead to a reduction in the number of individuals killed on highways, cities, and urban traffic. This reduction will likely take place as a direct result of these efforts. The term roadside weaponry refers to defensive equipment that is positioned along roadsides. Examples of roadside weaponry include computerized maps, alarm systems, and traffic monitors [6]. The incorporation of active safety features into motor vehicles is a critical part of the design process for collision warning systems.

It is possible to help reduce congestion by, among other things, locating bottlenecks, collecting estimates of the level of congestion, disseminating information on the current status of traffic, and offering alternate routes. Due to this, the method has to incorporate some kind of estimation of the traffic jams in order for it to be effective in cutting down on the amount of traffic congestion. When monitoring highways, it is helpful to make predictions about the frequency of occurrences based on the number of accidents that were recorded over a certain amount of time and in a particular location. The best course of action is to avoid sustaining head trauma as a result of being involved in an accident involving a motor vehicle [7]. The dissident is aware of the constant motion and frequent communication interruptions that occur within automobile networks.

Deep learning (DL) models are able to perform significantly better at predicting traffic accidents than other methods that use machine learning. These other methods include sampling, regressions, correlations, clustering algorithms, k-nearest neighbor algorithms, and artificial neural networks (ANNs). For the purpose of collision prediction, DL methods such as convolutional neural networks (CNN) [10], transpose CNN [11], and long short-term memory (LSTM) [12] are only a few examples of the approaches that are used [12]. The possibility for bias can be reduced by the use of systematic random sampling by collecting samples from automobilists, commuters, and desert residents, in that order. This can be performed by taking samples from each of these groups. When using intentional sampling [8], it is relatively easy to select traffic officers who focus on carrying out their duties on slow streets. This makes the selection of respondents for the study much more efficient. This is because the methodology places an emphasis on identifying respondents who pay attention to these specific activities or tasks.

When it comes to satisfying the requirements of a diverse variety of application needs, the adaptability of congestion clusters is unmatched and cannot be matched by any other technology. These groups are constantly changing their composition and reorganizing themselves into new patterns across the network. These groupings achieve intracluster similarity in order to demonstrate the progression of travel times in a manner that is parallel along the road segment [9]. The K-Nearest Neighbor (KNN) is first put to use to classify the various traffic circumstances, and then it gives preference to the classification that has received the most favorable input from local residents who live in the immediate region. A prediction of the occurrence of traffic accidents may be made using this method [10] by doing an examination of the conditions of the traffic as well as the aspects of the environment that function as limits. The application of ANN has been shown to be effective in a number of different contexts, including the extraction of features and the identification of situations that provide warning of potential shocks or impacts to passengers and operators [11]. In both of these spheres, the applicability of ANN has been established beyond a reasonable doubt.

A feedforward neural network that extracts picture information by using convolutional operations is referred to as a CNN. For the purpose of predicting traffic accidents from a sequence of photographs taken over time, a recurrent neural network is required. The LSTM refers to a sort of network that is used frequently and is one of the many types of networks. The cell state, the memory component, and three gates are all parts of this particular form of network. The production of predicted collision images is accomplished through the use of a transpose CNN.

5.2 Related works

The study examines the impact that geoinformation has had on the transportation system and offers examples of studies that are significant to the topic. A number of studies center their discussions on the question of how it has applied geoinformation and geospatial technologies in their operations.

The authors of [11] conducted research on the digitization of cities as well as the application of geoinformation in the process of SC implementation.

The writers of [12] looked into SC frameworks in addition to the impact that Information and Communication Technology (ICT) solutions have on the surrounding natural environment. Answers to some of the most pressing problems concerning the long-term viability of SC could be found in technologies involving geoinformation and communication (GeoICT). There is a study that was published in [13] that indicates the significance of GeoICT to the expansion of SCs. You can find this article by searching for it on the Internet. In the aforementioned reference, the authors provided the GeoSmartCity framework for readers to utilize. Their investigation made use of many different aspects, such as the location of the study, the paths that were taken, the correlations that were found, and the geographical relationships. The use of visualization technologies enables the production of visually appealing maps based on data depicting traffic in real time.

The authors of [14] discussed the potential applications of GeoDesign in SCs as well as the ways in which three-dimensional planning might improve environmentally conscious design. The authors of [15] describe a strategy that can be used in GIS for the purpose of fusing together different three-dimensional models (GIS). The authors of this study emphasized the benefits of using a three-dimensional model that is capable of providing input to other urban models for themes such as the design of telecommunications networks, disaster management, and the strategy for renewable energy. A multi-scale 3D-GIS method was presented by the authors of [16] as a means of analyzing and spreading the solar revenue of digital city models.

The authors of the article [17] proposed the introduction of location-based services, which are commonly referred to as LBS. LBS places a substantial degree of weight on the user current location as well as the environment that is immediately surrounding them [18]. There are numerous different uses for LBS in SCs, the majority of which concern security, the management of emergency situations, and the monitoring of mobile personnel.

The authors of [19] gave SCs access to a considerable amount of huge data as well as information that was spatial and temporal. Using geocomputing and spatial analysis, location analytics, also known as geospatial big data analytics, is an approach that aims to discover previously concealed insights hidden within spatiotemporal datasets. This approach was developed. The research of activity patterns, the evaluation of populations, and the management of natural disasters are just some of the many uses that may be made of the analysis of geo-tagged location data. Other applications include these and many more (such as Twitter). There is a chance that making use of satellite data and a variety of other forms of remote sensing technology will prove to be advantageous. The imagery that is collected by satellites is used as the basis for these GeoICTs, which, when combined, provide a digital representation of Earth with its position attached to it. Geospatial technology can be put to use in the service of city planning and management by evaluating and keeping track of important environmental indicators. This can be accomplished by assessing and mapping the city terrain. The application of software is required in order to achieve this goal.

The authors of [20] proposed a method that would assess the safety of public transportation in urban areas by making use of a wide variety of intricate network metrics. This method could be implemented. Metrics for complex networks are a form of measuring instrument that may be thought of as a mechanism for expressing high-dimensional interactions between things. The authors of [21] highlighted a significant variety of important smart transportation technologies that are currently accessible for SCs. These technologies are vital. The document contains a graphical representation of an intelligent transportation network in the form of a diagram. The system generates a digital map by making use of a wide variety of information and communication technologies. This map depicts the ways in which a large number of components, such as people, autos, and routes, communicate with one another and interact with one another. It is possible, for instance, to determine the route that will take the least amount of time to travel by taking into account the current state of traffic in addition to the locations of vacant parking spots and automobiles.

The authors of the paper [21] devised a method that they referred to as ELTRO for the goal of construction. As a result of a recent development in GIS, the idea that planning and localization can take place simultaneously has recently gained traction Simultaneous Localization and Mapping (SLAM). The authors of [22] devised a model that intelligent transport systems might use to increase their usefulness by combining

GIS and SLAM. As a component of their investigation into ways to improve the effectiveness of electricity distribution networks, they suggested making use of SLAM. As a result, this would be beneficial to urban transit systems as well as the process of charging electric automobiles (EVs). They constructed a centralized cloud-based SLAM on top of a GIS basis in order to guarantee a constant supply of electricity by basing it on load forecasts obtained from vehicle localization.

The authors of [23] noted that geostatistical approaches can be used in order to forecast the individual journey times, and this is something that has been supported by other researchers. The Kriging family of approaches, which takes into account actual city characteristics and contains regionally weighted regression algorithms, was the one that the researchers used in their investigation. The data collected in Novosibirsk was used in the tests that were carried out by the researchers. The authors of [24] proposed a method for identifying urban sprawl that was carried out with the use of image processing and GIS. This method was successful in accomplishing its goals. They used images collected by the Lansat satellite as a resource for their project so that they could extract various features.

The authors of [25] suggested a method for evaluating data regarding traffic trajectories that makes use of latent component modeling. You can learn more about this approach by reading the article. They built a generative model that they called TraLFM in order to find the human mobility patterns that lay beneath the surface of traffic pathways. This model name is TraLFM. Their approach was established on the basis of the following three observations: (1) the sequences of places indicated by the trajectories are suggestive of mobility patterns; (2) people display distinctive mobility patterns; and (3) mobility patterns are cyclical and evolve over the course of time. The authors conducted a comprehensive study with the use of data gathered from Vehicle Positioning Radio (VPR) and taxis. Their tests suggested, in contrast to the forecasts provided by other methods that are presently regarded as the most cutting-edge in the field, that the TraLFM strategy may be more likely to produce favorable outcomes.

The authors of the paper [26] developed a method for determining the actual distance between bus stops by making use of GPS data obtained from buses as well as information pertaining to bus stops. They were able to do this by combining this information with information about the bus stops themselves. The bus stop influence distance refers to the distance that must be traveled from the location of the bus stop entrance and exit points to the center of the zone where buses have a negative impact on the surrounding road traffic. The researchers wanted to find out how much of an impact the surrounding network has on the patterns of bus traffic that occur in the area immediately surrounding bus stops, and their study was designed to do just that. The purpose of this study was to determine whether or not the contextual factors had any effect on the behavior dynamics shown by motorists while they were driving.

5.3 Proposed methods

Researchers from a variety of institutions have come up with extending variants of the Self Organizing Map (SOM) in order to avoid the limits that were imposed by the SOM initial design. Growing Cell Structure is a form of SOM that is gaining popularity, and it involves the construction of a k-dimensional network space with the constant k being provided. Growing Cell Structure is an example of how SOM can be used. During each cycle, a new node and location are introduced to provide support for the node that has amassed the greatest number of faults over the course of the preceding cycles.

The network will continue to expand until the stop criterion is fulfilled, which might be the maximum cumulative error or the maximum network size. Both of these are possibilities. In the end, regardless of what happens, the network will reach its maximum capacity. A form of SOM grows over time and includes new nodes whenever the neural network does not correctly fit the input.

A more effective growing version of SOM, which they referred to the output network structure in this iteration of the algorithm begins with a limited number of nodes and gradually increases in size along the border, by making use of heuristics and the representation of the input data. The initial structure of the Growing Self-Organizing Map (GSOM) is typically made up of four nodes in the majority of instances. The neural network makes the necessary adjustments to its weights in the beginning of the GSOM process, which is referred to as "growing." This stage ensures that the weights accurately represent the input space. The second part of the process is called "smoothing," and it involves fine-tuning the weights of individual nodes by making adjustments to the weights of other individual nodes.

After the map has had the input vectors for a period of time, the neurons of the best matching units will begin to acquire quantization error based on the map in the growing phase. This mistake occurs when the map is in the process of learning its new features. When compared to the growth threshold, determining whether or not a neuron total quantization error is above that value indicates whether or not the neuron is under-representing the input space Growth Threshold (GT).

In order to address this issue, additional nodes will be added to the neural network that is currently being used. If the Best Matching Unit (BMU) neuron is discovered on the edge of the map, then additional neurons are added to the map beginning at the edge and working their way inward. This process continues until all of the space on the map is occupied by neurons. In the event that this does not happen, the erroneous information will be transmitted to the neurons that are located nearby. When a new neuron is introduced to the network, the weights of the initial connections for that neuron are adjusted to mimic the weights of the neurons that are located immediately adjacent to it.

$$GT = -D \times \ln(SF)$$

When computing the GT, a recently devised parameter known as the spread factor is used. This component value is determined by the total number of dimensions (D) that are contained within the input space. Regardless of the size or scope of the dataset, the SF can be applied to limit the spread of the network structure within the dataset. This can be done in any dataset.

The duties that are carried out during the smoothing phase are very comparable to those that were carried out during the growing phase. These responsibilities include providing inputs and making adjustments to weights. Due to the fact that the purpose of the smoothing phase is to eliminate any quantization error that may already be present, the generation of more neurons will not take place at this stage.

One of the key benefits of GSOM in comparison to SOM and its variants is the capacity to (self-build) self-structure, without requiring any prior knowledge of the data space. As a result of the fact that GSOM is able to self-structure on the latent space, it is able to both classify input into discrete categories and group inputs that have related qualities. This ability is made possible by the fact that GSOM is capable of analyzing the latent space. It is possible to achieve both structural adaptation and hierarchical grouping, both of which are key components of the human visual system, due to the fact that the map spread can be controlled.

5.3.1 Quantum modeling

The traffic lights that can be seen in urban areas are an exceptionally significant contributor to the overall reduction of traffic congestion. Urban planners have been forced to shift their focus from precisely determining the timing of lights at individual intersections to coordinating the flow of traffic through networks of arterial roads and, more recently, to area-wide scheduling that encompasses hundreds of intersections as a result of the exponential increase the traffic signals. This is because of the exponential increase the number of traffic signals. Congestion can be relieved on a worldwide scale by methodically planning the timing of traffic lights at various crossings in order to maximize the flow of traffic and eliminate bottlenecks. This will allow for the most efficient flow of traffic possible.

It is ludicrous to believe that the timing plan could be applied to a real-world urban road network in a manner that is both iterative and random. The strategy that has been proposed is to simulate the flow of urban traffic that is managed by traffic lights, and then use the data obtained from that simulation to establish the timing plan that is the most productive. The Boolean Model of Land Use (BML) is a streamlined model that illustrates in an exact manner the impact that metropolitan traffic signals have on the flow of vehicular traffic. However, the BML does not give a method to optimize the flow of traffic, and its relevance to actual cities is restricted due to the fact that it operates in a theoretical lattice space.

After the road network of the real-world metropolis has been mapped into Enhanced Bi-directional Map Learning (EBML) lattice space, simulation rule updates can be used to boost urban traffic flow. This will help improve the urban environment. This takes place once a map of the road network has been created. The proposed Q-Learning (QL) revises its testing schedule on an iterative basis using data from simulation in order to determine the best timing for traffic lights, which is then applied in the real-world equivalent of an urban area. This process is carried out in order to discover the optimal timing for traffic lights.

The rest of the terrain is effectively off-limits because the vehicles may only go on the city road network, which includes overpasses and tunnels. The lattice places that have been given varying degrees of unidirectional capability can be thought of as highways, and this is one way to think about them. Certain nodes in the lattice have been designed to perform the functions of bridges and tunnels, so that they can take advantage of the special ways in which they can interact with the other nodes. The block capacity is the one that is assigned to each of the lattice sites, unless the lattice sites additionally have the capacity to operate in a unidirectional or intersecting direction. On the lattice, locations known as roadblocks are those that have a high capacity for storing blocks. On the lattice, there are a number of junctions that perform the function of crossroads.

It is generally accepted that two roads are considered to have intersected when they meet at a point that resembles the letter T. The order of vehicles waiting in line to enter an intersection is determined by the sequence of the traffic lights that are located at that intersection. At each discrete time step, traffic lights are used to govern the flow of traffic, and the flow itself is determined by the regulations that are in place at that time. The reader is introduced to a variety of helpful parameters right at the beginning. The ascending lattice has a number of sites, and that number is denoted by the letter n. Starting at the bottom with site 1, the ascending lattice has a total of n sites. The value that is assigned to the number n represents the maximum number of units that can be housed at that location. The value of $max(n)$ is given to that number.

When the lattice that comes after it has the unoccupied vehicle unit that corresponds to the direction of travel, the vehicle that is located in the vehicle unit that is traveling either northbound or southbound will attempt to move ahead one site on the lattice. This happens whether the vehicle is traveling northbound or southbound. In the event that this does not occur, the vehicle will remain in the same spot. The traffic lights that show at even time steps whenever the following lattice will depict a junction are what decide the movement direction, and they do so anytime a junction is about to be depicted.

In order to ensure everyone safety, the traffic signals at a particular intersection need to be synced with one another and follow the same pattern throughout the entire intersection. The cumulative effect of all of the distinct color states that the traffic light shows at the intersection over the course of a particular amount of time is what is referred to as a phase of the intersection. A phase of the intersection can last for a certain amount of time. An established phase sequence is put into place for an intersection, along with the associated color state combinations for the traffic lights at each phase of the established phase sequence for the intersection. Adjusting the amount of time that elapsed between each light was one of the components of the game that required additional focus and care during the process of optimizing the quality of life.

The most cutting-edge navigational systems provide real-time route adjustments that are computed based on real-time traffic reports. Due to this, it will be feasible for users to receive information regarding alternative routes in the event that particularly long traffic delays develop.

For the sake of this investigation, we will be concentrating on one particular aspect of urban congestion, specifically, traffic. If daily traffic flow patterns can be predicted for a given urban environment, then travel times can be reduced based on historical data regarding the distribution of traffic density throughout the day. This is preferable to basing travel time reductions on accidents and other conditions that cause abnormally long delays. Due to the availability of historical data, it is feasible to ascertain the times when the volume of traffic is at its highest and lowest points, throughout the course of the day.

In particular, it facilitates interaction between clients and servers, with the process of route selection taking place on the route server in real time, making use of the route database as well as previous data. Multiple devices can participate in this interaction at the same time. The traffic analysis and visualization system not only enables the authorities that are in charge of traffic management to monitor the current state of traffic, but it also offers forecasts on the likelihood of congestion based on previous data. This provides a significant benefit to the authorities that are responsible for traffic management.

Customers contribute to the process of keeping the information contained in the route database up to date by providing input on the current state of traffic congestion in real time. This, in turn, makes it possible to maintain both a real-time map of the fluidity of traffic in a city as well as accurate historical data of how traffic behavior has changed over time. Using this strategy, it is possible to regulate traffic based on events and evenly disperse it everywhere.

This method results in significantly higher costs despite the fact that it offers significantly better routes because the estimated travel time for each path segment is no longer a fixed value that is determined by segment length and speed limit, but instead will fluctuate dynamically throughout the day. These charges could be used to generate revenue. These numbers were gleaned from the city various traffic records. In order to allow for smooth integration into the route server, the traffic analysis server needs to effectively summarize and synthesize such data. These logs provide hourly congestion measures for each and every induction loop detector in a city over the course of an entire year.

This would be done for each day of the year. In order to accomplish this, the pattern would need to be modeled for each day of the year (assuming a per-hour granularity). It possible that such a massive quantity of modeling work for a single city is unnecessary; also, it results in an extraordinarily high amount of computational cost for jobs on the server side that are linked to route recommendation.

Our objective is to achieve a deeper comprehension of the traffic situation by analyzing the distinct patterns that emerge in the movement of vehicles on different streets, depending on the day of the week, the time of day, and the type of road. In this article, we will offer a heuristic that uses observable traffic patterns to reduce the necessary number of models while preserving the bulk of the time-dependent modeling efficacy.

The first thing that we are going to do is evaluate the traffic volume for a number of different months to look for any clear seasonal shifts in the data. We will do this, so that we can determine whether or not there are any shifts at all. The monthly average number of visitors has relatively little variation from one month to the next. It is not hard to see that seasonal holidays invariably have an impact on the traffic patterns that take place on a daily basis. It is anticipated that a mean of around one million automobiles will be sold before the end of the year. The values for the remaining part of the year are relatively constant.

The findings presented here are derived from an investigation that was carried out in November and using data that was collected during that time period. This particular time period was chosen because, on average, November traffic flow is very stable around the mean, and it does not see any big peaks owing to major holidays. The major disparities occur between the weekdays and the weekends in terms of traffic patterns and other facets of ordinary commuter life, which compares and contrasts the two time periods. In addition, there is a general tendency for the volume of traffic to increase from Monday through Friday, with Friday having the highest volume among all the days of the week.

Not only does the overall number of cars that are operating on the road change on a daily basis, but the distribution of those vehicles also fluctuates throughout the course of the week. This phenomenon is known as vehicle traffic variability. There are times of the day when the vast majority of individuals are on the road on their way to work. Between the hours of two and three in the afternoon, there is a second rush that is not as large as the first. This rush may be suggestive of afternoon commuters and other staff who are on the move. The final traffic peak of the day occurs between the hours of six and eight o'clock, when people are leaving their places of employment and travelling home. The procedure is repeated on the weekdays that are left over.

On Sundays, for instance, rather than any other day of the week, there is a completely different pattern that can be observed: i) we can see that the traffic peaks that are frequently associated with working hours are not there; ii) the total volume of traffic is noticeably lower; and iii) the peak hours on weekends are different from those that occur during the week. The rush hour traffic toward food courts during lunchtime (between 1:00 and 2:00 p.m.) and the rush hour traffic away from lounge areas in the evening are now linked as peak hours. In particular, the rush hour traffic toward food courts during lunchtime (between 1:00 and 2:00 p.m. and between 6 and 8 p.m.).

It is common knowledge that the volume of traffic on major road in a city will be significantly higher than the volume of traffic on minor streets and side streets in the same general area. This is because major roads are designed to accommodate a significantly higher volume of vehicles. It is essential to make this distinction between them due to the fact that not all streets have the same level of foot traffic during rush hour.

Our time-dependent simulation showed that during peak hours, 31% of all roads had a traffic intensity that is lower than 700 automobiles per hour. These findings are based on the results of the simulation. It suggests that even during peak hours, the routes with low traffic intensity will not be affected by congestion due to the lack of drivers on the road. In addition to this, we see that an incredibly small proportion of the city highways and road are subjected to exceptionally large volumes of traffic (more than 10,000 vehicles during the peak hour).

The vast majority of city roads will experience quantities of traffic that are manageable, and the pattern of behavior that is seen at peak hours around the world will have no impact whatsoever on those roads. In spite of the fact that the two patterns have values for peak traffic intensity that are quite comparable to one another, it is fascinating to observe that the peaks in one pattern frequently coincide with the troughs in the other pattern. This phenomenon is fascinating to observe because it demonstrates how closely the two patterns are related to one another.

Therefore, it is vital to differentiate between the various streets based on the typical amount of daily traffic that they see on those routes. This may be done by looking at the quantity of traffic that is seen on each route. In order for us to achieve this objective, we will implement a clustering method that will enable us to automatically categorize streets according to the typical volume of traffic that they experience.

Researchers are investigating how to develop and deploy quantum software in order to achieve the aforementioned goals of machine learning on quantum computers being significantly faster and more efficient than their equivalent on classical computers. These goals are being pursued in order to achieve the potential benefits of quantum computing. This is due to the fact that it is anticipated that machine learning on quantum computers will be a lot quicker than its equivalent on classical computers. The application of quantum machine learning, which frequently involves the use of quantum algorithms, has the potential to outperform relevant classical machine learning techniques in certain cases. This is because quantum machine learning frequently involves the use of quantum algorithms.

A significant number of cutting-edge strategies for quantum machine learning have already been put into practice. A few examples of these methods include quantum principal component analysis, quantum support vector machines, and quantum neural networks. Previous research has demonstrated that certain quantum machine learning algorithms have the potential to achieve quantum speedups in their overall performance. Quantum reinforcement learning is a subsection of quantum machine learning in which a quantum agent learns through the course of its interactions with the world around it. This type of learning is referred to as reinforcement learning (RL). Two of the processes that can be incorporated into the building of a reinforcement strategy are the quantum measurement and the Grover operation. Using quantum superposition states allows for a more accurate description of the states and operations. It has been demonstrated that quantum RL, when compared to its classical forerunner, is capable of theoretically achieving a quadratic increase in speed.

The process of human decision-making can be described using quantum RL, and it has been demonstrated through experimentation that a quantum communication channel with the environment can significantly cut down the amount of time it takes for an agent to learn. When applied to a vector space of dimension, the Harrow-Hassidim-Lloyd algorithm (HHL) algorithm, which is also known as the quantum algorithm, has the potential to solve a system of linear equations in a polynomial amount of time. This is an order of magnitude faster than the classical algorithms that are currently known to be the most effective solution to this problem. The idea that matrices can be operated on vectors in high-dimensional vector spaces, which is important for quantum physics and that the quantum state of qubits is a vector in this space, provides the foundation for this technique. This technique was developed in order to solve some of the problems that arise in the study of quantum physics.

HHL has been an indispensable resource in the development of many other types of quantum machine learning algorithms, including quantum Bayesian inference, quantum principal component analysis, and quantum support vector machines, to name a few. Quantum neural networks are a fascinating approach to machine learning in quantum computing that is now gaining popularity. The ultimate goal of these networks is to construct quantum equivalents of neural networks and deep learning systems. Quantum information processing enables the development of novel models and characteristics, such as quantum entanglement and quantum coherence, which may allow for the creation of deep learning techniques that are superior to those that were previously produced using standard methods. For example, quantum entanglement and quantum coherence both fall into this category.

In the context of training a quantum Boltzmann machine, quantum coherence might, for example, cut the number of training samples needed to learn a target task by a factor of four. This would allow the machine to learn the task significantly faster. Due to this, the total amount of time spent on training may be cut down greatly. A further significant development in recent times has been the intensive study into variational quantum algorithms. This research, which tries to achieve a quantum edge using computers that will become available in the near future, has recently seen significant progress. Before being evaluated by a quantum computer, a job is often encoded into a parameterized cost function in these approaches. After that, the job is delivered to the quantum computer. The parameters of the cost function are then trained using a traditional optimizer in the next step. In addition, applications for quantum machine learning have been built by using the framework offered by variational quantum algorithms. These applications have been used in the development of these applications. Given that the study of quantum machine learning is only getting off the ground, there are a great many chances to make a difference right now.

Researchers have found that machine learning may be used to handle a range of difficult problems involving quantum estimation and control. Learning control, which is one of the most prominent methods of control design in quantum control, has demonstrated remarkable effectiveness in the field through its application to laser control of molecules and other fields of quantum technology. As a result of this, it is currently regarded as one of the most influential ways of control design in the field of quantum control.

Both quantum open-loop learning control and quantum closed-loop learning control are two perspectives that can be taken on the results that have already been achieved in the field of quantum learning control. In order to achieve outstanding results in the laser control of laboratory chemical reactions, using a quantum closed-loop learning control system that is founded on genetic algorithms (GA) or differential evolution (DE) has been shown to be effective. The use of the laser allowed for the acquisition of these results.

At the very beginning of a test, the input might either be a control pulse that has been meticulously arranged or it could be completely random. Both of these outcomes are entirely conceivable. The control target is defined in light of the practical necessity, and during the learning process, it is commonly transformed to the fitness function. This is done in order to facilitate the learning process. It is conceivable for this fitness function to be affected by the state of the system, the quantity of control energy, or the amount of control time.

In the process of learning, it is common practice to apply a trial input to a limited number of samples and then evaluate the change that occurs as a result of applying that input. This is done in order to facilitate learning. In the second stage of the procedure, a machine learning algorithm is used to the data that was acquired from the initial experiment in order to determine a control input that is more effective. This is done in order to achieve the best possible results. Thirdly, the improved input makes it possible to exert more control over the most recent samples. On a regular basis, this process is continued until either the desired level of control is reached or the end condition is satisfied, whichever comes first. Closed-loop learning control is particularly effective for overcoming issues connected with quantum control. This is due to the ease with which a large number of identical-state samples may be generated as well as the complexity of the system dynamics.

Closed-loop learning control is a helpful data-driven control strategy that can aid scientists and engineers working in systems and control to design effective experiments. Closed-loop learning control can be found in many modern control systems. A huge opportunity for collaboration between scientists and engineers working in systems and control and quantum physicists and quantum chemists arises in the form of the creation of quantum learning control algorithms that are both efficient and robust.

The tasks connected with quantum control are described as optimization problems within the framework of quantum open-loop learning control. The solutions to these problems can then be found with the use of an algorithm for machine learning that searches for the control inputs that are the most effective. It is essential to make the assumption of a certain level of prior knowledge regarding the system model and the dynamics of the system in order for this strategy to have any chance of being successful. The application of gradient algorithms in the research and development of quantum open-loop learning control is a logical fit for the properties of these algorithms because of the efficiency of these algorithms.

Even though the computation of the gradient information is required for gradient algorithms, it is frequently difficult to acquire this information in many real-world settings due to the complexity that is involved. This information might cause problems. In addition, many intricate scenarios involving quantum control frequently involve conditions that are considered to be the local optimum. In circumstances such as this one, methods of stochastic search have the potential to be applied in order to locate effective control fields that have increased performance. When the learnt control fields are applied to a quantum system that consists of uncertainties and noise, it is probable that the control fields will not be stable enough for open-loop control to function properly. Recent studies have shown that it is possible to include concepts from machine learning into the process of creating algorithms for quantum control systems in order to ensure consistent performance. This has been proved to be possible by the findings of these studies.

There is a substantial amount of potential that has not yet been realized in the field of using machine learning for the estimation and identification of quantum states and parameters. For instance, with the assistance of deep neural networks, it would be possible to reconstruct quantum states and detect parameters in noisy quantum systems. Those are just two of the applications of this technology. Due to their high level of generalizability and extensive processing capabilities, these networks could be regarded an alternate method.

You will not need a model to create controllers if you use RL or deep reinforcement learning, which are both types of learning. This is something that you should keep in mind whenever you are working on a controller, regardless of whether it is open-loop or closed-loop. It is now possible to detect parameters with a high level of precision, thanks to the incorporation of machine learning into adaptive techniques. Previously, this was not the case. Estimating the quantum state is difficult because the complexity of the problem grows at a pace that is exponentially proportional to the number of qubits. This makes the problem harder to solve as the number of qubits increases. Due to this, the extent to which machine learning may be used to recreate quantum states in their entirety is limited. Determining the level of precision that a learning algorithm is capable of achieving is another obstacle that must be overcome.

5.4 Results and discussion

In this section, we test the efficacy of our model by choosing the fewest patterns that appropriately define the amounts of traffic that occur at various times of the day. We do this by comparing the results to the original data. After that, we demonstrate how our traffic management platform may be able to benefit from the numerous models that we have created in order to estimate the monetary burden that is associated with a variety of routes. These models are used to compare and contrast the costs that are associated with the various travel options. In conclusion, we show the proposed QL in order to ensure that the provided approach may be used with any target city. This was done so that we can move forward with this research.

Table 5.1: Proposed classified results.

Vehicle flow	Accuracy	Sensitivity	Specificity	F1-score
10	0.8143	0.5187	0.9903	0.6987
20	0.9862	0.4450	1.0117	0.5330
30	0.9401	0.3427	1.0138	0.6680
40	0.9698	0.5115	1.0138	0.6496
50	0.8123	0.4143	0.9453	0.5217
60	0.9800	0.6496	1.0189	0.4890
70	0.9882	0.4829	1.0138	0.6670
80	1.0199	0.6138	1.0138	0.4092
90	0.7519	0.3355	0.9698	0.5729
100	0.9002	0.4552	0.9944	0.4419
110	0.8828	0.4532	0.9739	0.4327
120	0.9841	0.4706	1.0138	0.6210
130	0.9923	0.3887	1.0138	0.5708
140	0.9023	0.4133	0.9545	0.6905

We show the proposed classified results in Table 5.1. Also, given a street and an instant in time at which it is anticipated that a vehicle will enter the street, the four processes that are involved in calculating the trip time for that street specific route are shown here. The subindexes that correspond to the specified street and instant of time have not been allocated to the variables, since we wished to keep things as straightforward and uncomplicated as is humanly possible.

5.5 Conclusion

We concentrated on traffic flow and conducted an investigation of the traffic patterns that occur on the many streets and avenues of a city in order to determine how they shift throughout the course of the year, which days of the week have a pattern that is consistent, which streets have the most congestion, and how these streets can be clustered according to the daily traffic volume that they experience. Our research has shown that it is possible to predict how city traffic will behave if one puts together elements exhibiting similar characteristics within the same interpolation function. It is now possible to estimate how traffic will move across the city. We are able to achieve this by streamlining the model, which enables us to provide customers with travel itineraries that are both efficient and accurate. These itineraries take into account the amount of time necessary to traverse the major roads of the city.

References

[1]   Xu, D., & Ren, P. (2021). Quantum learning based nonrandom superimposed coding for secure wireless access in 5G URLLC. *IEEE Transactions on Information Forensics and Security, 16,* 2429–2444.

[2]   Derrouz, H., Cabri, A., Ait Abdelali, H., Oulad Haj Thami, R., Bourzeix, F., Rovetta, S., & Masulli, F. (2022). End-to-end quantum-inspired method for vehicle classification based on video stream. *Neural Computing and Applications, 34*(7), 5561–5576.

[3]   Jaiswal, A., Kumar, S., Kaiwartya, O., Kashyap, P. K., Kanjo, E., Kumar, N., & Song, H. (2021). Quantum learning-enabled green communication for next-generation wireless systems. *IEEE Transactions on Green Communications and Networking, 5*(3), 1015–1028.

[4]   Kalinin, M. O., & Krundyshev, V. M. (2021). Analysis of a huge amount of network traffic based on quantum machine learning. *Automatic Control and Computer Sciences, 55*(8), 1165–1174.

[5]   Wu, N., & Sun, J. (2022). Fatigue detection of air traffic controllers based on radiotelephony communications and self-adaption quantum genetic algorithm optimization ensemble learning. *Applied Sciences, 12*(20), 10252.

[6]   Zhang, M., Lv, B., & Liu, Z. S. (2022). Network Attack Traffic Recognition Based on Quantum Neural Network. In: 2022 7th International Conference on Computational Intelligence and Applications (ICCIA) (pp. 71–75). IEEE.

[7]   Majumder, R., Khan, S. M., Ahmed, F., Khan, Z., Ngeni, F., Comert, G., & . . . Chowdhury, M. (2021). Hybrid Classical-Quantum Deep Learning Models for Autonomous Vehicle Traffic Image Classification Under Adversarial Attack. *arXiv preprint arXiv:2108.01125.*

[8]   Majumder, R., Chowdhury, M., Khan, S. M., Khan, Z., Ahmed, F., Ngeni, F., & . . . Michalaka, D. Adversarial Attack-resilient Hybrid Classical-Quantum Deep Learning model for Traffic Sign Classification.

[9]   Meyer, J. J., Mularski, M., Gil-Fuster, E., Mele, A. A., Arzani, F., Wilms, A., & Eisert, J. (2022). Exploiting symmetry in variational quantum machine learning. *arXiv preprint arXiv:2205.06217.*

[10]   Wang, Y., Maniatakos, M., & Jabari, S. E. (2021). A trigger exploration method for backdoor attacks on deep learning-based traffic control systems. In: 2021 60th IEEE Conference on Decision and Control (CDC) (pp. 4394–4399). IEEE.

[11]   Lopez-Montiel, M., Orozco-Rosas, U., Sánchez-Adame, M., Picos, K., & Ross, O. H. M. (2021). Evaluation method of deep learning-based embedded systems for traffic sign detection. *IEEE Access*, *9*, 101217–101238.

[12]   Sabitha, R., Gopikrishnan, S., Bejoy, B. J., Anusuya, V., & Saravanan, V. (2022). Network based detection of IoT attack using AIS-IDS model. *Wireless Personal Communications*, 1–24.

[13]   Saravanan, V., Rajeshwari, S., & Jayashree, P. (2013). Security issues in protecting computers and maintenance. *Journal of Global Research in Computer Science*, *4*(1), 55–58.

[14]   Silvia Priscila, S., Sathish Kumar, C., Manikandan, R., Yuvaraj, N., & Ramkumar, M. (2022). Interactive Artificial Neural Network Model for UX Design. In: International Conference on Computing, Communication, Electrical and Biomedical Systems (pp. 277–284). Springer, Cham.

[15]   Manikandan, R., Sara, S. B. V., Yuvaraj, N., Chaturvedi, A., Priscila, S. S., & Ramkumar, M. (2022). Sequential pattern mining on chemical bonding database in the bioinformatics field. In: AIP Conference Proceedings (Vol. 2393, No. 1, p. 020050). AIP Publishing LLC.

[16]   Hu, X., Li, D., Yu, Z., Yan, Z., Luo, W., & Yuan, L. (2022). Quantum harmonic oscillator model for fine-grained expressway traffic volume simulation considering individual heterogeneity. *Physica A: Statistical Mechanics and Its Applications*, *605*, 128020.

[17]   Yadav, S. P. (2022). Blockchain Security. In: Baalamurugan, K., Kumar, S. R., Kumar, A., Kumar, V., Padmanaban, S., (eds.). Blockchain Security in Cloud Computing. EAI/Springer Innovations in Communication and Computing. Springer, Cham. https://doi.org/10.1007/978-3-030-70501-5_1.

[18]   Yadav, S. P., Bhati, B. S., Mahato, D. P., & Kumar, S. (eds.). Federated Learning for IoT Applications. EAI/Springer Innovations in Communication and Computing. Springer, Cham. https://doi.org/10.1007/978-3-030-85559-8.

[19]   Yadav, S. P., & Yadav, S. (2018). Fusion of medical images in wavelet domain: A discrete mathematical model. *Ingeniería Solidaria*, *14*(25), 1–11. https://doi.org/10.16925/.v14i0.2236.

[20]   Song, Q., Wang, W., Fu, W., Sun, Y., Wang, D., & Gao, Z. (2022). Research on quantum cognition in autonomous driving. *Scientific Reports*, *12*(1), 1–16.

[21]   Adil, M., Song, H., Ali, J., Jan, M. A., Attique, M., Abbas, S., & Farouk, A. (2021). EnhancedAODV: A robust three phase priority-based traffic load balancing scheme for internet of things. *IEEE Internet of Things Journal*.

[22]   Gobinathan, B., Mukunthan, M. A., Surendran, S., Somasundaram, K., Moeed, S. A., Niranjan, P., & . . . Sundramurthy, V. P. (2021). A novel method to solve real time security issues in software industry using advanced cryptographic techniques. *Scientific Programming*, *2021*.

[23]   Nithya, C., & Saravanan, V. (2018). A study of machine learning techniques in data mining. *International Science Refereed Research Journal*, *1*, 31–38.

[24]   Niranjan, D. R., & VinayKarthik, B. C. (2021). Deep learning based object detection model for autonomous driving research using carla simulator. In: 2021 2nd International Conference on Smart Electronics and Communication (ICOSEC) (pp. 1251–1258). IEEE.

[25]   Ferrag, M. A., Shu, L., Friha, O., & Yang, X. (2021). Cyber security intrusion detection for agriculture 4.0: Machine learning-based solutions, datasets, and future directions. *IEEE/CAA Journal of Automatica Sinica*, *9*(3), 407–436.

[26]   Hu, X., Niu, X., Qian, L., Pan, B., & Yu, Z. (2022). Analyzing the multi-scale characteristic for online car-hailing traffic volume with quantum walk. *IET Intelligent Transport Systems*.

Deepali Virmani*, T. Nadana Ravishankar, Mihretab Tesfayohanis

6 IoT attack detection using quantum deep learning in large-scale networks

Abstract: The probability of a cyberattack rises at an exponential pace in direct proportion to the size of the network-connected device population. Cybercriminals will concentrate their efforts on wireless networks because it is anticipated that more than half of all data on the Internet would originate from wireless networks. In this chapter, we develop an IoT attack detection using an intrusion detection system (IDS) framework that develops a quantum convolutional neural network-based Long Short-Term Memory (QCNN-LSTM) in large-scale networks. The collection of network logs is initially preprocessed and then it is classified using classifiers. The model is simulated to test its robustness against different scale of attacks, and the results show higher level of accuracy in detecting the attacks using QCNN-LSTM than other methods.

6.1 Introduction

The probability of a cyberattack rises at an exponential pace in direct proportion to the size of the network-connected device population [1]. Cybercriminals will concentrate their efforts on wireless networks because it is anticipated that more than half of all data on the Internet would originate from wireless networks [2]. There are currently four times as many spam emails as there were a year earlier, and IBM [3] reported a large increase in the number of account takeovers in 2016. According to the same survey, there are many various types of cyberattacks, some of which include brute force, phishing, SQL injection, distributed denial of service, malware, and others.

85% of the malicious software that was detected was ransomware. Those are some scary statistics. If such attacks were successful, there is potential for significant financial loss as a result of either the disclosure of confidential information or the disruption of regular business activities. Companies that are involved in the provision of financial services are always those that experience the most severe consequences as a result of data breaches. After that, come the wholesale and retail trade, followed

*Corresponding author: Deepali Virmani, B. Tech Programmes, Vivekananda Institute of Professional Studies Technical Campus, School of Engineering and Technology, Delhi, India,
e-mail: deepalivirmani@gmail.com
T. Nadana Ravishankar, Department of Data Science and Business Systems, SRM Institute of Science and Technology, Chennai, Tamil Nadu, India, e-mail: nadanart@srmist.edu.in
Mihretab Tesfayohanis, Department of IT, Dambi Dollo University, Dambi Dollo, Ethiopia,
e-mail: miremsc2011@gmail.com

https://doi.org/10.1515/9783110798159-006

by manufacturing, and then ultimately, the information and communications technology sectors [3].

In recent years, putting in place an IDS to safeguard sensitive information that is stored in online databases has evolved into a standard operating practice in the information security industry. The IDS is situated inside of the network, in contrast to the firewall, which is solely accountable for monitoring traffic entering the network. When it comes to the safety of a network, having both a firewall and an IDS might prove to be advantageous.

An IDS is an automated version of a method that was once carried out manually in order to identify situations in which security rules in a network environment were violated. This method was once carried out in order to identify situations in which unauthorized users gained access to a computer system. In addition to their primary role of event detection, IDS can also be used to record prospective threats and deter future adversaries [4]. This is in addition to the fact that its primary job is to identify events. IDS systems require a distinct collection of qualities because of their non-active nature, their concentration on network monitoring, and their aspiration simultaneously.

We are able to classify IDSs according to the methodologies that they employ and the locations in the network in which they are situated. IDSs can be classified into one of three groups depending on where the IDS module is located in the network. These categories are network-based, host-based, and hybrid-based. The network-based IDS, often known as NIDS, was the first type of IDS to function by embedding a monitoring module directly into the network that it was guarding. As it has a holistic perspective of the system, this intrusion detection software has an in-depth knowledge of how a computer network functions.

Host-based IDSs, on the other hand, install the IDS component locally on each network endpoint. In spite of the fact that the module can only monitor incoming and outgoing data of a client, it nonetheless performs extremely detailed monitoring of each client traffic. Both network-based and host-based IDSs offer benefits and suffer from drawbacks that are unique to each of them. While host-based IDSs need less labor but may not provide a network-wide perspective, network-based IDSs can be resource costly and may overlook some potentially harmful activities. As a result, hybrid-based IDSs install IDS modules not only in the network but also in the clients, allowing for simultaneous monitoring of both the individual clients and the entire network.

In the latter, there are three distinct types of IDSs that can be categorized based on the mechanism of detection. Each of these IDSs has its own set of capabilities. Abuse, anomaly, and specification-based categories are the names given to these groups. A type of IDS known as signature-based IDS is one that analyzes the traffic it is monitoring and compares it to known attack patterns, often known as signatures. [5] One that uses signatures to detect threats is called a signature-based IDS. This IDS is quite good at locating typical dangers; nevertheless, it is not up to the task of keeping up with the rapid pace at which zero-day exploits are being developed.

An anomaly-based IDS, is a type of security system that monitors for suspicious activity by generating a profile of typical user behavior and then sounding an alarm whenever this profile suggests that suspicious activity has occurred. One of the most impressive aspects of this IDS is its capacity to identify threats that have never been seen before. When it comes to detecting known threats, the detection performance of IDS systems that are based on misuse rather than anomalies is typically higher. This is because misuse is a more common occurrence than anomalies. An IDS known as a specification-based IDS is one that functions on the basis of rules and constraints that are personally established by an administrator. During the course of the execution, any deviation from the pre-determined parameters ought to be regarded as suspicious [6–10].

In this chapter, we develop an IoT attack detection using IDS framework that develops an QCNN- based LSTM in large-scale networks.

6.2 Related works

The development of the Neural Network (NN) algorithm, which may be regarded of as the theoretical foundation of deep learning, can be traced all the way back to the beginning of the field of deep learning. In order to get over the restrictions that are caused by neural network reliance on a single hidden layer, a variety of alternative approaches have been put into practice. These methods make use of a structured hierarchy of hidden layers that build on top of one another in an organized manner. In view of the multitude of readily available deep learning methods, we classify these methods into groups according to the strategy that is used [20]. Deep learning can be segmented into three separate categories: generative learning, discriminative learning, and hybrid learning. The function of the system being classified is either the architecture itself or the technology itself. Synthesis, generation, and recognition are three examples of distinct forms of goals.

In unsupervised learning, which makes use of generative architectures, to function correctly, it is necessary to make use of data that has not been labeled in any way. Unsupervised learning, which is often commonly referred to as pre-training, is a basic notion that drives generative structures [21] in the field of pattern recognition. This idea is what makes generative architectures possible. As it can be difficult to train the deeper layers of the networks of the future, deep generative architectures are absolutely important. Because of this, it is of utmost necessity to learn the lower layers independently of the top ones, in a layer-by-layer manner, while coping with a limited amount of training data. This must be done in order to achieve the best results.

There is an equal number of neurons in the network input and output layers. The Auto Encoder (AE) network is a typical example of an Artificial Neural Network (ANN).

This can be seen from the fact that the number of neurons in each of these layers is the same. On the other hand, the low-dimensional traits that are represented by the nodes in the hidden layer are completely original to this layer. After a significant amount of computer work has been done on the data, it is now possible to reconstruct the data. The purpose of artificial intelligence is to learn successfully with only a small quantity of information, and it is possible to combine it with other AE layers to produce very vast networks. The outcomes of the training that is completed by each consecutive layer of the buried structure are incorporated into that structure. A structure that is capable of delivering new characteristics at varying depths is referred to as a stacked auto-encoder (SAE). When there is a significant amount of data that has been labeled, it is possible to add another layer that also has labels in order to obtain more precise training [22]. This helps ensure that the model is being trained as accurately as possible. In order to reconstruct a clean corrective input from a noisy one, a denoising auto encoder (DAE) must first be trained to do so [15–19]. To accomplish this, the DAE is trained with the help of the noisy input. When constructing deep networks, the DAE can have additional layers placed on top of it for increased complexity.

A Restricted Boltzmann Machine (RBM) is a modified Boltzmann machine in which the concealed units are not connected to one another. As RBM takes into consideration both overt and covert data, it is possible to draw inferences regarding the links between the two types of variables. Deep belief networks (DBN) are a type of multi-layered neural networks. Dimensionality reduction is one of the potential applications for the feature extraction approach of DBN. All that is needed is a dataset that is not labeled, as well as back-propagation, which is another term for unsupervised training. On the other hand, DBN is the method of choice for classification [14] when training is conducted on a dataset that has been correctly labeled and that contains feature vectors. This type of training is also known as supervised training.

Convolutional Neural Network (CNN) makes use of a specific layout that has been determined to be the most effective for picture recognition. Due to the way CNN is structured, onboarding new workers is a straightforward and expedient process. CNN may be used to train multi-layer networks by employing gradient descent for high-dimensional and nonlinear mappings [13]. This allows for the possibility of using CNN to train multi-layer networks. The terms local receptive fields, shared weights, and pooling are the names of the three essential components that make up CNN [12].

The fact that generative and discriminative methods of design are both used in hybrid deep architecture is why the term "hybrid" is used. It is necessary to make use of the hybrid design in order to differentiate between the data and the discriminative method. On the other hand, it has proven of immense aid in the initial stages of the process, particularly with regards to the repercussions of generating structures. Deep neural networks (DNN) are an example of how hybrid architecture can be put to use in various contexts. It is important to keep in mind that DNN and DBN are frequently misunderstood to be the same. In the public literature, there are examples of DBNs that use back- propagation discriminative training for tuning [11].

We looked into a wide variety of algorithms, but we focused much of our attention on those that were quantum deep learning inspired due to the potential that these algorithms have in furthering IDS research. We are of the opinion that current procedures can be made more effective through the observation and analysis of natural occurrences.

6.3 Methods

This chapter presents an example of a system design that is capable of detection of system-based Internet of Things (IoT) botnets. The artificial intelligence (CNN-LSTM) model that is applied in this system is at the cutting edge of technology and is used to monitor devices connected to the IoT for indications of an intrusion.

The methodology was validated by using real-world traffic data that was obtained from nine commercial IoT devices that had been lawfully infected by a massive botnet attack, most notably Mirai. These devices were used to corroborate the methodology. In order for the security system to be able to spot common dangers, it was configured to recognize zero-day attacks that were carried out by devices connected to the IoT.

The architecture of the system is depicted in Figure 6.1, which shows how it is still in the process of being developed. In the following few paragraphs, we will delve deeper into the proposed organizational structure and discuss its finer points in greater depth.

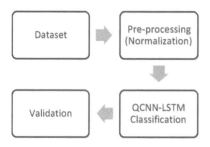

Figure 6.1: Proposed UAV.

6.3.1 Pre-processing technique

When the model is being trained, the values are represented in the features dataset using a wide variety of scales. This allows the loss function during the training process to be minimized as much as possible. While the procedure for gradient optimization is being carried out, these scales have a propensity to have an impact on the optimization of the learning rate.

These advantages include: in contrast to the signature-based approach that is used in NIDS, the min-max scaling method performs exceptionally well on our Network Security Laboratory - Knowledge Discovery in Databases (NSL-KDD) dataset. This is because applications for anomaly detection are not needed to conform to a certain distribution.

This can be done by using the Min-Max normalization method. This will make it possible to get more precise findings. The equation that is about to be presented takes into consideration both the value that is the lowest and the value that is the highest in the column. This is done, so that the resulting values will be between 0 and 1.

$$X' = X - Xmin/Xmax - Xmin$$

where Xmin is the smallest number, Xmax is the largest number, and X is original data.

6.3.2 Classification

The implementation of deep learning techniques, such as CNN, is necessary for the creation of photo classification systems that are both accurate and efficient. On the other hand, the CNN model may also be used in the process of assisting in the development of an effective security architecture. The four basic layers that comprise the CNN algorithm are the input layer, the convolutional layer, the pooling layer, and the fully connected layer. The fully connected layer is the last layer. A typical neural network is composed of these four primary layers in its structure.

(1) Convolutional layer
The first layer of the neural network is called the convolutional layer. In the convolutional layer, many filters, which are referred to collectively as convolution kernels, are used in order to explore, size, and filter the training sample. Before the weighted summation kernel layer can begin the process of recoding, it is required for the convolutional layer to first construct the weight matrix for the input sample.

These values are used to select particular pixels. Selecting optimal values for three fundamentals can assist in reducing the complexity of the neural network and boosting the overall performance of the system. The filter size, the stride, and the zero padding are all examples of these hyperparameters. The data entry form that is currently being used is: (115, 1). It has been agreed that a kernel size of 5 will be used, in addition to filter sizes of 64 and 128, respectively.

Nonlinear activation functions, such as rectified linear unit (ReLU), are used when applying the activation function of a feature map to the element of each individual convolutional layer. The ReLU function will always return 0 when it is applied to an input that is in the negative, but when it is applied to an input that is in the positive, it will return any number x.

(2) Pooling layer

A pooling layer can be of assistance in lowering when one is in the process of constructing a fit matrix average pool. This is accomplished by picking the values that are the highest in each region. The subsequent processing step will make use of the information that is stored within this matrix. That phase will come after this one. It has been decided that each pool can accommodate no more than five persons at a time.

(3) Fully connected layer

The third layer is one that is completely integrated with all of the other layers. Using layers that are totally connected to one another is the traditional method for representing the final phase of a CNN. Every single one of the nodes that are part of the layer that is entirely connected has a connection to every single one of the nodes that are part of level L as well as level L + 1, which is the level that comes after it. In contrast to the conventional ANN, there is no contact between the nodes that are located on the same layer. Training and examination on this layer both take a significant amount of time due to this reason.

6.3.3 Long short-term memory (LSTM)

The technique known as the recurrent neural network (RNN) is one of the more well-known models for deep learning, and it is implemented in a wide variety of applications that are used in the real world. One sort of RNN that can be used is referred to as the LSTM. It is a type of memory that is used to perform analysis on sequence data and that possesses a feedback loop that is not characteristic of feedforward neural networks.

The device for both long-term and short-term memory is dependent on three basic gates: the input gate, the forget gate, and the output gate. These gates are referred to collectively as the gates. The information that is gained throughout training is continuously incorporated into the input gate state of being via updates. The long-term memory is initialized using data from the most recent time step, and the short-term memory is also initialized using data from the most recent time step. The long-term memory is going to be initialized using the data that is now being supplied. After the training data have been filtered out of the input gate using filters, the helpful data are sent on to the sigma function. Irrelevant data, on the other hand, are discarded, and only the data that has the potential to be useful are advanced.

For the indicator variable, the sigma function is able to accept either the value 0 or the value 1 as an argument. In the context of this discussion, values that contain a 1 represent those with the highest priority, whilst values that contain a 0 suggest those with the lowest priority. The system short-term memory is where the results of the input layer are kept once they have been processed. The LSTM model places a significant amount of emphasis on its forget gate, which can be thought of as a fundamental component. By multiplying the values of the forget vector by the current input of the gate, the system is able to determine which bits of data should be saved and which should be discarded. This is done in order to optimize storage space. The output of the forget gate will be transferred into the cell that comes after it, and that cell will then contact long-term memory in order to obtain an updated version of the information.

Important information is passed on to the cell that comes after it by means of the activation function. It is the data that goes through the forget gate, the data that comes out of the forget gate, the cell that the data goes into, the data that comes out of the cell, and the data that goes through the forget gate. Likewise, the data that leaves the cell is the data that is sent into the forget gate.

6.4 Evaluation

The KDD Cup is widely recognized as being among the most prestigious data mining competitions in existence today. The NSL-KDD dataset was created with the purpose of addressing a major number of flaws that were present in the KDD Cup 1999 dataset. This was the motivation behind the construction of the dataset. Since the outset, the NIDS problem has been the focus of a great amount of study, and a large number of academics have relied on the NSL-KDD dataset for the purposes of testing and development. This collection features attacks of virtually every kind imaginable. The dataset contains 41 features, of which there are three primary types (basic feature, content-based feature, and traffic-based feature), each categorized as normal or attack, and the attack type further subdivided.

The authors suggest using a dataset known as NSL-KDD, which is divided into two parts: a training set and a test set. Both of these components are intended to be used independently. The construction of both sets makes use of a random sampling approach, and both kinds of information – numerical and symbolic – are included in both. The job becomes a more realistic illustration of an application problem that occurs in the real world when the training set and the test set each have different probability distributions.

Due to the fact that the NSL-KDD dataset does not include any duplicate data in either the training sets or the test sets, the opportunity for an algorithmic bias to occur during the phase of learning has been removed. The newly generated dataset, which comprises a total of 41 characteristics, includes a connection that is made between the training and test sets of the dataset. Learning algorithms are in a better position to effectively provide a higher detection rate because the test set of the NSL-KDD dataset does not include any duplicates.

This evaluation will be based on the accuracy measure, since it enables making an accurate comparison of the success of the developed method to the results of the

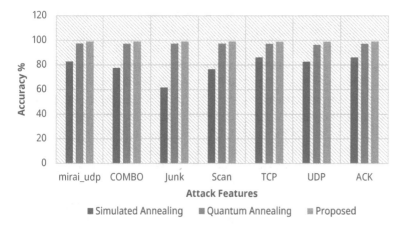

Figure 6.2: Training accuracy.

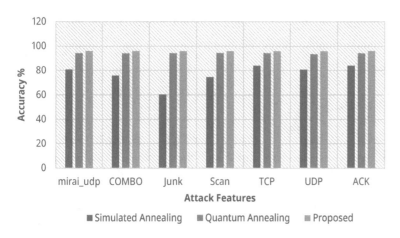

Figure 6.3: Testing accuracy.

binary classification issue. This comparison will serve as the basis for this evaluation. The degree to which the model is able to determine whether or not an attack is taking place in a specific network environment is represented by how well it performs on the binary classification job.

When compared to the deep neural network that used six features from the earlier approach, the CNN-LSTM method that was developed achieved a high accuracy score of 95.55% (shown in Figures 6.2–6.3). The QCNN was utilized for the purpose of making this comparison. In fact, we were successful in demonstrating that the proposed model had an accuracy of 92%.

Reproducibility and repeatability refer to the consistency with which the results of the classification task can be checked multiple times under the same conditions. Reproducibility and repeatability are sometimes used interchangeably. There is a positive correlation between these two terms and a greater degree of accuracy. When we take into account the findings from the previous research, we are in a position to assert that the solution that was provided for the binary classification problem yields satisfactory and reliable outcomes when it is applied to address the issue.

The area that is intended to be quantified by the area under the curve (AUC) is the whole area that lies beneath the two-dimensional ROC curve. The information that we get from the area AUC indicates the overall performance of the classification system across all of the different cutoffs. The AUC is a measure that is used in the process of determining how efficient a classifier is. It is unaffected by either the scale or the threshold, since it takes into account both the threshold and the entire range of values that can be predicted by the classifier. This makes it independent of both the scale and the threshold. When all four categories are taken into account at the same time, the AUC reaches 99.94%. By employing an alternative strategy for judging, it has been demonstrated that the proposed method is capable of performing as expected and meets the requirements for attack classification.

6.5 Conclusion

IDSs in IoT-based deep learning algorithms have attracted a considerable level of interest over the past two decades as a result of the different approaches and datasets that are developed in deep learning. These methods make use of a constrained number of attributes in order to improve their abnormality detection capabilities and provide superior and more efficient network security. Within the scope of this investigation, we train and evaluate our models using the reference dataset known as NSL-KDD, which is open to the general public. Methods such as feature normalization, feature selection, and data preparation are employed in order to increase the accuracy of the algorithm predictions, shorten the amount of time that is necessary for training, and lower the number of resources that are required.

The model decides on them based on a number of factors and compares and contrasts their positive attributes and negative characteristics. The performance of the developed QCNN-LSTM model was better than that of seven distinct algorithms that were previously being used in IDSs across all six different evaluation parameters. The method was developed with the goal of recognizing irregularities in real-time circumstances with the objective of providing protection for the IoT platform. The strategies that were proposed have the potential to detect the occurrence of an attack as well as determine the nature of the attack that is currently taking place concurrently.

References

[1]   Al-Hawawreh, M., Moustafa, N., Garg, S., & Hossain, M. S. (2020). Deep learning-enabled threat intelligence scheme in the internet of things networks. *IEEE Transactions on Network Science and Engineering, 8*(4), 2968–2981.

[2]   Yang, W., Jin, L., Tao, D., Xie, Z., & Feng, Z. (2016). DropSample: A new training method to enhance deep convolutional neural networks for large-scale unconstrained handwritten Chinese character recognition. *Pattern Recognition, 58*, 190–203.

[3]   Aminanto, M. E., Choi, R., Tanuwidjaja, H. C., Yoo, P. D., & Kim, K. (2017). Deep abstraction and weighted feature selection for Wi-Fi impersonation detection. *IEEE Transactions on Information Forensics and Security, 13*(3), 621–636.

[4]   Islam, U., Muhammad, A., Mansoor, R., Hossain, M. S., Ahmad, I., Eldin, E. T., & . . . Shafiq, M. (2022). Detection of distributed denial of service (DDoS) attacks in IOT based monitoring system of banking sector using machine learning models. *Sustainability, 14*(14), 8374.

[5]   Satheesh, N., Rathnamma, M. V., Rajeshkumar, G., Sagar, P. V., Dadheech, P., Dogiwal, S. R., & . . . Sengan, S. (2020). Flow-based anomaly intrusion detection using machine learning model with software defined networking for OpenFlow network. *Microprocessors and Microsystems, 79*, 103285.

[6]   Mao, Y., Huang, W., Zhong, H., Wang, Y., Qin, H., Guo, Y., & Huang, D. (2020). Detecting quantum attacks: A machine learning based defense strategy for practical continuous-variable quantum key distribution. *New Journal of Physics, 22*(8), 083073.

[7]   Liu, Y., Yuan, X., Xiong, Z., Kang, J., Wang, X., & Niyato, D. (2020). Federated learning for 6G communications: Challenges, methods, and future directions. *China Communications, 17*(9), 105–118.

[8]   Kwak, Y., Yun, W. J., Kim, J. P., Cho, H., Park, J., Choi, M., & . . . Kim, J. (2022). Quantum distributed deep learning architectures: Models, discussions, and applications. *ICT Express.*

[9]   Vashisht, V., Kumar Pandey, A., & Prakash, S. (2021). Speech recognition using machine learning. *IEIE Transactions on Smart Processing and Computing SCOPUS, 10*(3), ISSN: 2287–5255, 233–239. https://doi.org/10.5573/IEIESPC.2021.10.3.233.

[10] Booij, T. M., Chiscop, I., Meeuwissen, E., Moustafa, N., & Den Hartog, F. T. (2021). ToN_IoT: The role of heterogeneity and the need for standardization of features and attack types in IoT network intrusion data sets. *IEEE Internet of Things Journal, 9*(1), 485–496.

[11] Yadav, S. P. (2022). Blockchain Security. In: Baalamurugan, K., Kumar, S. R., Kumar, A., Kumar, V., Padmanaban, S., (eds.). Blockchain Security in Cloud Computing. EAI/Springer Innovations in Communication and Computing. Springer, Cham. https://doi.org/10.1007/978-3-030-70501-5_1.

[12] Lu, K. D., Zeng, G. Q., Luo, X., Weng, J., Luo, W., & Wu, Y. (2021). Evolutionary deep belief network for cyber-attack detection in industrial automation and control system. *IEEE Transactions on Industrial Informatics, 17*(11), 7618–7627.

[13] Rajalakshmi, M., Saravanan, V., Arunprasad, V., Romero, C. T., Khalaf, O. I., & Karthik, C. (2022). Machine learning for modeling and control of industrial clarifier process. *Intelligent Automation & Soft Computing, 32*(1), 339–359.

[14] Stergiou, C. L., Plageras, A. P., Psannis, K. E., & Gupta, B. B. (2020). Secure Machine Learning Scenario from Big Data in Cloud Computing via Internet of Things Network. In: Handbook of Computer Networks and Cyber Security (pp. 525–554). Springer, Cham.

[15] Gunjan, V. K., Vijayalata, Y., Valli, S., Kumar, S., Mohamed, M. O., & Saravanan, V. (2022). Machine learning and cloud-based knowledge graphs to recognize suicidal mental tendencies. *Computational Intelligence and Neuroscience, 2022.*

[16] Jia, Z., Shen, C., Yi, X., Chen, Y., Yu, T. & Guan, X. (2017). Big-data analysis of multi-source logs for anomaly detection on network-based system. In: 2017 13th IEEE conference on automation science and engineering (CASE) (pp. 1136–1141). IEEE.

[17] Yadav, B. P., Ghate, S., Harshavardhan, A., Jhansi, G., Kumar, K. S., & Sudarshan, E. (2020). Text categorization Performance examination Using Machine Learning Algorithms. In: *IOP Conference Series: Materials Science and Engineering* (Vol. 981, No. 2, p. 022044). IOP Publishing.

[18] Kim, K., Aminanto, M. E., & Tanuwidjaja, H. C. (2018). Network Intrusion Detection Using Deep Learning: A Feature Learning Approach. Springer.

[19] Chen, S. Y. C., & Yoo, S. (2021). Federated quantum machine learning. *Entropy*, *23*(4), 460.

[20] Siriwardhana, Y., Porambage, P., Liyanage, M., & Ylianttila, M. (2021). AI and 6G security: Opportunities and challenges. In: 2021 Joint European Conference on Networks and Communications & 6G Summit (EuCNC/6G Summit) (pp. 616–621). IEEE.

[21] Natarajan, Y., Srihari, K., Dhiman, G., Chandragandhi, S., Gheisari, M., Liu, Y., & . . . Alharbi, H. F. (2022). An IoT and machine learning-based routing protocol for reconfigurable engineering application. *IET Communications*, *16*(5), 464–475.

[22] Istiaque Ahmed, K., Tahir, M., Hadi Habaebi, M., Lun Lau, S., & Ahad, A. (2021). Machine learning for authentication and authorization in iot: Taxonomy, challenges and future research direction. *Sensors*, *21*(15), 5122.

S. Karthik*, Thenmozhi, R. M. Bhavadharini, T. Sumathi

7 Quantum transfer learning to detect passive attacks in SDN-IOT

Abstract: An attack on the network presents a potential risk to the integrity of the network security, which may or may not occur. As the field of quantum machine learning has made rapid strides in recent years, quantum learning (QL) has demonstrated quantum benefits in a variety of classification problems. This is due to the fact that variational quantum neural networks are also known as QL. When compared to an IDS that is based on quantum machine learning, an IDS that is based on classical machine learning is both less efficient and less accurate. This chapter discusses quantum transfer learning to detect the passive attacks in SDN-IoT. The use of quantum transfer learning makes the system detect the possible intrusions in the network before the data is traversed into the network environment. The results show an improved accuracy rate than those of state-of-art methods.

7.1 Introduction

There are over 26 billion linked devices, and over 80% of business apps are now hosted in the cloud. In addition, numerous new technologies have been developed in order to meet the expectations of businesses and the customers of those firms. Some examples of these new technologies are cloud computing, the Internet of Things, mobility, and virtualization. System designers frequently need to make alterations to existing networks, update existing software, and organize available computer and network resources in order to accommodate the ever-evolving requirements of these new technologies [1]. This is necessary in order to accommodate the proliferation of new technologies. In order to meet the demands of users and businesses while also reducing the level of complexity that is imposed by operations, a new network design that is both flexible and rapidly capable of implementing policies and supporting automation is required [2].

*Corresponding author: S. Karthik, Department of Computer Science and Engineering, SNS College of Technology, Coimbatore, Tamil Nadu, India, e-mail: profskarthik@gmail.com
Thenmozhi, Department of Computer Science and Engineering, SNS College of Technology, Coimbatore, Tamil Nadu, India, e-mail: then.shan.in@gmail.com
R. M. Bhavadharini, Department of Computer Science and Engineering, VIT Deemed University Chennai, 600037, Tamil Nadu, India, e-mail: rmbhavadharini@gmail.com
T. Sumathi, Department of Information Technology, Government College of Engineering, Erode, 641032, Tamil Nadu, India, e-mail: sumathiirtt@gmail.com

https://doi.org/10.1515/9783110798159-007

The concept of software-defined networking (SDN) began to take shape in people's minds. The development of the concept of SDN was sparked by the realization that there is a pressing requirement for open interoperability across all different kinds of devices [3]. An SDN is a type of network that is capable of having its architecture dynamically reshaped in response to events as they occur in real time. In order to achieve this goal, the network control plane and data plane must first be isolated from one another. Next, the intelligence and control of the network must be centralized, and finally, the applications must be kept in the dark regarding the specifics of the network underlying infrastructure [4].

(SDN has the potential to serve as the architecture for future networks due to the numerous advantages it provides such as agility, automation, loop avoidance, failure response, and management in a variety of domains. However, SDN architecture is vulnerable to a broad variety of attacks [5].

Due to the ease with which man-in-the-middle attacks can be carried out, particularly in an environment where they are centralized, as well as the fact that they are difficult to detect, SDN security is a primary issue that needs to be addressed. When an adversary eavesdrops on a conversation that is taking place between two legal users with the purpose of acquiring encryption keys and other sensitive information, this type of attack is known as Man in the Middle (MitM) [6].

An SDN) environment is rife with the prevalence of MitM attacks due to the ease with which they can be carried out, the difficulty in detecting them, and the fact that they are used to steal sensitive information that is being transmitted between controllers and SDN nodes. When an MitM attack takes place, the security of an SDN can be breached at any level, including the transport, application, and user levels. The effects of this could be felt for a long time [7–15].

A number of studies that have been published in recent years have made the detection and prevention of MitM attacks on SDN architecture the subject of their investigations. In these works, specific intrusion detection and prevention systems are used, in addition to some closed frameworks for anomaly detection. In addition, in order to authenticate SDN nodes, this study makes use of a variety of cryptographic and biometric methods that are already in use. When working with an SDN, it might be difficult to deploy traditional security measures due to the sheer quantity and variety of nodes that are present in the network. This can make conventional security measures more difficult to be executed [16, 17]. In fact, the great majority of the proposed MitM detection algorithms are founded on antiquated and redundant datasets that are better suited to an environment containing traditional networks rather than an SDN [18]. Furthermore, previous works focused their attention primarily on the control layer of the SDN rather than the data layer, and they did not provide effective mechanisms for automating filtration rules or feature selection methods that were appropriate to the context of the SDN for the purpose of rapid and efficient anomaly identification in real-time. This was a problem [19, 20].

7.2 Related works

When using SDN, the control plane and the data plane are separated from one another. Consolidated into a single, external piece of software known as the Controller, this control plane is now able to govern the network by leveraging a wide number of programmable services and application programming interfaces [21]. When using SDN design, the network was frequently partitioned into application layers, control layers, and infrastructure layers. In spite of the fact that the SDN architecture offers a lot of benefits, the process of putting it into practice presents operators and service providers with a number of challenges that they must overcome. Issues develop, which can be linked back to the root cause of the time lag in the deployment of an SDN network [22].

Multiple pieces of research, in addition to the perspectives of those who work in the field of information systems, have led researchers and industry experts to the same conclusion: security is the primary barrier to the widespread adoption of SDN services. This conclusion is supported by the viewpoints of those who work in the field of information systems [23]. Because of the centralized architecture of SDN networks, they have a single point of attack, and SDN networks inherit all of the vulnerabilities that are associated with traditional networks. As SDN nodes do not have any intelligence or oversight, it is considerably simpler to carry out attacks against the data plane [24].

The multiple flaws that are present in the architecture of the SDN can be exploited in a number of different ways. It is possible that one or more of these different sorts of attacks will be made against the SDN layers [25].

In actuality, an MitM attack is able to read and record conversations that are allowed to take place between two nodes, despite the fact that the MitM attack itself is not illegal. Before the signal reaches its intended destination, an adversary who is carrying out a MitM attack has the capability of stealing crucial information from the transmission, selectively modifying it, or engaging in some other kind of destructive action [26].

These concerns regarding safety have been the focus of a number of research that have been carried out as part of an effort to enhance and fortify the designs of SDNs. In the study that they published in [27], a literature review of earlier investigations that have been carried out on the topic of SDN security. The authors reach the conclusion that past research into control plane vulnerabilities has resulted in the development of several frameworks that guarantee the availability, scalability, and security of controllers. In addition, the authors indicate that an investigation of these potential flaws has been carried out. Sadly, none of the existing works offers any strategies that could actually work for rapidly detecting abnormalities and reacting to threats, particularly at the data plane level. In order to investigate and assess the performance of a variety of security countermeasures in the context of an SDN, the authors in [28] developed and implemented a secure autonomous response network.

The writers are of the opinion that the characteristics of the attack, in addition to the defense system that is currently being deployed, both have an influence on the effectiveness of detection, as well as the amount of time it takes to respond to an attack. According to the findings, there is potential for improvement in the degree of precision supplied by existing security solutions, particularly when applied to significant SDN installations.

MitM attacks are among the most worrisome threats to SDN infrastructures because they enable the capture of flows and the acquisition of sensitive data such as passwords, flow rules, encryption keys Public Key Infrastructure (PKIs), and network information. This makes MitM attacks one of the most worrisome threats to SDN infrastructures. Due to the fact that a MitM attack can be carried out discreetly and without having a negative impact on the performance of the traffic, it is not always feasible to recognize one of these attacks. The authors in [29] investigated the efficacy of pre-existing defensive methods in recognizing malicious or aberrant traffic by simulating a range of MitM attacks and then analyzing the results of their analysis. This allowed them to determine whether or not these methods were successful in recognizing malicious or aberrant traffic. The authors of this study provide evidence that an effective MitM attack can be carried out without the use of any security procedures or regulations. The authors in [30] examine the effectiveness of large-scale MitM attacks as part of their study to conduct an evaluation of the current state of secure frameworks. Their duty entails communicating the MitM standards for efficiency and robustness that must be met to a total of six tiers. It is also concerning that the majority of the models that were examined were at level 2 or lower. This places them in a position where they are more vulnerable to a wide variety of attacks, such as hijacking and DDoS attacks, amongst others.

The majority of existing efforts to avoid MitM attacks do so by introducing cryptographic defenses. This is the case for the majority of these efforts. This is the situation with nearly all of these different projects. As a kind of crypto-biometric authentication, fingerprints [31] to develop a system for generating encryption keys based on those fingerprints. This is done in order to ensure the safety of the communications that take place between the nodes that are a part of an SDN. Their efforts are mostly focused on warding off passive attacks such as replay, impersonation, privileged insiders, and MitM attacks. They also work to prevent active attacks. This serves as the primary focal point of all of their activities. The implementation of cryptographic protocols can frequently result in very fruitful effects. However, there is a danger that the combined cryptographic systems and biometric solutions will not function properly and will have a large percentage of false positives. This risk is increased when the two types of solutions are combined.

A lightweight method for identifying MitM attacks within the OpenFlow channel can be found in [32]. The authors propose a new set of standards for open flow communications as well as the use of a bloom filter as a technique to achieve this goal. It would appear that the authors have provided a logical framework in their discussion.

Having stated that, it is absolutely necessary to produce a new standardized version of the open flow protocol in order to make use of the new changes that have been suggested [33]. In addition, the authors claim that their approach is only capable of modeling a restricted number of MitM attacks, which is yet another contentious issue raised by the research. It is possible to regard these methods as a workable solution for detecting and preventing MitM attacks in large-scale SDN networks as a result of the fact that machine learning techniques make it possible to find anomalies through the examination of real-time and enormous data flows.

The authors [34] in made use of the NSL-KDD dataset and presented a Deep Learning Approach to Network Intrusion Detection in SDN. This approach was developed using the dataset. Even though it has some interesting potential applications, deep learning is difficult to implement and demands a lot of time and resources. This is despite the fact that it has become increasingly popular. An IDS that defends SDNs by leveraging signatures and a pattern recognition model that is acquired through machine learning is shown in [34]. The architects of the framework made it a top priority to check that it was resistant to denial of service (DoS) and MitM attacks, which are typically regarded as the dangers that pose the greatest risk to SDN configurations. Although these efforts have resulted in the production of some innovative insights, the deployment of those insights has mostly been limited to a simulation network that has a low level of traffic. In addition, the proposed models are dependent on signature-based IDSs that are currently in operation, which leaves them open to new types of MitM attacks.

7.3 Methods

As an immediate and unavoidable consequence of this quantum improvement, the volume of information that can be processed by computers has dramatically increased. It is believed that quantum computing can gain quantum advantages such as the exponential acceleration of computing performance by leveraging quantum effects such as interference and entanglement. This will allow it to efficiently address some problems that are challenging for classical computers to solve.

These issues include the following: even the most conventional approaches to nuclear computation are not particularly accurate. In the worst-case scenario, the sheer scope of the project will require quantum computing to expand on an exponential scale. This will be the case because of the nature of the undertaking. Quantum computing has the potential to improve not only the rate at which calculations can be carried out, but also the correctness and speed with which model training can be performed. In addition, quantum computing can accelerate the pace at which computations can be carried out, as in Figure 7.1.

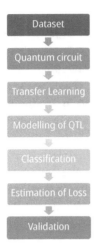

Figure 7.1: QTL model.

It has been shown that training support vector machines (SVMs) by using quantum computing has the potential to give exponential speedups in performance. This is partly attributable to the fact that inversion of the kernel matrix from a polynomial to a logarithmic level of complexity is made possible by the application of quantum techniques, which was previously impossible. The application of quantum computing to activities that are more conventional, such as image processing, has so far provided early results that are encouraging. As a direct result of this, the industry that deals with the detection of malicious code also needs the quantum advantage in order to make progress and break through the bottleneck that is currently in place. It is possible to simulate this kind of experiment on a regular computer even if we do not have access to the essential equipment.

Research that was conducted not too long ago in the field of natural language processing (NLP) has shown that transfer learning models that are based on the transformer architecture combine two benefits: attention and transfer learning. As a direct result of this, we created our model using a transformer in order to improve the semantic correctness of our findings. When we first began the process of training the model, we accessed the functions and comments contained inside the dataset that were used for pre-training. Then, in order to train the fine-tuning model based on the strategies that we identified from the malicious code dataset, we used position embedding in addition to word table mapping. This was done so that the model could be trained based on the strategies.

The feature vector was eventually obtained after going through a few different encoders first. After being formed by the encoder, the matrix vector was then sent into the decoder, so that comment vectors could be constructed on the fly. As we used bilinear pooling to carry out the feature fusion of the two vectors, we were able to accomplish our goal of producing a high-dimensional vector that was also improved semantically.

In the end, a layer that was fully linked was used in order to produce a vector representation in a fewer number of dimensions. This was done by reducing the number of dimensions that were being used. As it is built on the transformer as an extension of the pre-trained model architecture, the Android-SEM model has an O(n2) computational complexity, which is also satisfactory. This complexity can be linked to the fact that the Android-SEM model is satisfactory.

During the pre-training phase, we made use of a generative adversarial strategy with the goal of achieving the maximum amount of influence that could be obtained from the generator. We overcame the issue of processing sequence structures by applying the fundamental ideas behind generative adversarial networks, which are typically used in image processing. Due to this, we were able to find a solution to the problem. During the pre-training phase, we compared the generator to a fake coin maker, its output to fake coins, and the human-labeled comments in the dataset to real coins. All of these comparisons took place within the dataset. The dataset was used throughout each and every one of these comparisons. The fake coin factory and the police (which comprised of the encoder and the entirely linked layer) participated, which led to an improvement in the output quality of the generator as a result of the healthy competition between the two entities (the discriminator).

With the intention of preventing the development of erroneous remark vectors that insufficiently explain the semantics of the program, we offer a grading method that is founded on transfer learning. There is not much of a difference in the Euclidean distance between two vectors of source code and comments that are comparable in size and shape, since the semantics of the vectors are similar to one another. As a consequence of this, we made use of a linear regression model in order to acquire it.

This was done so that the model could be as realistic as possible in its representation of the world. After the model has been saved, inappropriate comments can be deleted by calculated discretion. This distance can be found by comparing the comment vector with the function vector. As a result, comments that are not pertinent to the model can be removed. Thus, we were able to eliminate spam comments during the process of feature fusion without making use of any annotated labels.

In contrast, we trained for accuracy using API sequences acquired from a dataset that included malicious code. This allowed us to better identify harmful code. Thus, we were able to deliver data that were more precise. In order to acquire the vector representation of the API sequence, we made use of the NLP concept to map it. This allowed us to learn the API semantics and context.

Obtaining the vector representation of the API sequence was therefore made possible. The ultimate result was a feature fusion vector, which was produced by combining the feature vector from the API sequence, the comments, and the method fusion vector. The identification and categorization of malicious code will be accomplished with the assistance of this vector. Multi layer Perceptron (MLP) and quantum feature mapping were the two approaches that were used in order to successfully complete the assignments that were given.

The majority of the investigations that have employed sequence formats have made use of a small number of very common features, and in recent years, there has been a substantial amount of research carried out on CNN-based image processing of Android code and its subsequent analysis. In this study, migration learning was used to transfer comments from the uncommented, potentially dangerous Android code that was originally used. We were successful in collecting data that had been overlooked in earlier investigations, thanks to the application of the semantic enhancement methodology. In following investigations, it was revealed that the transformer-based semantic improvement model resulted in an improvement in the classification of harmful code. This improvement was due to the fact that the model was able to take context into account.

7.3.1 Quantum transfer learning

There are several processes that are common to both classical and quantum neural networks. These stages include the preparation of data, the encoding of quantum states, the training of the network, parameter optimization, and the maximization of the probability of outputs.

Qubit registers are used to parameterize the input of quantum circuits when it comes to quantum neural networks. After then, measurement procedures are performed to identify the network output distribution of bit strings that occur with frequency (probability), i.e., to construct the totally positive map between the two. The likelihood of occurrence of a bit string is based on its frequency. For the purpose of finding solutions to challenges requiring quantum computing and quantum information processing, quantum neural networks are used.

It is possible for a conventional computer to communicate quantum state parameter encodings to a quantum neural network, which subsequently enables the quantum neural network to perform unitary transformations. The classical computer will then take a sample from the resulting distribution of output values for the variables that are being measured, using a random sampling method. The parameters are determined by the outcome, and any changes to those parameters are subject to review.

The output of the network can be formally described as the sum of a number of transition maps between layers, all of which are required to have a value that is unmistakably positive. Each layer of the quantum circuit makes use of the initial data that is fed into the circuit in order to construct the final data that is produced from the circuit. Incorporate some information from the past, Xi into a quantum circuit that possesses a parameter known as U, with U(0) acting as the starting point for the circuit.

When quantum circuits are measured, an output vector known as an "outcome" is generated. This output vector, in conjunction with the mapping function known as g, can then be used to provide a classification prediction known as yi for a particular collection of data.

Calculating the loss function requires comparing the expected classification result, yi, to the actual result, Yi, which was received from the training set. This is done so that the loss function may be determined.

After inserting the remaining training data Xj into the quantum circuit one at a time in order to obtain the related output vector, we can then calculate the cost function for that particular set of data by comparing the predicted classification yi to the true classification ti. We can then repeat this process for all of the training data in order to obtain the overall cost function. This process can then be used to optimize the parameters of the quantum circuit so that the overall cost function is minimized.

The parameters k of the quantum circuit should be updated iteratively (where k can range from 1 to n) until all of the conditions have been met and the cost function can be lowered using a conventional computer.

7.3.2 Quantum state encoding (QSE)

The formulation of any theory regarding a quantum neural network requires, first and foremost, the creation of a method for the construction of a quantum circuit. To get started, we will need to give some thought to the process of inputting classical data into a quantum circuit. This is the first step. Encoding can be done using either of the two most common approaches.

While the first technique encodes the parameters for quantum circuits, the second encodes the amplitudes of those parameters in a variety of different ways. The process of encoding correlations between quantum circuits and the parameters of those circuits:

Imagine that there are n different features in the data collection X and that each individual sample Xi possesses one of those properties.

Each characteristic can be encoded by using the parameter to correspond to a qubit initial state of $|0|$. This will complete the process of parameter encoding for statements concerning amplitude The data set is encoded into the state of the quantum system via the Sinput circuit, which is also known as the state preparation circuit. This is accomplished by transferring an input, to the logn2-dimensional amplitude vector S(x), which is used to represent the quantum state [S(x)].

The first method of encoding requires O(m) qubits for m-features of input data while only requiring a circuit depth of O. This means that the circuit depth can be as small as O(m). The second encoding approach offers the best possibility of generating the quantum state that is required.

This method of encoding requires $s = O(\log m2)$ qubits and a circuit depth of O before it can be put into practice.

Both of these prerequisites have to be satisfied. Evidently, the possibility that this encoding strategy will reduce the number of qubits that are thrown away is significantly higher. It could be an obstacle in the way of the development of Noisy Intermediate-Scale Quantum (NISQ) devices.

Although the method of variational encoding makes encoding more accessible to NISQ devices, this accessibility comes at the cost of requiring a higher qubit count than is required for amplitude encoding. The amplitude encoding method is the easiest to understand. Since variational encoding is able to significantly minimize the amount of depth that is required by quantum circuits, it is used in a significant number of technologies that are used for quantum machine learning.

7.3.3 Variational quantum circuit

After the classical data has been successfully encoded into a quantum state, we can begin the process of creating the quantum circuits by either making use of the qubits that are already available or by adding some additional qubits. This decision can be made after the classical data has been successfully encoded into the quantum state. The Variational Quantum Circuit (VQC) methodology is a hybrid quantum-classical method that utilizes both quantum and classical styles of computing.

This allows it to produce more accurate results than purely classical approaches. You can think of the changeable parameters as being comparable to the weights of an artificial neural network (ANN), because the circuit is a type of tunable quantum circuit that optimizes parameters via the iterative process of a classical computer. As the circuit in question is an illustration of an ANN, you are able to think of this.

The Virtual Quantum Computer (VQC), which plays a role in the process of permanently mapping quantum features, is built from a wide range of different quantum gates. VQC is commonly used as a quantum model for classification problems [30]. This is mostly due to the fact that it has been shown to have the ability to construct discrete probability distributions that are not adequately replicated by classical neural networks and that are somewhat noise-resistant. The procedure for converting between different quantum states is the same for each and every type of quantum gate, regardless of which one is used. Despite the fact that this mapping is carried out between the Euclidean space and the Hilbert space, it is unique from the mapping of classical functions due to the fact that it takes place between the two spaces. On the other hand, this mapping can still be interpreted in terms of a function, such as f(x), similar to how traditional machine learning works.

Encoding the bit string ak as a quantum state by making use of the quantum circuit U(|S(Xi)) and then performing measurements in the Z direction enables the computation of the probability pik that is associated with the bit string.

In an ideal world, the true outcome of the categorization, denoted by Yi, would be represented in a high likelihood of the occurrence of objects in category A, as would be the case after each measurement. In a perfect world, things would work out like this. It should be possible for any aka to satisfy the equation Yi = g(a), where g(a) is an encoding method that converts the measured string into the label Yi that is related to the input data Xi. Allowing this should be done allows any aka to be used. If you do so, you will end up with a categorization prediction that is more precise.

Using this strategy, the appropriate classification prediction may be obtained by switching to repeated measurement of quantum circuits, picking the bit string group that has the highest overall frequency, and so on. This will allow the prediction to be applied to the classification in question. Choosing the bit string group that has the lowest total frequency is just one of the several phases involved in this process.

As the cost function is a function of both the parameter and the training set X and Y, we can use a conventional computer to minimize the cost function and iteratively update the parameters until the termination condition is met. The fact that the cost function is a function makes this outcome tenable. The QNN education on traditional computers, which was carried out through the use of machine learning, is now over.

7.4 Results and discussion

We used the data set that was mentioned previously in the phrase to evaluate the quality of our model and assess whether or not it was accurate. In addition to this, we compared our technique to others that were currently being deployed and that were theoretically comparable to the one we had developed. The datasets that were available to the public were pretty analogous to those that we possessed. This offers ample basis for contrasting their findings with those of our recently constructed model.

In order to improve the program semantics, a transformer-based deep learning model was put through its paces during the pre-training phase, and then it was put to use to create comments from the source code of the program. Through the application of bilinear pooling and the process of filtering the pre-training vector that was produced by the encoder and decoder modules, feature fusion could be accomplished. It is important not to overlook the fact that the context relationship could be learned, thanks to the training provided by the API sequence.

In this groundbreaking piece of research, a pre-training model is used to create automated remarks. These comments are then used as semantic augmentation features following the fusing of feature sets. The findings of this study are the first of their kind. As it is the first system of its kind, it makes use of a generative adversarial network to improve the quality of generated semantics and migration learning. This enables a significant reduction in the amount of time that is required for training, in addition to the achievement of astoundingly high levels of accuracy.

Adjustments were made to the hyperparameters while keeping a close eye on the classification performance and decision boundary in order to ascertain the strategy that provided the greatest match for the data and to make some small changes. This proved that Quantum Transfer Learning (QTL) was just as effective as conventional Transfer Learning (TLs) in detecting and categorizing malicious Android code, and in certain circumstances, it was even more effective than standard TLs. The purpose of this project was to bring the accuracy of classification provided by the TL kernel up to a level that was higher than that provided by the QTL.

We created accuracy and confusion matrices in order to classify the many distinct kinds of quantum cores that are used to generate the QTL. It is the responsibility of the TL kernel to transform the data in such a way that it may be incorporated into the process of modeling.

A large number of algorithms, in order to do what they set out to do, make use of a wide range of kernel functions to choose from. For the purpose of our comparative methodology, we relied on the tried-and-true linear and Radial Basis Function (RBF) functions, which are the kinds of functions that are typically regarded as having the broadest appeal, overall.

Table 7.1: Results of accuracy.

IoT nodes	Time (s)	Accuracy (%)
10	12.75	65.35
20	30.39	88.66
30	65.69	90.18
40	113.73	89.90
50	180.39	91.20
60	265.69	92.42
70	404.90	93.39
80	648.04	95.89
90	824.51	89.67
100	1160.78	90.07

Table 7.2: Results of precision/recall and F1-measure.

IoT nodes	Precision (%)	Recall (%)	F1 (%)
10	65.06	98.04	77.91
20	90.08	91.45	91.68
30	91.88	93.04	92.31
40	90.66	93.26	91.80
50	92.25	93.52	92.80
60	93.66	94.39	92.31
70	93.86	94.25	92.66
80	95.30	97.60	96.42
90	93.45	89.75	91.21
100	89.76	95.80	92.46

The findings of the researcher investigation into the myriad of methods for categorizing possibly harmful Android applications are presented in the next section. The QTL test dataset displays accuracy that is comparable to that of traditional TL and can reach up

Table 7.3: Results of loss.

IoT nodes	Loss
10	0.2217
20	0.1130
30	0.0718
40	0.0622
50	0.0606
60	0.0594
70	0.0572
80	0.0546
90	0.0549
100	0.0556

to 99% when it comes to the detection of malicious code. This accuracy can go as high as 100% in some cases. If anything, the conclusions that can be drawn from using QTL with more complicated datasets are even more satisfying than those that can be drawn from using it with datasets that are simpler to analyze. If the dataset in question has a complex border that is not captured by normal classical kernels, then it is possible that QTL will be able to improve performance, which is shown in Tables 7.1–7.3.

It is impossible to avoid coming to the realization that there is a connection between the successes of today's deep learning models and those of the traditional models. Through the use of a transfer learning-based semantic improvement model and the pre-training of feature vectors, the accuracy of the QTL can be significantly enhanced.

In addition, the data that have been given in Table 7.5 and the confusion matrix that has been displayed in Table 7.4 demonstrate that the accuracy of QTL has been greatly improved. The findings of this experiment provide evidence that QTL may be a viable method for locating and categorizing possibly malicious code.

Table 7.4: Results of comparison between the proposed and existing methods.

Model	Training MSE
ANN	0.1016
SVM	0.2994
KNN	0.1033
NB	0.1261
DT	0.0630
Proposed QTL	0.0470

Model	Test MSE
ANN	0.1111
SVM	0.2647
KNN	0.1209
NB	0.1438
DT	0.1307
Proposed QTL	0.0577

Model	FPR
ANN	12.5882
SVM	25.1471
KNN	16.3333
NB	18.5000
DT	14.9608
Proposed QTL	6.7157

Model	FNR
ANN	5.1275
SVM	11.0980
KNN	9.5490
NB	10.7451
DT	8.6569
Proposed QTL	1.3333

Model	FAR
ANN	8.8627
SVM	18.1275
KNN	12.9412
NB	14.6275
DT	11.8137
Proposed QTL	4.0294

Model	Precision
ANN	88.2353
SVM	79.5784
KNN	86.0294
NB	83.0980
DT	85.9216
Proposed QTL	95.3039

Model	Recall
ANN	84.3235
SVM	63.4118
KNN	84.0490
NB	82.0392
DT	82.2353
Proposed QTL	97.5980

Model	F1
ANN	85.6569
SVM	62.9020
KNN	84.8333
NB	82.5000
DT	83.4804
Proposed QTL	96.4216

7.5 Conclusion

By using a generative adversarial strategy, we were able to enrich the comment vectors that were generated by the semantic enhancement module, which is the central component of our proposed model for the identification of potentially harmful code. Due to this, we are now in a better position to comprehend what is being said. In addition, we presented a comment filter that operates on the principle of linear regression, remembers comment vectors of a high quality, and makes use of them in conjunction with other features in order to recognize and categorize Android malware.

The findings showed that the method that we offered was effective in determining whether or not code samples were benign or harmful. We performed ablation experiments for the recommended model, which demonstrated the efficacy of our technique, demonstrated the improved accuracy our approach gave in detecting and classifying harmful code, and emphasized the value of each module. Moreover, these experiments highlighted the importance of each module individually. In addition, this work incorporated both quantum machine learning and more traditional types of machine learning into its methodology. Both conventional machine learning models and quantum machine learning models scored wonderfully in simulated malware detection tests; however, the QTL approach had a theoretical advantage.

References

[1] Luo, H., Zhang, L., Qin, H., Sun, S., Huang, P., Wang, Y., & . . . Huang, D. (2022). Beyond universal attack detection for continuous-variable quantum key distribution via deep learning. *Physical Review A, 105*(4), 042411.

[2] Rasool, R. U., Ahmad, H. F., Rafique, W., Qayyum, A., & Qadir, J. (2022). Quantum computing for healthcare: A review.

[3] Arooj, S., Zubair, M., Khan, M. F., Alissa, K., Khan, M. A., & Mosavi, A. (2022). Breast cancer detection and classification empowered with transfer learning. *Frontiers in Public Health, 10*.

[4] Meng, Y., Yuan, D., Su, S., & Ming, Y. (2022). A novel transfer learning-based algorithm for detecting violence images. *KSII Transactions on Internet & Information Systems, 16*(6).

[5] Pandita, P., Ghosh, S., Gupta, V. K., Meshkov, A. & Wang, L. (2022). Application of deep transfer learning and uncertainty quantification for process identification in powder bed fusion. *ASCE-ASME Journal of Risk and Uncertainty in Engineering Systems, Part B: Mechanical Engineering, 8*(1).

[6] Bale, A. S., Kumar, S. S., Yogi, S. V., Vura, S., Chithra, R. B., Vinay, N., & Pravesh, P. (2022). Network and Security Leveraging IoT and Image Processing: A Quantum Leap Forward. In: System Assurances (pp. 123–141). Academic Press.

[7] Chen, Y. A., Zhang, Q., Chen, T. Y., Cai, W. Q., Liao, S. K., Zhang, J., & . . . Pan, J. W. (2021). An integrated space-to-ground quantum communication network over 4,600 kilometres. *Nature, 589*(7841), 214–219.

[8] Tang, L. (2021). Integrity Protection Method for Trusted Data of IoT Nodes Based on Transfer Learning. In: Web Intelligence (No. Preprint, pp. 1–11). IOS Press.

[9] Islam, M., Chowdhury, M., Khan, Z., & Khan, S. M. (2022). Hybrid quantum-classical neural network for cloud-supported in-vehicle cyberattack detection. *IEEE Sensors Letters, 6*(4), 1–4.

[10] Yadav, S. P., Bhati, B. S., Mahato, D. P., & Kumar, S. (eds). Federated Learning for IoT Applications. EAI/Springer Innovations in Communication and Computing. Springer, Cham. https://doi.org/10.1007/978-3-030-85559-8.

[11] Yadav, S. P. (2022). Blockchain Security. In: Baalamurugan, K., Kumar, S. R., Kumar, A., Kumar, V., Padmanaban, S. (eds.). Blockchain Security in Cloud Computing. EAI/Springer Innovations in Communication and Computing. Springer, Cham. https://doi.org/10.1007/978-3-030-70501-5_1.

[12] Gobinathan, B., Mukunthan, M. A., Surendran, S., Somasundaram, K., Moeed, S. A., Niranjan, P., & . . . Sundramurthy, V. P. (2021). A novel method to solve real time security issues in software industry using advanced cryptographic techniques. *Scientific Programming, 2021*.

[13] Joshna, S. (2022). Melanoma classification using deep transfer learning. *International Journal of Data Informatics and Intelligent Computing, 1*(1), 11–20.

[14] Saravanan, V., Rajeshwari, S., & Jayashree, P. (2013). Security issues in protecting computers and maintenance. *Journal of Global Research in Computer Science, 4*(1), 55–58.

[15] Malamas, V., Dasaklis, T., Kotzanikolaou, P., Burmester, M., & Katsikas, S. (2019, July). A forensics-by-design management framework for medical devices based on blockchain. In: 2019 IEEE world congress on services (Services) (Vol. 2642, pp. 35–40). IEEE.

[16] Yuan, X., Zhang, Z., Feng, C., Cui, Y., Garg, S., Kaddoum, G., & Yu, K. (2022). A DQN-Based frame aggregation and task offloading approach for edge-enabled IoMT. *IEEE Transactions on Network Science and Engineering*.

[17] Bassi, G. S., Murchie, A. I., Walter, F., Clegg, R. M., & Lilley, D. M. (1997). Ion-induced folding of the hammerhead ribozyme: A fluorescence resonance energy transfer study. *The EMBO Journal, 16*(24), 7481–7489.

[18] Ji, B., Liu, Y., Xing, L., Li, C., Zhang, G., Han, C., & . . . Mumtaz, S. (2022). Survey of secure communications of internet of things with artificial intelligence. *IEEE Internet of Things Magazine, 5*(3), 92–99.

[19] Yin, X. (2010). Quantum evolutionary algorithm based network intrusion detection. In: 2010 3rd International Conference on Computer Science and Information Technology (Vol. 4, pp. 683–685). IEEE.

[20] Nithya, C., & Saravanan, V. (2018). A study of machine learning techniques in data mining. *International Scientific Refereed Research Journal, 1*, 31–38.

[21] Natarajan, Y., Raja, R. A., Kousik, N. V., & Saravanan, M. (2021). A review of various reversible embedding mechanisms. *International Journal of Intelligence and Sustainable Computing, 1*(3), 233–266.

[22] Liu, Y., Kang, J., Guo, C., & Bai, Y. (2022). Diesel engine small-sample transfer learning fault diagnosis algorithm based on STFT time–frequency image and hyperparameter autonomous optimization deep convolutional network improved by PSO–GWO–BPNN surrogate model. *Open Physics, 20*(1), 993–1018.

[23] Kwak, Y., Yun, W. J., Kim, J. P., Cho, H., Park, J., Choi, M., & . . . Kim, J. (2022). Quantum distributed deep learning architectures: Models, discussions, and applications. *ICT Express.*

[24] Liao, P., Song, W., Du, P., & Zhao, H. (2021). Multi-fidelity convolutional neural network surrogate model for aerodynamic optimization based on transfer learning. *Physics of Fluids, 33*(12), 127121.

[25] Vaidyan, V. M., & Tyagi, A. (2022). Towards Quantum Artificial Intelligence Electromagnetic Prediction Models for Ladder Logic Bombs and Faults in Programmable Logic Controllers. In: 2022 International Conference on Electronic Systems and Intelligent Computing (ICESIC) (pp. 1–6). IEEE.

[26] Angeline, R., Sajini, S., & Divakar, A. (2022). Segmentation of White Blood Cells with Colour Space Transformation and use of Transfer Learning for Optimization. *Central Asian Journal of Medical and Natural Science, 3*(3), 595–619.

[27] Niu, M. Y., Boixo, S., Smelyanskiy, V. N., & Neven, H. (2019). Universal quantum control through deep reinforcement learning. *Npj Quantum Information, 5*(1), 1–8.

[28] Khalil, M. I., Rehman, S. U., Alhajlah, M., Mahmood, A., Karamat, T., Haneef, M., & Alhajlah, A. (2022). Deep-COVID: Detection and analysis of COVID-19 outcomes using deep learning. *Electronics, 11*(22), 3836.

[29] Wiechers, C., Lydersen, L., Wittmann, C., Elser, D., Skaar, J., Marquardt, C., & . . . Leuchs, G. (2011). After-gate attack on a quantum cryptosystem. *New Journal of Physics, 13*(1), 013043.

[30] Schaffner, C. (2010). Simple protocols for oblivious transfer and secure identification in the noisy-quantum-storage model. *Physical Review A, 82*(3), 032308.

[31] Yamany, W., Moustafa, N., & Turnbull, B. (2021). OQFL: An optimized quantum-based federated learning framework for defending against adversarial attacks in intelligent transportation systems. *IEEE Transactions on Intelligent Transportation Systems.*

[32] Amaizu, G. C., Nwakanma, C. I., Bhardwaj, S., Lee, J. M., & Kim, D. S. (2021). Composite and efficient DDoS attack detection framework for B5G networks. *Computer Networks, 188*, 107871.

[33] Gao, Y. (2021). News video classification model based on ResNet-2 and transfer learning. *Security and Communication Networks, 2021.*

[34] Lo, H. K. (1997). Insecurity of quantum secure computations. *Physical Review A, 56*(2), 1154.

Kumari Manisha*, V. Dhanunjana Chari, Leta Tesfaye Jule

8 Intrusion detection framework using quantum computing for mobile cloud computing

Abstract: Mobile cloud computing (MCC) refers to a hybrid approach that brings together mobile computing, cloud computing, and wireless networks. The processing and storage of data are supposed to be moved away from the mobile device, which is its purpose. In MCC, mobile devices are not accountable for performing calculations or storing user data; rather, these responsibilities are transferred to the more powerful computing infrastructures of the cloud. In this chapter, an intrusion detection system (IDS) is developed to improve the detection of attacks in MCC. The model using quantum computing (QC) to detect the possible attacks in the MCC. Various types of attacks are proliferated and tested on the proposed QC and its detection rate is noted. The results show that the proposed QC has higher rate of accuracy and reduced computational burden than other methods.

8.1 Introduction

Mobile Cloud Computing (MCC), which uses Ethernet or the Internet to serve multiple mobile devices in a variety of settings, without limiting their access to a shared pool of cloud resources for unlimited storage, utility, and mobility, is one of the technologies that has the potential to alter the course of history [1–2]. MCC is one of the technologies that possesses the ability to alter the path that history will take in the future [3].

In order to become an expert in MCC, it is vital to have a comprehensive understanding of all there is to know about cloud computing and the services that it provides. As a result of cloud computing, the traditional client-server architecture, which is centered on the organization, has been supplanted by a data-centric strategy that is more scalable, efficient, and flexible [4]. This new method focuses on the data rather than on the organization. The cloud makes several computer resources, including

---

***Corresponding author: Kumari Manisha,** Assistant Professor, Department of ECE, Gokaraju Rangaraju Institute of Engineering and Technology, Hyderabad, Telangana, India,
e-mail: manisha.kx@gmail.com

V. Dhanunjana Chari, Professor and Dean of School of Sciences, Department of Physics, Malla Reddy University, Maisammaguda, Dulapally, Hyderabad, Telangana, India,
e-mail: dhanunjay@mallareddyuniversity.ac.in

Leta Tesfaye Jule, Physics Department, Dambi Dollo University, Dambi Dollo, Oromia Region, Ethiopia,
e-mail: laterajule@gmail.com

https://doi.org/10.1515/9783110798159-008

access to a shared pool of servers, data storage, and application software, available to users on an as-needed, pay-per-use basis. These resources include data storage, application software, and more. Computing on the cloud is also sometimes referred to as utility computing [5].

As all of the processing that calls for a considerable number of resources may be done in the cloud, it is not required for a mobile device to have a powerful CPU or a large amount of memory [6]. The amount of memory that can be stored on mobile devices, as well as the amount of bandwidth that can be accessed, are all subject to constraints [7].

Customers who subscribe to a software-as-a-service (SaaS) model are restricted to just using the cloud-based software offered by the supplier. Beyond the user-specific configuration settings, users of cloud-based apps such as salesforce.com need not be concerned about the administration [8]. Users are able to design and run their own apps in the cloud while utilizing Platform as a Service, which is also commonly referred to as PaaS. This is made possible with the assistance of the development tools and programming languages that are made available by the service provider [9].

They need not be concerned about the underlying cloud infrastructure; nevertheless, users do have some say in how their hosted applications, such as Google Apps, are organized and configured. Users have the ability to store and operate their own virtual computers in the cloud with Infrastructure as a Service (IaaS), which comes complete with pre-installed software such as operating systems and applications. Users also have the ability to store and operate their own virtual computers in the cloud with Amazon Web Services (AWS) [10].

Customers who use a service such as Amazon Elastic Compute Cloud (EC2) need not be worried about the underlying cloud architecture; nonetheless, these customers do have complete control over the operating system (OS), RAM, and any applications that have been installed on the server. MCC is different from cloud computing, which is still in its early stages, in a number of ways, including mobility, usage of bandwidth, fault tolerance, and security, to name a few of these differences [11].

8.2 Related works

The proliferation of mobile services is among the most rapid when compared to other areas of technological development. As a result of the advantages provided by MCC, a wide range of applications have made a significant contribution to the expansion of the international market [12–13]. The sale of financial services, the acquisition of event tickets online, and shopping done on mobile devices are just a few instances of the ways in which day-to-day lives of people have been impacted by mobile commerce. In order to be successful, these applications need to surmount a number of obstacles, such as restricted bandwidth and battery capacity, a complicated mobile design, and worries about the safety of their user data [14].

MCC addresses these challenges by integrating cloud computing and mobile commerce applications as a potential solution to these problems. Mobile learning, which blends e-learning with mobility, is laden with a number of intrinsic obstacles, such as poor data transmission rates and the prohibitively expensive nature of mobile devices. Despite these challenges, mobile learning is becoming increasingly popular [15]. It is strongly suggested that you use cloud computing, which provides customers with access to massive quantities of storage space as well as advanced processing capabilities. Mobile health care solutions, in contrast to more conventional forms of medical software, give mobile consumers speedy and uncomplicated access to pertinent medical information [16].

As a result of the on-demand services that are given by the cloud, mobile medical applications no longer have problems with the security of their data, the availability of storage space, or the performance of their applications. Mobile gaming offloads the processing of its graphics rendering and computing resources to servers that are situated in the cloud [17]. This is done so that the game engine module can be used on mobile devices. Both the development and hosting of mobile applications have opportunities that might be explored through the use of the cloud as an alternative. It is quite expected that mobile apps that are compatible with many mobile operating systems at the same time, such as Apple iOS, Google Android, and Microsoft Windows, would store their data in the cloud, analyze their data in the cloud, and make use of cloud fault tolerance [18].

Cloud service providers and their customers may have a tough time determining who is responsible for what, in terms of the security measures and controls that are installed in the cloud. Customers have the ability to configure and use the services in a manner that is compliant with the norms of their respective industries and geographic regions [19]. On the one hand, it is the responsibility of service providers to design their offerings, including any features, so that they satisfy the criteria for data protection and privacy. On the other hand, the capability to do so is available to customers. Despite the fact that service providers are able to put operational controls in place to protect the data of their customers who keep their data in the cloud, the final responsibility for ensuring that their data is not unintentionally shared lies with the consumers themselves [20].

Customers are responsible for ensuring that service providers meet the requirements for data privacy imposed by their own organizations by conducting audits and examining certificates that have been provided by service providers. On the other hand, it is the responsibility of the service providers to obtain the necessary certifications and to sign the service-level agreements. It is the responsibility of the customers to investigate the audit reports and certificates that are provided by the service providers (SLA) [21].

When it comes to the safety of the information, the customers and the providers of the PaaS and IaaS services share equal responsibility for everything that is above the virtual machine layer. This includes the obligation for ensuring data privacy. When using SaaS or cloud services, on the other hand, the user is held more directly responsible for executing duties such as access management and system monitoring. SaaS and cloud applications shift this obligation from the provider to the end user [22–23].

When using a private cloud, the customer is solely responsible for the cloud security; however, when using a public cloud, both the customer and the cloud service provider share responsibility for the cloud security. When a customer makes use of a platform or service that is hosted in the cloud, it is the customer's responsibility to implement the appropriate safety measures in order to protect the data and applications that are under their control [24].

8.3 Methods

The QC model is an explicit nonlinear feature mapping approach used in the implementation of the QC method that has been around for a while. In general, more hidden layer neurons are required for increasingly sophisticated pattern recognition tasks like as classification, regression, and other nonlinear pattern recognition tasks; as a consequence, the topology of the network becomes extremely complicated. This configuration makes use of a total of three levels, which includes the input layer, the concealed layer, and the output layer.

MCC requires careful consideration of both internal and external hazards, with internal hazards being the more essential category. Insider threats are the possible dangers that current or former workers of a company could potentially bring to the company computer network. Any component that poses a risk to the system yet originates from outside the system itself is referred to as an outsider threat. When the data are kept in the cloud, these concerns can put the data availability, privacy, and security at danger. Firewalls are one approach that may be used in order to protect against invasions of this kind. Another method that can be used is encryption.

Using a firewall may be necessary in order to stop potentially hazardous or undesired connections from accessing a network or computer system. It is possible to install a wide variety of different kinds of firewalls with the purpose of making the system more secure. An example of a firewall that is considered to be entry-level would be a stateless inspection firewall, which is also known as a packet filtering firewall, in some instances. Typically, these firewalls operate at the network layer and examine the information contained in the packet headers to ensure that it complies with the policies that have been defined. This includes checking the protocol type, the source IP address, and the destination IP address. When this is taken into account, firewalls that are based on packet filtering do not provide the best protection against attacks that involve fragmentation and spoofing.

The stateful inspection firewall is the second form of firewall, and it is differentiated from other types of firewalls by the fact that it keeps a separate table for the data that pertains to each connection. At this stage, the firewall decides which bits of information are going to be put in the header of the packet. Following this, the firewall analyzes the data to evaluate whether or not it is consistent with the information that is stored in the state table.

Application firewalls are able to operate at the application layer, which enables them to monitor and govern the inputs and outputs of any service or program. As application firewalls are able to operate at this level, they are also known as application layer firewalls. All of the communication that occurs between the lower layers and the application layer is controlled and regulated by this firewall. The method of communicating with users on different hosts by use of proxy agents is currently extremely common.

Depending on the terminology that is being used, this function may be referred to as a proxy or a gateway, while it is operating at the application layer. This functionality is included in firewalls. Proxy firewalls, in contrast to application firewalls, are better equipped to decode and analyze encoded payloads. A firewall that was built specifically for the purpose of securing virtualized network environments is also available for purchase, and this option is also open to users. The firewalls in this architecture are implemented as virtual machines (VMs), and their jobs are to manage traffic between VMs and filter data arriving from VMs. In other words, this design employs a software-based approach to firewall, which is shown in Figure 8.1.

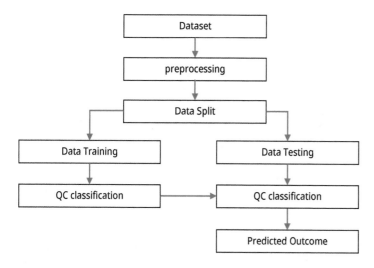

Figure 8.1: Proposed framework.

Methods for IDS in MCC can be placed into one of three categories: signature-based, anomaly-based, or hybrid intrusion detection. Each of these categories has its advantages and disadvantages. Approaches that are based on anomalies as well as signatures have been used in the development of methods for detecting intrusion.

For the purpose of managing and monitoring the status of guest operating systems, VMs, and application software, a collection of processes called virtual machine management (VMI) is used. These procedures are carried out at the hypervisor layer and have been given this name. Internal attacks are the kind of attacks that the VMI IDS is meant to recognize. These attacks can come from one VM against another VM or from a VM against the Virtual Machine Monitor (VMM), and they are the kind of thing that can originate from one VM. Due to the value it offers to the VMM in CC, the VMI is put to considerable use in order to monitor the operations of virtual machines.

The VMI IDS is able to conduct investigations that are particularly tailored to the condition and activities of a VM. Host-based detection systems are susceptible to attack despite the fact that they offer a high level of visibility. The IDS in this scenario has a considerably reduced visibility because it is placed on the network rather than the host. On the other hand, its sensitivity has been lowered, and it is more resistant to attacks than it was in the first scenario.

The VMI IDS analyzes the host for immediately observable events and the current condition of the connected hardware in order to ascertain the software current state. A Markov chain is used by this method in order to facilitate the generation of a dependency network for system calls. Since the authors achieved this and also employed a method called injection, they were able to recover the traces of a system call made by malware, which fortified the system against attempts to evade detection.

8.3.1 Quantum Intelligence

There is a similarity between the clustering that occurs in the swarm intelligence algorithm and the particle-bound state that can be discovered in classical physics. This similarity can be recognized through the use of swarm intelligence. The action of a potential field having an effect on individual particles ultimately leads to the formation of bound state pairs. When viewed in the context of a potential field centered on quantum particles, the behavior of particles in the world of quantum mechanics exhibits the same characteristics as the formation of bound state pairs.

At any given point in space, there is a region with a particular probability density where an occurrence involving a quantum-bound particle may take place. This region can be found anywhere in space. The probability density is at its peak when the particle is situated relatively close to the center p, but it starts to decrease as the distance between the particle and p gets closer and closer to infinity. It is not viable to reproduce the wave functions of competing potential energy models because these models are too intricate, and some of them have a tendency to reach maturity before they should. This prevents it from being possible to replicate the wave functions.

Since it is not possible to know both the position and the velocity of a particle in quantum space at the same time, the wave function is used to characterize the state of the particle rather than the position or the velocity themselves.

The implementation of the quantum version of the beetle swarm algorithm is the step that must be taken before moving on to the next step. We are able to apply quantum properties by looking at them from the perspective of quantum dynamics.

This allows one to get the desired result. It is now possible to search the entirety of the feasible domain space for particles that satisfy the aggregated state criterion. This is absolutely necessary in order to ensure that the algorithm converges everywhere in the globe, steers clear of problems with local optimal solutions, and speeds up the convergence process. In addition, the Monte Carlo simulation makes it feasible to determine the exact location of a particle at any specific point in time.

8.4 Evaluation

Anomaly detection systems have been evaluated on an annual basis using the dataset that was used in 1999 for the KDD Cup. The DARPA 1998 dataset, which includes military network breaches and is used by researchers to create machine learning-based classification and clustering algorithms with an emphasis on security, serves as the basis for these data. In the year 1998, the DARPA 1998 dataset was developed. In total, roughly five million connection records were used as training data for the KDD Cup 1999 dataset throughout the course of a period of time spanning around three weeks. The training data include categorical as well as statistical characteristics, and they are categorized as either typical traffic or as an assault of some kind.

The dataset for the KDD Cup 1999 is made up of many different features, some of which are traffic features, some are content features, and some are essential elements. Functions relating to Transmission Control Protocol (TCP) connections are handled by the basic class, which is accountable for this duty. Following the categorization of the features that are connected to a specific window size according to the type of traffic that they are intended to detect, the content features are consulted in order to validate the behavior of the data chunk that is causing the issue, which is shown in Figures 8.2–8.5.

This research makes use of both simple random sampling as well as stratified random sampling in order to reduce the amount of computer time needed for the massive data collection. The sum of all the data points that are present in the training set as well as the testing set takes the total to 20,121. After the data have been cleaned up by removing duplicates and gaps, the character information must be converted into numbers. This step must be completed before moving on to the next step. The second step is to normalize the data in such a way that the differences in the specific

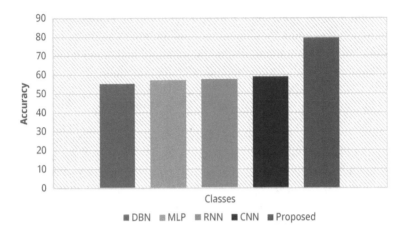

Figure 8.2: Detection rate.

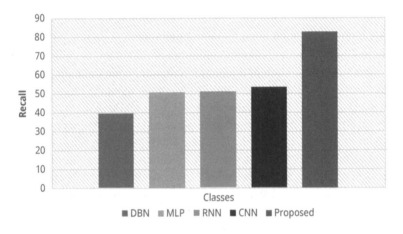

Figure 8.3: Computational time (s).

features do not have a negative impact on the categorization level of precision. The third step in the process of decreasing the dimensionality of the data is to determine, with the help of Pearson correlation coefficient, which characteristics are the most important to focus on.

The findings of this comparison make it abundantly clear that QC outperforms the other two algorithms in terms of accuracy and has a significantly lower rate of false positives than the other two algorithms. Figures 8.2–8.5 provide an illustration of a comparison of the convergence of and it does so in a manner that is analogous to this. According to the results of the experiments, QC is superior to QC in terms of its ability to converge quickly throughout the iterative process and to avoid becoming stuck on local optimal solutions. This is due to the fact that QC can prevent you from

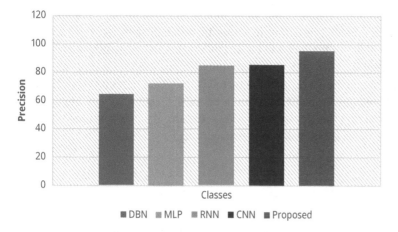

Figure 8.4: Precision.

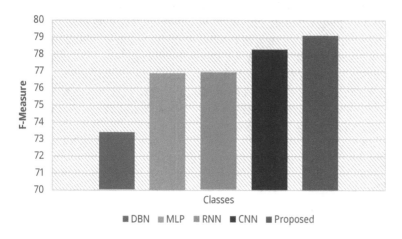

Figure 8.5: F-measure.

becoming preoccupied with finding optimal solutions at the local level. Due to this, QC provides a higher detection performance when it comes to the detection of intrusions using binary classification on the dataset.

Our first and primary step was to propose the quantum beetle swarm algorithm as the solution to the problem. The fundamental principle of quantum physics is used in this procedure, which results in a combination of the beetle swarm method and the particle swarm algorithm. It has been suggested that the Least Square QR (LSQR) decomposition method be used so that the performance of the extreme learning machine can be significantly enhanced.

The required number of calculations would be reduced and the rate at which the system would converge would pick up speed. In addition, a technique that is referred to as quantum beetle swarm optimization is implemented in order to make the most of the augmented extreme learning machine in terms of both its weights and its thresholds. At the end of the day, the approach that is used in quality control is the one that is utilized in the world of security monitoring. The findings of the experiments indicate that, in comparison to the methods that were used in the past, the QC algorithm possesses glaring benefits in a number of evaluation indices. This was determined by comparing the QC algorithm to the methods that were utilized. The finding of new applications for QC will be the primary focus of the second step.

8.5 Conclusion

It is proposed that the IDS be classified by making use of a quantum algorithm that incorporates a technique for estimating distribution. This was done so that the results could be more accurately predicted. Using the KDD dataset, a comparison was made between it and an additional QC-based classification algorithm. The data obtained from a variety of investigations demonstrate that the algorithm is capable of producing accurate categorization results. These results were shown by the algorithm. Its superiority to the other algorithm has been established through a plethora of experiments, which all point to the same conclusion. The next phase of our work will require us to conduct additional tests using a wide variety of different parameter values. These tests will ensure that the system is able to detect intrusions.

References

[1] Yin, X. (2010). Quantum evolutionary algorithm based network intrusion detection. In: 2010 3rd International Conference on Computer Science and Information Technology (Vol. 4, pp. 683–685). IEEE.

[2] Payares, E. D. & Martinez-Santos, J. C. (2021). Quantum machine learning for intrusion detection of distributed denial of service attacks: A comparative overview. *Quantum Computing, Communication, and Simulation, 11699*, 35–43.

[3] Dixit, V., Selvarajan, R., Aldwairi, T., Koshka, Y., Novotny, M. A., Humble, T. S., & . . . Kais, S. (2021). Training a quantum annealing based restricted Boltzmann machine on cybersecurity data. *IEEE Transactions on Emerging Topics in Computational Intelligence, 6*(3), 417–428.

[4] Nithya, C., & Saravanan, V. (2018). A study of machine learning techniques in data mining. *International Scientific Refereed Research Journal, 1*, 31–38.

[5] Nag-Chowdhury, S., Bellegou, H., Pillin, I., Castro, M., Longrais, P., & Feller, J. F. (2016). Non-intrusive health monitoring of infused composites with embedded carbon quantum piezo-resistive sensors. *Composites Science and Technology, 123*, 286–294.

[6] Pavithra, R., Srinivasan, R., & Saravanan, V. (2018). Web service deployment for selecting a right steganography scheme for optimizing both the capacity and the detectable distortion. *International Journal on Recent and Innovation Trends in Computing and Communication, 6*(4), 267–277.

[7]   Hou, Y., & Zheng, X. F. (2010). Quantum self organized map-based intrusion detection system. In: 2010 International Conference on Artificial Intelligence and Education (ICAIE) (pp. 140–145). IEEE.

[8]   Yadav, S. P. (2022). Blockchain Security. In: Baalamurugan, K., Kumar, S. R., Kumar, A., Kumar, V., Padmanaban, S. (eds.). Blockchain Security in Cloud Computing. EAI/Springer Innovations in Communication and Computing. Springer, Cham. https://doi.org/10.1007/978-3-030-70501-5_1.

[9]   Zeng, S., & Huang, Y. (2019). Collaborative quantum optimization network intrusion detection research. *Journal of Computational Methods in Sciences and Engineering*, *19*(1), 169–178.

[10]   Yadav, S. P., Bhati, B. S., Mahato, D. P., & Kumar, S., (eds). Federated Learning for IoT Applications. EAI/Springer Innovations in Communication and Computing. Springer, Cham. https://doi.org/10.1007/978-3-030-85559-8.

[11]   Wang, J., Liu, C., Shu, X., Jiang, H., Yu, X., Wang, J., & Wang, W. (2019). Network intrusion detection based on xgboost model improved by quantum-behaved particle swarm optimization. In: 2019 IEEE Sustainable Power and Energy Conference (iSPEC) (pp. 1879–1884). IEEE.

[12]   Gobinathan, B., Mukunthan, M. A., Surendran, S., Somasundaram, K., Moeed, S. A., Niranjan, P., & . . . Sundramurthy, V. P. (2021). A novel method to solve real time security issues in software industry using advanced cryptographic techniques. *Scientific Programming*, 2021.

[13]   Kolias, C., Kambourakis, G., & Maragoudakis, M. (2011). Swarm intelligence in intrusion detection: A survey. *Computers & Security*, *30*(8), 625–642.

[14]   Zhang, J., & Zhang, D. I nternet of things network intrusion detection model based on quantum artificial fish group and fuzzy kernel clustering algorithm. *Security and Privacy*, e220.

[15]   Thirumalairaj, A., & Jeyakarthic, M. (2020). Perimeter intrusion detection with multi layer perception using quantum classifier. In: 2020 Fourth International Conference on Inventive Systems and Control (ICISC) (pp. 348–352). IEEE.

[16]   Ling, Z., & Hao, Z. J. (2022). Intrusion detection using normalized mutual information feature selection and parallel quantum genetic algorithm. *International Journal on Semantic Web and Information Systems (IJSWIS)*, *18*(1), 1–24.

[17]   Chaudhary, H., Detroja, A., Prajapati, P., & Shah, P. (2020). A review of various challenges in cybersecurity using artificial intelligence. In: 2020 3rd International Conference on Intelligent Sustainable Systems (ICISS) (pp. 829–836). IEEE.

[18]   Feng, L. (2011). An intrusion detection approach based on multiple rough classifiers integration. *Journal of Experimental & Theoretical Artificial Intelligence*, *23*(2), 223–231.

[19]   Munawar, S., Hamid, M., & Lodhi, S. A. (2017). Quantum Bayesian game modeling for intrusion detection. *The Nucleus*, *54*(4), 214–218.

[20]   Wang, X. Y., Zhang, H. M., & Gao, H. H. (2008). Quantum particle swarm optimization based network intrusion feature selection and detection. *IFAC Proceedings Volumes*, *41*(2), 12312–12317.

[21]   Sarvari, S., Sani, N. F. M., Hanapi, Z. M., & Abdullah, M. T. (2020). An efficient quantum multiverse optimization algorithm for solving optimization problems. *International Journal of Advances in Applied Sciences*, *9*(1), 27–33.

[22]   Lindsay, J. R. (2020). Demystifying the quantum threat: Infrastructure, institutions, and intelligence advantage. *Security Studies*, *29*(2), 335–361.

[23]   Jasim Mohammad, O. K., El-Horbaty, E. S. M., & Salem, A. B. M. (2016). Ciphering of Cloud Computing Environment Based New Intelligent Quantum Service. In: New Approaches in Intelligent Control (pp. 241–272). Springer, Cham.

[24]   Nawaz, S. J., Sharma, S. K., Wyne, S., Patwary, M. N., & Asaduzzaman, M. (2019). Quantum machine learning for 6G communication networks: State-of-the-art and vision for the future. *IEEE Access*, *7*, 46317–46350.

Swati Tiwari*, Kamlesh Kumar Yadav, D. Palanikkumar

9 Fault-tolerant mechanism using intelligent quantum computing-based error reduction codes

Abstract: The chapter discusses the fault-tolerant mechanism using quantum computing that uses error reduction codes to reduce the possible faults. Building the circuits that make up a genuine quantum computer in order to get rid of delays that make the circuits more susceptible to noise was done in order to improve the performance of the computer. In addition, we have demonstrated that there will be no rise in the T-count as a direct consequence of carrying out this operation. We have provided three distinct iterations of a 4-digit carry lookahead adder that has been improved in terms of T-count, T-depth, and the number of ancilla qubits that can be used. These adders make use of a novel approach that performs operations with a smaller T-count, which speeds up the computation of carry by conducting operations more quickly.

9.1 Introduction

Traditional computers struggle to find solutions to specific problems that quantum computers would have no trouble handling [1, 2]. Large-scale quantum processing continues to be a serious experimental problem for the great majority of viable candidates, despite the fact that quantum computing at the microscale has been shown by exploiting a range of different physical systems [3, 4]. Using compressed vacuum states in an optical system, experiments have already attained states with more than a million modes [5]. When it comes to continuous-variable (CV) quantum computing on a massive scale, this kind of state is among the most promising options.

Only factoring and Hamiltonian simulations are two examples of the sorts of operations that it is believed that quantum computers would be able to do in an order of magnitude less time than classical computers [6]. This belief is based on only two examples of the kinds of operations. There are a great number of various kinds of procedures. Quantum systems, on the other hand, are inherently interactive, which causes them to make regular physical mistakes. These mistakes put the benefits of

---

***Corresponding author: Swati Tiwari**, Department of Computer Science, Kalinga University, Naya Raipur, Chhattisgarh, India, e-mail: swati.tiwari@kalingauniversity.ac.in
Kamlesh Kumar Yadav, Department of IT, Kalinga University, Naya Raipur, Chhattisgarh, India, e-mail: kamleshkuyadav05@gmail.com
D. Palanikkumar, Department of CSE, Dr. NGP Institute of Technology, Coimbatore, Tamil Nadu, India, e-mail: palanikkumard@gmail.com

https://doi.org/10.1515/9783110798159-009

quantum systems in peril of being made ineffective. Due to the fact that the rate of physical mistakes that can arise in quantum computers is still significantly higher than that which can occur in classical computers, the eradication of these faults is an absolute necessity.

In an effort to discover a solution to this issue, researchers have looked into fault-tolerant quantum computing (FTQC) in conjunction with quantum error-correcting codes [7–10]. On the FTQC, for instance, standard quantum algorithms like Hamiltonian simulation algorithms can be executed for a prolonged length of time [11]. To see clear quantum advantages based on the notion of computational complexity, the number of logical quantum operations will need to be of the order of 1,010, according to the most recent resource estimates [12]. This is the bare minimum number of processes that will be necessary to observe discernible quantum benefits.

We pass through a number of different intermediary regimes on the way to the actualization of the long-term FTQC because high-level encoding is not permitted due to the constraints of quantum resources such as qubits and magic state counts [13]. Because of these regimes, we are able to move in the direction of our ultimate aim of attaining the FTQC. The available code distance will be severely limited in the not-too-distant future due to the fact that quantum error correction (QEC) necessitates an enormous amount of classical computation for repeated error estimations [15–17].

This is going to be the situation because the use of QEC is obligatory. When all aspects of the development of quantum technology have been completed, we will have arrived at the point when we have achieved quantum superiority in logical-space computing [14]. The phrase early FTQC regime refers to the period of time that occurs after the accomplishment of logical quantum supremacy but before the proof of the viability of long-term applications. This period of time follows the achievement of logical quantum supremacy.

9.2 Related works

The connection overheads may not be worth it when compared to codes that allow communication over a shorter range. Other codes may provide communication over a longer range [15].

This is the case as a result of the fact that in the encoding rates of error-correcting codes, if vast quantities of quantum memory were readily available, then entanglement distribution might be a workable strategy for providing distant connectivity for large-scale machines that has only limited opportunities for physical connectivity. If the quantum memory reserves were sufficient in size, then this would be the outcome [16].

The term "transversal" refers to the property of error correction codes, whereby each code block is corrected independently of the others when an error arises. Error correction codes with a higher dimension have the advantage of accessing a wider variety of transversal gates, which can lead to a significant reduction in the overall time required to complete the error correction process. Photonic-interconnected modules may offer the most flexibility in terms of their potential connectivity graph. However, the maximum connection speeds that could be achieved would create a significant bottleneck in the system. Current quantum platforms may have difficulty realizing this level of 3D (or higher) physical connectivity [17]. This is due to the fact that the thickness can be reduced to a more manageable level than it now is [18].

Several of the most well-known quantum computing systems are analyzed, along with the error correction algorithms that are specific to each platform, and a comparison of the operational speeds of the various platforms is also presented. It has been estimated that the code cycle times, which refer to the fundamental sequence of hardware operations, will fall somewhere in the range of 0.2–10 s, and its name comes from the surface of a superconducting device [19].

It is feasible to implement designs for trapped ions in a variety of methods, each of which is quite distinct from the others, particularly in terms of the techniques that make it possible to establish connectivity. One study came to the conclusion that a scalable device using microwave-based gates and shuttling to give connectivity would have a coding cycle time of 235 s. The device would contain trapped ions and depend on shuttling to provide connectivity [20].

In this design that is based on shuttling, there is the possibility of a variable-mid-range connection. This indicates that various error correction protocols may have a better chance of succeeding than the surface code. However, it allows only the codes which are used the surface code. The extremely malleable nature of these connections suggests that higher-dimensional error-correcting codes may be used one day, despite the fact that the surface code was developed specifically for use with small trapped ion modules that are connected to one another by means of photonic interconnects [21]. One method that might be taken is to implement a notion that suggests using two layers. This, in turn, could influence the amount of time it takes for the code cycle time for trapped ions that make use of photonic interconnects [22].

Architectures that make use of trapped ions have been shown to provide some of the highest gate fidelity; however, these architectures require a smaller base area. The coding distance in the error correction technique will be reduced in proportion to the level of physical error that has been detected. Due to this, the number of physical qubits that are required to represent each logical qubit will be reduced [23]. On top of the surface code, which is anticipated to have a cycle time of 1.2 milliseconds, it has been proposed that a fault-tolerant silicon-based architecture might be developed. Depending on the design, the Raussendorf-Harrington-Goyal (RHG) lattice may be the most suitable option for a fault-tolerant solution in photonic devices [24]. The degree to which particular architectures and stages of development are scalable might vary greatly depending on the context.

As part of this project, we will be providing an estimate of the physical resources that a quantum computer must have in order for it to be able to properly run the surface code. This estimate will be provided in the form of a table. We investigate the connection that exists between the length of a code cycle and the maximum number of physical qubits that an underlying architecture is capable of supporting by utilizing cutting-edge techniques for time optimization. These techniques allow us to determine how closely these two variables are related to one another. This study was carried out with the purpose of achieving greater levels of productivity [20–25].

It is hypothesized that the use of these algorithms would result in a quantum advantage that will fundamentally alter the landscape of commercially significant applications.

9.3 Methods

Now that we have returned to the nine-qubit code, let us figure out exactly what needs to be done in order to resolve the concerns that have been brought up. First, we have to find out whether or not all three of the first qubits are identical, and if they are not, we have to figure out which one is the only one of its kind. If they are all the same, then we may move on to the next step. It is feasible to measure the parity of the first two qubits as well as the parity of the second and third qubits. Additionally, it is possible to measure the parity of the fourth qubit.

The first one informs us about whether or not qubits one and two have been affected by an X error, and the second one informs us about whether or not qubits two and three have been affected by an X error. It is absolutely necessary to be conscious of the fact that the error that was measured anti-commutes with the error that was discovered in both cases. After putting these two puzzle pieces together, we are immediately able to pinpoint the exact location of the mistake. The approach taken with each of the three groups of three is the same as the others. Following the completion of this expansion, the total number of operators in the sample has reached sixteen. It is essential to keep in mind that the information we need can only be gained by measuring Z by Z. This is the only way to get the information we need. This is an essential part of the solution to the problem of preventing the code superpositions from being rendered invalid. We shall be able to achieve this objective once we have added an ancilla qubit to our system.

The new codes can be described in a straightforward manner with the assistance of stabilizers. For instance, in the traditional theory of coding, a linear code is represented by a generator matrix or its antonym, the parity check matrix. Both of these matrices have the same name. Beginning with contemporary coding theory is another approach that might be used. Every other codeword can be described as a linear combination of the rows of the generator matrix, which are also codewords in their own right.

This is possible because every row of the generator matrix is a codeword. Each row of the parity check matrix has a list of parity checks that each of the classical codewords needs to pass in order to be considered legitimate. These checks are used to determine whether or not a codeword can be considered valid. (One might think of the stabilizer in quantum codes as a near analog to the parity check matrix that is employed in conventional computers.) The one-error-correcting Hamming code is an example of this type of code. It consists of seven bits and a parity-check matrix to ensure that there is only one error.

If we supply three operators that each execute the parity check measures, and one of those measures is to exchange the ones in this matrix for the Z operator and the zeros for the I operator, then we have not made any substantial alterations. In such a scenario, the parity check measures will be carried out in an appropriate manner. Therefore, the typical Hamming code only corrects one error because each bit-flip error has a weight of one or two anti-commutes with one of these three operators.

Once more, we are provided with three operators, and if there is any Z mistake with a weight of one or two, then the behavior of these operators will be anti-commutative. By combining the three Z operators and the three X operators into a stabilizer, we were able to generate a code that is capable of correcting a single qubit error. This was accomplished by merging these six operators into a single unit. Any faults that are associated with X will be discovered by the first three generators, any faults that are associated with Z will be discovered by the last three generators, and any faults that are associated with Y will be split evenly between the two groups. Having said that, there is one item that needs to be checked, and that is whether or not the stabilizer is abelian. The stabilizer uses a [1, 3, 7] code to encode a single qubit into its storage. The stabilizer has six generators and seven qubits.

The vast majority of quantum error-correcting codes are not stabilizer codes, and significant headway has been made in the research and creation of various kinds of codes besides stabilizer codes. Finding and using a code can be done in a variety of different ways, but in most circumstances, you will need to operate under the assumption that there is some degree of structure in order to do so. There are a few distinct approaches you might take to accomplish this goal.

The use of codes that operate across higher-dimensional registers, which are often referred to as qudits, can be a very profitable alternative to the use of qubits. Stabilizer codes can easily be generalized to this environment, and it is known that there are many different types of qudit stabilizer codes. One of the possibilities that can be taken into consideration is the endeavor to develop qubit codes that are more effective, which might be possible if the stabilizer structure were modified in some way, which is shown in Figure 9.1.

Figure 9.1: Quantum modelling.

In recent years, a method that goes by the name operator quantum error correction (which is also known as subsystem codes) has become the focus of a significant amount of research and development. As we are ignoring some degrees of freedom, this encoding makes it possible for us to successfully encode a state as a linear subspace rather than another state. This is because we are omitting certain degrees of freedom. In spite of the fact that the fundamental error-correcting features that have been stated cannot be enhanced by using subsystem codes, considering how fault-tolerant a system is can be aided by doing so.

Another potentially promising avenue is the investigation of fully degenerate code. If all of the possible errors for a code act as the identity on the code subspace, then there is no need for any active corrective action to be performed; in this scenario, the state will continue to be unaltered, regardless of which error occurs. The majority of the time, a Degenerate Fault-tolerant Subsystem (DFS) will undergo an analysis to look for situations in which errors occur continually throughout the course of time.

However, if the error rate is already sufficiently low, a more complete QECC can reduce the effective error rate for many different types of noise. This is only the case if the error rate is already sufficiently low. This is true provided, however, that the error rate is already at an acceptably low level.

Quantum error correction is not the only strategy for shielding qubits from the damaging effects of noise; naturally, there are other options accessible as well. For instance, in the method that is referred to as dynamical decoupling, the noise is reduced by performing a sequence of swift actions in rapid succession. In order for dynamic decoupling to be successful, it is required for the noise to vary at a pace that is noticeably slower than the rate at which humans are able to carry out activities. This rate must be much slower. It performs effectively even at quite high error rates, just like a DFS, and it does not require any additional qubits, in contrast to a DFS or a QECC, both of which require additional qubits to function properly. These are two of the many advantages that come with using dynamic decoupling.

The process of removing faults from a quantum computer is a complex one, and in order for us to find a solution to the problem, we will need to make use of every instrument that is available to us. The first line of defense will most likely consist of control methods such as dynamical decoupling. This cost can be divided into two categories: the first category refers to the overhead, while the second category refers to the errors. This cost may be broken down into two categories: first, there is the overhead that is tacked on, and second, there are the errors that are tacked on.

Nevertheless, there will be errors present in each and every action, each and every qubit that we add, and each and every extra gate that we complete. It is possible for the judgment of precisely which precautions are helpful and which create more effort than they are worth to become a complex exercise in striking a balance between several competing agendas.

9.4 Evaluation

Following the development of Python code for each of the suggested and state-of-the-art circuits, that code was run on IBM Quantum Experience hardware and simulators in order to verify and validate the circuits. After this replication was complete, in order to collect the metrics that are described further down, we tallied the number of qubits, T gates, and executions of T gates in consecutive order (while keeping in mind that some gates do not explicitly express their T-count and T-depth and making the necessary conversions). This was accomplished while keeping in mind that not all gates convey their T-count and T-depth in a clear and concise manner. One of the possibilities that can be taken into consideration is the endeavor to develop qubit codes that are more effective, which might be possible if the stabilizer structure were modified in some way (shown in Figures 9.2–9.5).

The T-count for each of Circuits 1, 2, and 3 is respectively 36, 51, and 41, and the T-depth for each of these circuits is accordingly 10, 11, and 11 respectively. This is something that can be concluded from the section discussion of the circuit technique and the graphical designs that are presented. It is necessary for them to possess 9, 5, and 6 ancilla qubits in this particular arrangement. The suggested circuits do not include any operations or trash outputs that, in a quantum setting, would be regarded as being invalid.

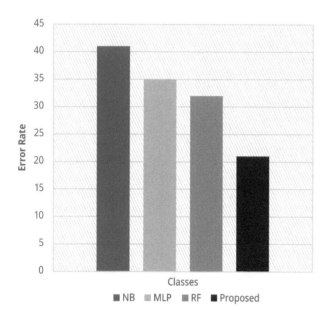

Figure 9.2: Error rate.

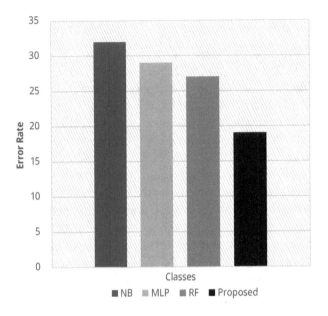

Figure 9.3: MAE.

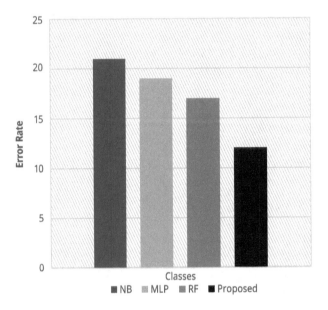

Figure 9.4: RMSE.

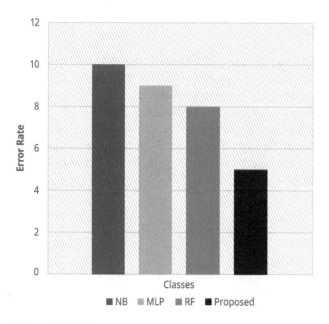

Figure 9.5: RRSE.

Given that a Toffoli gate has a T-count of 7 and a T-depth of 3, a temporary-logical gate has a T-count of 4 and a T-depth of 2, and no other gate in the circuit has either a T-count or a T-depth, it is not difficult to validate these numbers. However, it is important to note that there is no other gate in the circuit that has either a T-count or a T-depth.

For the most part, we have relied on two separate sites in order to evaluate the recommended circuits in comparison to circuits that have already been published. The first is a comprehensive analysis of quantum adders, in which several distinct incarnations of the algorithm are compared and contrasted with one another. Within the context of one of these evaluations, the carry lookahead adder functions as the principal focus of attention.

The second source that we investigated provides in-depth comparisons of the four different carry lookahead adders that are currently available. They examine a substantial number of adders from both publications and compare them. As we did not want to bloat this section with information that has already been compiled in a number of studies, the comparison that follows only takes into account the most effective circuits from the aforementioned sources. This decision was made because we did not want to repeat the work that has already been done.

9.5 Conclusion

In this chapter, an exhaustive analysis of the gate-based design of the three adders has been included for perusal. This description contains a detailed review of the stages, gates, and qubits that are required in order to construct them. This was done in order to ensure that it will function properly in a quantum setting.

In the end, we have compared our circuits to the most efficient adders stated in the previous research. This evaluation was carried out in order to determine how well our designs stack up. In light of these findings, it is clearly obvious that the recommended adders surpass the state-of-the-art circuits.

References

[1] Egan, L., Debroy, D. M., Noel, C., Risinger, A., Zhu, D., Biswas, D., & . . . Monroe, C. (2021). Fault-tolerant control of an error-corrected qubit. *Nature, 598*(7880), 281–286.

[2] Webber, M., Elfving, V., Weidt, S., & Hensinger, W. K. (2022). The impact of hardware specifications on reaching quantum advantage in the fault tolerant regime. *AVS Quantum Science, 4*(1), 013801.

[3] Hilder, J., Pijn, D., Onishchenko, O., Stahl, A., Orth, M., Lekitsch, B., & . . . Poschinger, U. G. (2022). Fault-tolerant parity readout on a shuttling-based trapped-ion quantum computer. *Physical Review X, 12*(1), 011032.

[4] Ryan-Anderson, C., Bohnet, J. G., Lee, K., Gresh, D., Hankin, A., Gaebler, J. P., & . . . Stutz, R. P. (2021). Realization of real-time fault-tolerant quantum error correction. *Physical Review X, 11*(4), 041058.

[5] Biswal, L., Rahaman, H., & Maity, N. P. (2021). Clifford+ T-based implementation of fault-tolerant quantum circuits over XOR-Majority graph. *Microelectronics Journal, 116*, 105212.

[6] Asaoka, R., Tokunaga, Y., Kanamoto, R., Goto, H., & Aoki, T. (2021). Requirements for fault-tolerant quantum computation with cavity-QED-based atom-atom gates mediated by a photon with a finite pulse length. *Physical Review A, 104*(4), 043702.

[7] Orts, F., Ortega, G., Cucura, A. C., Filatovas, E., & Garzón, E. M. (2021). Optimal fault-tolerant quantum comparators for image binarization. *The Journal of Supercomputing, 77*(8), 8433–8444.

[8] Walshe, B. W., Alexander, R. N., Menicucci, N. C., & Baragiola, B. Q. (2021). Streamlined quantum computing with macronode cluster states. *Physical Review A, 104*(6), 062427.

[9] Lin, L., & Tong, Y. (2022). Heisenberg-limited ground-state energy estimation for early fault-tolerant quantum computers. *PRX Quantum, 3*(1), 010318.

[10] Gobinathan, B., Mukunthan, M. A., Surendran, S., Somasundaram, K., Moeed, S. A., Niranjan, P., & . . . Sundramurthy, V. P. (2021). A novel method to solve real time security issues in software industry using advanced cryptographic techniques. *Scientific Programming, 2021*.

[11] Natarajan, Y., Raja, R. A., Kousik, N. V., & Saravanan, M. (2021). A review of various reversible embedding mechanisms. *International Journal of Intelligence and Sustainable Computing, 1*(3), 233–266.

[12] Wan, K., Choi, S., Kim, I. H., Shutty, N., & Hayden, P. (2021). Fault-tolerant qubit from a constant number of components. *PRX Quantum, 2*(4), 040345.

[13] Lin, C., Yang, G., Song, X., & Perkowski, M. (2021). Pieceable fault-tolerant conversion between Steane and Reed-Muller quantum codes with neural network decoders. *arXiv preprint arXiv:2105.07133*.

[14] Pavithra, R., Srinivasan, R., & Saravanan, V. (2018). Web service deployment for selecting a right steganography scheme for optimizing both the capacity and the detectable distortion. *International Journal on Recent and Innovation Trends in Computing and Communication*, 6(4), 267–277.

[15] Thomsen, F., Kesselring, M. S., Bartlett, S. D., & Brown, B. J. (2022). Low-overhead quantum computing with the color code. *arXiv preprint arXiv:2201.07806*.

[16] Sabitha, R., Gopikrishnan, S., Bejoy, B. J., Anusuya, V., & Saravanan, V. (2022). Network based detection of IoT attack using AIS-IDS model. *Wireless Personal Communications*, 1–24.

[17] Zhang, R., Wang, G., & Johnson, P. (2022). Computing ground state properties with early fault-tolerant quantum computers. *Quantum*, 6, 761.

[18] Yadav, S. P., & Yadav, S. (2018). Fusion of medical images in wavelet domain: A discrete mathematical model. *Ingeniería Solidaria*, 14(25), 1–11. https://doi.org/10.16925/.v14i0.2236.

[19] Delgado, A., Casares, P. A., Reis, R. D., Zini, M. S., Campos, R., Cruz-Hernández, N., & . . . Arrazola, J. M. (2022). How to simulate key properties of lithium-ion batteries with a fault-tolerant quantum computer. *arXiv preprint arXiv:2204.11890*.

[20] Yadav, S. P., & Yadav, S. (2019). Mathematical implementation of fusion of medical images in continuous wavelet domain. *Journal of Advanced Research in Dynamical and Control System*, 10(10), 45–54.

[21] Cetina, M. (2022). Scaling up quantum computing with ion chains. *Bulletin of the American Physical Society*.

[22] Shutty, N. & Chamberland, C. (2022). Finding fault-tolerant Clifford circuits using SMT solvers. *arXiv preprint arXiv:2201.12450*.

[23] Ayukaryana, N. R., Fauzi, M. H., & Hasdeo, E. H. (2021). The quest and hope of Majorana zero modes in topological superconductor for fault-tolerant quantum computing: An introductory overview. In AIP Conference Proceedings (Vol. 2382, No. 1, p. 020007). AIP Publishing LLC.

[24] Su, Y., Berry, D. W., Wiebe, N., Rubin, N., & Babbush, R. (2021). Fault-tolerant quantum simulations of chemistry in first quantization. *PRX Quantum*, 2(4), 040332.

[25] Tansuwannont, T., & Leung, D. (2022). Achieving fault tolerance on capped color codes with few ancillas. *PRX Quantum*, 3(3), 030322.

Kaushal Kishor*

10 Study of quantum computing for data analytics of predictive and prescriptive analytics models

Abstract: People now also earn money within a limited amount of time by spending it. This is going to happen when you make the correct decisions. In the coming years, quantum computing is expected to discover new patterns and solutions, as well as provide results faster and in a more energy- and cost-efficient fashion in selected analytics use case scenarios, but only if an integration of technology-affine business analysts and imposed researchers can effectively use and extend unique business and technology aware methods to "quantize" the business problem by developing a user accessible workflow. This quantification comprises two key problems to be overcome in terms of business needs on one side and R&D feasibility on the other. Despite difficulties in scaling quantum systems and integrating them into commercial data pipelines, the sector is rapidly approaching enterprise readiness. This chapter details and summarizes the existing language on prescriptive analytics, highlighting current problems and exploring possible solutions.

10.1 Introduction

We live in a world of growing global digital economy growth, where information digitization generates huge data assets and digital technologies become more powerful, accessible, and affordable. This is evident in whole new corporate operating models as well as the ways people connect, works, purchase, and receive services. This apparent acceleration and technological progress is the consequence of interconnected breakthroughs ranging from the internet, cloud and edge computing, mobile electronics, and open-source collaborations [1, 2]. Overall, the semiconductor sector is the backbone and major facilitator of this advancement. Based on several physics and engineering breakthroughs, as well as the invention of the transistor in the first half of the twentieth century, the industry has rapidly evolved from special- to general-purpose computing technologies, consistently following the performance predictions of Moore's Law 1, doubling the number of transistors in integrated computing circuits every two years [3].

*Corresponding author: Kaushal Kishor, IT Department, ABES Institute of Technology, Ghaziabad, Uttar Pradesh, India, e-mails: kaushal.kishor@abesit.in, kaushal.rastogi07@gmail.com

https://doi.org/10.1515/9783110798159-010

Stock market analysis is one of the most well-known applications in the world of science. Since this is a competitive medium, seeking an effective and productive approach remains a task, amid multiple attempts. The complexity of forecasting is proportional to the business dynamics models. Fundamental and technical [4] methodologies are encapsulated in the area of stock market analysis. Fundamental analysis is concerned with predicting stock price activity based on numeric historical evidence, while technological analysis is concerned with using simulation methods and maps to predict potential stock movements and prices. Natural language-based financial forecasting (NLFF) [5, 6] adds textual data analysis to the mix, recognizing that timely produced intelligence releases, news, and popular voice in social media and blogs have a substantial impact on the price and trend of a protection share. Pre-defining the application specific collection of keywords and determining the required machine learning methodology for sentiment analysis are among the tasks involved in text analysis for sentiment extraction.

Making good business decisions is challenging, particularly when there is not enough data to direct sound decision-making. Knowing what happened in the past does not help in predicting what will happen in the future, since assumptions relying solely on observational evidence are often wrong. To avoid these traps, business leaders use two innovative methods, predictive and prescriptive analytics. They combine historical data (descriptive analytics), laws, and market intelligence to better forecast the future and, in the case of prescriptive analytics, direct leaders to the best final decisions. Is there a difference between predictive and prescriptive analytics, or are they the same thing? We are now questioning if predictive and prescriptive analytics are separate or synonymous.

Despite the fact that both of the tactics are proactive, there is a significant difference between them. The following is the hierarchy of analytical methods, according to Gartner's Analytic Ascendency Model:
–   What happened to descriptive analytics?
–   Diagnostic analytics: What went wrong?
–   What Will Happen For Predictive Analytics?
–   How do we render predictive analytics a reality?

Prescriptive analytics demonstrates how to make things real, while predictive analytics indicates how to make things inevitable. In this way, predictive analytics is subordinate to prescriptive analytics. This is not to imply that predictive analytics are not valuable; it is just that the information they present is not equivalent.

The usage of mathematical and simulation tools to predict what will happen in the future is known as predictive analytics. It calculates the probability of a given occurrence or occurrences using historical data and simulation techniques. Predictive maintenance is a good example of predictive analysis, when it attempts to find out how a device has to be fixed by using multiple algorithms and computer data to approximate the presence of crucial components. While this knowledge is valuable and actionable, it does not dictate what action should be taken; however, it alerts the user of the need for maintenance.

Prescriptive analytics varies from predictive analytics in that it not only predicts what may happen, but also provides the customer with realistic choices and decides which market options are better, based on specific parameters. A model of the enterprise or company is generated using prescriptive analytics. This model is cross-checked against current and historical data to ensure that it accurately represents all aspects of the industry. Users should query the model to determine the best option based on predefined criteria such as profitability, SLAs, and throughput, rather than simply forecasting what would happen. Prescriptive analytics evaluates the right options for repair, substitution, or outsourcing to maximize net profitability and turnover in the case of predictive maintenance.

10.1.1 Predictive vs. prescriptive analytics

Predictive and prescriptive analytics are also useful market tools, but they have separate purposes. Predictive analytics, on the other hand, according to Gartner's analytics ladder, is equivalent to prescriptive analytics. This is due to the fact that predictive analytics predicts what will happen but does not provide guidance about how to make the necessary decisions. Prescriptive analytics, on the other hand, not only predicts what will happen, but also decides the right business judgment.

10.1.1.1 Predictive analytics

Predictive analytics is a branch of data analysis to help forecast possible results based on past data and analytical strategies such as mathematical simulation and deep learning. Predictive analytics science may produce potential insights with considerable accuracy. Using advanced predictive techniques and models, every organization may now use historical and present data to accurately estimate patterns and activities milliseconds, days, even years into the future.

Today, organizations use predictive analytics in almost infinite forms. The technology supports adopters in such varied fields as banking, healthcare, retail, and hospitality, pharmaceuticals, automotive, aerospace, and manufacturing.

Here are descriptions of how companies utilize predictive analytics:

- Aerospace: predict the reliability, fuel usage, affordability and uptime effect of complex maintenance operations.
- Automotive: record component robustness and malfunction in future car assembly plans. Study driver behavior to create improved driver assistance and automated vehicles.

– Energy: long-term price/demand ratios forecast. Determine effects on service costs of environmental conditions, system loss, rules, and other factors.
– Financial services: modeling default risk. Financial-market forecasts. Predict the effects of emerging industry and consumer strategies, rules, and legislation.
– Manufacturing: predict machine failure position and rate. Optimize deliveries of raw materials depending on potential needs.
– Enforcement: use criminal trend data to identify areas that can need extra security at certain times of the year.

10.1.1.2 Prescriptive analytics

Prescriptive analytics use similar modeling structures to forecast results and use a mixture of machine learning, market law, artificial intelligence (AI), and algorithms to replicate different approaches to these multiple outcomes. It then recommends best steps to optimize management activities. That is "what could happen."

If you are a senior leader, it is still top of mind to better maximize the quality and effectiveness of the organization's activities. Prescriptive analytics is the smartest, most effective platform used to scaffold the market intelligence of any company. Prescriptive analytics allows companies to:
– Effortlessly chart the achievement route. Prescriptive analytic models are built to collect data and operations and generate the roadmap that shows you what to do and how to do it first. AI takes business intelligence's reins to adapt simulated behavior to a situation to deliver the measures needed to prevent defeat or achieve achievement.
– Provide real-time, quick-term activities. Decision-makers should simultaneously interpret real-time and predicted data to make choices that promote sustainable development and performance. This streamlines decision-making by detailed recommendations.
– Think less and have more time. The instant turnaround in data collection and result predicting allows your staff to waste less time identifying challenges and planning the right solutions. In a fraction of the time, AI will curate and process data faster than the data engineering team.
– Reduce human error. Predictive analytics is an even more robust and precise means of data aggregation and interpretation than descriptive analytics, predictive analytics, or even individuals via sophisticated algorithms and machine learning processes.

Yeah, there is a difference between predictive and prescriptive analytics.

Some can question if the gap between these two analytics is relevant in use. They may also find out that optimizing a prescriptive analytics approach requires far more effort than optimizing a smaller-scale predictive analytics experiment. It is important to understand the market sophistication of potential buyers when addressing the query.

Although the bulk of organizations use business intelligence, not many of them have moved to predictive analytics. Prescriptive analytics is actually employed by just 11% of medium to large companies, according to Gartner. The prescriptive analytics applications industry, on the other hand, is expected to develop at a 20.6% CAGR between 2017 and 2022, according to Gartner. This means that approximately 37% of companies would begin to use predictive analytics [7].

These statistics show that the distinction between predictive and prescriptive analytics is becoming increasingly important for a rising number of businesses.

Predictive analytics excels at detecting future problems and obstacles, but only prescriptive analytics decides the right course of action for optimizing market opportunities. The two methods have completely different purposes. Predictive analytics is reactive in the sense that it stresses the need for management to adapt. Prescriptive analytics, on the other hand, are constructive in that they teach managers the path ahead.

Predictive and prescriptive analytics use actual data gathered by an organization, as well as other details. Predictive analytics actually interprets patterns, while prescriptive analytics determines the best path forward using heuristics (rules)-based automation and optimization modeling.

10.1.2 Problems that predictive analytics vs. prescriptive analytics will address

Predictive and prescriptive analytics are not stand-alone approaches that can be used separately. Both aspects of market analytics have a role in addressing multiple problems in enterprises. Predictive analytics is commonly used to detect short- to medium-term patterns, which are also used in isolation from larger trends. Here are a few examples:
- Sales patterns, particularly those for particular lines and products
- Vulnerability identification for short-term insurance
- Market research
- Consumer churn
- Inventory control
- Profitability

Prescriptive analytics requires a general perspective of the case. Prescriptive models, typically analyze whole firms, or at the very least discrete roles, units, or plants, while predictive analytics can calculate individual patterns. Prescriptive analytics has been used to address the following problems:

– Maximizing coal extraction through several mines to satisfy consumer needs while growing overall profitability.
– Creating the best packaging and inventory plan for consumer products firms.
– Choosing the appropriate operational strategy for a wastewater management utility that serves a large metropolitan area when adhering to regulations.

"How these techniques contribute to the organization's value:" Despite the fact that both approaches provide practical advantages, prescriptive analytics typically outperforms predictive analytics. While the size of activities plays a role, the kinds of decisions taken and the capacity of prescriptive analytics to refine decisions often play a role.

For short-term risk prediction, predictive analytics aims to rely on a very small range of criteria, such as the case above. While this form of study will produce substantial advantages by minimizing threats, it is unlikely to be on the same scope as a prescriptive analytics approach that models the insurance company's operations. A model like this will recognize the most attractive insurance products, the best opportunities, and the best plans for long-term business success. Additionally, instead of being restricted to pre-set situations, corporate leaders should use prescriptive analytics to consider a range of what-ifs, alternatives, and trade-offs. Prescriptive analytics is expected to be more costly than predictive analytics, but it has the ability to see a far better return on investment. This can be seen in the case of the coal mining firm above, which increased annual turnover by 4% ($250 million) while maintaining 100% consumer satisfaction [8].

10.1.3 Descriptive and exploratory analysis

Since their primary objective is to summarize and understand current data, descriptive analytics is the most popular method of data analytics. Since they aim to summarize measures in a data collection without much explanation, they are generally the simplest. Exploratory data analysis takes descriptive data analysis a step forward by looking for discoveries, patterns, associations, or interactions between measures in order to produce ideas or theories [9]. Categorical/discrete or continuous data may be used in analytical and exploratory data processing. Increment/decrement figures are finite or uncountable amounts in a countable set, which can be discrete (e.g., soldiers) or uncountable (such as people) (e.g., male or female). Continuous data refers to data that extends over time instead of discretely (e.g., temperature readings).

It can be summarized in a variety of ways. Counting values within a category or interval may be done using frequencies, distributions, or tabulations. measuring the underlying central value – the mean, median, and mode computes all values to form a normalized background Also known as the "the spread," "the variance," "the quartiles," or "the standard deviation." We should show or simulate these details and observations to the audience. Box charts, bar graphs, and scatter plots are also used to visualize this data.

Analytical prediction: Predictive analysis extends analytical and exploratory science by collecting knowledge from datasets in order to identify patterns and forecast possible outcomes and trends. Predictive analytics may be used to evaluate a specific hypothesis or to produce hypotheses in general [10]. These studies are carried out using a range of methods, some of which are briefly listed in the subsections below.

10.2 The distinction of technology needs

For prediction, several technologies are defined; data scientists have historically managed data analysis; but, in today's fast-paced market, line managers and executives need direct access to these computing resources. This does not imply that they should participate in programming or data cleansing, but it does imply that they should have access to end-user resources and dashboards that enable them to independently assess findings. This hands-on strategy fosters trust in the tools while still providing real-time data to aid decision-making. Prescriptive analytics can be accomplished using a variety of methods, including high-level programming languages, integrated ERP software, and solution-specific system kits. The first phase in getting the data accessible is to clean it up and combine it. Following that, a variety of methodological techniques are used, including:
- Regression models such as linear, time-based, and logistic
- Deep learning techniques
- Neural networks
- Naïve Bayes conditional likelihood

Prescriptive analytics brings things a step forward by integrating heuristics or optimization into the analysis. For organizational conditions that can be strictly described, heuristics are used. This procedure is a mathematical technique focused on laws. It is helpful in cases where identical choices are taken on a daily basis, such as buying raw materials. Heuristics are useful for automating choices but not so much for refining them. The need for continuous updating to prevent rules being out of date, as well as the fact that heuristics cannot evaluate any conceivable situation, are both flaws [11–14].

The optimal approach is sought using a blend of mathematical models and precise algorithms. To address specific questions, a mathematical model of the market or feature is developed, and an exact algorithm is used. An optimization model's target is to increase or decrease a parameter like benefit or cost.

Packaged solutions and modeling platforms are both available for prescriptive analytics applications. Packages are easier to customize and are often written to resolve a particular problem or sector. They are usually available as SaaS or PaaS solutions in the cloud. A modelling tool for identifying the problem and an optimization solver make up an optimization system. A drag-and-drop graphic interface or mathematics is used to construct models. The bulk of optimization platforms are run in-house, with a wide range of costs. They have highly customized solutions that accurately represent the issue. They may need master programmers to construct the model, and they often lack end-user interfaces. Others, such as River Logic's Microsoft Azure platform, need significant programming expertise [15].

10.3 A long-term decision-making guide using prescriptive analytics

Predictive analytics differs from prescriptive analytics in that the former uses short-term metrics to help describe what is going on in the organization, while the latter provides recommendations.

Predictive analytics examines metrics one at a time, but does not assess their total effect. They will, for example, calculate and forecast an organization's revenue output but not the effect of rising raw material prices on cost of sales and profitability.

Prescriptive analytics is a form of analytics that models companies by taking into account all of the inputs, procedures, and outputs. To ensure the models correctly represent business operations, they are calibrated and tested. Prescriptive analytics suggests the right course of action based on actionable data in order to increase overall returns and profitability. Prescriptive analytics frameworks help in making well-informed choices. For decision-making, several types of analysis are used. Few are listed below.

10.3.1 Sentiment analysis

Predictive analytics varies from prescriptive analytics in that the former uses short-term metrics that help understand what is going on in the company, while the latter makes predictions about what should be done.

Predictive analytics tests indicators one at a time and does not recognize their overall effect. They may, for example, calculate and estimate an organization's revenue efficiency, but they will not generally adjust for the effect of rising raw material prices on sales costs and profitability.

Prescriptive analytics is a form of analytics that models companies by taking into account all of their inputs, procedures, and outputs. To ensure the templates correctly represent business operations, they must be configured and tested. Prescriptive analytics uses actionable data to recommend the right course of action for maximizing overall returns and profitability. Prescriptive analytics frameworks aid in making better decisions.

10.3.2 Machine learning provides prediction

Predicting using results sequentially: this can be achieved by inputting many segments in different sequences; calculations describe an upcoming attribute on the basis of the previous values.

10.3.2.1 Sequence prediction model

Figure 10.1 shows anticipation of the next value on the basis of previous series.

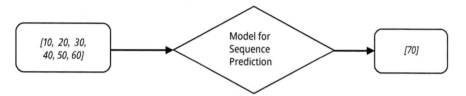

Figure 10.1: Example of a sequence prediction problem.

10.3.2.2 Sequence learning model

Predicts using a series labeled dataset. A series may be assigned a class name by using this method shown in Figure 10.2.

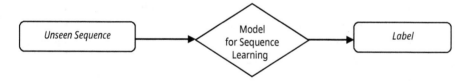

Figure 10.2: Example of a sequence classification problem.

Examples of sequence learning include sequence classifier and sentiment analysis.

10.3.2.3 Sequence generation model

It converts one or more input sequences into a new output one. Automatic text generation and picture text/abstracting images are examples of sequential prediction models shown in Figure 10.3.

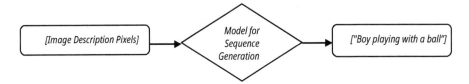

Figure 10.3: Example of sequence generation problem.

10.3.2.4 Sequence-to-sequence prediction

As shown in Figure 10.4, speaking and solving queries are sequential processes that store the order of input prediction.

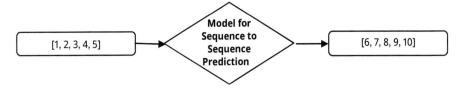

Figure 10.4: Sequence-to-sequence prediction problem.

10.4 Materials and methods

Data and models had similar significance in their contribution to advancing empirical theory; the data itself may have provided most of the input as well as the methods. The feature set can be built entirely on the basis of the functionality as well as the requirements of the customer. For a stronger and more precise stock forecast, many variables must be taken into consideration. Statistical approaches are extended to currently accessible past stock details in the early days to forecast potential price/movement. To approximate the price/movement of the stock, the financial technical analysis used many predefined technical indicators. Human emotions are often factored into the prediction phase in addition to historical evidence.

Pre-processing: In the modern world, data may be insufficient, noisy, and unreliable. Initial data processing, also known as pre-processing, is needed to increase the consistency of the data, mining performance, and the simple, efficient processing of data. Cleaning, integration, transition, elimination, and discretization are some of the steps of pre-processing. In the data transformation level, normalization is the most critical pre-processing technique. It is a method used for reducing the size of an attribute's data. A few materials and method-related algorithms are described below.

10.4.1 Algorithms for deep learning

The selection of Machine Learning methods that can be used is determined by the program in question. Loan eligibility, for example, may be assessed using the decision tree algorithm. The main algorithms, regression, Support Vector Machines (SVM) [16], Naïve Bayes, and K-Nearest Neighbors (KNN), were covered in this section, and the choice of algorithm is solely based on the application in question [17, 18].

10.4.2 Regression

Regression may be used to explain the relationships between variables. A continuous stream of incoming data is required for supervision through regression [13]. In this way, the program would be able to distinguish the most popular data stream trends. As a consequence, the data allows correct assumptions regarding future sources.

10.4.3 K-Nearest neighbors

KNN stands for Knowledge Network, and it is based on equivalence. This ensures that the assigned test documents are contrasted to records from the training set that are identical. An n-dimensional pattern space is used to store a training collection of n attributes. Each record represents an n-dimensional point in space. When a new record is sent, the KNN classifier uses the nearest neighbor mechanism to scan the pattern space for similarly matching input [19].

Building economic models and a modular classification system are two benefits.

Unknown records classification is a time-consuming procedure owing to the scale of the training collection.

10.4.4 Naïve Bayes

KNN stands for learning by equivalence and is abbreviated as K-nearest neighbor. This ensures that the test documents are linked to records from the training collection that are identical to the test records. An n-dimensional pattern space is used to store a training collection of n-attributes. Each record represents an n-dimensional point. When a new record is sent, the KNN classifier uses the nearest neighbor mechanism to scan the pattern space for input that is similarly matched [16].

Economic model creation and a modular classification scheme are two advantages.

In terms of the training set scale, the classification of unknown records is a time-consuming process.

10.4.5 Support vector machine

Support Vector Machine (SVM) is another commonly employed state-of-the-art AI methodology focused on the theory of margin estimation. SVM can handle both classification and regression problems, although it is more often used for classification. It effectively establishes class boundaries. The boundaries are drawn in such a manner that the difference between the boundary and the groups is the largest, thereby reducing the classification error shown in Figure 10.5. SVM focuses on correctly classifying objects in the training data collection that are based on models [20].

Advantages: SVM can accommodate both structured and semi-structured data, there is less chance of over fitting when generalization is used, and high-dimensional data scales up.

Disadvantages: Accuracy suffers when dealing with massive data sets, choosing the right kernel function is complicated, it is not good for noisy datasets, and it doe snot have likelihood estimates.

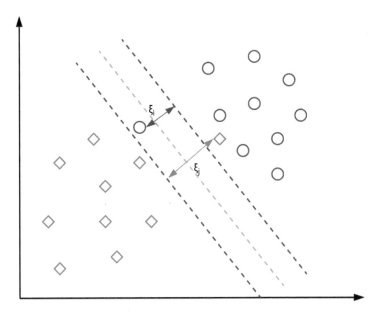

Figure 10.5: SVM's soft margin formulation technique.

10.4.6 Artificial neural networks

Artificial neural networks contain artificial neurons, also known as units. These units are stacked on top of one another to form the whole artificial neural network of a system. Depending on how the intricate neural networks are to be utilized to find the hidden patterns in the data set, a layer may include a dozen or millions of units. In addition to the input, output, and output layers, artificial neural networks frequently incorporate hidden layers. The input layer gathers data that the neural network must process or learn from the outside environment. This data is converted into meaningful information for the output layer after passing via one or more hidden layers. Last but not least, the output layer generates an output in the form of a reaction to the incoming input from an artificial neural network. Units are connected from one layer to another in the majority of neural networks. These linkages each have weights that regulate how much one unit influences another. As it advances from one unit to another, the neural network gains more knowledge about the data, finally resulting in an output from the output layer [21].

Benefits: Compatible with both linear and nonlinear data; needs no reprogramming and works even though one or a few nodes fail to respond to the network.

Disadvantages: Takes a wide range of instruction; requires a lot of computing and computing power; and the consumer has no way of knowing what is going on within the network.

10.4.7 Hybrid models

It is a type of construction that combines two or more techniques to produce a better result. Homogeneous models are built with the same type of learner(ing)s, whereas heterogeneous models use different classes of learners instead of using a single prediction model; many models can be employed to form a blend for diverse purposes of modeling, simulation, and optimization [22, 23]. Classification of hybrid model is given below.

10.4.7.1 Construction of the model

Bootstrap Aggregation (Bagging): To minimize uncertainty, a variety of machine learning algorithms are run in parallel, each utilizing training data and bootstrap sampling. The final classifier is chosen by a voting process.

Boosting: A series of machine learning techniques are applied in order to minimize bias. The slow learners are strengthened in the step-by-step process, resulting in improved results. Only the misclassified data points from the previous stage were handled in a corresponding step.

Stacking: A variety of machine learning algorithms are applied in serial fashion to improve precision. The result of one move may be used as feedback for the next step.

10.4.7.2 Application areas of hybrid models

Modeling entails a mathematical representation mechanism of concepts discovered and understood for a given model configuration, such as the model's purpose, variables, and constraints. A goal is a measurable metric that can be reduced or maximized depending on the application and is used to assess the model's efficiency. Reduce the cost, time, and variance objective functions as far as possible. Benefit maximization is the target, and similarity is the objective function. The model's components are represented by variables, which must be identified and assigned appropriate values. Bounding with the given constraint functions defines the relationships between variables and the required values for variables. Machine learning algorithms may be used to train a model that predicts label location. The model should be tuned to suit the market requirements and should also consider revised input data.

Machine learning algorithms may be used to automate computational models by simulation. These algorithms may be used to build models, change them in real time, and make predictions. Artificial intelligence (AI) is a simulated paradigm that aims to characterize human intelligence. In activities like understanding, preparation, thinking, interpretation, problem solving, and decision making, this model mimics human brain capacity [19, 24].

10.5 Optimization technique

It is a comparative-iterative method for achieving the most efficient and best use of the planned model, which is the optimum or satisfactory solution. There should be a target, such as cost savings or improved performance.

The optimization algorithms used to achieve a better solution vary depending on the type of problem. As a result, optimization algorithms are classified.
- Continuous Optimization, Discrete Optimization focused on variable value form.
- Unconstrained Optimization and Restricted Optimization are two types of optimization based on vector constraints.
- Optimization based on the amount of target tasks –none, more, or several objectives.
- Deterministic and stochastic optimization based on data specificity.

Some optimization techniques and approaches used for prediction are discussed below.

10.5.1 Demystification of optimization techniques

Solution techniques can be classified as population-specific or solution-specific (evolutionary methods, swarm intelligence methods). Meta-equations are combinatorial subsets of techniques [25].

Figure 10.6 illustrates stages of this taxonomy. A first differentiation is made between a mixture of several solutions (solution creation) or an alternative solution (differential vector movement). Solution formulation can rely on mixed solution or stigmergy. Differential vector movement may use the entire population as a basis for a different solution, more only within a population group or culture. The group can contain subpopulations or communities [26].

This taxonomy provides a valuable first metaheuristics differentiation. Its implementation offers meaningful metaheuristics grouping and encourages their behavior evaluation. Thus, all metaheuristic publications should be a routine. However, there are several problems by using this taxonomy to further compare metaheuristics. [26] introduced the most influential algorithms together with strong similarities. For e.g., the Particle Swarm Optimization (PSO) algorithm has 57 other related metaheuristics [26]. If distinctions between these must be illustrated in order to clarify the respective performances, pick them for comparison, or analyze their functionality, it is also important to evaluate both of them individually. This takes time and commitment. Thus, we consider it important to extend this taxonomy through more precise standards listed in the following paragraphs.

Look for: Third-level classification concerns the metaheuristic framework's intensification including diversification (and exploitation and exploration) capabilities. The criteria must enable defining the capabilities and measuring them in some way.

Examples of how criteria could represent the processes of intensification and diversification are provided by [27], Dokeroglu[28], and Blum[29]. Fausto et al. attribute discovery and exploitation behavior to metaheuristic characteristics. They concentrate on selection process, attraction managers, and reliance on iteration. In this stage, these factors may be used as classification criteria. Dokeroglu et al. have multi-algorithm discovery and exploitation stages. However, they characterize these steps as underlying metaphors of metaheuristics. This helps in finding standardized definitions for these stages, as metaheuristics similarities can be found. Blum and Roli's incision and drainage (I&D) components provide easier grouping criteria. Especially basic (or intrinsic) components are essential as inherent in a metaheuristic framework classification. Strategic elements are algorithm-dependent, providing ways to distinguish metaheuristic algorithms. Again, some of the intrinsic components in metaphor-specific terminology are presented and must be translated for general use. Examples are evolutionary computation with simulated annealing cooling schedule, replication, recombination and selection, pheromone transition, and ant colony optimization. However, the remaining components may be used as criteria in the classification process, e.g., black box scan and identification criterion.

The second component of this categorization is the measurement of metaheuristic intensification and diversification [29]. In their I&D system, they give a partial quantification. They balance their directions based on the objective property, other characteristics, or randomness. Thus, components controlled only by the goal purpose give the greatest potential intensification, but components controlled by factors other than the objective and random features provide the greatest diversity.

Combining a metaheuristic's intensifying and diversifying elements and weighing their results provides appropriate classification requirements. However, standardized definitions of these components are essential. It may also be checked if the I&D framework describes the weighting of their results accurately or if some more detailed metric must be sought.

The fourth classification criterion employs fundamental metaheuristic components that are classified as such in a metaheuristic sense [30]. This study looked at metaheuristics to uncover basic algorithmic structures. To differentiate their essential metaheuristic components, he began analyzing metaheuristics using local search, evolutionary algorithms, PSO, and ant colony optimization.

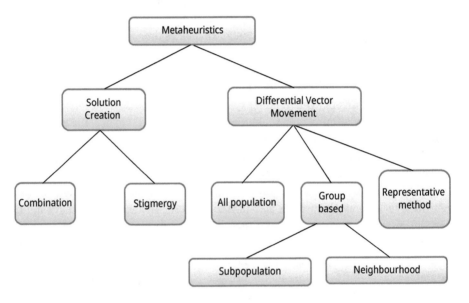

Figure 10.6: Subset classification of metaheuristics with different combinations of solutions [26].

10.5.2 Strategies based on one-of-a-kind solutions

Present metaheuristics that are dependent on a single solution are referred to as trajectory approaches. This approach is initialized with a solution and defines a trajectory direction for a full solution, close to how it is used in space science. Tabu search, simulated annealing, and other variants are among these techniques. These approaches are often referred to as "smart additions" to local search algorithms.

10.5.3 Approaches focused on the population

These methods are built to handle the community instead of the primary remedy. Such approaches are related to studies of the Darwin's hypothesis, in which the population is modified by Species-Survival Leveling Intelligence (SI), and association is used to support social experiences as an analogy to computational experiences. Forms of population-based optimization and animal-inspired optimization are two different approaches.

10.5.4 Complexity in mathematical optimization

When considering different constraints, the aim of mathematical optimization is to find a set of decisions or acts that has the best potential outcomes in terms of stochastic interest system models. A single-period decision-making optimization problem is defined as minimizing or maximizing measurable interest functionality, while considering various constraints. Using stochastic models of interest for these and similar variables, the objective and restriction functions specify the criteria for determining the best possible outcomes in terms of judgement variables and other dependent variables. The interactions between these precisely classified components are vital and so difficult to comprehend [31].

Mathematical optimization is a set of evolutionary ruling policies for dynamic variations in decisions or behaviors over time while instability arises, coming up with the best possible results in the form of stochastic representations of the concerned system and subject to a number of constraints. Minimizing an observed functional of interest over time while considering several restrictions is a general approximation of a multi-period decision-making optimization challenge. The functional and constraint functional time-dependent target describes the criteria for deciding the best possible outcomes over a given time span with reference to time-dependent controller parameters and other dependent variables, focusing on stochastic interest mechanism models. Interactions between these optimization formulation components are critical and can be complicated and difficult to understand.

As a consequence, mathematical optimization also yields filtration-friendly strategies that determine a series of bad decisions or behavior at the beginning of the time period or a range of functional decision-making procedures for complicated doings over time to achieve the best possible results in stochastic model. These answers can be sought using a variety of mathematical methods that focus on the system's stochastic representation properties and implementation methods that go with them. The complexity of the underlying stochastic instability models and the complexity of formulating the optimization issue of concern inside stochastic models both decide the most effective approaches. Probability theory, optimization theory, control theory, and simulation theory require domain knowledge in stochastic systems.

Where only point projections are used, methods such as linear programming ([32], convex optimization [33], combinatorial optimization ([34], integer programming, nonlinear optimization ([35], and deterministic dynamic programming and optimum control ([36], are always the better options. A stronger choice centered on the characteristics of the analytical solutions, owing to the richer probabilistic characterizations of analytical solutions of stochastic processes and procedures, is based on mathematical programming, stochastic optimization ([37], stochastic programming ([38], stochastic dynamic programming, and stochastic optimal control ([39]. Since simulation approaches are the only way to test the stochastic representations of a structure and the resulting decision processes, simulation optimization of stochastic approximation ([40–42]) is always the best choice. Finally, robust optimization [43] is often used, which translates deterministic heterogeneity in the value of the parameters of the decision-making issue itself or its solution as a measure of the mechanism's and its underlying decision processes' robustness against ambiguity.

A more sophisticated variant of what-if and scenario analysis is another statistical modelling approach used in prescriptive analytics, which searches for the best option based on a collection of goals, parameters, outcomes, and other facets of the issue formulation. For instance, a mathematical optimization under uncertainty strategy may be used to find the answer to a single-period optimization problem that maximizes the goal in anticipation for the random variables involved under a certain set of standard deviations, and then this process could be replicated for different sets of standard deviations. Any of these options determines the decisions or acts that, with a certain amount of variation, will result in the best possible performance. The efficient frontier of the current portfolio theory can be represented by this series of solutions, where no other portfolio solution has a higher expected return and the same standard deviation as this one (level of risk). More generally, this approach encourages the examination of the sensitivity of the optimal solution to aspects of the formulation and relevant trade-offs in a mathematical optimization under ambiguity challenge, which aids decision-making and enables particular forms of risk hedging. The methodology was implemented in a decision-support paradigm widely used by the U.S. Army TRADOC Research Center (White Sands Missile Range, New Mexico). The U.S. Army TRADOC Research Center (Salt Flats Missile Range, New Mexico) designed the device in a control system commonly used in army review. Laferriere [44] suggests a related approach using stochastic computation ideas to calculate hedged decisions; the strategy was applied by the U.S. Army TRADOC Research Unit (Salt Flats Missile Range, New Mexico) in a decision process commonly employed in army study.

10.6 Methods for statistical optimization

It is the method of picking the right facet from a range of choices. Stochastic Gradient Descent (SGD), Stochastic Gradient Descent with Momentum, AdaGrad, and RMSProp are among the optimization strategies in this group. We can predict the data for using some method which is given below-

10.6.1 Stochastic gradient descent (SGD)

It is an optimization strategy that includes assigning values at random to chosen parameters in order to minimize the cost function. Each parameter must be modified with a numerical value derived from a derivative equation, referred to as gradient. Gradients are tested through an iterative method before the lowest cost function is identified. The learning rate is the shift in a parameter's value, with each iteration. It depicts the objective's speed of convergence. The higher the training process, the more repeats, and the smaller the learning rate, the more variants are required.

10.6.2 Naturally inspired optimization techniques

These are optimization strategies influenced by real beings and environmental variables, and they are split into two categories: evolutionary algorithms and swarm optimization techniques, as seen in Figure 10.7.

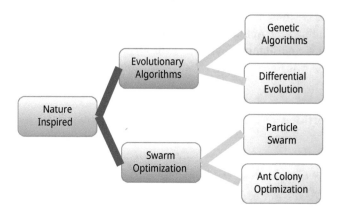

Figure 10.7: Classification of naturally inspired algorithms.

10.6.3 Evolutionary methods

Evolutionary methods are focused on Darwin's concepts and are influenced by living organisms that will respond to their environments. It serves as shorthand for a group of optimization algorithms. To achieve improved alternatives, these approaches include genetic programming, comparative evolution with a principle of exchanging in the type of structure, recombination, and mutation breeding. As a means of problem solving, evolutionary methods mimic the ideas of natural selection. In genetic programming, the principle of mutation is performed by spreading numbers of zero mean and standard deviation, which allows for a versatile interpretation of the distribution parameters when evaluating the output of a search algorithm [45]. Matrix of covariance The Adaption Evolution Technique has been shown to be an efficient tool for executing global optimizations in a number of evolutionary algorithms. Using this method, a community of candidates was selected for the optimization challenge [46, 47]. Differential evolution is commonly used to address linear regression questions. In this method, individuals are produced using the mutation and crossover operators, and their respective results used to determine the next generation's responses. Differential evolution has less regulation settings, an approach that has been widely used for single-objective optimization that can be extended to multi-objective problems.

10.6.4 Strategies of Swarm Intelligence

The Swarm Intelligence model discusses distributed intelligence technique and a revolutionary solution to problem optimization focused on the mutual actions of living beings. They consist of a population of agents that execute different roles when communicating with the world. In the absence of a management system or local connections, they contribute to the creation of self-organizing global habits. The simulation uses many algorithms including PSO, Ant Colony Optimization, Bee Colony Optimization, Bat Herdation, Immune, and Immune Systems, Krill Algorithm, in addition to Gravitational Search. The following sections describe the algorithms.

10.6.4.1 Optimization of particle swarms (PSO)

It is seen as a global optimization strategy to use behavioral models of birds travelling to far-away locations, creating a type of interconnectedness in-structure with candidate solutions placed in space.

10.6.4.2 Optimization of ant populations (ACO)

It is a useful metaheuristic method that is based on the action of ants in forming the best direction from the source (nest) to the destination (food sources) and back to the nest. This approach aids in the identification of suitable solutions to complicated optimization issues. In this approach, a swarm of artificial ants (software agents) search for better solutions to the problem at hand. This technique is based on identifying the right route using a weighted graph, and the ant builds the answer incrementally by traversing the weighted graph. This creation method is known as a stochastic process and is inspired by the pheromone model, which implies that the parameters at the graph elements, such as nodes and edges, can be randomly changed by the ants at runtime.

10.6.4.3 Bee hive (BCO)

BCO's philosophy is to create a multi-agent method that uses the honey bee theory to find a good solution among different combinations of optimization problems. The quest is carried out in an iterative fashion before a stop criterion is reached. This method has been implemented in two ways. In the first method, a positive action is taken piece by piece. The second method, known as BCO, involves improving the whole solution in order to find the correct final solution.

10.6.4.4 Annealing simulation

Simulated annealing is a method of optimization that has a good solution. It aids in the detection of global optima within local optima. The word annealing relates to the likelihood of conforming to the thermodynamic theorem. Rather than using material energy, this method employs the objective feature of an optimization problem. This technique is based on hill climbing, in which the best step is selected at random rather than because it is the best move. If the change strengthens the solution, it is approved. If not, the algorithm chooses a pass with a chance of less than one.

10.6.4.5 Bee colony (artificial) (ABC)

Karaboga implemented a swarm-based metaheuristic algorithm in 2005 to optimize numerical problems, which was influenced by honeybee behavior. There are three aspects of this model: working bees, unemployed bees, and food supplies. To live, the first two components look for the third part. This paradigm distinguishes between two self-organizing and intelligent modes, based on the bees' reviews, whether good or negative. To use this model, first transform the issue to find the best parameter vector for minimizing the objective function. The neighbor search technique iteratively increases the random discovery of population with initial solution vectors.

10.7 Case study about predictive analytics in finance

There are also more communication options for customers, which results in increased amounts of financial data for the firms. AI will be used to get these perspectives from this info. Financial firms have developed data and AI/digital innovation centers to leverage their data; many institutions believe that to be able to provide high-quality products and tailor their offerings while lowering prices, they need to develop technological skills [48, 49].

Predictive analytics may be useful in helping banks to support activities while still reducing expenses and providing fewer resources; We can elucidate the concept of predictive analytics in finance by using four case studies. Classified below are the following:

- Statistical insights to identify minute variances in transactions.
- Credit default rates would be expected if a credit card issuer declines to recover debts.
- Examining the lifetime value provided by a consumer and his or her bank.

In order to better predict fraud, we will start by looking at Dataiku's fraud detection solution.

It was founded in 2013 and claims to have used machine learning techniques on raw data in various formats in order to generate predictive models. Firms claim that their solutions help businesses understand data relationships, which save them money in the following ways:

Therefore, as an example, banks like Wells Fargo collect large amounts of raw customer data from surveys, tweets, postings on social media, and websites. In this manner:

- Marketing and internal departments at the bank may use the Dataiku anomaly detection dashboard for accessing predictive analytics data.
- Along with the company's stated capabilities, it also collects, disinfects, and analyzes actionable observations like this:
- Untapped advertising markets can be tracked by monitoring social media content.
- Foreign transaction and consumer data patterns can help detect fraud.

Upon an end user signing up, the app gives them access to the data they have been given the ability to send and apply. According to the business, the information on the spreadsheet occurs in text and is well-presented. This data will be connected to the software with regard to a person's characteristics. For example, the company asserts that such data would be consistent with the gender of customers over and below a certain age, making this an example; the company asserts that it has found correlation among customers of a specific age demographic. In order to increase the probability of being able to correct, per column has a small percentile value that displays how many non-invasive values were detected for the current data and their counts to serve as an organizing scale, such as for example, gender.

The user should click on the headings to expand these entries to see a variety of data visualization options; this would then bring up a menu, allowing them to view the data in charts or graphs. Additionally, they may also produce graphs that connect different data sets. If the consumer suspects outlier results, the app offers ways to handle and train the data, gives feedback to the person using the software, and encourages the person to improve their technique.

In 2017, Dataiku conducted a case study for the BNP Paribas (Luxembourg) Group Fraud Identification and Prevention Service Intelligence Unit, which found that it had improved the group's detection and reporting of internal fraud.

When a user is signed in, they can include or enter data that the app will use. According to the business, the data is in a spreadsheet. The information will be assigned to characteristics. For example, the company can decide whether particular information is associated with males or females under a given age. To display the number of missing values in each column, as in this one that shows age or gender, there is a percentage at the top.

After clicking on the column headings, you may choose to view the data in various types of charts or graphs. Column relationships can also be created. If the consumer believes that an outlier is found, the app has instructional choices on fixing and training the application.

According to a case study conducted in 2017, Dataiku worked with BNP Paribas (located in Luxembourg) to upgrade the internal fraud detection mechanism.

Based on our study, we were able to identify the following as the most popular predictive analytics applications for AI in the finance sector:

- Identification and prediction of fraud for financial companies and banks
- Predicting whether or not a borrower would default on a loan or credit bill
- Predicting consumer behavior in order to optimize a company's capital distribution for customers that can have the highest ROI over their lifetimes
- Using consumer and industry data to refine financial product and service pricing

10.8 Conclusions

As a result, the need for developing and piloting high potential use cases is a vital check that must be undertaken on a regular and frequent basis. Several elements must be addressed throughout this discovery process, ranging from data encoding and loading methods to the use of new quantum computing tools or processors. The foundation of success is rigorous due diligence in analyzing data quality and structure, which helps the selection of appropriate algorithms / solvers for the instance at hand.

The first practical benefits will be based on hybrid approaches, which will be efficiently coordinated by a mix of quantum computers interfaced with conventional computers. This method combines the best of both worlds, combining simple pre-processing and extremely flexible cloud configuration with innovative quantum techniques. As a consequence, we looked at various opinion analysis and data mining methods for stock market prediction. Opinion mining has been an active study field as a result of its utility and demand from the public. Analysis and summarization of opinionated data are becoming highly necessary as the amount of opinionated data increases. In the chapter, we have discussed some Analytic Ascendency Models, various types of analytical models, and some optimization models, as well as their benefits and drawbacks. In this chapter, we have also described many methods to categorizing metaheuristics. Most methods are somewhat insufficient and can only be implemented with a particular classification target in mind rather than a systematic classification of all metaheuristics. Only recently has a more comprehensive taxonomy, focusing on the general behavior of the metaheuristics, been presented. Although this is more useful for identifying parameters for categorizing metaheuristics based on their general behavior, it is also important to analzse them deeply, when the cause of this behavior is found or appropriate metaheuristics for a comparison are desired.

References

[1]   McCarthy, B. H., & Ponedal, S. (2021). "IBM Unveils World's First 2 Nanometer Chip Technology, Opening a New Frontier for Semiconductors". [Online]. Available: https://newsroom.ibm.com/2021-05-06-IBM-Unveils-Worlds-First-2-Nanometer-Chip-Technology,-Opening-a-New-Frontier-for-Semiconductors.

[2]   Alsop, T. (2021). "Statista". [Online]. Available: https://www.statista.com/statistics/993634/quantum-computers-by-number-of-qubits/.

[3]   Weigold, M., Barzen, J., Leymann, F., & Salm, M. (2021). Expanding Data Encoding Patterns For Quantum Algorithms. In: Institute of Architecture of Application Systems University of Stuttgart, Germany. Available https://ieeexplore.ieee.org/document/9425837/.

[4]   Dash, R., & Dash, P. K. (2016). A hybrid stock trading framework integrating technical analysis with machine learning techniques. *The Journal of Finance and Data Science*, 2(1), 42-57.

[5]   Xing, F. Z., Cambria, E., & Welsch, R. E. (2018). Natural language based financial forecasting: A survey. *Artificial Intelligence Review*. 50(1), pp. 49–73.

[6]   Miah, M. B., Hossain, M. Z., Hossain, M. A., & Islam, M. M. (2015). Price prediction of stock market using hybrid model of artificial intelligence. *International Journal of Computer Applications*, 111(3), 1

[7]   Yadav, S. P. et al. (2022). Survey on machine learning in speech emotion recognition and vision systems using a recurrent neural network (RNN). *Archives of Computational Methods in Engineering*, 29(3), 1753–1770.

[8]   Vashisht, V., Kumar Pandey, A., & Prakash Yadav, S. (2021). Speech recognition using machine learning. *IEIE Transactions on Smart Processing & Computing*, 10(3), 233–239.

[9]   Hastie, T., Tibshirani, R., & Friedman, J. (2008). The Elements of Statistical Learning: Data Mining, Inference, and Prediction. New York: Springer-Verlag.

[10] NRC. (2013). Frontiers in Massive Data Analysis. Washington, D.C: The National Academies Press.

[11] Kishor, K. (2022). Communication-Efficient Federated Learning. Yadav, S. P., Bhati, B. S., Mahato, D. P., Kumar, S. (eds.). Federated Learning for IoT Applications. EAI/Springer Innovations in Communication and Computing Springer, Cham. https://doi.org/10.1007/978-3-030-85559-8_9.

[12] Kishor, K. (2022). Personalized Federated Learning. Yadav, S. P., Bhati, B. S., Mahato, D. P., Kumar, S. (eds.). Federated Learning for IoT Applications. EAI/Springer Innovations in Communication and Computing Springer, Cham. https://doi.org/10.1007/978-3-030-85559-8_3.

[13] Sharma, A., Jha, N., & Kishor, K. (2022). Predict COVID-19 with Chest X-ray. In: Gupta, D., Polkowski, Z., Khanna, A., Bhattacharyya, S., Castillo, O. (eds.). Proceedings of Data Analytics and Management.

Lecture Notes on Data Engineering and Communications Technologies Vol. 90 Springer, Singapore. https://doi.org/10.1007/978-981-16-6289-8_16.

[14] Sharma, R., Maurya, S. K., & Kishor, K., (2021). Student Performance Prediction using Technology of Machine Learning. In: (July 3, 2021). Proceedings of the International Conference on Innovative Computing & Communication (ICICC), Available at SSRN: https://ssrn.com/abstract=3879645 or http://dx.doi.org/10.2139/ssrn.3879645.

[15] Anish, C. M., & Majhi, B. (2016). Hybrid nonlinear adaptive scheme for stock market prediction using feedback FLANN and factor analysis. *Journal of the Korean Statistical Society*, 45, 64–76. Mar pp.

[16] Kishor, K., Sharma, R., & Chhabra, M. (2022). Student Performance Prediction Using Technology of Machine Learning. In: Sharma, D. K., SL, P., Sharma, R., Zaitsev, D. A. (eds.). Micro-Electronics and Telecommunication Engineering. Lecture Notes in Networks and Systems Vol. 373 Springer, Singapore. https://doi.org/10.1007/978-981-16-8721-1_53.

[17] Jain, A., Sharma, Y., & Kishor, K. (2020). Financial supervision and management system using ml algorithm. Solid State Technology, 63(6), 18974–18982.

[18] Tyagi, D., Sharma, D., Singh, R., & Kishor, K. (2020). Real time 'driver drowsiness' & monitoring & detection techniques. *International Journal of Innovative Technology and Exploring Engineering*, 9 (8), ISSN 2278–3075.

[19] Jain, A., Sharma, Y., & Kishor, K. (2021). Prediction and analysis of financial trends using ml algorithm (july 11, 2021). In: Proceedings of the International Conference on Innovative Computing & Communication (ICICC), Available at SSRN: https://ssrn.com/abstract=3884458 or http://dx.doi.org/10.2139/ssrn.3884458.

[20] Ouahilal, M., El Mohajir, M., Chahhou, M., & El Mohajir, B. E. (2017). A novel hybrid model based on Hodrick–Prescott filter and support vector regression algorithm for optimizing stock market price prediction. *Journal of Big Data*, 4(1), 31. 1 Dec.

[21] Sherstinsky, A. (2020). Fundamentals of recurrent neural network (RNN) and long short-term memory (LSTM) network. *Physical D: Nonlinear Phenomena*, 4, March.

[22] Kara, M., Ulucan, A., & Atici, K. B. (2019). A hybrid approach for generating investor views in Black–Litterman model. *Expert Systems with Applications*, 15(128), 256–270. Aug.

[23] Kia, A. N., Haratizadeh, S., & Shouraki, S. B. (2018). A hybrid supervised semi-supervised graph-based model to predict one-day ahead movement of global stock markets and commodity prices. *Expert Systems with Applications*, 1(105), 159–173. Sep.

[24] Kishor, K., Nand, P., & Agarwal, P. (2018). Notice of retraction design adaptive subnetting hybrid gateway manet protocol on the basis of dynamic ttl value adjustment. *Aptikom Journal on Computer Science and Information Technologies*, 3(2), 59–65.

[25] Chou, J. S., & Nguyen, T. K. Forward forecast of stock price using sliding-window metaheuristic-optimized machine-learning regression. *IEEE Transactions on Industrial Informatics*, 14(7), 3132–3142. 18

[26] Molina, D., Poyatos, J., Del Ser, J., García, S., & Hussain, A. Herrera F (2020). Comprehensive taxonomies of nature- and bio-inspired optimization: Inspiration versus algorithmic behavior.

[27] Fausto, F., Reyna-Orta, A., Cuevas, E., Andrade, Á. G., & Perez-Cisneros M. (2019). From ants to whales: metaheuristics for all tastes. *Artificial Intelligence Review*, 53(1), 753–810.

[28] Fausto, F., Reyna-Orta, A., Cuevas, E., Ág, A., & Perez-Cisneros, M. (2019). From ants to whales: metaheuristics for all tastes. Artificial Intelligence Review, 53(1), 753–810.

[29] Blum, C. (2003). Roli a metaheuristics in combinatorial optimization. *ACM Comput Surv*, 35(3), 268–308.

[30] Lones MA metaheuristics in nature-inspired algorithms. (2014). In: Proceedings of the 2014 conference companion on Genetic and evolutionary computation companion – GECCO Comp'14, ACM Press.

[31] Melvin, M., Panb, W., & Wikstrom, P. (2020). Retaining alpha: The effect of trade size and rebalancing frequency on FX strategy returns. *Journal of Financial Markets*, 51.

[32] Vanderbei, R. J. (2013). Linear Programming: Foundations and Extensions. 4th ed. New York: Springer-Verlag.

[33] Boyd, S., & Vandenberghe, L. (2004). Convex Optimization. New York: Cambridge University Press.

[34] Nemhauser, G. L., & Wolsey, L. A. (1999). Integer and Combinatorial Optimization. Hoboken, N.J: Wiley.

[35] Ruszczynski, A. (2006). Nonlinear Optimization. Princeton, N.J: Princeton University Press.

[36] Bertsekas, D. P. (2005). Dynamic Programming and Optimal Control. Vol. I. 3rd ed. Nashua, N.H: Athena Scientific.

[37] Chen, H., & Yao, D. D. (2001). Fundamentals of Queueing Networks: Performance, Asymptotics and Optimization. New York: Springer-Verlag.

[38] King, A. J., & Wallace, S. W. (2012). Modeling with Stochastic Programming. New York: Springer-Verlag.

[39] Bertsekas, D. P. (2012). Dynamic Programming and Optimal Control. Vol. II. 4th ed. Nashua, N.H: Athena Scientific.

[40] Asmussen, S., & Glynn, P. W. (2007). Stochastic Simulation: Algorithms and Analysis. New York: Springer-Verlag.

[41] Handbooks in Operations Research and Management Science, Chapter 19. (2007). In: Nelson, B. L., Henderson, S. G. (eds.). Elsevier Science

[42] Dieker, A. B., Ghosh, S., & Squillante, M. S. (2016). Optimal resource capacity management for stochastic networks. *Operations Research, Submitted*, http://www.columbia.edu/~ad3217/publica tions/capacitymanagement.pdf.

[43] Ben-Tal, A., El Ghaoui, L., & Nemirovski, A. (2009). Robust Optimization. Princeton, N.J: Princeton University Press.

[44] Laferriere, R. R., & Robinson, S. M. (2000). Scenario analysis in U.S. Army decision making. Phalanx, 33(1), 11–16.

[45] Kim, H. Y., & Won, C. H. (2018). Forecasting the volatility of stock price index: A hybrid model integrating LSTM with multiple GARCH-type models. *Expert Systems with Applications*, 1(103), 25–37. Aug.

[46] Huang, K. Y., & Jane, C. J. (2009). A hybrid model for stock market forecasting and portfolio selection based on ARX, grey system and RS theories. *Expert Systems with Applications*, 36(3), 5387–5392.

[47] Dietrich, B. L., Plachy, E. C., & Norton, M. F. (2014). Analytics Across the Enterprise: How IBM Realizes Business Value from Big Data and Analytics. Indianapolis: IBM Press.

[48] Jain, A., Sharma, Y., & Kishor, K. (2020). Financial supervision and management system using Ml algorithm. *Solid State Technology*, 63(6), 18974–18982. http://solidstatetechnology.us/index.php/JSST/article/view/8080.

[49] Gupta, S., Tyagi, S., & Kishor, K. (2022). Study and Development of Self Sanitizing Smart Elevator. In: Gupta, D., Polkowski, Z., Khanna, A., Bhattacharyya, S., Castillo, O. (eds.). Proceedings of Data Analytics and Management. Lecture Notes on Data Engineering and Communications Technologies (Vol. 90). Springer, Singapore. https://doi.org/10.1007/978-981-16-6289-8_15.

B. Aruna Devi*, N. Alangudi Balaji, Mulugeta Tesema

11 A review of different techniques and challenges of quantum computing in various applications

Abstract: Since its inception in the 1980s and early proof of principle for hardware in the 2000s, quantum computing has made tremendous strides. Despite the fact that the technology is still in the process of being developed, there are a number of people who believe that machines known as Noisy Intermediate Scale Quantum (NISQ) could soon outperform conventional computers. This is the result of the rapid development of hardware connected to quantum computing as well as the significant financial expenditures that have been made in many countries all over the world. In this chapter, a deep review of various applications of quantum computing is conducted.

11.1 Introduction

Quantum computing does not feature a significant number of actual qubits to make it possible to develop robust error correction systems. As a consequence of this, they can only be used for lightweight jobs until more powerful quantum computers are made available. NISQ machines have already proven that they are more effective than conventional computers at tackling a subset of tasks that are ideally suited for quantum computing [1]. This has been shown through a series of demonstrations that have taken place over the past few years.

The algorithms that can be run on them may only require a small number of qubits, demonstrate some degree of noise resilience, and are commonly modeled as hybrid algorithms, in which some steps are done on a quantum device and others on a regular computer [2]. This is because of the limited capabilities of the quantum devices themselves. This is due to the fact that these algorithms are able to be executed, despite the inherent limitations of the quantum device in terms of their capabilities [3].

It is important to keep the number of operations, which are also known as quantum gates, to a minimum because the longer it takes to perform them, the more errors

---

*Corresponding author: **B. Aruna Devi**, Department of Electronics and Communication Engineering, Dr. NGP Institute of Technology, Coimbatore, Tamil Nadu, India, e-mail: arunadevi@drngpit.ac.in
N. Alangudi Balaji, Department of CSE, Koneru Lakshmaiah Education Foundation, Vaddeswaram, Vijayawada, Andhra Pradesh, India, e-mail: alangudibalaji@gmail.com
Mulugeta Tesema, Department of Chemistry (Analytical), Dambi Dollo University, Dambi Dollo, Ethiopia, e-mail: efa.ntust@gmail.com

https://doi.org/10.1515/9783110798159-011

are introduced into the quantum state, and the more likely it is to decohere. Due to this, it is essential to perform as few tasks as possible throughout the entire process. As a direct consequence of these constraints, the choice of algorithms that can be implemented is drastically narrowed down [4].

Well-known quantum approaches, such as Shor algorithm for factoring prime numbers and Grover algorithm for unstructured search problems, are inappropriate for the task at hand. These two algorithms are neither useful nor applicable. In the field of NISQ algorithms, the Variational Quantum Eigensolver (VQE) stands out as one of the most promising instances [5]. This is because it can solve problems with a large number of variables simultaneously. It is due to the fact that it is capable of solving problems that involve a significant number of variables all at once. The process of determining the energetic characteristics of molecules and materials often begins with the calculation of an upper bound for the ground-state energy of a Hamiltonian. This step is typically the first stage in the process. A Hamiltonian is what is needed to get this done [6].

Conventional computational chemistry, which is built on findings from studies carried out over the course of more than a century, provides effective methods for approximating the aforementioned features. This strategy, on the other hand, can become unmanageably expensive when it comes to doing exceedingly accurate computations on progressively massive systems. Implementing such tactics can be fairly difficult because of this particular factor [7].

The application of computational chemistry to the study of molecular systems can frequently lack sufficient precision for a variety of reasons. One of the most important of these reasons is an insufficient treatment of the correlations that exist between the electrons that make up the system. Due to the intricacy of the underlying electron interactions, accurate approaches to quantum chemistry are often intractable with the technology that is available at this time. This is due to the exponential nature of the development in computational complexity that occurs with an increase in system size [8].

This limitation is driving research into other ways such as the VQE, which might one day prove to be more successful than the current computer paradigm for dealing with problems of this sort [9]. The best way to simulate quantum systems would be to take control of and make adjustments to a separate quantum system. Pelucchi et al., believed that this would be the strategy that would produce the most accurate results. A collection of qubits, like an electronic wavefunction, is subject to the rules of quantum physics in the same way that an individual electronic wavefunction is [10].

The superposition principle [11, 12] in quantum physics makes it possible for the same information to be encoded on conventional devices at a cost that is prohibitively expensive while using only a linearly rising number of qubits to do so. This is made possible by the fact that it is possible for the same information to be encoded on conventional devices as qubits. The attractiveness of quantum computing rests in the fact that, in the context of electronic structure theory [13–15], it enables the accurate modeling and manipulation of quantum wavefunctions, which is not feasible with classical computing. Due to this, quantum computing has emerged as an appealing alternative to traditional computing.

The various applications have been used to solve a variety of different quantum mechanical problems with scaling difficulties equivalent to those of the study of electronic structure, which has garnered the vast majority of attention over the course of the past few years.

11.2 Taxonomy

In this section, we will organize the various quantum computing technologies into the several groups that they belong to, according to the criteria outlined in the introduction. Each of these categories is differentiated from the others by its own particular set of activities and attributes. The quantum computing taxonomy takes into account all of the relevant elements, including the fundamental features, the algorithmic features, the time and gate features, and the extra features: A) Features that are fundamental, B) Features that are algorithmic, C) Features that are time and gate, and D) Features that are additional. Figure 11.5, which can be accessed through this link, provides a diagrammatic representation of the classification technique that applies to quantum computers [16].

Implementation of qubits, the categorization of quantum computing technologies, and the evaluation of performance are three examples of the essential components that make up quantum computing. Quantum computing is made up of a great deal of other fundamental elements as well. One of the most important parts of quantum computing is the research that is conducted into the myriad of various ways that quantum bits, sometimes referred to as qubits, can be implemented and represented. Representing qubits can be done in a variety of ways, some of which include doing it on the ground, in the air, or while moving [17].

When it comes to programming, the fixed strategy is more comparable to the way that it has always been done, but the mobile approach is more akin to the way that it has always been done when designing conventional circuits. In addition, the selection of a quantum computing technique offers additional categorization, in particular with reference to singleton computing and ensemble computing. An ensemble computing system is a system that consists of many quantum computers that are all the same in design and operation. A singleton computing system, on the other hand, is made up of nothing more than a solitary quantum computer that serves as the system's nerve center. There is a second subgroup of quantum computing methods that is based on performance measurements [18]. Approaches such as mechanical vibrations, fluorescence, and concurrency are examples of the types of methods that come under this subcategory.

The incorporation of quantum algorithmic frameworks into the pre-existing classical computer infrastructure is necessary for the practical application of quantum computing approaches. It is crucial to have a discussion regarding quantum computing technologies and to classify them according to the qualities supplied by quantum algorithms. Parallelism, the total number of available qubits, topologies, methodology for locating the qubits, and qubit operations are all examples of algorithmic components that are included in quantum computing system architectures [19].

Parallelism is the defining characteristic because parallelizing the implementation of quantum gates is required for preventing or at least significantly reducing decoherence in qubits. The parallelization of the implementation of quantum gates is crucial for improving the efficiency and scalability of quantum computation. This is due to the inherent need for parallelization in the development and execution of quantum gates. This is the situation as a result of the necessity of employing parallelization in the development of quantum gates. When it is put into action, the quantum computer has a variety of qualities that contribute to its dependability and scalability. One of these qualities is the total number of qubits that may be used. The optimization of the architecture of quantum computers is of utmost importance because it ensures the efficient transfer of data and information between the various physical units that make up the system [20].

Quantum computers are expected to play a crucial role in the development of artificial intelligence. Topologies, which are configurations of the physical components that make up the architecture of quantum computers, can take on a wide range of forms and can be built in a number of different ways. The user needs to put a significant amount of logical thought into the process in order to take advantage of the addressing technique that is used to locate a specific qubit. When it comes to the hardware of a quantum computer, having this capability permits a study of the states of the qubits that is substantially more nuanced. In addition, in order for any operation to take place, the qubits need to be relocated from their storage location to the area where the qubit gates are working [21]. This movement of the qubits is required before any operation can take place.

Time and entryways share the following characteristics: The properties of time and gates, which include elements such as decoherence time and measurement time, make it feasible to further classify the technologies used in quantum computing. This is made possible because of the characteristics of time and gates. Find the length of time that must pass before a qubit can no longer be sustained in a particular state. This is the amount of time that constitutes the decoherence time. The determination of the decoherence time is currently receiving the majority of the attention and focus of those individuals whose work focuses on the subject of quantum computing. When classifying, one more crucial aspect that needs to be taken into consideration is the measurement time, also known as the length of time that needs to elapse before it is possible to determine the exact state of a qubit [22].

Scalability, timing, and control of gate-level qubits are some of the other features that are used in the classification of the many kinds of quantum computing technologies. Scalability refers to the ability to increase the number of qubits in a system without increasing its overall size. All of the qualities that have been covered up to this point are beneficial to the process of scaling up the number of qubits to bigger quantities. On the other hand, in order to avoid always representing a single ion or photon, it is recommended to employ a large number of qubits. By using a greater number of qubits, this issue can be resolved. Since changing the state of qubits is a process that takes time, precise computation of gate timing is an imperative requirement. This is because the transition between states of qubits is time-dependent. The arrival times of the qubits need to be fine-tuned in order to successfully place a large number of qubits in their respective phases, simultaneously [23].

11.3 Challenges

There are particular problems in developing a large-scale quantum computer. The term "decoherence of qubits" refers to the process by which qubits lose their coherent properties as a result of interaction with their surroundings. This is one of the most significant challenges that must be overcome before developing quantum technology, and it is considered to be one of the most difficult problems to solve. As a result of this, quantum bits that are in a superposition state would decohere into classical bits, which will render null and void any possible benefits that could be reaped from making use of quantum bits. The term noisy in the acronym Noisy Intermediate Scale Quantum (NISQ) refers to the fact that the instruments will be impacted by interference from the environment in which they are located. It is possible for external influences such as shifting temperatures and stray electric or magnetic fields to degrade quantum information that has been stored in a computer [24]. This is a possibility since environmental conditions can cause information to become corrupted.

The development of effective error correction strategies for NISQ devices is now receiving a large amount of interest in the field of quantum computing research, which is spending a significant portion of its attention on the production of quantum computers. Second, the interconnection of qubits is one of the most significant technical problems that contemporary quantum systems need to conquer in order to function properly. This issue is connected to the fact that current quantum devices have only a limited number of connections between their qubits. This challenge becomes increasingly critical when the mapping of large-depth quantum circuits with many two-qubit gates that require inter-qubit interactions via direct couplings gets more complex. These gates are required because they require inter-qubit interactions [25]. Despite the fact that there are still some technological hurdles to overcome, NISQ quantum computers are proving that they have a computational advantage over traditional computers. In the realm of quantum computing, the recent demonstration of quantum supremacy that was carried out by the Google team constitutes a watershed event.

The entire world is currently engaged in cutthroat competition to build the first application of practical quantum computing that will be able to solve a real-world problem in a way that cannot be done by classical computers. The topic of how to solve it using quantum computers is the focus of this competition, and the goal is to find a solution to that problem. We will require error-corrected quantum hardware in addition to developments in quantum algorithms in order to achieve this goal in the not-too-distant future. On the hardware provided by NISQ, completely original quantum algorithms are being designed and are being put through their paces as rapidly as is humanly possible [26].

One of the types of quantum algorithms that sees the most application is the variation quantum algorithm class. Some of the most important categories of quantum algorithms are search, which includes amplitude amplification and Grover, and variational, which includes discrete logs and verifying matrix products. The construction of such a computer will take several years of research and development. In spite of this, prototype applications are already making use of the quantum speedup on already existing NISQ-era devices, and the results have been encouraging thus far.

The majority of research and development efforts relevant to NISQ devices are being concentrated on the disciplines of variational quantum algorithms and quantum machine learning. This is because quantum machine learning makes use of quantum entanglement. This idea has been put up by researchers. There have been some encouraging discoveries made in recent research, but it is not yet feasible to say for sure whether or not the implementation of quantum machine learning will result in greater computational efficiency in comparison to that of conventional machine learning.

Using quantum machine learning algorithms to find solutions to situations that require a large amount of data will assist in lowering overall energy expenditures and reducing our reliance on fossil fuels. The amount of data that needs to be processed can be cut down, which will allow for these benefits to be realized. As quantum computers may be reprogrammed to handle a specific task, the quantum circuit model is regarded as the most practicable solution out of the other options that are now accessible.

11.4 Models in QC

The Turing Machine is a computing device that is also referred to as the Machine Logic Circuit for Quantum Information Algorithmic Barriers, QPL, and other programming languages that are used in academic settings. It will be considerably simpler to undertake an analysis of the articles described here due to the fact that there are only four major categories of quantum models. On the other hand, the process of assessing articles frequently leads to the discovery and development of more categories, which adds variation to the process. These classifications, which include both tabular and graphical analysis, provide light on the numerous different sorts of models that are at issue. Due to the widespread application of these models in the quantum sector, the authors have taken them into consideration because of the importance of this topic.

Table 11.1: Various applications of quantum computing.

Subfield	Advantages in construction
Machine learning	Relevant prescriptive insights Increased efficiency Improved safety Efficient resources Cost savings Reduced omissions
Computer vision	Faster monitoring Better transparency Increased productivity Cost-effective Increased safety
Automated planning and scheduling	Reduced planning effort Increased productivity Simplified control Cost savings Optimal schedules
Robotics	Increased safety Improved quality Increased productivity Better accuracy Faster humans
Knowledge-based systems	Easy, relevant information Ability behind solution Easy update Availability Consistency
Natural Language Processing	Cost-effectiveness Increased productivity Time efficiency
Optimization	Increased efficiency Increased productivity Cost savings

In spite of this, the authors admit that there are still other models that have not been fully investigated, shown in Table 11.1. Due to this, they have added a section that is called others in the report. This study aims to give useful knowledge to the field of quantum computing as well as to readers and researchers by providing a discussion of as many of the most recent state-of-the-art models of quantum computing as feasible, spanning as many diverse application fields as possible.

11.4.1 Circuit models

The question is how to predict advancement in the field of quantum computing by compiling a dataset of quantum computer systems, assigning points based on the number of physical qubits and the gate error rate, and defining an index that combines these two criteria. Ultimately, the researchers conducting the study came to the conclusion that the best way to predict advancement in the field of quantum computing is to define an index that combines these two criteria.

They tested a variety of different hypotheses related to technological forecasts, quantum computing, and estimation of timelines. Ultimately, they arrived at the conclusion that defining an index that combines the number of physical qubits and the gate error rate is the most effective method for predicting advancements in the field of quantum computing.

11.4.2 Quantum perceptron

It is possible to create standard quantum processors and quantum chips using the circuit models. These models can be of assistance in this endeavor. It is necessary to have a paradigm that is capable of doing quantum algorithm mapping for the construction of quantum hardware schemes in order for there to be a functional and practical possibility of using quantum computers. This is due to the necessity of doing quantum algorithm mapping in the process of designing quantum hardware schemes. In addition, the process of building quantum logical matrices may find these models to be helpful, which is a possibility.

11.4.3 Quantum automata

Raychev built a model of a quantum circuit for the purpose of discovering complex eigenvalues of Hamiltonian matrices on quantum computers, an iterative method for phase estimation and a demonstration of resonant state simulation for quantum systems. On quantum computers, this model was used to find the complex eigenvalues of Hamiltonian matrices.

11.4.4 Quantum neural computation

A quantum perceptron is a quantum neural network that is a direct generalization of a conventional perceptron. The deployment of a quantum perceptron across a field is done with the purpose of optimizing the weights and topologies of neural networks.

The mathematical model of quantum neural networks (QNNs) is well-defined; it is an improvement upon the Deutsch concept of a quantum computational network, which included the introduction of a non-reversible and linear gate analogous to the speculative operator.

Entangled quantum neural processing is immune to both noise and loss of coherence. It is not necessary for the system to be near any one state in order to employ the neural network entanglement predictor, and the amount of additional training that is required lowers as the size of the system increases. A standardized technique to building neural networks using these powerful processors when quantum computers first became accessible; this method was made possible by the introduction of quantum computing. A classical network was proven to be incorporated into a quantum framework, and numerous specialized models, such as convolutional, recurrent, and residual networks, were offered as viable candidates for quantum implementation. In conclusion, they provide a range of modeling experiments that were developed by the deployment of the Strawberry Fields software package.

This is done in order to retrieve the probability distribution over the classes that were predicted. A dissipative quantum brain model provided a full introduction to contemporary quantum neural processing for readers of all levels of experience. The theory that a fundamental component of quantum brain processing is an appreciation for and utilization of entanglement. Trained conventional neural networks to aid with the parameters of numerous sets of quantum variational algorithms in order to speed the process of quantum learning. This was done in order to speed up the learning process.

A Quantum Neural Network (QNN) that can be taught by supervised learning and can represent either classical or quantum labeled input. The models were put into use for a wide variety of different reasons. There are a few data and arguments that, when integrated, suggest that these novel models are more effective and efficient than standard ANNs. Understanding the power of QNN requires that you have a clear understanding of these results and justifications.

11.4.5 Abelian quantum double models

Abelian quantum double models coupled with matter that has topological and algebraic order are an extension of a class of discrete bidimensional models. These models for entangled quantum states are abelian.

11.5 Conclusion and future work

This article provides a thorough analysis of the research that has been done on quantum computers. According to the findings of this study, quantum mechanical phenomena such as entanglement and superposition are very likely to play an important part in the problem-solving process involving computers. We developed taxonomy of quantum computing and then used it in a number of different studies that are connected to the field in order to establish which areas require additional investigation. A conversation is had regarding the numerous quantum software resources and technologies that are currently available. Additionally covered are quantum computers for use in industry as well as post-quantum cryptography. There are a lot of unresolved issues that are brought to light, and some possible solutions are presented.

On the other hand, it is not yet clear how to include all of these various performance characteristics into a single method of quantum computing. Constructing a quantum computer that is capable of conducting concurrent operations requires a method of quantum computing that enables quantum I/O and has all of the necessary classification features. Using the taxonomy framework that is proposed, one is able to examine the various quantum computing methods that are currently being used in order to determine the most efficient strategy that can be implemented on traditional computer hardware. The field of quantum computing is still in its infancy, and as such, there are many unanswered problems regarding how to scale qubits and how to strike a balance between speed and decoherence time.

Developing quantum computers with the intention of reducing the amount of time needed for computing in order to increase the percentage of secure communication and calculations is the objective. Post-quantum cryptography procedures are being developed in order to protect the cryptographic primitives and protocols of classical cryptography from the threat posed by quantum computers. In addition, in order to ensure the safety of the cryptography primitives and protocols used in asymmetric key cryptography, it was necessary to find solutions to three difficult mathematical problems. These problems were integer factorization, discrete logarithmic and elliptic-curve discrete logarithmic problems. In conclusion, the features of post-quantum cryptography improve the computing efficiency as well as the safety of a wide variety of possible future applications.

In addition, because of the challenges involved in efficiently expanding the number of qubits that can presently be realized, classical supercomputers cannot yet be fully replaced by commercial quantum computers at their current state of development. There is no clear answer to the question of when something like that might take place. Despite the fact that the next decade will be an extremely exciting time for industrial quantum computers, the question of when quantum computers will begin to replace their conventional counterparts in challenging jobs remains unanswered. Despite this, digital supercomputers will continue to exist, regardless of whether or not quantum computing becomes a reality in the future, because they will serve as a supplement to future quantum computers.

It is necessary to maintain a connection between the classical platform and the quantum processor in order to avoid an excessive amount of control overhead brought on by the huge quantity of physical qubits that are required. One of the subfields of research that falls under the umbrella of quantum computing is energy management. The use of a hybrid computing system that combines quantum and classical computing can drastically cut down not only the amount of energy that is consumed but also the costs that are associated with it. This can greatly improve energy efficiency. However, more study needs to be done before hybrid computing can be practically deployed to solve the most important problems that organizations are facing today. Complex quantum experiments can be simulated with the aid of specially developed quantum simulators, which can make use of helpful aspects of quantum computing such as entanglement and superposition. This allows for the simulation of previously inaccessible quantum phenomena. Graph search is currently being used by robots that are powered by artificial intelligence to solve a wide variety of problems. However, as data volumes continue to grow, so does the difficulty of these tasks. Quantum computing can use quantum random walks in place of graph search, which will allow for the simplification of robotic processes. The advancement of quantum computing will have repercussions in a great number of other fields, including computer security, biology, the discovery of novel materials, and the economy, among others.

References

[1] Gambetta, J., Sutter, D., Piveteau, C., Annunziata, A., Zuckerman, R., & Sarango, S. (2022). How to prepare yourself for an IBM Quantum internship. *Quantum*, *10*, 8.
[2] Luckow, A., Klepsch, J., & Pichlmeier, J. (2021). Quantum computing: Towards industry reference problems. *Digitale Welt*, *5*(2), 38–45.
[3] Andersson, M. P., Jones, M. N., Mikkelsen, K. V., You, F., & Mansouri, S. S. (2022). Quantum computing for chemical and biomolecular product design. *Current Opinion in Chemical Engineering*, *36*, 100754.
[4] Ma, W. L., Puri, S., Schoelkopf, R. J., Devoret, M. H., Girvin, S. M., & Jiang, L. (2021). Quantum control of bosonic modes with superconducting circuits. *Science Bulletin*, *66*(17), 1789–1805.
[5] Phalak, K., Ash-Saki, A., Alam, M., Topaloglu, R. O., & Ghosh, S. (2021). Quantum puf for security and trust in quantum computing. *IEEE Journal on Emerging and Selected Topics in Circuits and Systems*, *11*(2), 333–342.
[6] Fedorov, A. K., & Gelfand, M. S. (2021). Towards practical applications in quantum computational biology. *Nature Computational Science*, *1*(2), 114–119.
[7] Mosteanu, N. R. and Faccia, A. (2021). Fintech frontiers in quantum computing, fractals, and blockchain distributed ledger: paradigm shifts and open innovation. *Journal of Open Innovation: Technology, Market, and Complexity*, *7*(1), 19.

[8] Vietz, D., Barzen, J., Leymann, F., & Wild, K. (2021). On decision support for quantum application developers: Categorization, comparison, and analysis of existing technologies. In: International Conference on Computational Science (pp. 127–141). Springer, Cham.

[9] Carrega, M., Chirolli, L., Heun, S., & Sorba, L. (2021). Anyons in quantum hall interferometry. *Nature Reviews Physics*, *3*(10), 698–711.

[10] Pelucchi, E., Fagas, G., Aharonovich, I., Englund, D., Figueroa, E., Gong, Q., & . . . Jöns, K. D. (2022). The potential and global outlook of integrated photonics for quantum technologies. *Nature Reviews Physics*, *4*(3), 194–208.

[11] Silvia Priscila, S., Sathish Kumar, C., Manikandan, R., Yuvaraj, N., & Ramkumar, M. (2022). Interactive artificial neural network model for UX design. In: International Conference on Computing, Communication, Electrical and Biomedical Systems (pp. 277–284). Springer, Cham.

[12] Yarkoni, S., Raponi, E., Bäck, T., & Schmitt, S. (2022). Quantum annealing for industry applications: introduction and review. *Reports on Progress in Physics*.

[13] Manikandan, R., Sara, S. B. V., Yuvaraj, N., Chaturvedi, A., Priscila, S. S., & Ramkumar, M. (2022). Sequential pattern mining on chemical bonding database in the bioinformatics field. In: AIP Conference Proceedings, (Vol. 2393 No. 1, p. 020050). AIP Publishing LLC.

[14] Bale, A. S., Khatokar, J. A., Singh, S., Bharath, G., Mohan, M. K., Reddy, S. V., & . . . Huddar, S. A. (2021). Nanosciences fostering cross domain engineering applications. *Materials Today: Proceedings*, *43*, 3428–3431.

[15] Saravanan, V., Rajeshwari, S., & Jayashree, P. (2013). SECURITY issues in protecting computers and maintenance. *Journal of Global Research in Computer Science*, *4*(1), 55–58.

[16] Kumar, N., Philip, E., & Elfving, V. E. (2022). Integral transforms in a physics-informed (Quantum) neural network setting: applications & use-cases. *ArXiv Preprint arXiv:2206.14184*.

[17] Sabitha, R., Gopikrishnan, S., Bejoy, B. J., Anusuya, V., & Saravanan, V. (2022). Network based detection of IoT attack using AIS-IDS model. *Wireless Personal Communications*, 1–24.

[18] Bova, F., Goldfarb, A., & Melko, R. G. (2021). Commercial applications of quantum computing. *EPJ Quantum Technology*, *8*(1), 2.

[19] Yadav, S. P., Bhati, B. S., Mahato, D. P., & Kumar, S. (eds.). Federated Learning for IoT Applications. EAI/Springer Innovations in Communication and Computing. Springer, Cham. https://doi.org/10. 1007/978-3-030-85559-8.

[20] Nimbe, P., Weyori, B. A., & Adekoya, A. F. (2021). Models in quantum computing: A systematic review. *Quantum Information Processing*, *20*(2), 1–61.

[21] Vashisht, V., Kumar Pandey, A., & Prakash, S. (2021). Speech recognition using machine learning. *IEIE Transactions on Smart Processing and Computing SCOPUS*, *10*(3), 233–239. ISSN: 2287–5255. https://doi.org/10.5573/IEIESPC.2021.10.3.233.

[22] Uppu, R., Midolo, L., Zhou, X., Carolan, J., & Lodahl, P. (2021). Quantum-dot-based deterministic photon–emitter interfaces for scalable photonic quantum technology. *Nature Nanotechnology*, *16*(12), 1308–1317.

[23] Yadav, S. P., & Yadav, S. (2018). Fusion of medical images in wavelet domain: A discrete mathematical model. *Ingeniería Solidaria*, *14*(25), 1–11. https://doi.org/10.16925/.v14i0.2236.

[24] Marx, V. (2021). Biology begins to tangle with quantum computing. *Nature Methods*, *18*(7), 715–719.

[25] Piattini, M., Serrano, M., Perez-Castillo, R., Petersen, G., & Hevia, J. L. (2021). Toward a quantum software engineering. *IT Professional*, *23*(1), 62–66.

[26] Jiang, W., Xiong, J., & Shi, Y. (2021). A co-design framework of neural networks and quantum circuits towards quantum advantage. *Nature Communications*, *12*(1), 1–13.

Kaushal Kishor*

12 Review and significance of cryptography and machine learning in quantum computing

Abstract: Quantum machine learning, which combines quantum computers with regular machine learning, is a much contested field of research. The goal of quantum ML is to provide light on the possible applications of quantum mechanical findings to ML challenges. The exponential growth of data that must be taught to a typical computer paradigm implies that the present cutting-edge computing equipment cannot keep up with the pace. Quantum computing might be useful in this context for continuous training with enormous datasets. Scientists have resorted to quantum machine learning to reduce the development time for new learning algorithms. Traditional machine learning seeks patterns in data and uses those patterns to forecast the future. This is machine learning's ultimate objective. However, the new patterns created by quantum techniques imply that quantum computers may be more successful in machine learning than traditional computers. One of the most significant uses of cryptography is assuring user anonymity and data security over unsecure networks. In this section, we examine the history of quantum machine learning and summarize the most current results in the field.

12.1 Introduction

Our classical understanding is founded on human experiences, not nature's core process. Our environment is the evolution of basic quantum mechanics. Quantum events defy common sense. In science and human mind, these essential processes were hidden for a long time. The previous century was when we noticed this natural phenomenon. As the inquiry progressed, our professionals produced concepts and mathematical tools. Probabilistic quantum theory has provoked philosophical debates. Quantum superposition, quantum tunneling, etc. continue to fascinate us. Quantum technologies aim to utilize these laws to our advantage. Quantum mechanics-based applications rules have developed leaps and bounds in the last 10 to 20 years, with the goal of replacing or running alongside conventional devices.

Quantum computing, quantum storage, and quantum cryptography are the three primary specialties of quantum technologies today. The broad premise is that with the

---

*Corresponding author: Kaushal Kishor, IT Department, ABES Institute of Technology, Ghaziabad, Uttar Pradesh, India, e-mails: kaushal.kishor@abesit.in, kaushal.rastogi07@gmail.com

https://doi.org/10.1515/9783110798159-012

addition of each qubit, quantum computers will have double the memory capacity. We will need N bits of binary integers to describe an N-bit classical bits system. In quantum systems, we now know that there are two potential definite states: $|0>$ and $|1>$. A bipartite quantum system's general state may be written as $= |00 + |01 + |10 + |11$, and we can readily consider how a two-qubit quantum system yields four traditional pieces of information (α, β, γ, δ). Similarly, we may extract 2^N bits of classical information from an N-qubit quantum system. A strip, an automaton containing certain a collection of rules, symbols, and a read-write head (included within the transition function) that may alter the strip's symbols, make up a Turing machine. Universal Turing machines are quantum computers. Quantum computers are recognized to solve issues that a traditional computer cannot. Factorization of big integers using the Shor's technique [1] is one such example. Moreover, if traditional and quantum are used for the same task at the same time, there may be instances when quantum algorithms show improved efficiency. These algorithms pertain to the BQP complexity class [2]. Solving the Pell's equation, which is a difficult task in the classical computation paradigm, is also efficiently solved in the quantum computation model. Similarly, a quantum algorithm is proven to handle the Non-Abelian hidden subgroup issue efficiently [2]. In the fields of optimization and simulation, quantum computers have made significant advances – calculate partition function characteristics, optimize approximations, simulate quantum systems, etc. Quantum optics and condensed matter physics use quantum simulations [3].

Arthur Samuel remarked in 1955, "Give robots the drive to identify without training." This claim explains machine learning. A machine learning program examines enormous amounts of data, finds patterns, and predicts future events. The techniques used to maximize a multivariate function with restrictions are at the basis of current data mining and visualization. Decision functions map inputs and outputs. Optimization yielded this. Optimizations like these are fundamental in learning theory. These algorithms create AI. Common machine learning techniques are:

1. Supervised Machine learning [4] – trains computers to use labeled data.
2. Unsupervised Machine learning [5], in which machines are not given labeled data and must assess data, based on similarities and differences across classes.
3. Reinforcement learning [6], in which machines assess and discover from our comments. The most prevalent supervised machine learning approach in Quantum Support Vector Machine is a kind of machine learning. [7], It sorts tagged data using a vector space optimal boundary. Another prominent algorithm is PCA [8]. This is the essence of the quantum. Quantum computing can also help with financial modeling [9]. Quantum computers' intrinsic randomness is comparable due to the erratic nature of financial markets [10]. Quantum computers can solve such issues. Weather forecasting has long been a scientific aim, but many aspects must be considered, making standard simulations too long. Quantum computers' parallel processing benefits climate simulations. Traditional computers have trouble simulating complex molecules. Chemical processes produce quantum superposition states, showing they are quantum [11]. Quantum computers can accurately characterize such conditions.

12.2 Quantum cryptography

Quantum cryptography is another exciting specialty in the world of quantum technology. The use of quantum mechanical events to accomplish cryptographic operations is known as quantum cryptography. The birth of this field was sparked by the publication of Wiesner's work in 1983. The quantum key distribution is a well-known example of quantum cryptography – Quantum Machine Learning: A Retrospective and Current Status (QKD). Bennett and Brassard were responsible for developing the complete methodology for exceptionally secure quantum key distribution in 1984. The BB84 protocol [12] is what it is now as. This protocol garnered a lot of interest from the cryptography world since it provided security that could not be achieved by traditional methods [13].

Authentication is the process of verifying one's identity using cryptography. Only the intended recipient sees the message. Integrity: Proof a message was delivered.

12.2.1 Cryptography's advantages

Encryption can prevent unauthorized access to and disclosure of conversations and stored data. Spoofing and message forgeries can be protected using other cryptographic techniques such as authentication procedures and digital signatures.

12.2.2 Cryptography's various forms

Quantum cryptography is indeed a method of encryption that makes use of quantum physics to ensure encrypted messaging. It allows two individuals to create a unique randomized bit string that is only visible to them, and can also be used to encode and decode messages. The capacity of the communication between two users to identify the presence of any 3rd person attempting to obtain information of the key is a significant and unique feature of quantum cryptography. This is because a basic tenet of quantum physics states that monitoring a quantum state impacts the entity as a whole. An external entity trying to intercept the key must assess, causing discrepancies. Quantum strangeness and quantum information transmission may be used to detect espionage. If eavesdropping falls below a certain threshold, a private key may be generated; otherwise, the connection is broken. Quantum cryptography generates and redistributes keys, not data. This key is used to encrypt (and decode) a message, which is subsequently sent over ordinary data transfer. Only one pad technique is most usually linked with QKD [14] because it is probably safe, when combined with a secret random integer.

12.2.3 Cryptography using elliptical curves

ECC provides quicker, smaller, and more efficient cryptographic keys using the elliptic curve theory. ECC creates keys using the elliptic curve equation. The system supports most public key encryption methods, including RS. Some researchers think ECC can give the same level of security as other methods, with a 164-bit key. ECC is popular for mobile applications because it provides equivalent security with less power and battery. In 1985, UW's Neal Koblitz and IBM's Victor Miller created the elliptic curve cryptography. An elliptic curve is a looping line between two axes. ECC is based on a mathematical group's equation, obtained from points where a line crosses the axis. Elliptic curve equations are easy to perform but difficult to reverse [15].

12.2.4 Visual cryptography

Visual cryptography encrypts visual data (images, text, etc.) such that humans can decode it without computers. Overlapping the transparent sheets' shares decrypted them. All n overlapped shares showed the top picture [16].

12.2.5 Financial cryptography

FC refers to encrypting communications when subversion might cause financial loss. Dr. David Chaum's blindfolded signature is credited with starting cryptography. This unique cryptographic signature allows digital token money to be signed without the signer seeing the currency. Digital Cash is another name for this type of currency. Aside from the creation of new kinds of money, financial cryptography encompasses the procedures and algorithms necessary for cash transfer security. Financial cryptography encompasses proof of work and a variety of auction mechanisms. Hashcash is being utilized to keep spam to a minimum. Financial cryptography is often thought to have a wide range of applications. Financial cryptography, according to Ian Grigg, is made up of seven levels; Each level consists of seven distinct disciplines: security, software engineering, rights, accountancy, governance, value, and banking transactions. The failures of many companies can be attributed to a lack of several of these disciplines, or to their incorrect use. FC is seen as a sufficiently multidisciplinary subject [17].

12.2.6 Cryptography in games

Crypto! (TM) is a Windows version of the standard Cryptogram problems encountered in puzzle books and Sunday newspapers. Crypto! selects a statement or term from its 50-strong database, encrypts it, and sends it to you to resolve. Cryptograms are more enjoyable to solve since Crypto! allows you to test different letters and erase errors. There are letter frequencies supplied, as well as a variety of pointers and tips to help you get started fast.

This free flash game improves your word understanding for faster reading while also allowing for slow scanning on any Windows machine. This free flash game strengthens your comprehension of words for fast reading and also allows for slow scanning on any Windows computer. A flash version of the cryptogram puzzles may be found in this game. Break the code and find out what the message is. From the list, Crypto-gram chooses a phrase. It then encrypts it and provides it for decryption. The intellect is challenged in this cryptogram game. Its goal is to solve the puzzles by choosing letters and placing them on the cryptogram map [18].

12.3 Classical machine learning

In this part, we examine fundamental machine learning types and models in order to provide a foundation for the wide variety of methods through which computers learn. A computer may often learn new information either from data or via human contact. We cover both of these instructional methods thoroughly. Then, the most popular machine learning models that employ these various types of learning are explored. When rapid processing was a challenge, machine learning methods were developed decades ago. With today's enhanced processing power, correctly implementing these algorithms is a pretty doable challenge. For ML algorithms, a classification may be made, based on their simplicity or difficulty of implementation, as well as by the computer resources required for implementation.

12.3.1 Data-driven learning and interaction-driven learning

In machine learning, there are three ways of learning: supervised, unsupervised, and reinforcement learning. The sections that follow go over each type of learning.

12.3.2 Supervised learning

An input–output device pairing set D is provided to us for supervised learning, and we are to use it (x, t). In most cases, the input x is a vector of n dimensions; however this is not always the case. The goal is to assess whether inputs and outputs have a linear or nonlinear connection, and to forecast the outcome for unknown inputs. We wish to forecast t from x. An example is spam classifier. The Figure 12.1 shows the process of a classifier – it evaluates whether future emails are spam, based on a training set [19].

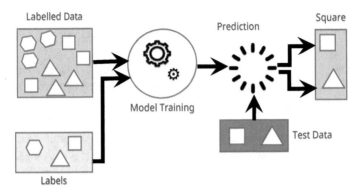

Figure 12.1: Working of supervised learning.

Loss functions measure prediction accuracy. Various loss functions may be used to measure the distance between $t(x)$ and t. An example is to minimize $f(t(x), t(x))$. The probability function prediction, $p(x, t)$, has three phases.

12.3.2.1 Model selection

We choose a PDF from a vector of capabilities. An inductive bias describes this. We parameterize the predictive distribution $p(t|x, t|)$ in discriminative models.

12.3.2.2 Learning

Second, maximize a learning parameter (loss function $f(t(x), t)$), given training set D. (x). Parameter and distribution family parameterized by.

12.3.2.3 Inference

The main downside of these models over discriminative models is their proclivity for outliers. The mathematics behind generative models is also relatively simple. The procedure is not as straightforward as in discriminative models. To compute $P(Y|X)$, first estimate the prior probability $P(Y)$ and the probability $P(X|Y)$ using the data presented.

12.3.3 Unsupervised learning

Unsupervised learning does not use labeled data points. D includes inputs x. We just have input data. The procedure extracts important data attributes. We need these jobs:

12.3.3.1 Density estimation

Through using data for training, we attempt to decision-make the probability distribution $p(x)$.

12.3.3.2 Clustering

Users may want to split into separate groups, based on similarities and differences, unless the initial data set lacks labels or categories – a limit imposed on us to readily segregate the pieces of data into groups.

12.3.3.3 Methods for reducing dimensionality

To better identify the parameter linkages, dimension reduction entails portraying the data point x in many spaces. This is generally done in a lower-dimensional space to help retrieve component relationships.

12.3.3.4 Generation of new samples

We want new D samples with the same likelihood function as the training data. Sports scientists utilize it to predict player behavior. A three-stage procedure similar to supervised learning is used – modeling choices, model learning, and model-based grouping and sampling.

12.3.4 Reinforcement learning

Using the information gained from previous judgments, Reinforcement Learning attempts to maximize a set of variables. In contrast, supervised learning employs "correct" input responses from a training set D of input-output pairs. It is not necessary to immediately fix suboptimal routes taken by a reinforcement learning system.

12.3.5 Machine learning models

12.3.5.1 Artificial neural networks

There are artificial neural networks that are focused on the central nervous system in animals, and are used to replicate biological models. The main aspects of neural networks are deep learning and pattern detection. It is a system of interconnected neurons, with adjustable weights associated with each link, and an activation mechanism specified at each node. An artificial neural network is used to deal with constant contingent variables – a layer-based unit, one hidden layer, or two output layers. Passive nodes in the input layer are to repeat rather than change the content. Processing occurs in the secrete layer, utilizing layer weight activation measurements. The output layer receives the single numbers generated by each hidden node in the last hidden layer. The answer is the variable's final forecast, as returned by the output sheet [20, 21].

Benefits: Compatible with both linear and nonlinear data; needs no reprogramming; and works even though one or a few nodes fail to respond to the network

Disadvantages: Takes a wide range of instructions; requires a lot of computing and computing power; and the consumer has no way of knowing what is going on within the network.

12.3.5.2 Convolutional neural networks

Images may be categorized using Convolutional Neural Networks. The output is calculated using a set of weights and biases applied to inputs. Between the input and output layers are the hidden layers. Next comes a layer with an activation function (the RELU Layer), and then, a series of pooling levels. The phrase derives from kernel-based convolution. The distribution of weights might be improved by backpropagation [22].

12.3.5.3 A recurrent neural network

Here, the current step's input is the previous step's output. Predictive text is one such example. Foreseeing the next word requires storing the preceding word. RNNs make autonomous activation by distributing weights and biases across layers.

12.3.6 Support vector machines for supervised learning

Boser, Guyon, and Vapnik created the Support Vector Machine (SVM) idea at COLT-92 in 1992. SVMs are one of the numerous models in the family of supervised learning-based generalized linear classifiers, utilized in classifying data and predicting outcomes. SVMs are high-dimensional feature storage systems that are based on a linear function's parameter space. They are trained utilizing learning bias optimization techniques. Handwriting recognition is a powerful example of SVM. Such classifiers are given pixel maps as inputs, and their performance is equivalent to that of complex neural networks with specific features for handwriting detection. Several applications, particularly those reliant on pattern recognition and regression, have emerged as a result of promising characteristics such as SVMs' improved empirical performance. Handwriting analysis, facial analysis, and other techniques are examples of SVMs.

12.4 Application quantum computing in ad hoc networks

Traditional MANETs use 0 and 1 for QoS [23, 24]. When a node moves and tries to access a service via an SP, these services may be lost [25]. Quantum adaptation involves using QKD with superdense coding. Quantum MANETs increase quantum communication by superimposing EPR pairings, or bell states. If we measure these stacked states qubits, we can determine the equal distribution of 0 or 1. This helps distribute network services. Using qubits, we can deliver messages. Einstein's use of the EPR conundrum helps identify qubit quantum entanglement. Several research works imply that quantum internet can carry quantum and conventional data across large distances. MANET [26] uses this kind of network. Due to QUMANET's increasing number of states, more services will be provided by more service providers.

12.5 Computational learning theories

Because there are so many machine learning algorithms, it is important to define their strengths and weaknesses. How hard is it to train a machine? [27] Assessing the efficacy of a machine learning approach in a given situation may be challenging. The effectiveness of an algorithm may be affected by factors such as sample complexity, computational complexity, mistake bound, etc. The field of study known as "computational learning theory" (COLT) [28], which explores the theoretical boundaries of machine learning methods. First, analyze a problem or environment, then utilize learning algorithms, and finally assess the best algorithm's performance [29]. PAC analyses COLT. Valiant's PAC evaluates learner competence [30].

12.5.1 Quantum machine learning

Machine learning teaches computers new abilities by observing how algorithms interpret data. This field uses AI and computational statistics. With its supervised and unsupervised deep learning subsets, the traditional machine learning technique facilitates the classification of images, recognition of patterns and voices, and the administration of massive data sets. Currently, a tremendous quantity of data is being produced. To handle, organize, and categorize enormous data, new ways are necessary. Traditional reinforcement learning can often discover patterns in data, but it cannot address unusual challenges that need huge volumes of data quickly. Companies that maintain enormous databases are aware of these limits and are actively trying to find solutions, most of which are quantum machine learning-based.

Quantum phenomena such as quantum entanglement may be used to address typical machine learning issues [30].

12.5.2 Quantum machine learning algorithms implementation

In algorithm development, we consider supervised and unsupervised learning [20]. In supervised learning, patterns are learnt by observing training samples. Unsupervised learning reveals the structure of clustered data.

12.5.3 Quantum clustering [31]

Quantum clustering uses Lloyd's method to solve k-means clustering. It employs various ways to calculate the distance between the cluster centroid and the origin. Pick a random starting centroid and assign each vector to the cluster with the closest mean. Calculate and update the cluster's centroid, until stationary. Quantum algorithms speed up the classical method. Quantum method takes O(Mlog(MN)) time in N-dimensional space.

12.5.4 The quantum neural network (QNN) [32]

The QNN paradigm is a deep supervised learning technique that may be used to teach a computer to organize data, find patterns, or recognize images. It is, in fact, an intake network. Qubits (like neurons) and spinning gates are used to build circuits. Network training uses training instances. Each thread is labeled. The network must retrieve the label value from the data collection, while minimizing label divergence. To find the least error-prone training parameter, each iteration updates the training parameter. Backpropagation, based on conjugate gradient, reduces errors.

12.5.5 Quantum decision tree [33]

It separates the quantum states into categories. Similar to other types of tree topologies in computer science, decision treesdecision trees begin with a root node that receives no incoming connections, and has only edges that branch out to leaves. Classification of solutions occurs as we progress through the various frameworks. Each leaf in a classification tree is assigned an output class, depending on the qualities that were originally used to create the tree. Quantum machine learning is the use of quantum computers to run traditional machine learning algorithms.

12.6 Machine learning is used in learning and renormalization procedures

Machine learning finds patterns in unrecognisable data. Certain traits defy numerical modeling. Machine learning fixes such issues. Recent improvements in machine learning offer promise for classifying matter phases or approximating arbitrary functions, using neural networks. Machine learning is used in search engines, recommendation engines, program management, smartphone and camera software, and more. These programs need deep neural networksdeep neural networks (with hidden layers and neurons).

12.6.1 Quantum support vector machine

Categorization is a key machine learning technology. It identifies, organizes, and investigates new data. Computer vision [34], medical imaging [35, 36], and other applications use machine learning categorization. Machines classify data to decide how to react to it. SVM is a popular data categorization approach in machine learning. It is helpful because it qualifies into one of two groups by using a training set and support vectors shown in Figure 12.2. Quantum SVMs have been recreated logically and practically. These technologies solve problems using qubits. Quantum and computational SVM methods are created.

12.6.2 Quantum classifier

A quantum classification is a quantum information approach that uses current data's subatomic particles to recognize or characterize incoming data. In the following paragraphs, we will talk about the groundwork for quantum classifications and how it has been used on a quantum computer.

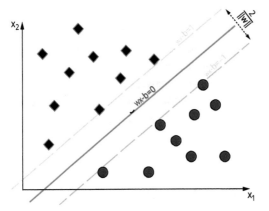

Figure 12.2: The best possible SVM margin hyperplane.

12.6.2.1 Current work on quantum classifiers

Microsoft recently introduced a variation-based quantum paradigm for supervised methods in a study (Figure 12.3).

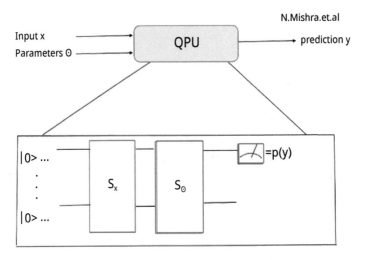

Figure 12.3: Concept of the Quantum Classifier as a Printed-Circuit Board [37].

Further operations, such as a measuring device and a state preparation circuit, S_x, which maps input x to the amplitude of a model circuit U, are carried out by the QPU (quantum processing unit). By keeping an eye on the amplitudes generated by the state preparation circuit and by reacting the model circuit, this kind of QPU may also do model inferences or calculate $f(x,) = y$ analytically. These tests provide a binary result of either 0 or 1, allowing for a yes/no diagnosis, shown in Figure 12.4. The parameters of a classification circuit may be learned and mastered with the help of a discretization approach. As can be seen in Figure 12.3, the prototype circuit sends an n-dimensional ket vector representing an encoding feature to another ket = U(x), where U should be unitary.

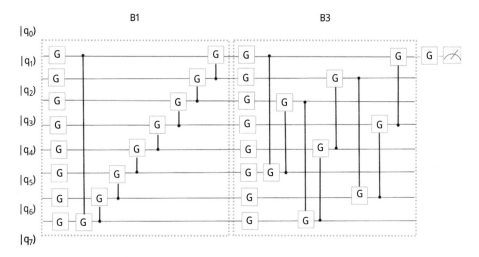

Figure 12.4: Generic model circuit architecture for 8 qubits [37].

12.6.2.2 The use of quantum machine learning in physics

There are several applications of machine learning in the quantum world, including quantum metrology, Hamiltonian estimation, quantum signal processing, and quantum control. Quantum computers employ AI and machine learning. Machine learning and re-inforcement learning produce entangled states. By performing simple gates, automated systems may govern quantum computing. Machine learning techniques can handle decoherence or noise in quantum computing and optimizing QKD-type cryptography procedures in noisy channels [38]. Online machine learning optimization can discover the optimal Bose-Einstein condensate evaporation ramps [39]. Machine learning and quantum theory have similar statistical basis. Condensed matter physics uses unsupervised learning to detect phases and order parameters. Model thermal state configurations may be solved via unsupervised learning. Along with phases, order parameters (magnetization) may be detected. Using these tactics, we can get phase information without knowing the Hamiltonian.

12.6.3 Quantum computing, quantum learning, and quantum artificial intelligence

Quantum Machine Intelligence is controversial. In the following parts, we will try to comprehend fundamental AI and machine learning concepts before looking at how quantum information processing and quantum computing might augment them. We mention recent advancements at the conclusion of this section.

12.6.3.1 Quantum artificial intelligence

Can quantum contribute to AI? We will simulate quantum information processing and AI. Quantum Computing (QC) simulates quantum data for faster search and optimization. It helps AI govern algorithms, and its variants speed up search jobs quadratically, whereas Quantum Machine Learning discoveries enhance machine learning issues exponentially. Projective Simulation is being studied (PS). The agent operates in an environment that responds with physical inputs. Agents learn via experience. PS's primary component is ECM (ECM). ECM helps the agent project into episodic memoryepisodic memory, resulting in a random wander. PS is quantified. Quantum-enhanced autonomous agents interact with conventional environments but have quantum memories. Quantum-walking agent now navigates memory. Created transitions are interference-prone quantum superpositions. Clip states produce quantum jumps. Quantizing the PS model helps speed up memory searches. The PS model's application to the quantum world introduces embodied quantum agents.

12.6.4 Classical neural networks

"Neural Networks" (together with "Artificial Neural Networks" and "Connectionist Models") is a word that is used to refer to a variety of models, although there is no precise definition of the phrase [40].

12.7 Conclusions

This chapter discusses quantum computers and learning algorithms. After years of speculation, quantum machine learning is finally validated. As expected, these new algorithms are faster and more efficient. Combining machine learning with quantum computing speeds up many algorithms. Quantum computers might revolutionize machine learning. When more quantum computers with more qubits are accessible, we can fully understand quantum computers' influence on machine learning. Real quantum computers could not do many of these tasks. Future developments may include quantum computers and machine learning algorithms. If a more successful technique for dealing with machine learning challenges is discovered in the future, it is possible. As long as quantum algorithms remain illogical, this will likely remain one of the most difficult challenges of dealing with quantum computers. For conventional machine learning classifiers, we can use quantum computers to improve speed and accuracy. Even though we do not yet know how quantum computers will affect computer vision, the possibilities are unlimited, and with each new technique, machine learning seems to be the one that will help quantum computers get better.

References

[1]   Shor, P. W. (1994). Algorithms for Quantum Computation: Discrete Logarithms and Factoring. In: Proceedings 35th Annual Symposium on Foundations of Computer Science IEEE Comput. Soc. Press.
[2]   Bermejo-Vega, J., & Zatloukal, K. C. (2015). Abelian hypergroups and quantum computation. arXiv:1509.05806.
[3]   Somma, R. D. (2016). Quantum simulations of one dimensional quantum systems. *Quantum. Inf. Comput*, *16*, 1125.
[4]   Kishor, K., Sharma, R., & Chhabra, M. (2022). Student Performance Prediction Using Technology of Machine Learning. In: Sharma, D. K., SL, P., Sharma, R., Zaitsev, D. A. (eds.). Micro-Electronics and Telecommunication Engineering. Lecture Notes in Networks and Systems (Vol. 373). Springer, Singapore. https://doi.org/10.1007/978-981-16-8721-1_53.
[5]   Kishor, K. (2022). Communication-Efficient Federated Learning. In: Yadav, S. P., Bhati, B. S., Mahato, D. P., Kumar, S. (eds.). Federated Learning for IoT Applications. EAI/Springer Innovations in Communication and Computing Springer, Cham. https://doi.org/10.1007/978-3-030-85559-8_9.
[6]   Kishor, K. (2022). Personalized Federated Learning. In: Yadav, S. P., Bhati, B. S., Mahato, D. P., Kumar, S. (eds.). Federated Learning for IoT Applications. EAI/Springer Innovations in Communication and Computing Springer, Cham. https://doi.org/10.1007/978-3-030-85559-8_3.
[7]   Gupta, S., Tyagi, S., & Kishor, K. (2022). Study and Development of Self Sanitizing Smart Elevator. In: Gupta, D., Polkowski, Z., Khanna, A., Bhattacharyya, S., Castillo, O. (eds.). Proceedings of Data Analytics and Management. Lecture Notes on Data Engineering and Communications Technologies (Vol. 90) Springer, Singapore. https://doi.org/10.1007/978-981-16-6289-8_15.
[8]   Yadav, S. P. (2020). Vision-based detection, tracking, and classification of vehicles. *IEIE Transactions on Smart Processing & Computing*, *9*(6), 427–434.
[9]   Orus, R., Mugel, S., & Lizaso, E. (2019). Quantum computing for finance: Overview and prospects. *Review Physical*, *4*, 100028.

[10] Palsson, M. S., Gu, M., Ho, J., Wiseman, H. M., & Pryde, G. J. (2017). Experimentally modeling stochastic processes with less memory by the use of a quantum processor. *Science Advances, 3*.

[11] Yadav, S. P., & Yadav, S. (2018). Fusion of medical images in wavelet domain: A discrete mathematical model. *Ingeniería Solidaria, 14*(25), 1–11.

[12] Bennett, C. H., Bessette, F., Brassard, G., Salvail, L., & Smolin, J. (1992). Experimental quantum cryptography. *Journal Cryptography, 5*(3), 13. A. Pathak, Elements of Quantum Computation and Quantum Communication (CRC Press, 2018.

[13] Kishor, K. Cryptography's role in securing the information society. *International Journal of Communication and Media Studies, 1*(1), 46–59. Dec 2011.

[14] Pathare, A., & Deshmukh, D. B. (2022). Review on cryptography using quantum computing. *International Journal for Modern Trends in Science and Technology, 8*, 141–146. https://doi.org/10. 46501/IJMTST0801024.

[15] Goya, A., Sharma, S., Tiwari, U., & Kishor, K. (2018). Intrusion detection in wireless sensor networks. *International Journal of Creative Research Thoughts (IJCRT), ISSN, 6*(2), 120–125. 2320–2882. Available at http://www.ijcrt.org/papers/IJCRT1892020.pdf.

[16] Pandey, A., & Som, S. (2016). Applications and Usage of Visual Cryptography: A Review. In: 2016 5th International Conference on Reliability, Infocom Technologies and Optimization (Trends and Future Directions) (ICRITO) (pp. 7784984) IEEE, DOI: 10.1109/icrito.2016.

[17] This paper was presented at FC00 and is originally published in the Proceedings of Financial Cryptography Fourth International Conference, Anguilla, British West Indies, 21st – 24th February 2000. A web copy is located at http://www.iang.org/papers/.

[18] Kol, G., & Naor, M. Cryptography and game theory: designing protocols for exchanging information, full version, www.wisdom.weizmann.ac.il/%7enaor/PAPERS/cryptogames.html.

[19] Sharma, A., Jha, N., & Kishor, K. (2022). Predict COVID-19 with Chest X-ray. In: Gupta, D., Polkowski, Z., Khanna, A., Bhattacharyya, S., Castillo, O. (eds.). Proceedings of Data Analytics and Management. Lecture Notes on Data Engineering and Communications Technologies (Vol. 90). Springer, Singapore. https://doi.org/10.1007/978-981-16-6289-8_16.

[20] Sharma, R., Maurya, S. K., & Kishor, K. (2021). July Student Performance Prediction using Technology of Machine Learning (3, 2021). In: Proceedings of the International Conference on Innovative Computing & Communication (ICICC), Available at SSRN: https://ssrn.com/abstract=3879645 or http://dx.doi.org/10.2139/ssrn.3879645.

[21] Jain, A., Sharma, Y., & Kishor, K. (2021). Prediction and Analysis of Financial Trends Using Ml Algorithm (July 11, 2021). In: Proceedings of the International Conference on Innovative Computing & Communication (ICICC). Available at SSRN: https://ssrn.com/abstract=3884458 or http://dx.doi. org/10.2139/ssrn.3884458.

[22] Tyagi, D., Sharma, D., Singh, R., & Kishor, K. (2020). Real time 'driver drowsiness'& monitoring & detection techniques. *International Journal of Innovative Technology and Exploring Engineering, 9*(8), 280–284. DOI: 10.35940/ijitee.H6273.069820.

[23] Kishor, K., Nand, P., & Agarwal, P. (2018). Secure and efficient subnet routing protocol for MANET. *Indian Journal of Public Health, Executive Editor. 9*(12), 200. DOI: 10.5958/0976-5506.2018.01830.2.

[24] Kishor, K., Nand, P., & Agarwal, P. (2018). Notice of retraction design adaptive subnetting hybrid gateway MANET protocol on the basis of dynamic TTL value adjustment. *Aptikom Journal on Computer Science and Information Technologies, 3*(2), 59–65. https://doi.org/10.11591/APTIKOM.J.CSIT.115.

[25] Kishor, K., & Nand, P. (2013). Review performance analysis and challenges wireless MANET routing protocols "international. *Journal of Science, Engineering and Technology Research (IJSETR), 2*(10), 1854–185. ISSN 2278-7798.

[26] Kishor, K., & Nand, P. (2014). Performance evaluation of AODV, DSR, TORA and OLSR in with respect to end-to-end delay in MANET. *International Journal of Science and Research (IJSR), 3*(6), 633–636. ISSN 2319-7064.

[27] Kishor, K., & Pandey, D. (2022). Study and Development of Efficient Air Quality Prediction System Embedded with Machine Learning and IoT. In: Gupta, D. et al (eds.). Proceeding International Conference on Innovative Computing and Communications. Lect. Notes in Networks, Syst (Vol. 471). Springer, Singapore. https://doi.org/10.1007/978-981-19-2535-1.

[28] Angluin, D. (1992). Computational Learning Theory: Survey and Selected Bibliography. In: Proceedings of 24th Annual ACM Symposium on Theory of Computing (pp. 351–369).

[29] Kishor, K., Nand, P., & Agarwal, P. (2017). Subnet based ad hoc network algorithm reducing energy consumption in manet. *International Journal of Applied Engineering Research, 12*(22), 11796–11802.

[30] Bansal, A., Kumar, S., Pandey, A., & Kishor, K. (2018). Attendance management system through fingerprint. *International Journal for Research in Applied Science & Engineering Technology (IJRASET), 6*(9), DOI: 10.22214/ijraset.2018.4368, http://ijraset.com/fileserve.php?FID=15925.

[31] Lloyd, S., Mohseni, M. & Rebentrost, P., Quantum algorithms for supervised and unsupervised machine learning. arXiv:1307.0411.

[32] Yadav, S. P., & Yadav, S. (2020). Image fusion using hybrid methods in multimodality medical images. *Medical & Biological Engineering & Computing, 58*, 669–687.

[33] Yadav, S. P. et al. (2022). Survey on machine learning in speech emotion recognition and vision systems using a recurrent neural network (RNN). *Archives of Computational Methods in Engineering, 29*(3), 1753–1770.

[34] Rai, B. K., Sharma, S., Kumar, G., & Kishor, K. (2022). Recognition of different bird category using image processing. *International Journal of Online and Biomedical Engineering (Ijoe), 18*(07), 101–114. https://doi.org/10.3991/ijoe.v18i07.29639.

[35] Yadav, S. P., & Yadav, S. (2019). Fusion of medical images using a wavelet methodology: A survey. *IEIE Transactions on Smart Processing & Computing, 8*(4), 265–271.

[36] Erickson, B. J., Korfiatis, P., Akkus, Z., & Kline, T. L. (2017). Machine learning for medical imaging. *Rad. Graph, 37*, 505–515.

[37] Yadav, S. P. (2020). Vision-based detection, tracking, and classification of vehicles. *IEIE Transactions on Smart Processing & Computing, 9*(6), 427–434.

[38] Krawec, W. O., Nelson, M. G., & Geiss, E. P. 2017. Automatic Generation of Optimal Quantum Key Distribution Protocols. In: Proceedings of Genetic and Evolutionary Computation (pp. 1153). ACM, New York.

[39] Wigley, P. B., Everitt, P. J., Van den Hengel, A., Bastian, J. W., Sooriyabandara, M. A., McDonald, N. P., Hardman, G. D., Quinlivan, K. S., Manju, C. D., Kuhn, P., Petersen, C. C. N., Luiten, I. R., Hope, A. N., Robins, J. J., & Hush, M. R. (2016). Fast machine-learning online optimization of ultra-cold-atom experiments. *Scientific reports, 6*, 25890.

[40] Vashisht, V., Kumar Pandey, A., & Prakash Yadav, S. (2021). Speech recognition using machine learning. *IEIE Transactions on Smart Processing & Computing, 10*(3), 233–239.

Shally Nagpal, Puneet Garg*, Shivani Gaba, Alankrita Aggarwal

13 An improved genetic quantum cryptography model for network communication

Abstract: Any wireless or open space network's biggest problem is security. When the network has limited coverage and high-speed mobility, communication becomes even more crucial. One similar network with a lower sensing limit and designed for indoor use is WPAN. In order to increase the communication's dependability and security, this paper suggests a quantum-inspired encoded communication. The work model is established for a highly mobile, randomly scattered WPAN network. The initial step of this model performs node-level characterization under the parameters of coverage, stability, and load. Based on this analysis, the initial population sequence is generated and based on this generation, communication can be performed. The genetic model applied on this population pool is processed to generate the effective communication pair. After generating the population pair, quantum technique is applied to capture the characteristics of the node pair to generate the key. Finally, the data is encoded using the quantum key-based SHA. Over the network, this encoded communication is carried out.

13.1 Introduction

Cryptographic methods are available to provide encoded communication between distributed users in the public environment. It protects information from intruders who want to snoop on it. Cryptography is about having an integrated authentication policy that protects the communication from various kinds of network attacks [1].

There are a number of methods to provide security and protect the communication in an open environment. Anti-virus are software programs that secure a system from viruses. Firewalls can also be used for a specific application, program or a system to provide a secure gateway adaptive communication.

*Corresponding author: **Puneet Garg**, ABES Engineering College, Ghaziabad, Uttar Pradesh, India, e-mail: puneetgarg.er@gmail.com

Shally Nagpal, Panipat Institute of Engineering and Technology, Samalkha, Panipat, Haryana, India, e-mail: shally.ngpl@gmail.com

Shivani Gaba, Panipat Institute of Engineering and Technology, Samalkha, Panipat, Haryana, India, e-mail: sgsgknl@gmail.com

Alankrita Aggarwal, Panipat Institute of Engineering and Technology, Samalkha, Panipat, Haryana, India, e-mail: alankrita.agg@gmail.com

https://doi.org/10.1515/9783110798159-013

To provide safe and reliable communication along with the preventive and defensive approaches, attack detection methods are also applied. The node behavior analysis and the activity pattern can be monitored to identify the attack type over the network.

13.1.1 Cryptography

Cryptography is the traditional and the most reliable communication method that provides security at the user level, group level, data level, and communication level. Cryptography is about transforming the transmitting data to some other form that is not readable by other users. To ensure security, the data is transformed to a form that is either block-specific or stream-specific. Encoding is applied here by using some key or measure or method. Some of the encoding techniques are based on media types. Image encoding is one such common media form that provides biometric information communication over the global medium.

13.1.2 Quantum cryptography

Quantum cryptography is a continuous encoding method that uses correspondence behavior or the organization's true depiction to execute information encoding. This covers the vast majority of an organization's vulnerability problems in correspondence. The quantum cryptography method really uses a representation that includes energy, force, and exact variation.

13.1.2.1 Network formation

The standard provided by IEEE is high-speed data communication over Wireless PAN. This standard is identified by 802.15.3. This standard is designed to provide high-speed communication of different types of media like auto data transmission, video data transmission, etc.

Network Connectivity: The connectivity in a network depends on the communication range. Maximum communication connectivity is provided by Line of Sight (LOS). Maximum coverage-based analysis is used to identify the virtually connected nodes.

Line of Sight (LOS): Frequency-specific estimation is defined to identify the maximum coverage, based on which the connectivity-eligible nodes can be identified. Frequency, bandwidth, and interference analysis-based connectivity observation can be applied to generate an effective network connectivity.

Non-Line of Sight (NLOS): This kind of range analysis is defined for lower frequency-based observation. The frequency band is defined with smaller units, and the communication under the obstacle can be defined to achieve an effective communication.

13.1.2.2 Personal area network

An Individual Region Organization is the adhoc network characterized without the detail of any particular regulator or framework. The dynamism is the primary component of this organization structure that is accessible in various structures. These types of organizations are essentially characterized to give an undeniable level of agreeable correspondence between sets of savvy hubs that can be accessible in various mathematical areas. This weighty correspondence is attracting ongoing attention, with respect to real-life situations and applications. This continuous availability additionally expands the organization's criticality. Along these lines, these organizations are experiencing a weighty correspondence load.

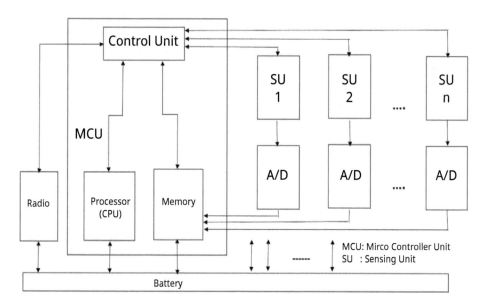

Figure 13.1: Smart node architecture.

13.1.2.3 Communication architecture

An Individual Region Organization has numerous limitations related to correspondence, design, and conventions. Correspondence can be drawn by including a few significant mechanical terms in the organization, including WPAN, outline transfer correspondence, and VAN (Virtual Region Organization). Edge hand-off unambiguous correspondence can be drawn by specific cells. The correspondence control strategy with the cell detail can be characterized as a successful correspondence control.

The correspondence control with information parcel detail is completed. Source, base, and size are the key vectors that are characterized while empowering correspondence. The correspondence can be empowered by determining the innovation; so the central organization can be seen with directing the table development. The standard form of this enabled Personal Area Network is shown in Figure 13.1.

13.2 Related study

This includes a study of the existing technology that is used for secure communication. We will study the existing methods to identify the loopholes.

Bencheikh [22] has suggested a quantum cryptography technique based on continuous variouss. There have been a few suggested continuous various quantum cryptography methods. They are constrained by a number of things, including the 50% data rejection, resulting from the random selection of bases and the conventional construction of the random bits of the key. Furthermore, certain protocols require considerable (irrational) squeezing in order to be implemented [1].

Kartalopoulos [37] has defined the work on optical data processing in a secure way to recover the error in quantum cryptography method. The author reviewed quantum cryptography and the author identifies the various steps in the quantum key identification process. The author then analyzes and discusses the problems that occur in key generation and distribution in fiber optics networks. The topological formulation and communication in the network are provided by the author. The author also observed the network capabilities, and relatively maps it with different attacks to achieve the adaptive network communication [2].

Goel [34] identified new research directions for quantum cryptography method. This is a substantial difference from classical cryptographic techniques. This article also characterized the formulation of quantum cryptography as well as available extensions to it to achieve the different levels of security [3].

Teja et al. [40] has provided the study-based work for exploring the various aspects of quantum cryptography. Two of the most common quantum key distribution protocols have been explained. The author also defined the key-specific experimentation to recognize and resolve the technological challenge in the network [4].

Vignesh [35] has provided work to identify the limitation of quantum cryptography and observed the advantages over traditional cryptography. The author presents here some of the quantum's theoretical weaknesses, including the algorithmic formulation for signature generation, real-time implementation, and capability-driven estimation [5].

Sharbaf [28] has proposed a new technological model for improving the quantum cryptography approach. The author has included the technological improvement to the network using quantum cryptography modeling. Real-world security was provided to obtain the future-directed security. The behavior analysis at a higher level is provided to achieve secure communication within the network [6].

Kurochkin [39] provided a work on the exploration of the various aspects of quantum cryptography. The work also applied the cryptography method to telecom communication security. The network setup and the security implementation were provided by the author. Quantum key generation, with behavior, and network characterization were provided [7].

Zorbas et al. [11] has proposed an algorithm for computing the desired cover set formation to improve the coverage performance. The characteristics-driven node structure analysis is applied based on topology parameter specification with an extensive network life mapping. An experimentation is provided here to achieve topology-independent network tracking to improve the target coverage to optimize the network lifetime. The author provided the work on complete and the partial target coverage, based on cluster formation. A heuristic algorithm is integrated here to provide the phase-specific constraint-specific weight assignment. The formation of the path tree with cover set construction is defined here to improve the target coverage [8].

Zhang et al. [21] has provided work on the 1-hop target coverage to provide critical node observation for a sensor network. A local environment analysis method is defined to provide the node dimension analysis with a scalability vector to improve the coverage criteria. The author observed the energy and waiting time to improve the optimization of the distributed coverage algorithm. The author processed the design constraints to improve the computational complexity and communication. The work model also achieved scalability and stability for this real-time network [9].

Jamali et al. [32] has defined an algorithmic model, based on region analysis, to generate the cover set and provide activation of the covers, based on the base station connectivity. The subset-based activation is observed based on the target node monitoring. Sensor cover-based lifetime analysis is provided for the transformation of the connected cover problem. The method has improved the computational complexity and generated the solution, using the proposed heuristic algorithm. The work is defined to generate effective covers under energy- and distance-level observation, so that the connected communication will be improved and energy consumption will be reduced [10].

Kurochkin et al. [38] has defined work on security improvement method using quantum cryptography approach. Theoretical analysis demonstrated an increased opportunity for security. This protocol was experimentally implemented on a quantum cryptography system, based on polarization encoding through a free space quantum channel [11].

Nirmala et al. [25] has defined an improved secure broadcast method in a clustered sensor network. The author defined the phase-driven analysis to compute the key and to provide communication at the prior analysis defined at the time of deployment.

Immediate and independent authentication was provided with base station specification and cluster-specific communication. A compromised node generation for the mobile agent was provided to evaluate the security responsibility and the performance measure. The author defined a secure key distribution method with specification of shared secret key so that there is a paired communication between the node and cluster head. The author achieved secure authenticated communication in the clustered sensor network [12].

Sharbaf et al. [29] has proposed the quantum as the energy technology for improving the security aspect. This research paper concentrates on quantum cryptography and how this technology contributes to network security. The paper has identified the limitations in the existing cryptography method in reference to quantum cryptography modeling. The application, usage, characterization, and scope of quantum cryptography were provided by the author [13].

Shrivastava et al. [3] has given the quantum cryptography model an enhancement. This research developed a novel technique that gives the quantum cryptography system two phases of security. The suggested algorithm uses the idea of prime factor to modify the secret key bits at both the sender and receiver ends, so the existence of an eavesdropper has no impact on the system's security [14].

Kim et al. [8] has developed a new heuristic algorithm based on the communication weight assignment, and applied a probabilistic measure for target cover generation. The greedy weighted algorithm is defined, based on the connectivity and coverage constraints analysis, to improve the communication connectivity. Diverse sensing and characterization are provided to improve the probabilistic coverage model with constraint specification. The author improved the network deployment, energy sensing, and sink node tracking to improve the coverage, and defined an optimized scheduling method. A probabilistic investigation is provided here to improve the coverage model for improving the coverage under an uncertainty parameter [15].

Mandal et al. [36] has defined a multi-photon-based three-stage model for improving the aspect of quantum cryptography. This paper presented an implementation of the three-stage model to provide the free space-specific communication modeling. The model required the environment and the network information to generate keys based on which the encoded information was communicated within the network [16].

Borzoi [2] has established a protocol for using quantum cryptography in communications. The author presented an examination of the techniques and measures used to establish the related uncertainty vector, and create key parameters for quantum cryptography. The author also covered the key restrictions used to enhance the modeling of cryptography [17].

Niemen [27] has specified the quantum cryptography method's security management. To create the keys and give a reasonably adaptable network communication, the laws and procedures of physics are combined with network characteristics. To accomplish the channel-specific security, multiple layers of rule-specific analysis were offered. In order to enable dependable communication over insecure channels, channel state-based quantum bit creation was made available [18].

Lei Zhou et al.'s [24] Zigbee protocol work has been established to ensure effective network security. Interconnection analysis was given design-specific estimation so that sub-network adaptive communication could be carried out. In order to increase communication dependability, security was included into the protocol design and assessment. The author [19] supplied the simulated observation and communication analysis.

Adam Dahlstrom et al. [4] have produced research on several routing protocols designed especially for sensor networks. AODV and DYMO protocols were used to observe the Zigbee network standard, and communication is mostly based on measurements. To accomplish an adaptive cooperative communication, a realistic density analysis and beacon-enabled communication were offered. Throughput and loss of communication were both increased by the strategy [20].

Meng-Shiuan Pan et al. [31] has done research on the creation of cover sets for sensor networks and has developed tree-adaptive communication. The event slot-based communication that is offered to set up the communication slots is what is meant by the term "job." To accomplish frequent and event-supported communication, design tree formulation and design time observation were offered. To enhance communication dependability, improvements in operating and design times were offered.

Shazly et al. [26] has developed a node-uncertainty analysis piece of work to enhance the target network coverage in real time. The probabilistic estimate has been defined by the author under various limitations. To enhance the node connection, a grid-specific coverage analysis is provided here. This computational solution corrects the deployment and placement issues. To obtain the optimal coverage solution, the coverage-level and block-level target mapping are supplied. To enhance the interval-specific communication, connection processing with a target set is defined [22].

Alexandru-Corneliu Olteanu et al. [5] formed the Zigbee network, and carried out device-specific improvements. For the purpose of providing various communications, the investigation was carried out at the node level. To achieve the layered estimate, direct communication, that is channel-specific, is offered. To increase the job effectiveness, layered abstraction with channel communication is offered [23].

Chaturvedi et al. [33] developed a target coverage problem observation, based on trust measures that effectively addresses the fundamental communication challenge. To guarantee the coverage and give an energy-conserving method to deliver an integrated communication in the network, a trust metric is formulated. To monitor the node stage and achieve the target region-based node monitoring, a target cover-based preservation protocol is designed. A communication confidence is provided is here for a defined neighborhood analysis to estimate the trust level. A convenient trust node is identified here to reduce the overhead and the energy consumption in the network [29].

13.3 Genetic and quantum-improved group adaptive communication

A wireless network provides an open environment in which nodes can communicate freely and cooperatively. When the nodes are mobile and are defined under infrastructure restrictions, the communication criticality increases. The criticality can be identified in terms of internal or external network attacks. This particular work is focused on a more critical network form called WPAN (Wireless Personal Network). This network is formed using smart sensor devices with mobility. The infrastructure devices are also defined to provide an effective network communication. The random mobility within a network is defined along with a smaller coverage. The restricted network features increase the network criticality. There is the requirement of some encoded communication method so that the secure communication will be drawn for the network. The dynamic nature of the network results in a communication loss. If the node is not within the zone or if some attack occurs, communication loss occurs. The infrastructure-driven communication defined in an earlier work is discussed in this section. Data is encoded here using the fixed hash key algorithm. The fixed key-based communication cannot always ensure reliable data delivery.

13.3.1 Significance of work

The work has used the genetic adaptive quantum cryptography to improve the communication reliability. The significance of the work is given here under.
- The dynamic constraint analysis approach is effective to the environment and will not change with network configuration.
- The genetic approach identifies the most effective communication pairs so that the communication reliability is improved.

13.3.2 Model to optimize network communication

The introduced work here is characterized as a coordinated work model in which the correspondence network is framed, and later on applied to the encoded correspondence over it, utilizing quantum cryptography. The work likewise coordinated the hereditary, demonstrating the creation of more versatile correspondence coordinates so dependable that the correspondence will be drawn over the organization. The comparative work stages with this given work are displayed in Figure 13.2.

Step 1: Network generation
To implement the work model, the first requirement is to generate the network with random placement of nodes. The nodes are characterized here with the specification of

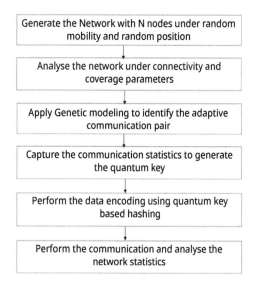

Figure 13.2: Work model.

random position, mobility, and fixed coverage range. Base stations are defined to provide controlled communication.

Step 2: Node-level analysis
Once the network is formed, the requirement is to observe the network at the node level. The coverage, distance, and connectivity level analysis are applied to identify the controller node. The maximum connectivity within the region is the main criterion along with the mobility map. The centralized node is selected to achieve the maximum communication and connectivity.

Step 3: Genetic modeling
After obtaining the parameter-level statistics, the next requirement here is to identify the main controller node using genetic modeling. Genetic is an evolutionary process that accepts the connectivity and coverage statistics of the network as the initial population. Later on, pairs are identified to communicate. Each node works as the source, and the controller node is considered as the receiver for that group.

Step 4: Quantum key-based encoded communication
Once the node pairs are obtained, the final work defined here is to carry out the communication. To securely communicate, node-level characterization is obtained and the quantum key is formed relatively. Finally, this quantum key is applied to the hashing algorithm to encode the data.

The work is defined here based on parametric analysis. The parameters considered in this work are
1. Velocity
2. Connectivity analysis
3. Load

The aspects covered in this work are
– Group generation
– Group leader selection

13.3.3 Group generation

Due to the increased mobility of the nodes in the specified network, base station tracking of these nodes is challenging and adds to the overall burden. Taking this issue into account, the group-driven quantum encoding model presented in this study dynamically divides the network into groups. A geographical area with density observation serves as the basis for the groupings. A group of nodes are those that are located in the same region. Here, group selection is described in terms of the load and coverage restrictions. It indicates that the group size is flexible, so that the overall burden is not raised. Density limit is used to regulate the load situation as well.

13.3.4 Group leader selection

After the groups have been split up, the next task is to choose a leader who can keep track of the group nodes and will assume responsibility for the group nodes. To find the leader, a parameter-specific estimation is done to each zone node. The primary factors for selecting a group leader are coverage, connection, and average distance. The leader is the node with the highest connection and the shortest average distance.

13.3.5 Genetics-based key pair selection

By using some efficient integrated processes on the initial and the existing population, genetics is an evolutionary process model that works on the biological process stages to develop new population. The specification of the fitness function results in a regulated definition of the data-driven generations. In order to develop useful and practicable data members, prospective data analysis is used to apply the fitness criteria to this input data. The evolutionary method used in this study accepted node pairs as potential connections and determined the most economical network connectivity. The goal is to increase the dependability of communication. After the initial population is specified, a number of iterative procedures are used to produce the next level population and to offer the efficient choice of efficient key pairs. For the generation of the ultimate solution, the next level generation and the definition of the goal function are defined. An effective ranking map under load, coverage, and failure characteristics is used in this study. To produce the following potential effective value, the population is processed using the crossover and mutation vectors. The procedure is repeated until the ultimate optimum result cannot be found.

13.3.6 Initial population

To process the genetic algorithm, the first stage is to generate or define the population in an organized form. This organized data form is defined with a specification of the number of possible connectivities for each smart node. In this work, the effective key pair identification is defined by the genetic process.

13.3.7 Fitness function

The fitness function is defined as the control method to select the feasible solution as well as to achieve the optimized results. In this work, an optimization function is defined based on the distance and cost-based analysis. The work is defined here to improve the connectivity and reliability over the network.

13.3.8 Crossover function

The crossover function is applied on the generated parent values to identify a new child. The crossover operation is applied for this generation of child element. The child generation is distance-based in this work. This DPX crossover has provided the optimized result with minimum error.

13.3.9 Mutation function

The mutation function is defined to converge the population, relative to the defined objective function. For this, the random or the selective change in the new child can be performed. In this work, random mutation function is applied.

13.3.10 Application area

The application areas associated to the work are listed here under.

- In vehicular network, the vehicle communication control is defined within the coverage of RSU (Road side units). The RSU controller adaptive dynamic switching can be handled to provide an effective solution to hand off for different networks, including Wi-Fi and WiMAX.

13.4 Algorithm

This section explains the algorithm used for Genetic and Quantum encoding in WPAN. Table 13.1 explains the working of algorithm.

13.5 Conclusion

In this chapter, we discussed a genetic-improved quantum cryptography model to optimize the network communication, and we studied scenario in which the network with random placement of nodes were created. Blue nodes are smart sensor nodes defined under the mobility vector. The nodes are able to perform cooperative communication even when the network is defined with integrated group and area controllers. Red circles represent the group leader. The work is defined here specifically for grouped communication with mobility. Once the group is formed, effective communication pairs are identified by the genetic approach. From these pairs, key characteristics are taken as used as the quantum key. Finally, by using these quantum keys, hash-based encoded communication is performed. The work is implemented here on a mobile WPAN network for a random network scenario. Results shows that the model has improved the communication and improved the network life.

Table 13.1: Algorithm for genetic and quantum encoding In WPAN.

Communication(SmartNodes)
/*SmartNodes is the array of n SmartDevices, with specification of node-level features, including positional and energy constraints*/
    {
       1. Set Decision Constraints for Group control including GroupLoad, GroupLimit, EnergyLimit and CoverageRange
       2. For round = 1 to CommRounds [Define the communication for Fix number of Communication Rounds]
       {
       3. For I = 1 to SmartNodes.Length
       [For eaGL round, the sensing nodes are analyzed under different vectors for Group formation]
       {
       5. Cnodes = GetCoverageNodes(SmartNodes(i),CoverageRange)
       6. if(Any(Cnodes)<>Cleader)
       [GLeck no other Group present in the range]
       7if (Cnodes.Length>LoadLimit)
       [GLeck for the Group leader load]
       {
       8. if (GL.Length>GroupLimit)
       {
       Print "Max Groups are formed"
       }
       9. else
       [The Group Formation is possible]
       {
       10. GL.Add(SenNode(i))
       }
       }
       11. [EligibleNodes GLs] = Genetic(SmartNodes,GL)
       [Apply the Genetic Modeling on Smart Nodes for generating effective node pairs]
       12. For I = 1 to SmartNodes.Length
       [Process the Nodes]
       {
       13. For j = 1 to GL.Length
       [Process the Group leaders]
       {
       14. key = GenerateQuantumKey(GL(j),SmartNodes(i))
       [Generate the key based on the smart node and the leader specific features]
       15. Edata = HashEncode(data,key,Smartnodes(i),GL(j))
       [Generate the Quantum Encoded Hash Encoding on source for secure transmission]
       16. data = HashDecode(Edata,key,Smartnodes(i),GL(j))
       [Apply the quantum key constraints at leader end for decoding]
       17. if (Coverage(SmartNodes(i),GL(j))>Range)

Table 13.1 (continued)

```
    [Check for Failure]
    {
18. CommFailure = CommFailure+1
    [Increase the number of communication failures]
    }
19. Else
    [Identify the valid communication]
    {
20. Comm = Comm+1
    [Apply Packet Communication ]
    }
}
}
```

References

[1] Dahane, N. E. B., & Loukil, A. (2015). Homogenous and Secure Weighted Clustering Algorithm for Mobile Wireless Sensor Networks. In: Control, Engineering & Information Technology (CEIT), 2015 3rd International Conference on (pp. 1–6).Tlemcen.

[2] Porzio. (2014). Quantum Cryptography: Approaching Communication Security from a Quantum Perspective. In: Photonics Technologies, 2014 Fotonica AEIT Italian Conference on (pp. 1–4). Naples.

[3] Shrivastava, & Singh, M. (2012). A Security Enhancement Approach in Quantum Cryptography. In: Computers and Devices for Communication (CODEC), 2012 5th International Conference on (pp. 1–4). Kolkata.

[4] Dahlstrom, A. (2013). Performance Analysis of Routing Protocols in Zigbee Non- Beacon Enabled WSNs. In: Internet of Things: RFIDs, WSNs and beyond. 978-1-4673-3133-3/13 ©. IEEE.

[5] Olteanu, A.-C. (2013). Enabling mobile devices for home automation using ZigBee. In: 2013 19th International Conference on Control Systems and Computer Science. 978-0-7695-4980-4/13 ©. IEEE.

[6] Diop, D. D., & Thiare, O. (2014). A weight-based greedy algorithm for target coverage problem in wireless sensor networks. In: Computer, Communications, and Control Technology (I4CT), 2014 International Conference on (pp. 120–125). Langkawi.

[7] Beniwal, S., Saini, U., Garg, P., & Joon, R. K. (2021). Improving performance during camera surveillance by integration of edge detection in IoT system. *International Journal of E-Health and Medical Communications (IJEHMC)*, *12*(5), 84–96.

[8] Kim, M., Kim, Y. H., Kang, I. S., W. Lee, K., & Han, Y. H. (2012). A scheduling algorithm for connected target coverage under probabilistic coverage model. In: The International Conference on Information Network 2012 (pp. 86–91. Bali.

[9] Chaudhary, A., & Garg, P. (2014). Detecting and diagnosing a disease by patient monitoring system. *International Journal of Mechanical Engineering and Information Technology*, *2*(6), 493–499.

[10] Chauhan, S., Singh, M., & Garg, P. (2021). Rapid forecasting of pandemic outbreak using machine learning. *Enabling Healthcare 4.0 For Pandemics: A Roadmap Using AI, Machine Learning, IoT and Cognitive Technologies*, 59–73.

[11] Zorbas, D. G., & Douligeris, C. (2009). Connected Partial Target Coverage and Network Lifetime in Wireless Sensor Networks. In: 2009 2nd IFIP Wireless Days (WD) (pp. 1–5). Paris.

[12] Dixit, A., Garg, P., Sethi, P., & Singh, Y. (2020). TVCCCS: Television Viewer's Channel Cost Calculation System On Per Second Usage. In: IOP Conference Series: Materials Science and Engineering (Vol. 804, No. 1, pp. 012046). IOP Publishing.

[13] Garg, P., Dixit, A., & Sethi, P. (2021). Performance comparison of fresh and spray & wait protocol through one simulator. *IT in Industry, 9*(2).

[14] Garg, P., Dixit, A., & Sethi, P. (2021). Opportunistic networks: Protocols, applications & simulation trends. In: Proceedings of the International Conference on Innovative Computing & Communication (ICICC).

[15] Garg, P., Dixit, A., Sethi, P., & Pinheiro, P. R. (2020). Impact of node density on the qos parameters of routing protocols in opportunistic networks for smart spaces. *Mobile Information Systems, 2020*.

[16] Garg, P., Pranav, S., & Prerna, A. (2021). Green Internet of Things (G-iot): A Solution for Sustainable Technological Development. In: Green Internet of Things for Smart Cities (pp. 23–46). CRC Press.

[17] Gupta, A., Garg, P., & Sonal, Y. S. (2020). Edge detection based 3D biometric system for security of web-based payment and task management application. *International Journal of Grid and Distributed Computing, 13*(1), 2064–2076.

[18] Gupta, M., Garg, P., & Agarwal, P. (2021). Ant Colony Optimization Technique in Soft Computational Data Research for NP-Hard Problems. In: Artificial Intelligence for a Sustainable Industry 4.0 (pp. 197–211). Springer, Cham.

[19] Gupta, M., Garg, P., Gupta, S., & Joon, R. (2020). A novel approach for malicious node detection in cluster-head gateway switching routing in mobile ad hoc networks. *International Journal of Future Generation Communication and Networking, 13*(4), 99–111.

[20] Gupta, S., & Garg, P. (2021). An insight review on multimedia forensics technology. *Cyber Crime and Forensic Computing: Modern Principles, Practices, and Algorithms, 11*, 27.

[21] Zhang, H., Wang, H., & Feng, H. (2009). A Distributed Optimum Algorithm for Target Coverage in Wireless Sensor Networks. In: Information Processing, 2009. APCIP 2009. Asia-Pacific Conference on (pp. 144–147). Shenzhen.

[22] Bencheikh, K., Jankovic, A., Symul, T., & Levenson, J. A. (2001). Quantum cryptography with continuous variables. In: Quantum Electronics and Laser Science Conference, 2001. QELS '01. Technical Digest. Summaries of Papers Presented at the (pp. 239–240). Baltimore, MD, USA.

[23] Khanna, A., Rani, P., Garg, P., Singh, P. K., & Khamparia, A. (2021). An enhanced crow search inspired feature selection technique for intrusion detection based wireless network system. *Wireless Personal Communications*, 1–18.

[24] Zhou, L. A Simulation Platform for ZigBee-UMTS Hybrid Networks. In: IEEE Communications Letters 1089-7798/13@ 2013. IEEE.

[25] Nirmala, M. B., & Manjunath, A. S. (2010). Secure program update using broadcast encryption for clustered wireless sensor networks. In: Wireless Communication and Sensor Networks (WCSN) 2010 Sixth International Conference on (pp. 1–6). Allahabad.

[26] Shazly, M. H., Elmallah, E. S., & Harms, J. (2013). Location Uncertainty and Target Coverage in Wireless Sensor Networks Deployment. In: 2013 IEEE International Conference on Distributed Computing in Sensor Systems (pp. 20–27). Cambridge, MA.

[27] Niemiec, M., & Pach, A. R. (2013). Management of security in quantum cryptography. *IEEE Communications Magazine, 51*(8), 36–41.

[28] Sharbaf, M. S. (2009). Quantum Cryptography: A New Generation of Information Technology Security System. In: Information Technology: New Generations, 2009. ITNG '09. Sixth International Conference on (pp. 1644–1648). Las Vegas, NV.

[29] Sharbaf, M. S. (2011). Quantum Cryptography: An Emerging Technology in Network Security. In: Technologies for Homeland Security (HST), 2011 IEEE International Conference On (pp. 13–19). Waltham, MA.

[30] Malik, K., Raheja, N., & Garg, P. (2011). Enhanced FP-growth algorithm. *International Journal of Computational Engineering and Management, 12,* 54–56.

[31] Pan, M.-S. (2013). Convergecast in ZigBee Tree-Based Wireless Sensor Networks. In: 2013 IEEE Wireless Communications and Networking Conference (WCNC): Networks. 978-1-4673-5939-9/13 ©. IEEE.

[32] Ali Jamali, M., Bakhshivand, N., Easmaeilpour, M., & Salami, D. (2010). An Energy-efficient Algorithm for Connected Target Coverage Problem in Wireless Sensor Networks. In: Computer Science and Information Technology (ICCSIT), 2010 3rd IEEE International Conference on (pp. 249–254). Chengdu.

[33] Chaturvedi, P., & Daniel, A. K. (2015). An Energy Efficient Node Scheduling Protocol for Target Coverage in Wireless Sensor Networks. In: Communication Systems and Network Technologies (CSNT), 2015 Fifth International Conference On (pp. 138–142). Gwalior.

[34] Goel, R., Garuba, M., & Girma, A. (2007). Research Directions in Quantum Cryptography. In: Information Technology, 2007. ITNG '07. Fourth International Conference on (pp. 779–784). Las Vegas, NV.

[35] Vignesh, R. S., Sudharssun, S., & Kumar, K. J. J. (2009). Limitations of Quantum & the Versatility of Classical Cryptography: A Comparative Study. In: Environmental and Computer Science, 2009. ICECS '09. Second International Conference on (pp. 333–337). Dubai.

[36] Mandal, S. (2013). et al. Multi-photon Implementation of Three-stage Quantum Cryptography Protocol. In: Information Networking (ICOIN), 2013 International Conference On (pp. 6–11). Bangkok.

[37] Kartalopoulos, S. V. (2005). Identifying vulnerabilities of quantum cryptography in secure optical data transport. In: Military Communications Conference, 2005. MILCOM 2005 (pp. 2788–2796). IEEE, Atlantic City, NJ.

[38] Kurochkin, V., & Kurochkin, Y. (2010). Quantum Cryptography Security Improvement with Additional States. In: Micro/Nanotechnologies and Electron Devices (EDM), 2010 International Conference and Seminar On (pp. 231–233). Novosibirsk.

[39] Kurochkin, V. L., & Neizvestny, I. G. (2009). Quantum Cryptography. In: Micro/Nanotechnologies and Electron Devices, 2009. EDM 2009. International Conference and Seminar on (pp. 166–170). Novosibirsk.

[40] Teja, V., Banerjee, P., Sharma, N. N., & Mittal, R. K. (2007). Quantum Cryptography: State-of-art, Challenges and Future Perspectives. In: Nanotechnology, 2007. IEEE-NANO 2007. 7th IEEE Conference on (pp. 1296–1301). Hong Kong.

Swati Gupta*, Puneet Garg

14 Code-based post-quantum cryptographic technique: digital signature

Abstract: In order to prevent engineers, even those hazardous entertainers who have quantum enrolment of their own, from accessing information, quantum cryptography adds quantum mechanics standards to information encryption and transmission. The more widespread application of quantum cryptography similarly streamlines the development and performance of numerous cryptographic operations, leveraging the intriguing capabilities and power of quantum computers. Possibly, this type of PC can aid in the development of new, more sophisticated, and more effective encryption structures that are unable to comprehend using the current, conventional recruitment and communication methods. Quantum computer systems may cap in a position to interrupt all presently deployed public-key cryptographic algorithms. As those algorithms are critical to run a stable IT infrastructure, we urgently want to transition to the Malware capable of disrupting any active public-key cryptography algorithms that may face assaults from attackers to enter into large-scale quantum computer systems. Quantum computing is an upcoming era that targets to take advantage of quantum phenomena, consisting of superposition and entanglement, to carry out certain computational duties a lot extra effectively than currently feasible with conventional computing. Unlike conventional computer systems, quantum computer systems may be employed exponentially in many states at any moment, unlike classical computers, which can be used in some well-defined state at any point in time. The challenges of quantum computing has reinvigorated study efforts in all the areas of post-quantum cryptography, especially closer to making cryptosystems sensible by optimizing algorithms, featuring concrete parameter sets, and writing green and side-channel steady implementations.

14.1 Introduction

Quantum cryptography is a framework that is totally secure against being compromised without the information on the message sender or the recipient. That is, it is difficult to duplicate or view information encoded in a quantum state without cautioning the sender or the recipient. Quantum cryptography ought to likewise stay protected against those utilizing quantum registering.

*Corresponding author: Swati Gupta, Vaish College of Engineering, Rohtak, Haryana, India, e-mail: swati.mangla.555@gmail.com
Puneet Garg, ABES Engineering College, Ghaziabad, Uttar Pradesh, India, e-mail: puneetgarg.er@gmail.com

https://doi.org/10.1515/9783110798159-014

Quantum cryptography transmits data across fiber optic wire using individual light particles or photons. Photons deal with two issues. The system's security is dependent on quantum mechanics. These safe properties incorporate the accompanying:

1. Particles can exist in more than one spot or state.
2. A quantum property cannot be seen without changing or upsetting it.
3. Whole particles cannot be duplicated.

These properties make it difficult to gauge the quantum condition of any framework without upsetting that framework.

Photons are utilized for quantum cryptography since they offer every one of the essential characteristics required: their way of behaving is surely known, and they are data transporters in optical fiber links. One of the most incredibly known instances of quantum cryptography right now is quantum key circulation (QKD), which gives a solid strategy to trade keys.

Example: Assume there is a snoop present, named Eve. Eve endeavors to tune in and has similar devices as Bounce. However, Bounce enjoys the benefit of addressing Alice to affirm which polarizer type was utilized for every photon; Eve does not. Eve winds up delivering the last key erroneously. Alice and Weave would likewise be aware of the off chance that Eve was listening in on them. Eve noticing the progression of photons would then change the photon places that Alice and Sway hope to see [4] (shown in Figure 14.1).

QUANTUM CRYPTOGRAPHY MODEL : THE CASE OF ALICE, EVE AND BOB

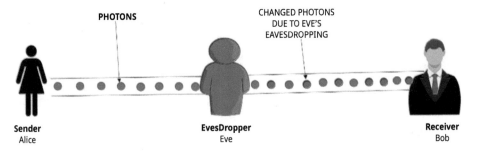

Figure 14.1: Quantum cryptograph [4].

A couple of huge applications where encryption systems merge with quantum figuring are critical for a surefire component of an organization's security. Two popular, yet obviously remarkable cryptographic applications that are work in progress using quantum properties include:

Quantum-safe cryptography: The advancement of cryptographic operations, frequently referred to as "post-quantum cryptography," which are resistant to attack by a quantum computer and are used to transmit quantum-safe statements [7].

Quantum key conveyance: The technique involves using quantum correspondence to distribute a typical key between two trusted parties so that an eavesdropper cannot learn anything about that message [8].

Need: A quick improvement in the ability of quantum laptops to overcome solid computer programming limits so as to tackle a broad assortment of fundamental issues that customary computers basically cannot. Sadly, they are not yet suitable for taking on new risks at phenomenal scale and speed. For instance, we would like quantum computers do quantum calculations like the Shor's estimate, which can resolve complicated mathematical situations in minutes that currently take conventional laptops months or even more to resolve. It is anticipated that within the next 5–10 years, structures will be ready for cracking common math-based cryptographic computations [2].

Engineers need to use this method to quickly address the attacks against the current encryption standards that are in use. Particularly fast numerical conditions are the RSA and ECC encryption calculations, which are essential to symmetric key and public-key cryptography, respectively, in laptops. This compromises most present day network security, correspondence, and high-level characters.

Ensuring PKI courses of action can give adequate assurance to these systems and data against quantum-based attacks. This infers that new quantum-safe estimations ought to be made and that associations ought to move to new, quantum-safe announcements. The endeavor of moving to new electronic supports requires a particularly organized work to update PKI systems and the applications using these statements [3].

Advancement of and migration to quantum-secure validations need to manifest hastily and may slightly cling on till RSA and ECC calculations are broken. Today engineers are able to use uncertain data that has been encoded using modern tests and decode it later on when the quantum workstations are available. Associations want to address this risk today in order to ensure that the data, applications, and IT infrastructure of their associations are covered going forward, indefinitely, for quite some time.

How does quantum-safe cryptography work?

Quantum cryptography works by handling absolutely different issues. For example, cross segment cryptography is based on a numerical procedure rather than a logarithmic one, conveying a quantum PC's remarkable success at breaking quantum encryption structures. This type of cryptography is critical for every dated PC and quantum one to deal with, making it a nice contender to as the rationale for a post-quantum cryptographic calculation [1].

14.2 Types of certificates

There are four types of certificates, as show in Table 14.1

Table 14.1: Type of certificates.

Certificate type	Encryption algorithms	Description	Purpose
Traditional	RSA or ECC	Traditional non-quantum secure certificates	Traditional PKI and to identify systems
Quantum secure	New quantum-secure algorithms	Quantum secure certificates	Implementing Quantum-Secure PKI and to identity systems
Hybrid	Traditional and quantum-secure algorithms	Contain both traditional and quantum-secure keys	Used for migration to Quantum-secure algorithms that systems can use either traditional or quantum-secure keys.
Composite	Multiple traditional and quantum-secure algorithms	Contains multiple traditional and quantum-secure keys	Used in systems requiring the highest level of security and protection, while recognizing the provenance of some encryption algorithms that are still unknown

14.2.1 Traditional certificates

Traditional PKI statements are currently the greatest level of affirmation for encryption of cutting edge characters. These confirmations are suggested as "regular" because they utilize the existing ECC or RSA encryption estimations. The vast majority of PKI structures will continue to use regular PKI statements for a surprisingly long time to come. They give effective affirmation for handling existing attacks, but in the future, they will be made vintage due to the use of quantum PCs and attacks on ECC and RSA encryption [6].

There are three kinds of cutting edge confirmations that are significant while looking for quantum-safe decisions. Each type is at this point adherent to X.509 progressed confirmation rules that are essential to public key cryptography. These types shift especially according to their inspiration and the encryption estimation used to make the declaration.

14.2.2 Quantum-secure certificates

Quantum-secure endorsements are X.509 verifications that use quantum-secure encryption estimations. While NIST is an existing approach but as per the latest encrypting computations, Quantum-secure Certificates are better approach as it may identify as well as compute numerous metrics as per the current requirements [8].

14.2.3 Types of quantum-secure certificates

There are three kinds of modernized statements that are appropriate while looking for quantum-safe decisions. Each type is at this point adherent to X.509 modernized statement rules that are integral to public key cryptography. These types change indisputably as shown by their inspiration and the encryption estimation used for adherence [7].

14.2.4 Hybrid certificates

Creamer confirmations are cross-stamped; they contain a regular (RSA or ECC) key and an imprint, and a quantum-secure key and an imprint. Blend confirmations interact in a migration manner for structures with exceptional components that cannot be all-round upgraded or displaced at the same time. This kind engages in a slow improvement of structures, but subsequently all systems that use the ECC or RSA encryption must proceed to the new quantum-secure cryptographic estimations [23].

14.2.5 Composite certificate

Composite testaments resemble cross variety supports in that they contain different keys and checks, yet are different in that they utilize a mix of existing and quantum-safe encryption calculations. Composite backings are in every way that really matter, similar to having a particular entry with various locks [29]. The target of composite keys is to address the concern that any single encryption estimation, be it in the long run or any time in the future, may be broken using quantum workstations [9]. Enduring that one of the encryption appraisals shows to have an exploitable shortcoming, Figure 14.2 shows the feature of various certificates. While NIST is working to vet and pick quantum-safe cryptographic calculations, these new ones have not yet been thoroughly established as secure. It is conceivable that security specialists or programmers could find weaknesses in something like one of these proposed solutions eventually. Regardless, making different encryption keys and a short time later, solidifying them to give a composite statement requires noteworthy computational power.

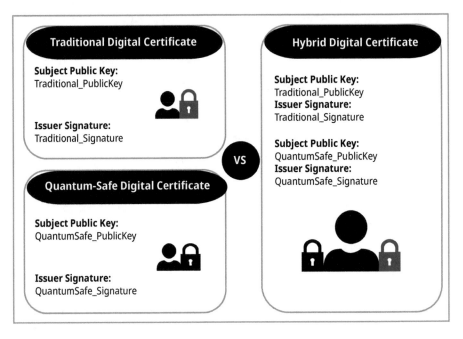

Figure 14.2: Features of various certificates.

Figure 14.3: Relocating quantum safe cryptography.

How does a cross breed TLS endorsement vary from a customary one?

All TLS authentications contain computerized marks, keys, and calculations. The distinction between a customary TLS endorsement and a Sectigo half-breed TLS declaration is that notwithstanding those conventional parts:

1. The half and half declaration would contain extra X.509 endorsement fields for quantum-safe keys and marks [26].
2. The cross breed endorsement would incorporate the encoding for a quantum-safe calculation [27].

How a cross breed TLS testament functions in validation

Tim Callan expects utilizing crossover advanced authentications for bilingual applications. Fundamentally, in the event that you communicate in English and French, and the individual you are speaking with does too, then, at that point, you could decide to utilize either of the languages [28]. Moreover, in the event that you are bilingual and you are talking with somebody who just communicates in English or just communicates in French, you can, in any case, also speak with them effectively.

Grau depicts it with the relationship of changing the lock on the front entryway of a motel that has numerous occupants. If by some stroke of good luck, one of those occupants is there to get the new more grounded and safer key (quantum safe crypto calculation), they would have the option to utilize the front entryway [13]. However, in the event that others are not there when the lock is traded out, then they would, in any case, need to utilize the secondary passage and the less-safe key.

Stage 1: Action to quantum-safe PKI establishment – The underlying move toward migrating is to overhaul an affiliation's PKI structure, including the statement authority (CA) to help quantum-safe estimations. Rather than endeavoring to upgrade inside PKI structures without assistance from any other person, IT security gatherings could zero in on a business CA, for instance, Sectigo, which can offer business help for giving and managing statements. At this point, when an affiliation refreshes its ongoing CA, or picks another CA, the underwriting authority ought to give another quantum-safe root and moderate confirmation [22].

Stage 2: Update server cryptographic computations – Next, cryptographic libraries used by server applications ought to be invigorated to help both the new cryptographic estimations and the new quantum-safe announcement plans. Accepting cream confirmations are used; server applications ought to see and process both the regular RSA or ECC statements as well as the hybrid supports containing quantum-safe cryptographic keys [21]. This requires the server applications to perceive the two different validation types and suitably use the two types with the right algorithmic method for the connected underwriting type.

Stage 3: Update client cryptographic computations – Gatherings then, can revive client applications. Realize that a client application could talk with different server applications, including external circumstances, and no less than one of those server applications could not have been refreshed as of now. For this present circumstance, creamer confirmations license the client to work with servers supporting the standard RSA and ECC estimations, while using quantum-safe computations with servers that help these fresher computations [16].

Stage 4: All designs should have roots that are quantum-safe. Every PKI-using framework has a recognized root store. The backings for the root and the intermediate CAs that provide authorizations inside the PKI framework are contained in this root store [18]. These root stores should be restored in order to incorporate the updated root and the midway declarations after the client and server frameworks have been strengthened to support quantum-safe assessments.

Stage 5: Issue and present quantum-safe certs for all contraptions/applications – After IT bunches have revived an association's all's structures to help quantum-safe cryptography. At the point when gotten done, each contraption is defended by the new announcements [20].

Stage 6: Condemn standard encryption evaluations and reject RSA/ECC-based approvals – The final stage of development involves blocking the common RSA and ECC encryption calculations. This should be gradually feasible on applications and designs when they are transferred to the new evaluations. The root RSA and ECC articulations should be refused after all designs have been relocated to ensure that no frameworks are using them [19].

Quantum figuring is ready to disturb the mechanical world as far as we see. Also, in spite of the fact that quantum processing – and the benefits it offers – is all still sensibly years away, organizations and associations need to set themselves up for its unavoidable disadvantage: broken cryptosystems.

Quantum PCs will break our current uneven cryptosystem – something that cybercriminals will be prepared for and anxious to exploit. For this reason it will be important to relocate your current IT and cryptosystems to their quantum-safe or quantum-safe counterparts [11].

Be that as it may, obviously, moving up to post-quantum cryptographic (PQC) frameworks and foundation takes time and assets. Thus, one of the ways of future proofing your network through this interaction is by using half and half computerized testaments, for example, a crossover TLS declaration.

14.3 Quantum cryptography vs. post-quantum cryptography

There are innumerable terminologies used to describe quantum cryptography, including quantum encryption, post-quantum encryption, quantum-safe encryption, quantum-confirmation encryption, quantum-safe encryption, quantum security, and quantum correspondences to portray comparative, yet altogether different ways to deal with safeguarding data and guaranteeing secure interchanges in the period of quantum figuring [17].

14.3.1 Quantum cryptography

Quantum security, often known as quantum encryption or quantum cryptography, is the application of quantum physics to secure and detect pariahs who are tuning in to correspondences. Quantum encryption makes use of fundamental principles of physics, such as the observer effect, which expresses the perception that an atom's region is infinite, without affecting the molecule itself [14].

14.3.2 Quantum key dispersion

The most well-known implementation of quantum cryptography in use today is known as quantum key scattering, or QKD. Associations can take advantage of photons' no-change and no-cloning properties to transmit data instead of bits, which means that a secret key moved in this way between two social gatherings cannot be duplicated or discreetly hampered. In this system, the photon delivering the key changes state and will thereafter crash and burn, alerting the two social events that their correspondence is not safe. This is because it anticipates that an untouchable spying on their correspondences tries to learn about the key being disseminated out [12].

While conventional public key encryption can be bypassed or cracked in a variety of ways, QKD gives businesses and government agencies the ability to transmit confidential, strategic information.

14.3.3 Post-quantum cryptography

A term that is similarly confusing is post-quantum cryptography. While post-quantum cryptography (sometimes referred to as quantum-proof, quantum-safe, or quantum-safe) proposes cryptographic computations (typically, open key estimations) that are

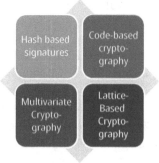

Figure 14.4: Post-quantum-based cryptography.

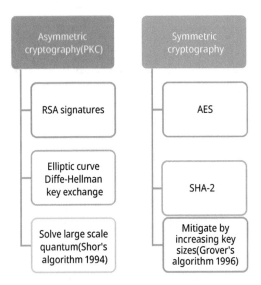

Figure 14.5: Post-quantum SSH.

accepted to be secure against an attack by a quantum PC, quantum cryptography depicts using quantum peculiarities as the focal point of a security method [32]. By reinvigorating current mathematically based estimates and principles, post-quantum cryptography is related to preparing for the era of quantum figuring.

14.4 Applications of quantum cryptography

Quantum encryption as of now safeguards each sensitive public record within the side the public place, and economic records within the side of the non-public place. Its protection is confirmed. The functions of quantum cryptography are here. Beginning around 2007, Switzerland has been using quantum cryptography to guide online voting, shaping the choice of locals and authorities. In Geneva, votes are blended at a vital vote-counting station. The results are then sent to a far-off facts storage across a given optical fiber line. The majority rule results are obtained via quantum cryptography, and the most helpless aspect of the data exchange occurs when the vote moves uninterrupted from the counting station to the crucial storage location.

This improvement will soon unfold everywhere on the planet as numerous international locations face the phantom of bogus races. B [25]: Secure correspondences with space-secure correspondences with the help of satellites and area explorers is a growing concern, and an affiliation referred to as Essence Labs is dealing with NASA to make sure that there are stable communication exchanges between the Earth and satellites as well as with area voyagers. The goal of the assignment is to carry out a conference that guarantees the safety of correspondences, irrespective of the innovation or information for which an enemy approaches. Additionally, it has a directive to gather each fact "very still" and in the proper place. This may eventually provide protection to explorers in space and, ideally, stop the need for supplies to change in the future beyond small speed increments [30]. C: A more incredible power network: It has been predicted that the American electricity community is one of the maximum vulnerable for a virtual attack [14].

Some prominent U.S. executives mention that utilities are under "steady" attack from virtual foes. A little encryption machine assists the experts with conveying very well stable messages, making use of public record groups to manipulate clever electricity networks. Shrewd lattices are essential for adjusting the marketplace hobby for productivity. Also, with valid protection measures set up, they may be essentially more secure than traditional matrices. D [24]. Quantum Web – The gift that internet is exceedingly brief, but in comparison to quantum-scrambled transmissions, its security is paltry. The internet could magically start up again thanks to quantum encryption. However, in the future, it may be possible for us to seamlessly switch between "standard" and "quantum encoded" internet, allowing our most important information to be sent through in a very secure manner [14]. This might accomplish the correct of an on the identical time short and stable internet.

14.5 Conclusion

In the case of captured photons, which are through all debts safeguarded, there may be a problem with the cost, but there is also a problem with keeping them sufficiently captured to cope with the issues of this gift reality. Another issue is that the disturbance seems to be most noticeable at distances of more than 50 kilometers or more, at which point error prices also sharply increase. This leaves the channel totally powerless for busybodies, and makes the channel nearly difficult to transmit data. Be that it may, in future, it is far possible for quantum keys to be traded via the air [33]. Little telescopes will probably adjust to pick out the signs. By combining such schemes, additional constructions such as identity-based, threshold rings, or blind signatures can be obtained. However these schemes also inherit the disadvantages of the underlying protocols.

A few estimations even advocate that photons may be outstanding through a satellite, which lets in correspondence to any place on the planet. Since QKD is the primary application of quantum mechanics' foundational theories, it proves the need of critical technological research [31]. The assumption that Quantum Key Conveyance will be employed by and through its protection at any point must be proven, and ultimately, a thorough analysis of the quantum mechanics principles upon which its security is founded is essential.

References

[1]   Ford, J. (1996). "Quantum cryptography tutorial." http://www.cs.dartmouth.edu/~jford/crypto.html.
[2]   "Quantum cryptography." Wikipedia, the free encyclopedia. (17 September 2004). http://en.wikipe dia.org/wiki/Quantum_cryptography.Modified.
[3]   "The BB84 Quantum Coding Scheme", (June 2001). http://www.cki.au.dk/experiment/qrypto/doc/Qu Crypt/bb84coding.html.
[4]   Gisin, N., Ribordy, G., Tittel, W., & Zbinden, H. (2002). Quantum cryptography. *Reviews of Modern Physics, 74,* 146–195.
[6]   Hughes, R. J., et al. (1995). Quantum cryptography. *Contemporary Physics, 36*(3), 149–163.
[7]   Bernstein, D. J., Chou, T., & Schwabe, P. (2013). Mcbits: Fast Constant-time Code- Based Cryptography. In: International Workshop on Cryptographic Hardware and Embedded Systems (pp. 250–272). Springer.
[8]   Phesso, A. & Tillich, J.-P. (2016). An Efficient Attack on a Code-based Signa- Ture Scheme. In: International Workshop on Post-Quantum Cryptography (pp. pages 86–103). Springer.
[9]   Moody, D. & Perlner, R. (2016). Vulnerabilities of "Mceliece in the World of Escher. In: International Workshop on Post-Quantum Cryptography (pp. 104–117). Springer.
[10] Galbraith, S. D., Petit, C., & Silva, J. Signature schemes based on supersingular isogeny problems. Cryptology ePrint Archive, Report 2016/1154, 2016.
[11] Yoo, Y., Azarderakhsh, R., Jalali, A., Jao, D., & Soukharev, V. A post-quantum digital signature scheme based on supersingular isogenies. Cryptol- ogy ePrint Archive, Report 2017/186, 2017. https://eprint.iacr.org/2017/186.
[12] Howe, J., Pöppelmann, T., O'Neill, M., O'Sullivan, E., & Güneysu, T. (2015). Practical lattice-based digital signature schemes. *ACM Transactions on Embedded Computing Systems (TECS), 14*(3), 1–24, ISSN 1539–9087.
[13] Nguyen, P. Q. & Regev, O. (2009). Learning a parallelepiped: Cryptanalysis of ggh and ntru signatures.(report). *Journal of Cryptology, 22*(2), ISSN 0933–2790.
[14] Ducas, L. (2014). Accelerating bliss: The geometry of ternary polynomials. IACR Cryptology ePrint Archive, 2014, 874.
[15] Saarinen, M.-J. O. (2017). Arithmetic coding and blinding countermeasures for lattice signatures. *Journal of Cryptographic Engineering,* 1–14.
[16] Soni, E., Nagpal, A., Garg, P., & Pinheiro, P. R. (2022). Assessment of compressed and decompressed ECG databases for telecardiology applying a convolution neural network. *Electronics, 11*(17), 2708.
[17] Chauhan, S., Singh, M., & Garg, P. (2021). Rapid forecasting of pandemic outbreak using machine learning. *Enabling Healthcare 4.0 For Pandemics: A Roadmap Using AI, Machine Learning, IoT and Cognitive Technologies,* 59–73.
[18] Gupta, S. & Garg, P. (2021). An insight review on multimedia forensics technology. *Cyber Crime and Forensic Computing: Modern Principles, Practices, and Algorithms, 11,* 27.
[19] Shrivastava, P., Agarwal, P., Sharma, K., & Garg, P. (2021). Data leakage detection in Wi-Fi networks. *Cyber Crime and Forensic Computing: Modern Principles, Practices, and Algorithms, 11,* 215.
[20] Pustokhina, I. V., Pustokhin, D. A., Lydia, E. L., Garg, P., Kadian, A., & Shankar, K. (2021). Hyperparameter search based convolution neural network with Bi-LSTM model for intrusion detection system in multimedia big data environment. *Multimedia Tools and Applications,* 1–18.

[21] Khanna, A., Rani, P., Garg, P., Singh, P. K., & Khamparia, A. (2021). An enhanced crow search inspired feature selection technique for intrusion detection based wireless network system. *Wireless Personal Communications*, 1–18.

[22] Meenakshi, P. G. & Shrivastava, P. (2021). Machine learning for mobile malware analysis. *Cyber Crime and Forensic Computing: Modern Principles, Practices, and Algorithms*, *11*, 151.

[23] Garg, P., Pranav, S., & Prerna, A. (2021). Green Internet of Things (G-iot): A Solution for Sustainable Technological Development. In: Green Internet of Things for Smart Cities (pp. 23–46). CRC Press.

[24] Nanwal, J., Garg, P., Sethi, P., & Dixit, A. (2021). Green IoT and Big Data: Succeeding Towards Building Smart Cities. In: Green Internet of Things for Smart Cities (pp. 83–98). CRC Press.

[25] Garg, P., Dixit, A., & Sethi, P. (2021, May). Link Prediction Techniques for Opportunistic Networks using Machine Learning. In: Proceedings of the International Conference on Innovative Computing & Communication (ICICC).

[26] Garg, P., Dixit, A., & Sethi, P. (2021). Opportunistic networks: Protocols, applications & simulation trends. In: Proceedings of the International Conference on Innovative Computing & Communication (ICICC).

[27] Garg, P., Dixit, A., & Sethi, P. (2021). Performance comparison of fresh and spray & wait protocol through one simulator. *IT in Industry*, *9*(2.

[28] Gupta, M., Garg, P., & Agarwal, P. (2021). Ant Colony Optimization Technique in Soft Computational Data Research for NP-Hard Problems. In: Artificial Intelligence for a Sustainable Industry 4.0 (pp. 197–211). Springer, Cham.

[29] Malik, M., Singh, Y., Garg, P., & Gupta, S. (2020). Deep learning in healthcare system. *International Journal of Grid and Distributed Computing*, *13*(2), 469–468.

[30] Gupta, M., Garg, P., Gupta, S., & Joon, R. (2020). a novel approach for malicious node detection in cluster-head gateway switching routing in mobile ad hoc networks. *International Journal of Future Generation Communication and Networking*, *13*(4), 99–111.

[31] Garg, P., Dixit, A., Sethi, P., & Pinheiro, P. R. (2020). Impact of node density on the qos parameters of routing protocols in opportunistic networks for smart spaces. *Mobile Information Systems*, *2020*.

[32] Gupta, A., Garg, P., & Sonal, Y. S. (2020). Edge detection based 3D biometric system for security of web-based payment and task management application. *International Journal of Grid and Distributed Computing*, *13*(1), 2064–2076.

[33] Dixit, A., Garg, P., Sethi, P., & Singh, Y. (2020). TVCCCS: Television viewer's channel cost calculation system on per second usage. In: IOP Conference Series: Materials Science and Engineering (Vol. 804, No. 1, p. 012046). IOP Publishing.

Annapantula Sudhakar*, G. R. S. Murthy, Thirukumaran S.

15 Post-quantum cryptography for the detection of injection attacks in small-scale networks

Abstract: In this chapter, we develop a post-quantum cryptography for the detection of injection attacks in small-scale vehicular ad hoc networks. The model is designed using genetic algorithm-based convolutional neural network to test the efficacy of the network against mitigating the attacks. IoT devices in vehicular networks are easily prone to attacks and hence the research uses the deep learning model to train and classify the attacks. A simulation shows the efficacy of the model in detecting the attacks over various layers of attacks.

15.1 Introduction

The increasing prevalence of Internet of Things (IoT) devices has opened the door to a wide variety of commercial prospects that were previously inconceivable. Unfortunately, producers are unable to guarantee the safety of their products at this time because they are still developing them [1]. Therefore, despite all the benefits, concerns regarding the safety of these devices are a big impediment in the way of enabling this paradigm to have a significant impact on people's lives [2].

Attackers are presented with a wonderful opportunity to carry out distributed denial-of-service attacks as a direct result of the unplanned deployment of a huge number of unsecured and susceptible IoT nodes (also known as DoS and DoS variants) [3]. These devices create issues when it comes to privacy, guaranteeing secure communication and storage, implementing access control, and authenticating users. This is because of the open nature of these devices and the vast acceptance that they enjoy [4].

Between the people who use the devices and the people who develop them, there is still a significant amount of misconception regarding who is responsible for the security gaps that are present in these devices. Changing their passwords regularly and keeping their devices up-to-date with the latest security patches are seen as consumer responsibility by the manufacturer [5]. On the other hand, customers consistently

*Corresponding author: Annapantula Sudhakar,** Department of ECE, GMR Institute of Technology, Rajam, Andhra Pradesh, India, e-mail: sudhakar.a@gmrit.edu.in

G. R. S. Murthy, Department of CSE, GVPCDPGC(A), E & T Program, Rushikonda Campus, Visakhapatnam, Andhra Pradesh, India, e-mail: murthy.grs@gmail.com

Thirukumaran S., Data Science Department, SoS.B2, Jain University, Bangalore, Karnataka, India, e-mail: s.thirukumaran@jainuniversity.ac.in

https://doi.org/10.1515/9783110798159-015

voice their dissatisfaction with the fact that manufacturers do not include adequate safety features in the products they sell. These devices do not have a centralized security system, and they are still operating on the older network infrastructure, which relies on insecure firmware, complicated cryptographic protocols, and weak passwords [6].

In order to support the efficient deployment of these devices and successfully solve the new difficulties that have emerged as a result of the convergence of computing technologies in the future generation, the construction of an architecture that is universally secure is required [7]. It is feasible to arrive at the conclusion that each device within an IoT network should be given equal priority in terms of the level of security that it requires. This is due to the fact that attackers favor breaking into networks by attacking the firmware, and passwords of devices that have a weakly configured configuration [8, 9]. This is the reason why this situation has arisen. Researchers are putting in a lot of effort to design a secure architecture that is capable of withstanding attacks, even in the event that culprits obtain access to the system through another channel.

Establishing reliable cryptographic systems that are able to protect sensitive information as well as private communications is an essential initial step. The standard cryptography methods, on the other hand, take up a disproportionate amount of the available resources while in opetaion, in contrast to new cryptographic methods that only use a small portion of the available resources while executing. Some of the encryption challenges in IoT are also challenges in more traditional security solutions. This is because IoT is a network of interconnected devices [10].

This domain encompasses not only the authentication and authorization of users but also of safeguarding data while it is being transmitted and while it is being stored. The two basic categories of these cryptographic solutions for security are those that are based on a symmetric key and those that are based on an asymmetric key. Symmetric key solutions and asymmetric key solutions are both cryptographic solutions for security. Researchers are looking for a solution that will work for devices connected to IoT, despite the limited resources that are now accessible [11].

A greater quantity of energy is necessary for asymmetric key mechanisms to function properly, despite the fact that these mechanisms have a higher breaking strength. In the past, people have explored ways to reduce the amount of computational work required by cryptographic primitives, such as elliptical curve cryptography (ECC) and advanced encryption systems (AES). These protocols are based on the discrete logarithm (DL) and integer factorization (IF) problems, which serve as their conceptual basis. The amount of difficulty that was used in the formulation of the challenge is directly related to the level of difficulty that was used in the development of the algorithm resistance to various sorts of assaults. The development of algorithmic systems that are not only more effective but also more reliable is the primary emphasis of researchers [12].

In contrast, quantum computers are swiftly approaching the realm of feasibility in this day and age of information, and this trend is expected to continue for the foreseeable future. Quantum computing, like any other growing technology, raises a number of new questions and concerns with regard to safety. Nevertheless, it also has the capability of resolving certain issues that have existed for a considerable amount of time [13].

These machines are able to quickly tackle the tough mathematical problems that are required to crack existing public key infrastructures. This makes it possible for hackers to steal private information. Even though the majority of the information regarding large-scale quantum computers is still unclear, some researchers believe that the present time is an ideal opportunity to begin developing new cryptographic strategies that can provide security in a post-quantum future [14].

They believe this even though the majority of the information regarding large-scale quantum computers is still unclear. There are answers to problems that are believed to be predicated on quantum physics and some related mathematical concerns, which can generate proof that cannot be broken in the world that came after quantum theory. These solutions exist in the world that came after quantum theory. At this point in time, however, it is difficult to say whether or not such strategies will prove to be successful [15].

Therefore, in order to investigate the potential security flaws and risks, it is necessary to become familiar with the underlying cryptographic algorithms that are appropriate for the IoT environment, and it is also necessary to determine how successful they will be in the realm of quantum computers. This is because the IoT is a network that connects everyday objects to the internet. In this body of work, we investigate the ways in which the adoption of insecure encryption methods can put IoT at risk, as well as the ways in which quantum cryptography can protect post-quantum IoT networks from being compromised.

15.2 Related works

The issues that have been raised with regard to the safety of resources, apps, and devices connected to the IoT will be investigated in this study. Cybercriminals frequently direct their attacks toward devices that are connected to an IoT. The exponential rise of devices connected to the Internet of Things is adding another layer of complexity to these issues. It is anticipated that there will be 7.6 billion IoT devices in operation in 2019, and it is very possible that this number will more than quadruple to reach 24.1 billion by the year 2030 [16]. This includes sensors, actuators, and networked devices, in addition to mobile devices that have GPS capabilities and mobile connectivity. Examples of technologies that contribute to the building of hybrid networks include the IoT smart grids, and several other sensor networks.

Because of the constraints caused by elements such as low power, poor capacity, and limited performance, the authors of [17] advocate collaborating between the Internet of Things and cloud computing. This is done in order to circumvent these problems. By combining cloud computing and devices that are connected to the Internet of Things, it is feasible to develop new services that can be of great benefit to users (IoT). The idea that the internet can be thought of as a cloud is explored in greater depth in the article [18]. When traditional approaches are taken, it is not possible to accomplish either low cost or simplicity in respect to Internet of Things without making a sacrifice in regard to at least one of these qualities. Computing on the cloud, on the other hand, offers an alternate solution that could meet the needs of any of these two groups. Cloud computing is an option that gives the Internet of Things with a nearly unlimited pool of computer resources that are easily accessible via the internet. In addition, these resources have a greater level of reliability and may be accessed at a reduced cost.

As in [19], the combination of the cloud and the internet of things has an impact on the level of security that is present. The Internet of Things has given rise to a new set of security issues as a result of its heavy reliance on cloud computing services.

Recent publications have placed a greater emphasis on examining the security problems raised by cloud computing and IoT. The authors in [20] examines this brand new and intriguing set of issues that have come up as a result of the situation that is created. The proliferation of Internet of Things infrastructure has brought to the foreground as significant impediments, the problems of data privacy and data security. The combination of cloud computing with the Internet of Things raises even more issues, despite the fact that there has been a lot of discussion about the difficulties associated with cloud security.

The article [21] provides a summary of the IoT as well as cloud computing, with the primary focus being on the potential dangers that are associated with both of these technological advancements. Mobile cloud computing is the name of the other technology that they connect (MCC). The term mobile cloud computing refers to a computer model in which cloud computing is combined with mobile devices to increase the utility of mobile devices in areas such as processing speed, data storage, battery life, and awareness of its surroundings. This model was given the name mobile cloud computing because it combines cloud computing with mobile devices. The fact that this approach incorporates cloud computing with mobile devices is the reason why it was given the label mobile cloud computing.

The author in [22] claims that because the idea of networking appliances and other devices is still in its infancy, safety considerations have not always been taken into mind during the design process of products. This is due to the fact that the concept of networking is still relatively new. One of the most common problems associated with these goods is the fact that many IoT devices ship with embedded software and operating systems that have not been updated in a significant amount of time and, as a result, do not any longer receive security fixes. In addition, a sizeable percentage of people who buy smart devices do not bother to change the passwords that are set by the manufacturer, and the majority of people who do change the passwords choose passwords that are not robust enough for the device.

When it comes to the creation of established standards on the protection and safety of data, the IoT poses a number of unique difficulties that need to be addressed. Some devices do not have the processing capability or storage space, necessary to utilize the industry-standard safety safeguards. These devices may pose a potential risk to users. Efficiency in energy utilization is of utmost importance for most Internet of Things devices because the majority of these devices are powered by relatively small batteries. When securing a device, connected to IoT, against certain types of attacks, it is essential to first identify potential threats, and then apply appropriate countermeasures that are tailored to the specific architecture of the built IoT system. This is done in order to protect the device from being compromised. If this is not done, it is possible that there is a need for a large quantity of energy to maintain the device functioning properly.

15.3 Methods

In the field of quantum computer development, there are extremely unsettling ramifications. Both the enemies and the threats are more technologically advanced now compared to how they were in the past. The development of quantum computers has made it possible to open up new vectors of attack against the algorithms that are used to secure devices that are connected to the IoT. These new vectors of attack are particularly effective against algorithms that are used for key exchange and digital signatures. Traditional computers, such as desktops and laptops, have an additional factor that needs to be taken into consideration. This factor is known as the operating system. In this aspect, touch screens are included. While the amount of processing power that can be accessed by attackers continues to rise, we have relatively few tools that can be deployed against them on IoT devices.

In order to protect the user privacy and maintain the integrity of their data, IoT makes extensive use of a variety of encryption protocols. However, a closer inspection of the specific cryptographic algorithms employed by these protocols reveals that only a small portion of the possible ciphers are actually put to use by these protocols. This finding is based on the fact that these protocols are designed to protect sensitive information.

We offer a demonstration of the protocol and make use of novel cryptographic techniques for each layer, including the following:

- **Physical Layer**: The AES-128 encryption standard is used by the great majority of physical layer protocols, such as DASH7 and LoRa, to ensure that data is kept private and secure. This is done to prevent unauthorized access to the data.

- **Data Link Layer**: The Advanced Encryption Standard is the basis for all the cryptographic options that are specified in IEEE 802.15.4. This standard provides protection at the Data Link Layer by defining a number of different cryptographic options, and the Advanced Encryption Standard is the foundation for all of these options (AES-32–AES-128).
- **Network Layer**: The IPsec protocol is required for IPv6 on the network layer because it supports methods such as Diffie–Hellman, ECDH, RSA, and AES. This makes IPsec a vital component of IPv6. The only thing that the 6LoWPAN protocol, which is a component of the network layer, relies on is the safety of the transport layer.
- **Transport Layer**: The Transmission Control Protocol (TCP) and the User Datagram Protocol (UDP) are the two primary protocols that are used in the transport layer.
    - **TCP**: Transport Layer Security (TLS) provides an additional layer of protection, and as of version 1.3, it supports both temporary Diffie-Hellman and Advanced Encryption Standard (AES).
    - **UDP – DTLS or QUIC**: These protocols make it possible to use the ephemeral Diffie-Hellman for the purpose of key exchange and AES for the purpose of data secrecy. This protocol makes it possible to use QUIC.
- **Application Layer**: When it comes to keeping data secure, the usage of DTLS is strongly encouraged by CoAP, whereas AMQP relies on TLS at the application layer. As a direct result of this, the processes that are carried out in this layer are precisely the same as those carried out in the transport layer.

The distinction between benign and malicious network activity can be made by intrusion detection systems that are based on machine learning classifiers. These systems employ data from the past. A big drawback is the likelihood that hackers will, at some point, devise an attack that is not recognized as an attack by the system, but, which nevertheless, enables them to bypass security measures. Coevolution is a theory that proposes that two populations of the same species, such as predators and prey, would evolve together if they are mutually dependent on one another.

In this scenario, genetic algorithms are employed to develop novel adversaries (who play the role of predators), which are then used to teach an artificial immune system to identify them. In other words, the adversaries serve as a training ground for the artificial immune system. They were able to successfully protect themselves against a specific type of attack, called as interest cache poisoning, because they concentrated their attention more narrowly. According to the findings of this study, vulnerabilities can be identified before an attacker has a chance to take advantage of them by traversing the attack space. Figure 15.1 below shows the GA-CNN Model flow diagram.

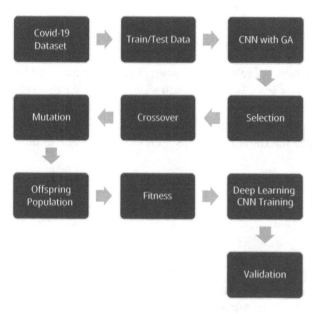

Figure 15.1: GA-CNN Model.

15.3.1 GA-CNN model

Convolution is employed in the model that we provided, with the specified kernel K, and it is applied to the input X.

$$(X^*K)(i,j) = \sum_m \sum_n K(m,n)X(i-m,j-n)$$

where $*$ – discrete convolution operation.

The kernel matrix, denoted by K, is slid over the input matrix as the convolutional procedure is carried out. This makes it possible to derive features from the data. Following the phase of convolution, the characteristics that were gathered are then corrected by means of a nonlinear activation function. This stage takes place after the step of convolution.

The Leaky ReLU activation function has lately gained traction as a preferred activation function due to its ability to maintain input size while also being immune to the vanishing gradient problem. This is due to the fact that Leaky ReLU can maintain the input size. ReLUEach and every one of the convolutional layers makes use of a rectifier that is made of leaking ReLU.

$$L(\text{size}(L) > \text{size}(M)$$

L is significantly more substantial than M when the two are examined side by side.

$$
\mathrm{Re}\,LU\,(x) = \begin{cases} 0.01x & for\,x < 0 \\ x & for\,x \geq 0 \end{cases}
$$

Because the traditional GA operators of selection, crossover, and mutation are used to maximize a single fitness value or score (that is, classification accuracy for the training and validation datasets), the genetic algorithm that is currently being utilized has a single goal that it strives to achieve. The CNN classification kernel is available in a number of different sizes, and the GA chromosome is an example of one of those sizes.

15.4 Evaluation

In order to evaluate the usefulness and safety of messages, an investigation of both the qualitative and quantitative characters is carried out. This is done in an effort to assess how effective and safe the messages are. When compared to other frameworks, the amount of time that it takes for transmissions is also discussed here, along with the impact that this particular framework has on that amount of time.

Comparisons that are made theoretically and mathematically do not take into account the additional time needed to perform cryptographic calculations. These comparisons assist in putting into perspective the benefits of the design that we have proposed as well as the amount of money that is required to convey huge amounts of information. These comparisons assist in throwing light on our alternative approach to security, which focuses on post-quantum protection, and has low storage and transmission requirements.

The transmission of noticeably larger payloads that are capable of encrypting more information is made possible by the utilization, which does away with the necessity of slicing up data into numerous messages. In addition to this, our system keeps the public key of the server within the data that is kept locally. This key is located within the data that was generated by the server. It is feasible to utilize this in order to validate information without transferring any public keys in the course of the authentication operation.

This is made possible by the fact that this is a reversible authentication method. When both of these advantages are combined, the resultant message counts are comparable to those of lightweight pre-quantum algorithms, despite the fact that the key sizes are greater. Even if the key sizes have been increased, this is still the case. For the data transmission to be verified, there is only a need for three messages of length n, where n is the total number of nodes in the network.

Figure 15.2 shows the results of class accuracy vs. learning rate, Figure 15.3 shows the results of class accuracy vs. batch size, and Figure 15.4 shows the results of class accuracy vs. training samples for GA-IDS in PL, GA-IDS in DLL, and GA-IDS in NL.

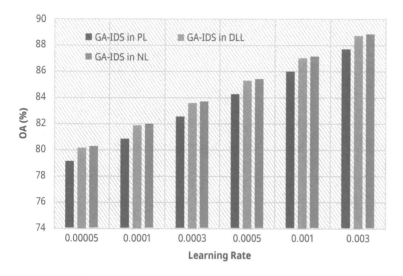

Figure 15.2: Class accuracy vs. Learning rate.

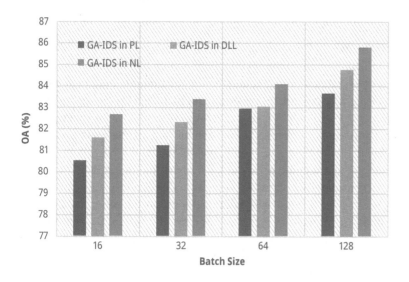

Figure 15.3: Class accuracy vs. Batch_size.

From the results, it is seen that with increasing training samples, the overall accuracy increases; however, with increasing batch size and learning rate, the accuracy of the classifier reduces at a varying rate. Further, from the results, it is found that the GA-IDS in NL achieves higher rate of accuracy than other methods.

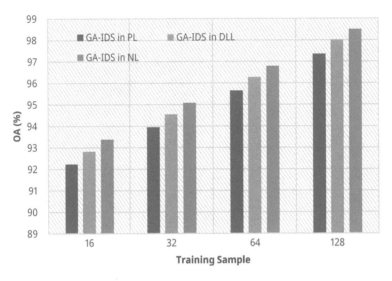

Figure 15.4: Class accuracy vs. Training samples.

15.5 Conclusion

The development of IoT has made it possible for everyday items to exchange information and communicate with one another over the internet. This IoT capability enables previously inaccessible levels of interconnectivity. However, the use of a wide variety of technologies brings about a host of new problems, one of the most pressing of which is the problem of maintaining adequate levels of safety.

Other GA-based cryptographic primitives have been devised and put into use, and they are being considered as potential solutions to these concerns. Because quantum computing is a fact now, such encryption methods, on the other hand, can no longer be used in a secure manner in this day and age. By carefully optimizing the flow of traffic and taking into consideration the storage of public keys locally, our architecture is able to deliver bus performance that is on par with or even better than that of existing pre-quantum and post-quantum frameworks. This is possible because of the use of quantum computing.

References

[1] Kumar, A., Ottaviani, C., Gill, S. S., & Buyya, R. (2022). Securing the future internet of things with post-quantum cryptography. *Security and Privacy*, 5(2), e200.

[2] Ulitzsch, V. Q., Park, S., Marzougui, S., & Seifert, J. P. (2022). A Post-Quantum Secure Subscription Concealed Identifier for 6G. In: Proceedings of the 15th ACM Conference on Security and Privacy in Wireless and Mobile Networks (pp. 157–168).

[3] Taha, M. & Eisenbarth, T. (2015). Implementation Attacks on Post-quantum Cryptographic Schemes. *Cryptology ePrint Archive*.

[4] Ravi, P., Chattopadhyay, A., & Baksi, A. (2022). Side-channel and Fault-injection Attacks over Lattice-based Post-quantum Schemes (Kyber, Dilithium): Survey and New Results. *Cryptology ePrint Archive*.

[5] Chowdhury, A. B., Mahapatra, A., Soni, D., & Karri, R. (2022). Fuzzing+ hardware performance counters-based detection of algorithm subversion attacks on post-quantum signature schemes. *IEEE Transactions on Computer-Aided Design of Integrated Circuits and Systems*.

[6] Saravanan, V., & Neeraja, A. (2013). Security issues in computer networks and stegnography. In: 2013 7th International Conference on Intelligent Systems and Control (ISCO) (pp. 363–366). IEEE.

[7] Fritzmann, T., Sharif, U., Müller-Gritschneder, D., Reinbrecht, C., Schlichtmann, U., & Sepulveda, J. (2019). Towards reliable and secure post-quantum co-processors based on RISC-V. In: 2019 Design, Automation & Test in Europe Conference & Exhibition (DATE) (pp. 1148–1153). IEEE.

[8] Gill, S. S., Kumar, A., Singh, H., Singh, M., Kaur, K., Usman, M., & Buyya, R. (2022). Quantum computing: A taxonomy, systematic review and future directions. *Software: Practice and Experience*, 52(1), 66–114.

[9] Kumari, S., Singh, M., Singh, R., & Tewari, H. (2022). Post-quantum cryptography techniques for secure communication in resource-constrained internet of things devices: A comprehensive survey. *Software: Practice and Experience*, 52(10), 2047–2076.

[10] Jati, A., Gupta, N., Chattopadhyay, A., & Sanadhya, S. K. (2019). Spqcop: Side-channel Protected Post-quantum Cryptoprocessor. *Cryptology ePrint Archive*.

[11] Gunjan, V. K., Vijayalata, Y., Valli, S., Kumar, S., Mohamed, M. O., & Saravanan, V. (2022). Machine learning and cloud-based knowledge graphs to recognize suicidal mental tendencies. *Computational Intelligence and Neuroscience*, 2022.

[12] Mus, K., Islam, S., & Sunar, B. (2020). QuantumHammer: A practical hybrid attack on the LUOV signature scheme. In: Proceedings of the 2020 ACM SIGSAC Conference on Computer and Communications Security (pp. 1071–1084).

[13] Yuvaraj, N., Raja, R. A., Ganesan, V., & Dhas, C. S. G. (2018). Analysis on improving the response time with PIDSARSA-RAL in ClowdFlows mining platform. *EAI Endorsed Transactions on Energy Web*, 5(20), e2–e2.

[14] Cintas-Canto, A., Mozaffari-Kermani, M., Azarderakhsh, R., & Gaj, K. (2022). CRC-Oriented Error Detection Architectures of Post-quantum Cryptography Niederreiter Key Generator on FPGA. In: 2022 IEEE Nordic Circuits and Systems Conference (NorCAS) (pp. 1–7). IEEE.

[15] Kousik, N. V., Sivaram, M., Yuvaraj, N., & Mahaveerakannan, R. (2021). Improved Density-based Learning to Cluster for User Web Log in Data Mining. In: Inventive Computation and Information Technologies (pp. 813–830). Springer, Singapore.

[16] Azouaoui, M., Kuzovkova, Y., Schneider, T., & Van Vredendaal, C. (2022). Post-Quantum Authenticated Encryption against Chosen-Ciphertext Side-Channel Attacks. *Cryptology ePrint Archive*.

[17] Hannah, S., Deepa, A. J., Chooralil, V. S., BrillySangeetha, S., Yuvaraj, N., Arshath Raja, R., & . . . Alene, A. (2022). Blockchain-based deep learning to process IoT data acquisition in cognitive data. *BioMed Research International*, 2022.

[18] Canto, A. C., Sarker, A., Kaur, J., Kermani, M. M., & Azarderakhsh, R. (2022). Error detection schemes assessed on FPGA for multipliers in lattice-based key encapsulation mechanisms in post-quantum cryptography. *IEEE Transactions on Emerging Topics in Computing.*

[19] Yadav, S. P., Bhati, B. S., Mahato, D. P., & Kumar, S., (eds). Federated Learning for IoT Applications. EAI/Springer Innovations in Communication and Computing. Springer, Cham, https://doi.org/10. 1007/978-3-030-85559-8.

[20] Wang, L. J., Zhou, Y. Y., Yin, J. M., & Chen, Q. (2022). Authentication of quantum key distribution with post-quantum cryptography and replay attacks. *arXiv preprint arXiv:2206.01164.*

[21] Gélin, A. & Wesolowski, B. (2017). Loop-abort Faults on Supersingular Isogeny Cryptosystems. In: International Workshop on Post-Quantum Cryptography (pp. 93–106). Springer, Cham.

[22] Yadav, S. P. (2022). Blockchain Security. In: Baalamurugan, K., Kumar, S. R., Kumar, A., Kumar, V., Padmanaban, S. (eds.) Blockchain Security in Cloud Computing. EAI/Springer Innovations in Communication and Computing. Springer, Cham. https://doi.org/10.1007/978-3-030-70501-5_1.

Sreelatha P.*, Nitin Purohit, S. Chandra Sekaran

16 RSA security implementation in quantum computing for a higher resilience

Abstract: The public key cryptosystem is widely used in the current scenario. The possibility of breaking this system by a quantum algorithm would pose a significant threat to the confidentiality of the data and assets held by all participants in the digital economy. This is because the public key cryptosystem was designed specifically for the purpose of encrypting information. The chapter discusses the security implementation in quantum computing using RSA to improve the security against vulnerabilities. The RSA is designed in such a way that it mitigates all possible attacks in the system, and provides better resilience against attacks. The results shows reduced computational time in detecting attacks and mitigating them than with other methods.

16.1 Introduction

There is a large range of experimental systems that have been identified as possible candidates for quantum computing. Trapped ion systems are yet another possibility in the field of quantum computing. These systems have a very high level of fidelity and extraordinarily fast operation times. In 2018, IonQ created a 11-qubit quantum processor with the goal of determining the energy level of water molecules when they are in their ground state [1–6]. In addition, the business carried out a trapped ion quantum computation that comprised 79-bit single-qubit operations and 160-bit storage qubits [7]. The advent of quantum computing paved the way for the achievement of both these goals.

Quantum algorithms can shorten the amount of time needed for calculation, but their applicability in the actual world is still limited to a certain extent. Especially in the sphere of cryptography, the results that were obtained are useless if the cracking time takes longer than a particular length of time that was defined beforehand [8]. This time limit was determined before the results were obtained. To give you an example, if the amount of time required to break a cipher text is longer than the term of confidentiality, then it is evident that the cracking was a waste of time. Another

---

*****Corresponding author: Sreelatha P.**, Department of Biomedical Engineering, KPR Institute of Engineering and Technology, Arasur, Tamil Nadu, India, e-mail: sreelathaselvaraj@gmail.com
Nitin Purohit, Department of Computer Science, Kebri Dehar University, Kebri Dehar, Somali Region, Ethiopia, e-mail: nitinpurohit111@kdu.edu.et.
S. Chandra Sekaran, Department of CSE, PSV College of Engineering and Technology, Krishnagiri, Tamil Nadu, India, e-mail: chandrudpi@gmail.com

https://doi.org/10.1515/9783110798159-016

example would be if the term of confidentiality is shorter than the amount of time required to break the cipher text [9].

It is anticipated that 2100 qubit processes were carried out when these exceptionally huge inputs were active in the environment. The public key cryptosystem, on the other hand, might not be able to deal with it if the length of the input key is one terabyte (TB). This is owing to the fact that the extended period of time required to decode the data would significantly reduce how efficiently the data could be transmitted [10]. On the other hand, 2100 qubit operations can result in a time overhead that is substantially higher than the level of security that is required. This can be an issue. Consequently, in the field of RSA public key cryptography and even in public key cryptography, it is an intriguing matter to discover a key length that can rapidly encrypt and decrypt while still guaranteeing security in the face of quantum algorithm attacks. This is because RSA public key cryptography was developed by RSA, the company that invented public key cryptography [11].

The execution of quantum algorithms is aided by physical norms, but the processing capabilities of quantum computers will be bound by the same physical factors that aid in the execution of quantum algorithms. This relation specifies the minimum amount of time required to complete a quantum operation. This is going to take place as a result of the fact that quantum computers have a cap placed on their processing speed by the physical laws that govern the universe. If it would take a quantum computer that is now in production, more time to crack the key than the key level of secrecy warrants, then the key is secure. If it would take a classical computer less time to crack the key, then the key is not secure [12].

The chapter discusses the security implementation in quantum computing using RSA to improve the security against vulnerabilities.

16.2 Related works

At the moment, a sizeable number of research projects concerning post-quantum cryptography and traditional algorithms are being carried out. You can make use of the reference number [13] to search for the study that compares and contrasts the performance of RSA and ECC. The authors have discovered that both the process of encrypting data and decrypting it takes far longer than they had anticipated. In research, classical algorithms were the only kind of algorithms that were looked at. You can find an analysis [14] that is quite similar to this one, comparing the performance of ECDSA and RSA. This particular investigation focuses on the Name Data-Link State Routing Protocol. The results of the comparison testing revealed that RSA is noticeably more expedient than ECDSA.

One of the primary topics of study [15–17] has been establishing which approach, between RSA and ECDSA, is the method that is utilized the most frequently. In order to establish whether or not RSA and ECDSA were effective in meeting their intended purpose, the authors looked at both the effectiveness of the algorithms and the amount of energy used by each one. There has been a demonstration of the reliability and efficacy of the MSS system through the use of mathematical proof [18, 19]. One of the shortcomings of MSS is that it can only generate a specific amount of signatures at once. This is one of its limits.

The authors in [20] tested whether or not MSS could be used to generate address signatures in mobile Internet Protocol version 6 by deploying it in software (IPv6). The authors of the study found that MSS is a more secure alternative to ECDSA, which led them to conclude that MSS is a viable replacement to ECDSA. They did this by analyzing the differences between the two algorithms. In [21], a dependable and space-saving sign-ing scheme for the distributed ledger is outlined. This is another illustration of how the recurring subject is progressing. When putting the authors' hypotheses to the test, they used both a model of a conventional cryptocurrency and advanced petri nets. Both of these tools were quite helpful. On the other hand, the authors' proposed form of W-OTS-S has key sizes that are noticeably bigger than those of the standard algorithm.

Signature systems that make use of post-quantum hashes were the primary focus of the research that was presented in [22]. It examined the similarities and differences between a number of these systems. The study investigated the Lamport, Winternitz, and Merkle systems with relation to the prices they demand as well as the results they produce. The work done by the authors of [23] is comparable to the work done while analyzing the efficacy of various hash functions that can be employed in the signature scheme.

There has been a significant amount of research and development put into the creation of various cryptographic systems as a form of protection against attacks on ordinary methods [24].

It likely that research communities would find the findings of this work useful as a starting point for designing cryptosystems that are resistant to quantum computing. This study looked at hash-based signature schemes as a potential candidate for use in the post-quantum era because their security properties are well established; they do not rely on number-theoretic security or structural hardness assumptions, and they provide forward security.

16.3 Methods

Currently, security relies mostly on asymmetric and symmetric cryptosystems for its communications; it still needs to defend itself against a number of different attacks. A cryptosystem is said to have 256-bit security if an attacker would need to spend the same amount of time and effort as they would need to break a 256-bit key. This strength can be measured in bits of security. Other researchers have also described quantum birthday attacks that generate 3 N-size tables and use Grover (however, relevant hash functions like SHA-2 and SHA-3 will remain quantum-resistant by increasing their outputs).

Messages that have been encrypted with the public key and then delivered to a particular user can only be decoded using the private key that corresponds to that particular user. The user messages that are directed at them will be encrypted using the public key. The amount of computational effort required to perform a brute-force key search attack, which attempts to determine the private key by using only the public key, is referred to as the work factor in the field of cryptography. This attack attempts to determine the private key by using only the public key.

Given the mathematical connection that exists between a public key and the private key that corresponds to it, the security of a public-key cryptosystem can be evaluated based on how much work is required to carry out an attack of this kind. This is the case because of the nature of the problem. The proposed model of QRSA is shown in Figure 16.1.

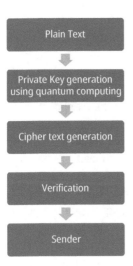

Figure 16.1: Proposed QRSA.

It is impossible to decode messages utilizing the public key since public-key cryptosystems are asymmetric in nature. This prevents this from being a possibility. Because of this trait, public-key cryptosystems are fantastic for use in insecure networks. This is because they solve the problem of key distribution, which is a common issue in such networks. Because it uses the same key for encrypting and decrypting communications, symmetric cryptography requires safe means of keeping keys among the peers interested in exchanging information.

This is because the key is always used in symmetric cryptography. In contrast to symmetric cryptosystems, which frequently use k-bit strings that are generated at random as their keys, public-key cryptosystems require their keys to have a certain structure, which makes the production of these systems significantly more expensive. Symmetric cryptosystems, on the other hand, use keys that are generated at random.

On the other hand, an elliptic curve of 160 bits could be broken by a quantum computer with 1,000 qubits, while a key of 1,024 bits would require a system with 2000 qubits. The capabilities of the quantum computers that are now in use are not even close to being enough for either of these jobs. As a consequence, the transition to post-quantum cryptographic protocols that are immune to conventional computer attacks has taken a higher position on the list of priorities than has the modernization of antiquated cryptographic protocols.

These cryptosystems are derived from a protocol known as the isogeny protocol, which was originally conceived for use with ordinary elliptic curves. Supersingular curves are an option worth considering for the construction of post-quantum systems; but in order to defend themselves against quantum attacks, they have to be noncommutative.

16.3.1 Quantum key distribution

The application of the law of mechanics enables the QKD to make the transfer of the secret key completely risk-free for both parties that are involved. This is made feasible by the QKD. The majority of the time, the construction of an exhaustive protocol is achieved by completing a variety of separate cryptographic jobs. The employment of a one-time pad, in conjunction with a key distribution mechanism, enables the construction of encrypted communication to take place. This is made possible by the fact that both these components are present. When each cryptographic task that two protocols undertake can be employed independent of the other, we refer to those protocols as being composable and secure. Composability refers to the ability of two protocols to work together securely. Because of this, there is no longer a requirement that either protocol demonstrates its commitment to security. Additionally, the QKD does not make use of the composable definition; yet, when utilized in conjunction with the one-time pad, the resulting security proof is far less robust.

The idea of composability was first proposed in the classical context of cryptography. After further development in the classical setting, the idea was eventually introduced into the quantum setting of cryptography. It was important to first establish a solid foundation in order to set the basis for the construction of the ideal protocol. As a result, a new composable security specification was designed in order to fulfill this requirement. This faultless technique guarantees that security is maintained at all times, and is practically monitored during the process of carrying out the actual execution of any given scenario. During the course of the procedure, this monitoring may take place at any point.

Because of the capabilities of the Distinguisher, it is possible to check, modify, or snoop on any type of information. Everyone else is only allowed to view the results of the procedure, and they are not permitted to view any information that has not been made public yet. Only Alice and Bob have access to the information that is being communicated between the two of them and transmitted back and forth. When using the QKD protocol, an unexpected key is first generated, and it is then disseminated around the network in a manner that is distinct from how the encrypted data is moved around. It is the job of a quantum engine to produce the keys, and a fiber-optic quantum link is the medium via which they are transmitted in the form of a stream of photons.

Due to the fact that it was generated using a key that was entirely arbitrary, the quantum information can be decoded by no one other than the solitary reader who was supposed to receive it. In the event that the continuous flow of photons that is communicated across the quantum link is ever disrupted or altered in any way, there is a chance that a security flaw has been introduced. We are able to send messages without having to worry that they will be intercepted, thanks to a secure fiber connection, and we are able to extend this network across the country by connecting dependable nodes in order to break free of the constraints that are imposed by the distance limitation.

Every operation that is performed on a quantum computer requires the investment of time, and has the ability to affect the current state of the system. It is believed that quantum states will change over the course of this period of time, and all that is required is a single action to bring about this change. It can be recorded as the amount of time that must pass in order to complete an operation in the least possible amount of time. This is true regardless of whether the gate in question is a single qubit or a multi-qubit one. This is the case regardless of the number of qubits that the gate may or may not include. In the context of this discussion, the phrase total time refers to the sum of the times that are required for each separate operation.

Modular addition serves as the foundational network for the implementation of modular exponentiation, which is necessary for the later successful operation. The addition operation can be finished with the help of two controlled-not gates; the carry can be managed with the assistance of two gates, and the normal addition network can be finished with the assistance of a third controlled-not gate. In addition to this, the modular addition network might be constructed out of a grouping of the adders discussed when the basic building block of a modular addition circuit is the two-qubit gate. This is due to the fact that modular addition uses the two-qubit gate as its fundamental building block.

16.4 Evaluation

Every operation that is performed on a quantum computer requires the investment of time, and has the ability to affect the current state of the system. It is believed that quantum states will change over the course of this period of time, and all that is required is a single action to bring about this change. The evolution time of the controlled qubit can be recorded as the amount of time that must pass in order to complete an operation in the least possible amount of time. This is true regardless of whether the gate in question is a single qubit or a multi-qubit one. This is the case regardless of the number of qubits that the gate may or may not include. In the context of this discussion, the phrase total time refers to the sum of the times that are required for each separate operation.

Modular addition serves as the foundational network for the implementation of modular exponentiation, which is necessary for the latter successful operation. The addition operation can be finished with the help of two controlled-not gates, the carry can be managed with the assistance of two gates, and the normal addition network can be finished with the assistance of a third controlled-not gate. In addition to this, the modular addition network might be constructed out of a grouping of the adders discussed. When the basic building block of a modular addition circuit is the two-qubit gate, the circuit time complexity of modular addition is linear in the input n for a chain design of this kind. This is due to the fact that modular addition uses the two-qubit gate as its fundamental building block.

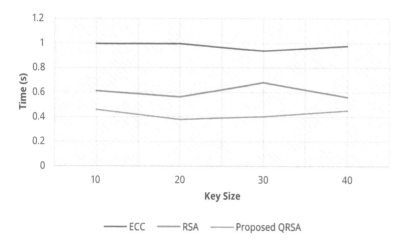

Figure 16.2: Run Times (s).

It should be possible to arrive at a better solution as in Figure 16.2–16.4 for the normal amount of time required to finish each necessary process. Because all universal quantum gates may be split into single-bit gates and two-bit gates, and controlled-not gates are the two-bit gates that are most typically used in adders, we will perform the calculation using the operating time of a single-bit gate rather than of a two-bit gate.

The following is a list of some of the reasons why not only is our paradigm reasonable, but also why it is practical: (1) The amount of time necessary to run a single qubit gate is a large fraction of the amount of time necessary to operate a two-qubit gate, and (2) the amount of time that we are estimating here is the very minimum amount of time that is necessary.

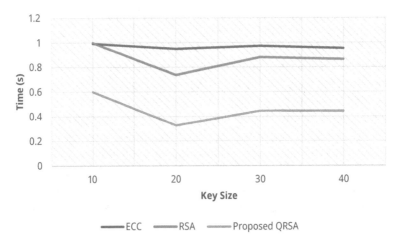

Figure 16.3: Encryption Times (s).

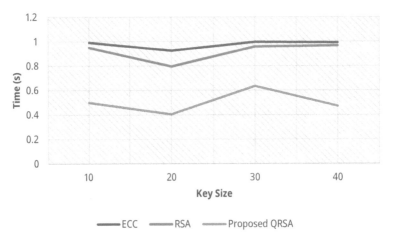

Figure 16.4: Decryption Times (s).

It is vital to bear in mind that the processing speed of a traditional computer is limited by a factor that is directly related to its clock speed. This is something that you should keep in mind at all times. In the realm of quantum computing, the frequency of a clock is typically conceived of in terms of the amount of time it takes for a system to transition from one of several potential states to another, or more specifically between 0 and 1. This is because the quantum state of a system can exist in a number of different states at the same time, shown in Figure 16.5. In the next section, we will investigate in further depth the question of whether or not the period of time needed for the operation of the quantum gates may be construed as the period of time needed for the transition between orthogonal states.

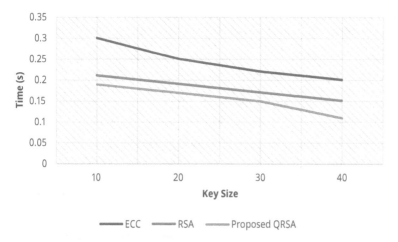

Figure 16.5: Computational Times (s).

16.5 Conclusion

The chapter demonstrated that hash-based signature algorithms are efficient in terms of the amount of time that is required to generate keys, the amount of time that is required to generate signatures, and the amount of time that is required to verify signatures. This research also sheds light on the difficulties of using traditional methods rather than hash-based signatures in settings. When compared to the strategies utilized by its rivals, RSA reveals itself to be the strategy with the highest level of efficiency. Following a side-by-side comparison of the two time-tested approaches, we came to the conclusion that the RSA protocol generates keys and signatures in a significantly shorter amount of time. On the other hand, it was found that the RSA method was the one that was the most effective when checking signatures.

References

[1] Mosca, M. (2018). Cybersecurity in an era with quantum computers: Will we be ready? *IEEE Security & Privacy*, *16*(5), 38–41.
[2] Mustafa, I., Khan, I. U., Aslam, S., Sajid, A., Mohsin, S. M., Awais, M., & Qureshi, M. B. (2020). A lightweight post-quantum lattice-based RSA for secure communications. *IEEE Access*, *8*, 99273–99285.
[3] Tosh, D., Galindo, O., Kreinovich, V., & Kosheleva, O. (2020). Towards security of cyber-physical systems using quantum computing algorithms. In: 2020 IEEE 15th International Conference of System of Systems Engineering (SoSE) (pp. 313–320). IEEE.

[4] Fritzmann, T., Sharif, U., Müller-Gritschneder, D., Reinbrecht, C., Schlichtmann, U., & Sepulveda, J. (2019). Towards reliable and secure post-quantum co-processors based on RISC-V. In: 2019 Design, Automation & Test in Europe Conference & Exhibition (DATE) (pp. 1148–1153). IEEE.

[5] Ravi, P., Chattopadhyay, A., & Bhasin, S. (2022). Security and quantum computing: An overview. In: 2022 IEEE 23rd Latin American Test Symposium (LATS) (pp. 1–6). IEEE.

[6] Tang, Z., Zhang, P., & Krawec, W. O. (2021). A quantum leap in microgrids security: The prospects of quantum-secure microgrids. *IEEE Electrification Magazine, 9*(1), 66–73.

[7] Zhou, Y., Tang, Z., Nikmehr, N., Babahajiani, P., Feng, F., Wei, T. C., & . . . Zhang, P. (2022). Quantum computing in power systems. *IEnergy*.

[8] Sadeeq, M. A., Zeebaree, S. R., Qashi, R., Ahmed, S. H., & Jacksi, K. (2018). Internet of things security: A survey. In: 2018 International Conference on Advanced Science and Engineering (ICOASE) (pp. 162–166). IEEE.

[9] Mavroeidis, V., Vishi, K., Zych, M. D., & Jøsang, A. (2018). The impact of quantum computing on present cryptography. *ArXiv Preprint arXiv:1804.00200*.

[10] Nahed, M. & Alawneh, S. (2020). Cybersecurity in a post-quantum world: How quantum computing will forever change the world of cybersecurity. *American Journal of Electrical and Computer Engineering, 4*(2), 81–93.

[11] Vashisht, V., Kumar Pandey, A., & Prakash, S. (2021). Speech recognition using machine learning. *IEIE Transactions on Smart Processing and Computing, SCOPUS, 10*(3, ISSN: 2287-5255. https://doi.org/10.5573/IEIESPC.2021.10.3.233.

[12] Kachurova, M., Shuminoski, T., & Bogdanoski, M. (2022). Lattice-Based Cryptography: A Quantum Approach to Secure the IoT Technology. In: Building Cyber Resilience against Hybrid Threats (pp. 122–133), IOS Press.

[13] Rani, P., Verma, S., Yadav, S. P., Rai, B. K., Naruka, M. S., & Kumar, D. (2022). Simulation of the lightweight blockchain technique based on privacy and security for healthcare data for the cloud system. *International Journal of E-Health and Medical Communications (IJEHMC), 13*(4), 1–15, http://doi.org/10.4018/IJEHMC.309436.

[14] Rosch-Grace, D. & Straub, J. (2021, November). Analysis of the necessity of quantum computing capacity development for national defense and homeland security. In: *2021 IEEE International Symposium on Technologies for Homeland Security (HST)* (pp. 1–8). IEEE.

[15] Yadav, S. P., Bhati, B. S., Mahato, D. P., & Kumar, S., (eds.). Federated Learning for IoT Applications. EAI/Springer Innovations in Communication and Computing. Springer, Cham, https://doi.org/10.1007/978-3-030-85559-8.

[16] Martonosi, M. & Roetteler, M. (2019). Next steps in quantum computing: Computer science's role. *arXiv preprint arXiv:1903.10541*.

[17] Saravanan, V. & Raj, V. M. (2016). A seamless mobile learning and tension free lifestyle by QoS oriented mobile handoff. *Asian Journal of Research in Social Sciences and Humanities, 6*(7), 374–389.

[18] Lacerda, F. G., Renes, J. M., & Renner, R. (2019). Classical leakage resilience from fault-tolerant quantum computation. *Journal of Cryptology, 32*(4), 1071–1094.

[19] Natarajan, Y., Kannan, S., & Mohanty, S. N. (2021). Survey of various statistical numerical and machine learning ontological models on infectious disease ontology. *Data Analytics in Bioinformatics: A Machine Learning Perspective*, 431–442.

[20] Zohuri, B. (2020). What is quantum computing and how it works. *Journal of Material Sciences & Manufacturing Research. SRC/JMSMR/105, 3*, 3–5.

[21] Gobinathan, B., Mukunthan, M. A., Surendran, S., Somasundaram, K., Moeed, S. A., Niranjan, P., & . . . Sundramurthy, V. P. (2021). A novel method to solve real time security issues in software industry using advanced cryptographic techniques. *Scientific Programming*, 2021.

[22] Yuvaraj, N., Chang, V., Gobinathan, B., Pinagapani, A., Kannan, S., Dhiman, G., & Rajan, A. R. (2021). Automatic detection of cyberbullying using multi-feature based artificial intelligence with deep decision tree classification. *Computers & Electrical Engineering*, *92*, 107186.

[23] Yuvaraj, N., Raja, R. A., Karthikeyan, T., & Kousik, N. V. (2020). Improved Privacy Preservation Framework for Cloud-based Internet of Things. In: Internet of Things (pp. 165–174), CRC Press.

[24] Saravanan, V., Thirukumaran, S., Anitha, M., & Shanthana, S. (2013). Enabling self auditing for mobile clients in cloud computing. *International Journal of Advanced Computer Technology*, *2*, 53–60.

Kaushal Kishor*

17 Application of quantum computing for digital forensic investigation

Abstract: In the current technological climate, there is an increase in the number of instances of cybercrime. In the real world, it is never simple to track down and apprehend a cybercriminal. Even if the perpetrator is captured, it will be challenging to secure his conviction since there are not enough standardized digital investigation models. As a consequence of a badly handled forensic investigation, a person who committed a cyber crime may go free, while an innocent person may be subject to adverse ramifications as a result of the inquiry. Forensic investigators are required to adhere to consistent and well-defined forensic methods in order to successfully capture and prosecute cyber criminals. In recent years, a number of new investigating models for digital forensics have been developed; nonetheless, the percentage of cases that result in a conviction remains low since the same investigation model is not relevant in all nations. This chapter introduces a one-of-a-kind Digital Forensic Investigation Model that is built on the architecture and cyber regulations of the Indian subcontinent.

17.1 Introduction

A system of information exchange is one of the most fundamental foundations of contemporary society. It requires new concepts to be developed in order to ensure secure transmission and archive for the future. The goal of cryptography has not changed. Cryptography is the practice of encrypting and decrypting communications in order to ensure their confidentiality, non-repudiation, validity, and integrity. Kryptós, the Greek word for hidden or secret, and graphein, the Greek word for writing, are the roots of the term. The practice of deciphering codes is known as cryptanalysis, whereas the word "cryptography" refers to a combination of the terms. Many scientific paper contacts have already been supplanted by digital communication, making it difficult to find digital passports, enclosures, and signature counterparts. More work is required when there are more applications. Let us take a look at a few. Encryption is all about preventing unauthorized third parties from deciphering the content of a communication between two authorized parties. Identification is used to verify the identities of those conversing.

*Corresponding author: Kaushal Kishor, IT Department, ABES Institute of Technology, Ghaziabad, Uttar Pradesh, India, e-mail: kaushal.kishor@abesit.in, kaushal.rastogi07@gmail.com

https://doi.org/10.1515/9783110798159-017

Another type of cryptography challenge is exchanging information in secret, which involves dividing a secret, such as a password, into numerous parts so that when a particular minimal subset of the pieces is assembled, the secret may be retrieved. Digital signatures, communication authentication, negligible proofs, and other cryptography applications are examples. Nonetheless, current cryptographic methods only guarantee conditional security, which is dependent on the adversary's computational and technical powers. In contrast, this thesis gives three experimental prototypes whose security is total and assured by basic physics laws. The first research paper is an application of interferometric quantum key distribution (QKD), which allows multiple senders and receivers to remotely create a secret cryptographic key. Quantum-state particles called photons encode evidence in the form of weak coherent states [1]. We can identify eavesdropping and transmission errors, thanks to the Heisenberg uncertainty principle. If the amount of listening does not reach a specific threshold, all eavesdropper data is securely erased using an additional augmentation of privacy approach. After that, the created key is utilized to secure communication with the Vernam cypher.

17.2 Literature review

People have always desired the ability to converse in private, so that no one might overhear their communications. Archeological digs have revealed that ancient civilizations in Mesopotamia, India, and China utilized various types of encryption. Ancient Egyptians employed modified hieroglyphs to disguise their communications four thousand years ago [2].

The Spartans of Greece created a Skytale crypto system, based on letter transposition in the fifth century BC. The message was inscribed over a sliver of paper or leather wrapped around a baton made of wood. When the line came to an end, the baton was twirled. The letters appeared jumbled once the parchment was unwrapped, and only the individual who owned a baton of the same form was able to retrieve the message [3].

The substitution cypher is another common and easy encryption method that substitutes every character of a document between another letter, integer, or symbol. The Caesar cypher is one example.

Most cryptosystems in the middle ages relied on transposition, substitution, or a mix of the two. Some writers like Edgar Allan Poe used some of these methods in his novel. However, neither of these cyphers is safe since they may be broken by utilizing numerous linguistic aspects, for example, the frequency of particular clusters of letters. The introduction of the telegraph in the 1830s greatly increased interpersonal communication. This predecessor of current communications, however, has a significant handicap in terms of cryptography. The telegraph operator was aware of the substance of the sent message. As a result, people and corporations desiring to keep their interactions private developed a number of codebooks [4].

Key terms and phrases were rewritten into gibberish in the codebooks. The codes had two purposes: first, they reduced the number of messages transmitted, decreasing costs since telegrams were charged per character sent; and second, the codes formed a cypher if the coding process was secret.

The two world conflicts of the 21st century accelerated the development of new encryption techniques. Cyphers such as the One-time Pad use a random number of locations to advance each letter ahead in the alphabet. In order to create the cryptographic key, the sender and receiver must exchange a series of random integers. No matter how powerful an attacker's computer or technological skills, the Vernam cypher still faces the challenge of securely disseminating the key. As a result, it was not as widely disseminated as Vernam had anticipated. The severe key management concerns are not an issue in certain military and diplomatic applications, though.

The famed spies Theodore A. Hall, Klaus Fuchs, the Rosenbergs, and others utilized the Vernam cipher to smuggle atomic secrets to Moscow. Ché Guevara also used the One-time Pad to encrypt his letters to Fidel Castro. It is said to be deployed for nuclear submarine transmissions and even for some official conversations, and it was used to safeguard the hot line connecting Washington and Moscow. We will come back to the Vernam cypher later since it is great for quantum key distribution.

17.3 Cryptography using public keys

In the late 1970s, digital telecommunications boosted interest in encryption. Safe contact between strangers without a cryptographic key was crucial. Safely transferring the key remained a concern. Whitfield Diffie and Martin E. Hellman solved the problem in 1976 [5]. Public-key encryption's simplicity spurred the 1990s ecommerce boom. Public-key cryptography needs two keys. The receiver of a message creates two keys, publicizes the public key, and keeps the secret key concealed. Anyone with the public key can encrypt data, but only the recipient with the private key may decode it.

Public-key cryptography's security relies on insoluble computational difficulties. Encryption and decryption are one-way processes. One-way measurements are straightforward to calculate in one direction but hard to reverse. Multiplying two primes is easy, but dividing their product is difficult. Other public-key cryptosystems employ discrete logarithms in Abelian groups on elliptic curves and finite groups. No other function has been proven one-way; it is only presumed. Public-key cryptography is not secure. It is algorithmic security. RSA is the most popular public-key cryptosystem. Ronald Rivest, Adi Shamir, and Leonard Adleman established RSA in 1977 [6]. RSA exploits the difficulty of factoring large integers. The receiver chooses two large prime numbers and makes their products public. The modulus produces the public key. Anyone with the key can encrypt data. To invert the approach, the modulus primes must be known. Dividing the modulus is the most promising way to attack RSA. Richard Guy [7] remarked in 1996, "I'd be shocked if someone frequently factors 1,080 without special form this century." Scientific American presented the first 425-bit RSA hacking challenge in 1977. While it took a huge amount of equipment to crack the 425-bit RSA in February 1999, just 185 machines were able to factor a 465-bit RSA module in 9 weeks. 512-bit keys protected 95% of the Internet e-commerce at that time (155-digit number). 292 computers analyzed a 512-bit integer in August 1999. That is, neither the 512-bit keys nor the 256-bit keys provide sufficient protection for anything besides extremely short-term security requirements. All these difficulties have helped to estimate the amount of time and money required to crack a certain key size using public efforts. Estimating what can be accomplished by corporate and governmental endeavors with considerably higher funds is obviously much more challenging.

A computer network is not really the sole method for factoring large numbers. In 1999, Adi Shamir invented the TWINKLE device. a parallel processing optoelectronic factorization device that can factor 512- and 768-bit keys and is substantially faster than a normally fast PC. Larger key lengths and key sizes of 1,024 bits for corporation keys and 2048 bits for costly keys are now recommended.

The emergence of a quantum computer might pose another danger to the public-key cryptography's security. Decryption would take nearly the same amount of time as encryption with a quantum computer, rendering public-key cryptography useless. Algorithms that can achieve this have already been developed, and pilot testing with narrow quantum computers have effectively cleared the way for more complex systems.

17.3.1 Secret-key cryptography

If users communicate a sufficiently lengthy secret key in advance, secret-key cryptography can provide them with unquestionable security. Later, the shared key is utilized for both encryption and decryption. The fundamental disadvantage of secret-key cryptosystems is secure key distribution. Telecommunications security is reduced to secret-key distributing security. Some users distribute the secret key through public-key cryptography. It is then utilized in a cryptosystem with a secret key. To avoid this need, human meetups or courier services interchange the secret key. As a result, the system's unconditional security is limited to computational security. Even though they mix the secret-key systems' response time with the efficiency of the public key exchange, hybrid systems have gained favor. They were used for electronic transactions, financial transactions, ATM transactions and PIN encryption techniques, cellular phone conversations identifying and verification, electronic signatures, and an increasing number of other purposes.

The Digital Encryption Standard (DES) and its variants are the most widely used secret-key cryptosystems. It is the most often used cryptosystem in history due to its extensive application in hybrid systems. DES was created in 1975 by IBM and the US government, and became a benchmark two years later. Because it uses extremely basic arithmetic operations, it can be implemented using a simple hardware and achieve very fast encryption speeds. DES has been subjected to the same wave of assaults as public-key cryptosystems. The technique employs a 56-bit key to encrypt the full message. As a result, it is just secure in terms of computing [8]. A new award was presented in January 1998. The contest winners made use of idle time of computers connected to the Internet. Over 50,000 CPUs were networked together. After 41 days [9], the key was discovered. Another set of code breakers went a different route. They created a single machine that decrypted the encrypted communication. It's time to get out the 128-, 192-, and 256-bit keys was only 56 h of trying at a rate of 88 billion keys per second [10]. Based on the current technology, an identical machine would take only 100 s [11]. The thorough search is not the only way to tackle DES. Other effective attacks that leverage the internal structure of the encryption were presented in the 1990s [12]. Cryptographers worked to improve DES's security. Triple DES, DESX, and more variants were created. A four-year effort to replace the ageing DES ended in the release of a new standard, the Advanced Encryption Standard (AES), in October 2000 [13]. This standard was adopted in December 2001 and became effective in May 2002.

Another typical issue with traditional cryptography approaches is what is known as side-channel cryptanalysis [14]. Side channels are undesired methods for information about the cryptographic device's activities to leak out. The attacks based on side-channel information target specific implementations of cryptosystems rather than their mathematical basis. Information can be obtained by monitoring the time necessary to perform an operation, energy consumption, thermal radiation, or magnetic emission.

17.4 Quantum approach

The basic challenge of secret-key cryptosystems, as described in the preceding chapter, is safe key distribution. Here, quantum mechanics come in help and provide an easy answer. While technological advancements and mathematical formulae can weaken the security of standard encryption systems, the quantum method can provide unconditional protection. The Heisenberg uncertainty principle ensures security by stating that we cannot confidently discriminate non orthogonal states. It is difficult to expose probable eavesdropping within the framework of classical physics since information stored in any attribute of a classical object may be collected without altering the item's state. All conventional transmissions can be passively monitored. In classical transmission, one piece of information is encoded in billions of photons, electrons, atoms, or other carriers. Passively listening in is always possible by diverting a piece of the transmission and monitoring it.

The goal of cryptography [15] is to send material in such a way that access to it is completely limited to the intended receiver, even if the communication is intercepted. With the advent of broadcast and total, such as online transfers, the Internet, e-mail, and mobile phones, this science has grown in prominence; crucial monetary, business, political, and intimate talks are sent across public channels. The sender uses cryptography to scramble or encrypt the original comment or plaintext, obscuring its meaning. The message is recovered after the encrypted communication or crypto text has been sent by breaking or decrypting the transmission. Existing encryption algorithms are divided into two categories: "traditional" and "modern." Traditional procedures use coding (the use of alternate words or phrases), transposition (the rearranging of plaintext), and substitution operations (alteration of plaintext characters). Traditional approaches for manual encoding and decoding were supposed to be easy. Modern approaches, on the other hand, rely on computers and incredibly lengthy keys, intricate algorithms, and insoluble difficulties to establish security guarantees. There are two alternatives to conventional cryptographic approaches: public key encryption [16] and cryptographic key encryption [15, 16]. Messages are delivered using Public Key Cryptography, which utilizes an encryption process so complicated that even full disclosure of the jumbled technique offers no relevant information on how to undo it. Each participant has a "public key" and a "private key," the former of which is used to encrypt and the latter to decode talks.

Providing a secret key is the biggest practical problem in secret key encryption. In theory, any two users who wanted to communicate may meet beforehand to agree on a key, but this could be time-consuming in practice. Any argument over how the key should be chosen that occurs over a public data transmission might possibly be accepted and exploited by an eavesdropper. Light waves are distinct particles called as photons, according to quantum theory [17]. In electrical waves, a photon is an inextensible particle that carries energy, momentum, and angular momentum. Photon pairs formed by certain particles processes are referred to as "entangled pairs" [18]. Each pair is made up of two photons with different but related linear polarization as shown in Figure 17.1. Measurement randomness is influenced by entanglement. When we employ a polarization filter to observe a photon beam E1, half of the incident radiation will pass through to the filter, irrespective of their direction. It is impossible to forecast whether a given photon will pass through the filter.

The cornerstone of quantum cryptography is the Heisenberg uncertainty principle, which states that some pairs of physical properties are linked in such a way that measuring one prevents the observer from concurrently knowing the value of the other. When measuring the polarization of a photon, the direction of measurement has an impact on all subsequent measurements. Quantum cryptography, also known as quantum key distribution (QKD), employs quantum physics to provide secure communication. It

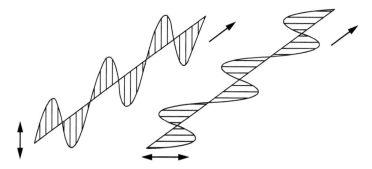

Figure 17.1: shows a representation of horizontally and vertically polarized light.

allows two parties to generate a shared random bit string that is only known to them, and may be used as a key to encrypt and decode communications. The capacity of the two communicating users to identify the existence of any third party attempting to obtain knowledge of the key is a significant and unique aspect of quantum cryptography.

Quantum cryptography is solely used to generate and distribute keys, not to send messages. Quantum cryptography differs from standard cryptographic systems in that it bases its security model on physics rather than mathematics. Quantum cryptography employs current physics knowledge to create a cryptosystem that cannot be defeated – that is, one that is entirely safe against being compromised without the knowledge of the transmitter or recipient of the messages. The genius of quantum cryptography is that it addresses the key distribution problem. By transmitting a succession of photons with random polarizations, a user can suggest a key. This sequence may then be used to construct a number sequence. This is referred to as quantum key distribution. If an eavesdropper intercepts the key, this can be noticed, but it is of little importance because it is merely a series of random bits that can be disregarded. The sender may then send another key.

17.4.1 Quantum bits (qubits)

In traditional informatics, digital signals are represented by classical bits. These fundamental bits, or "bits," can still have two states, 0 and 1, yielding in an n number of bit vectors. A qubit (short for quantum bit) is the fundamental unit of information in quantum computing and its classical equivalent, the bit (binary digit). When it comes to storing information, a qubit is comparable to a bit, but it operates quite differently due to the quantum qualities on which it is built. A superposition is defined in Figure 17.2:

$|\psi\rangle = \alpha|0\rangle + \beta|1\rangle$ Where α and β are complex number.

A coin toss might represent a traditional bit's notion. Every time a coin is tossed, the notion of a 0 or a 1 is the same as receiving a "Head" or a "Tail." However, a qubit can persist in a series of states between and until it is detected.

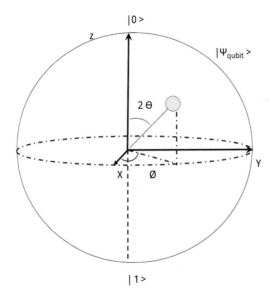

Figure 17.2: The Bloch sphere.

17.4.2 Quantum gates

Four types of quantum gates are required to accomplish quantum operations – Pauli X, Pauli-Z, Hadamard barriers, and U Gate. Their block diagram is shown in Figures 17.3 and 17.4.

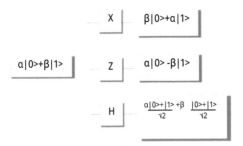

Figure 17.3: Hadamard gates.

Figure 17.4: Controlled U-gate & uncontrolled U-gate.

17.4.3 Quantum cryptography

This is the most important aspect of the project. It begins by presenting the fundamental concepts of quantum cryptography as well as the physical and technical principles of quantum cryptography, and then explores the differences between quantum cryptography and classical encryption.

17.4.3.1 Brief overview

Quantum cryptography is a technology that uses principles of quantum mechanics to create a cryptosystem that allows two parties to communicate random strings of qubits that may be used as keys to encrypt and decode messages sent between them.

The most significant characteristic of quantum cryptography is the ability to determine whether or not a third party is attempting to intercept the key. Since quantum bits cannot be copied, if Alice gives the secret to Bob and an eavesdropping Eve tries to acquire the key, Eve must delete the qubits because a quantum process cannot be measured without changing the system, according to quantum physics. Assume you are an eavesdropper. Eve is attempting to listen in on Alice and Bob's conversation. Because of the no-cloning theorem, quantum key distribution is effective. Eve cannot collect knowledge if she tries to discriminate between two non orthogonal states without collapsing at least one of them.

17.4.4 Physical and technical principles

17.4.4.1 Heisenberg uncertainty principle

Werner Heisenberg, a German physicist, was born in 1927 (1901–1976). His principle states, "A specific pair of physical attributes cannot be assessed simultaneously." In this situation, measuring one property (for example, particle location) will affect the other property, momentum. As a result, it cannot be properly quantified."

17.4.4.2 No-Cloning theorem

It is frequently advantageous for Eve in a cryptographic system to replicate the communication between Alice and Bob. Eve may have collected enough knowledge later in the protocol, or at a far later period, to extract meaningful information from these communications. Data copying is a concept that many of us take for granted. However, in the field of quantum information, William Wootters and Wojtek Zurek demonstrated that quantum mechanics principles disallow this easy job [19]. It claims that "given an arbitrary, unknown quantum state, no legitimate quantum operation can make a second, independently measurable duplicate of the state."

Ref. [20] provides a straightforward demonstration of the no-cloning theorem. As a result of this discovery, only orthogonal states can be properly discriminated. We would have to disrupt the system in order to obtain information from two non orthogonal states.

17.4.4.3 Entanglement property

It states that "a quantum of two or more items must be described in relation to each other, even if the individual objects are physically separated." The measurement taken on one system may have an immediate impact on the other systems involved.

17.4.4.4 Differences with classical cryptography

Classic cryptosystems have been demonstrated to be safe for decades, and enough effort has gone into implementing them for communication security. Despite the use of RSA, El-Gamal, and ECC cryptosystems [21], each of these systems might be compromised. If the transmission is intercepted and stored, emerging technologies may equip us with the computing capacity to decipher such information. However, quantum cryptography does not allow for the decoding of the quantum key. The important components of security are contrasting, in that, conventional cryptography relies on computer capacity, while quantum cryptography relies on a basic property of quantum physics that asserts that a qubit cannot be detected before collapsing it and therefore damaging the key. Another distinction between traditional and quantum encryption is that in quantum cryptography, qubit transmission is continual since qubits cannot be reproduced and stored. Traditional cryptography, on the other hand, does not require the encrypted message to remain continuous. It may be stored and sent in parts or in any order desired, something quantum cryptography may not be able to achieve. Quantum repeaters were invented in the 1990s to store photon states, and they have now been improved to be more reliable. It has not, however, been widely adopted and remains a source of conjecture.

17.5 Quantum convolutional neural network

Convolutional Neural Network is a deep neural network design inspired by animal visual brain [22]. CNNs excel in a range of tasks, including object tracking [23], text detection and identification [24], posture estimation, action recognition [25], and saliency detection, using multicontext deep learning. [26, 27] refers to a more detailed discussion of deep convolutional deep learning. CNNs' power originates from several convolutional layers, maxpooling, and a few densely, fully connected layers, which assist in reducing the large quantity of different picture matrices to a few thousand nodes, which may then be used for the output data layer of a few nodes [28–30].

17.6 Quantum key distributions

The purpose of quantum key distribution (QKD) is to securely transfer a random binary string (a key) between two people (often referred to as Alice and Bob) through a public quantum channel, shown Figure 17.5. The key obtained by QKD can be used in a variety of ways, but it is most commonly utilized by Alice and Bob to interact traditionally and securely. Alice, in particular, adds the created key to a conventional binary message and transmits the encrypted message to Bob. Bob then adds the key to the encrypted text in order to decode the original message. An eavesdropper cannot decipher the encrypted communication since it is simply a collection of random 0s and 1s. This technique of communication, known as the One-time pad or Vernam cypher may be demonstrated to be more rigorously safe [31]. Three conditions are put on the key in order for this system to be unconditionally secure: The key must be as lengthy as the message; it must be completely random; and (3) it may only be used once [31].

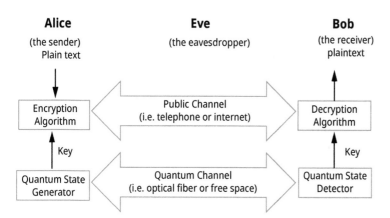

Figure 17.5: A quantum cryptography form of communication for safely exchanging random keys.

The Vernam cipher's fundamental disadvantage is the requirement to distribute a secret key as lengthy as the message, which prevented it from being widely used. So far, the cypher has largely been used in military and diplomatic agencies. As will be demonstrated in the next section, quantum key distribution can alleviate the challenge of safe key distribution. Because of its capacity to guarantee absolute security and also because of its simplicity of use, the Vernam cypher becomes important.

17.7 Quantum computing in ad hoc networks

In a traditional MANET, the network delivers QoS using 0 and 1 [33, 34]. When a node moves from one location to another and attempts to access a service through a service provider (SP), these services may be lost owing to mobility [35]. However, with the introduction of quantum adaptation, applications such as quantum key distribution (QKD) and superdense coding are being deployed. Quantum MANETs can improve on the notion of quantum communication by employing EPR pairs, also known as bell states, in a superimposed state. We can discover the equal distribution of 0 or 1 with equal probability if we try to measure these stacked states of qubits. This possibility will aid in the distribution of services in a network. As a result, we will be able to send messages using these qubits. Einstein and his colleagues' utilization of the EPR paradox aids in identifying quantum entanglement behavior of qubits.

17.7.1 Comparison

Several studies suggest that quantum internet may be utilized for long-distance transfer of quantum and conventional information. This form of network may be used in modern technologies, such as MANET [36–38]. Services supplied by various service providers and the quantity of services will be more in QUMANET than in standard MANET due to the increased number of states in QUMANET. The block diagram of Classical MANET versus QUMANET is shown in Figure 17.6.

17.8 Quantum cryptographic protocols

The most popular quantum cryptography protocols will be described in this section. This comprises Bennett and Brassard's BB84 and B92 protocols, as well as the EPR and KCQ protocols. The theoretical evidence of QKD's security is excellent.

17.8.1 BB84 protocol

Charles H. Bennett and Gilles Brassard suggested utilizing quantum mechanics to reliably release a random cryptographic key in 1984, which led to the development of quantum key distribution (QKD) [39]. As a result, the protocol is referred to as BB84.

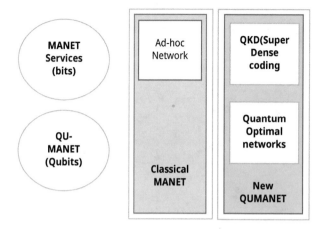

Figure 17.6: Classical MANET versus QUMANET.

Based on Stephen Wiesner's notions on immutable quantum money [40], Bennett and Brassard created a method that allows users to establish an identical and fully random stream of characters at two remote sites while disclosing any eavesdrop with a high possibility.

17.8.2 B92 protocol

In 1992, Charles Bennett developed the B92 encoding technique. This quantum encoding system is similar to BB84, except it only employs two of the four BB84 states to represent 0 and 1, and 0 and 45, respectively. The bits would be encoded in two non orthogonal BB84 states using B92 in such a way that no one could confidently distinguish a bit since no measuring could discriminate between two non orthogonal quantum states. Any quantum particle characterized by a two-dimensional Hilbert space H that reflects the polarization states of a single photon can be used to create the B92 protocol. B92 can be used on any non-symmetrical premise.

17.8.3 KCQ protocol

Keyed communication in quantum noise (KCQ) is a classical information transfer technique based on quantum detection and communication theory. In a classical universe, where a single universal observation is best for all signal sets, this KCQ technique does not exist. The key difference between KCQ and the BB84-type QKD protocol is that intrusion-level estimates can be removed as a result of the optimum quantum receiver concept. Although KCQ key production is fundamentally different from the quantum-noise-randomized direct encryption protocols Alpha Eta () or Y-00 [41, 42], it would ease the use of physical key generation methods in real optical systems, shown in Figure 17.7

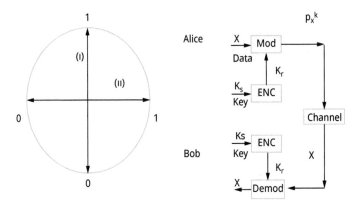

Figure 17.7: The system Qb-KCQ (Left) There are two causes for this: I and II. (Right) The encryption approach illustrated by the box requires modulation with bases specified by a running key Kr produced from a seed key K. ENC.

17.9 Conclusions and future work

Because of system losses and the presence of an attacker, the key cannot be produced and transferred simply by utilizing the existing model, which must be supplemented with a non-quantum process, new methodology, and numerous additional steps in QKD. The work improves the quantum key distribution technique, particularly in the areas of mistake removal, authentication, estimating the attacker's knowledge, and privacy amplification. This improves the whole transmission process, from identification through quantum key creation and distribution. It will be useful for future research on quantum keys.

While quantum cryptography has made considerable breakthroughs in the last decade, there are still substantial barriers to overcome before quantum cryptography can be extensively used as a key distribution method for governments, organizations, and people. Among these challenges is the advancement of more current technology to enable higher quality and longer broadcast distances for quantum asymmetric key. However, advances in computer processing capabilities and the fear of aging for today's encryption techniques will drive quantum cryptography studies and development in the future. Quantum cryptography is still in its infancy, but it appears to be quite promising thus far. If quantum cryptography lives up to even part of its lofty promises, it will have a dramatic and transformative impact on all of our lives.

As a result, there is a need to update the Quantum Key Distribution protocol (QKD) and improve the BB84 protocol. The primary goal of future study is to identify more possible attacks on the BB84 protocol as well as the impact of the MAN-IN-THE-MIDDLE ATTACK on the protocol. Future study will look into the influence of MAN-IN-THE-MIDDLE ATTACK on the efficiency, accuracy, authentication, and integrity of the protocol. The investigation includes determining [43–45].

The goal of future study is to determine the impact of another attack on the protocol, such as the TROJAN HORSE ATTACK. What effect does the BB84 protocol have on BANDWIDTH and COMPUTATIONAL POWER? Research also answers the issue of whether a DOS (denial of service) attack is conceivable on the BB84 protocol, and if so, how. The study also includes developing protocols that are less reliant on hardware resources and can communicate over vast distances effectively and efficiently.

References

[1] Orus, R., Mugel, S., & Lizaso, E., Quantum computing for finance: Overview and prospects. *Review Physical. 4,* 100028 (2019)

[2] Palsson, M. S., Gu, M., Ho, J., Wiseman, H. M., & Pryde, G. J. (2017). Experimentally modeling stochastic processes with less memory by the use of a quantum processor. *Science Advances. 3.*

[3] Cryptography/Scytale. (2022). Wikibooks, The Free Textbook Project. Retrieved 06:31, June 10, 2022 from https://en.wikibooks.org/w/index.php?title=Cryptography/Scytale&oldid=4028986.

[4] Vashisht, V., Pandey, A. K., & Yadav, S. P. (2021). Speech recognition using machine learning. *IEIE Transactions on Smart Processing & Computing, 10*(3), 233–239.

[5] Bennett, C. H., et al. (1999). Experimental quantum cryptography. *Journal of Cryptology, 5*(3), pp. 3–28.

[6] Rai, B. K., Sharma, S., Kumar, G., & Kishor, K. (2022). Recognition of different bird category using image processing. *International Journal of Online and Biomedical Engineering (IJOE), 18*(07), 101–114. https://doi.org/10.3991/ijoe.v18i07.29639.

[7] Bennett, C. H., et al. (2003). Experimental quantum cryptography. *Journal of Cryptography, 5*(3), 3–15.

[8] Bennett, C. H., Brassard, G., & Mermin, N. D. (1992b). Quantum cryptography without Bell's theorem. *Physical Review Letters, 68,* 557–559.

[9] Bennett, C. H., Brassard, G., Cr'epeau, C., & Maurer, U. M. (1995). Generalized privacy amplification. *IEEE Transactions on Information, 41,* 1915–1923.

[10] Yadav, S. P. (2021). Emotion recognition model based on facial expressions. *Multimedia Tools and Applications, 80*(17), 26357–26379.

[11] Bethune, D., & Risk, W. (2000). An auto compensating fiber-optic quantum cryptography system based on polarization splitting of light. *IEEE Journal of Quantum Electronics, 36,* 340–347.

[12] Gisin, N., & Wolf, S. (1999). Quantum cryptography on noisy channels: Quantum versus classical key-agreement protocols. *Physical Review Letters, 83,* 4200–4203.

[13] Bennett, C. H. (1992). Quantum cryptography using any two non orthogonal states. *Physical Review Letters, 68,* 3121–3124.

[14] Ch.H, B. & Brassard, G. (1984). Quantum Cryptography: Public Key Distribution and Coin Tossing. In: Int. Conf. Computers Systems & Signal Processing, Bangalore, India. December 10–12 175–179.

[15] Fung, C.-H. F., Tamaki, K., & Lo, H.-K. Performance of two quantum key- distribution protocols. *Physical Review A, 73,* 2006.

[16] Elliott, C., Pearson, D., & Troxel, G. (2003). Quantum Cryptography in Practice. Karlsruhe, Germany: Proceedings of the 2003 Conference on Applications, technologies, architectures, and protocols for computer communications.

[17] Kishor, K., & Pandey, D. (2022). Study and Development of Efficient Air Quality Prediction System Embedded with Machine Learning and IoT. In: Gupta, D., et al (ed.), Proceeding International Conference on Innovative Computing and Communications. Lect. Notes in Networks, Syst (Vol. 471). Springer, Singapore, https://doi.org/10.1007/978-981-19-2535-1.

[18] Yadav, S. P., & Yadav, S. (2018). Fusion of medical images in wavelet domain: A discrete mathematical model. *Ingeniería Solidaria*, *14*(25), 1–11.

[19] Yadav, S. P., et al. (2022). Blockchain-based cryptocurrency regulation: An overview. *Computational Economics*, *59*(4), 1659–1675.

[20] Kishor, K. Cryptography's role in securing the information society. *International Journal of Communication and Media Studies*, Vol. *1*(1), 46–59.

[21] Mayers, D. (2001). Unconditional security in quantum cryptography. *Journal of the ACM, 48*(3), 351–406.

[22] Kishor, K., Sharma, R., & Chhabra, M. (2022). Student Performance Prediction Using Technology of Machine Learning. In: Sharma, D. K., Peng, S. L., Sharma, R., Zaitsev, D. A. (eds.) Micro-Electronics and Telecommunication Engineering. Lecture Notes in Networks and Systems (Vol. 373). Springer, Singapore, https://doi.org/10.1007/978-981-16-8721-1_53.

[23] Sharma, A., Jha, N., & Kishor, K. (2022). Predict COVID-19 with Chest X-ray. In: Gupta, D., Polkowski, Z., Khanna, A., Bhattacharyya, S., Castillo, O., (eds.). Proceedings of Data Analytics and Management. Lecture Notes on Data Engineering and Communications Technologies (Vol. 90). Springer, Singapore. https://doi.org/10.1007/978-981-16-6289-8_16.

[24] Sharma, R., Maurya, S. K., & Kishor, K. Student Performance Prediction Using Technology of Machine Learning (July 3, 2021). In: Proceedings of the International Conference on Innovative Computing & Communication (ICICC) 2021, Available at SSRN https://ssrn.com/abstract=3879645, or http://dx.doi.org/10.2139/ssrn.3879645.

[25] Jain, A., Sharma, Y., & Kishor, K. Prediction and Analysis of Financial Trends Using Ml Algorithm (July 11, 2021). Proceedings of the International Conference on Innovative Computing & Communication (ICICC) 2021, Available at SSRN: https://ssrn.com/abstract=3884458 or http://dx.doi.org/10.2139/ssrn.3884458.

[26] Kishor, K. (2022). Communication-Efficient Federated Learning. In: Yadav, S. P., Bhati, B. S., Mahato, D. P., Kumar, S., eds. Federated Learning for IoT Applications. EAI/Springer Innovations in Communication and Computing. Springer, Cham. https://doi.org/10.1007/978-3-030-85559-8_9.

[27] Kishor, K. (2022). Personalized Federated Learning. In: Yadav, S. P., Bhati, B. S., Mahato, D. P., Kumar, S. (eds.) Federated Learning for IoT Applications. EAI/Springer Innovations in Communication and Computing. Springer, Cham. https://doi.org/10.1007/978-3-030-85559-8_3.

[28] Gupta, S., Tyagi, S., & Kishor, K. (2022). Study and Development of Self Sanitizing Smart Elevator. In: Gupta, D., Polkowski, Z., Khanna, A., Bhattacharyya, S., Castillo, O. (eds.). Proceedings of Data Analytics and Management. Lecture Notes on Data Engineering and Communications Technologies (Vol. 90). Springer, Singapore, https://doi.org/10.1007/978-981-16-6289-8_15.

[29] Tyagi, D., Sharma, D., Singh, R., & Kishor, K. (2020). Real time 'driver drowsiness'& monitoring & detection techniques. *International Journal of Innovative Technology and Exploring Engineering*, *9*(8), 280–284. doi:. 10.35940/ijitee.H6273.069820.

[30] Jain, A., Sharma, Y., & Kishor, K. (2020). Financial supervision and management system using Ml algorithm. *Solid State Technology*, *63*(6), 18974–18982. http://solidstatetechnology.us/index.php/JSST/article/view/8080.

[31] Vernam, G. S. (1926). Cipher printing telegraph systems for secret wire and radio telegraphic communications. *Journal All India Engineering Entrance Examination AIEE 45*, 109–115. *Cryptology*, 18, 133–165, 200.

[32] Wang, X. B. (2005). Beating the photon-number-splitting attack in practical quantum cryptography. *Physical Review Letters*, *94*, 230503 .

[33] Yadav, S. P., et al. (2022). Survey on machine learning in speech emotion recognition and vision systems using a recurrent neural network (RNN). *Archives of Computational Methods in Engineering*, *29*(3), 1753–1770.

[34] Kishor, K. & Nand, P. (2013). Review performance analysis and challenges wireless MANET routing protocols. International *Journal of Science, Engineering and Technology Research (IJSETR)*, *2*(10), 1854–185. ISSN 2278-7798.

[35] Kishor, K., Nand, P., & Agarwal, P. (2017). Subnet based ad hoc network algorithm reducing energy consumption in manet. *International Journal of Applied Engineering Research*, *12*(22). 11796–11802.

[36] Kishor, K., Nand, P., & Agarwal, P. (2018). Secure and efficient subnet routing protocol for MANET. *Indian Journal of Public Health, Executive Editor*, *9*(12), 200, DOI: 10.5958/0976-5506.2018.01830.2.

[37] Kishor, K., Nand, P., & Agarwal, P. (2018). Notice of retraction design adaptive subnetting hybrid gateway MANET protocol on the basis of dynamic TTL value adjustment. *Aptikom Journal on Computer Science and Information Technologies*, *3*(2), 59–65. https://doi.org/10.11591/APTIKOM.J.CSIT.115.

[38] Kishor, K., & Nand, P. (2013). Review performance analysis and challenges wireless MANET routing protocols. International *Journal of Science, Engineering and Technology Research (IJSETR)*, *2*(10), 1854–185, ISSN 2278-7798.

[39] Makarov, V. (2009). Controlling passively quenched single photon detectors by bright light. New Journal of Physics, *11*, 065003.

[40] Lamas-Linares, A., & Kurtsiefer, C. (2007). Breaking a quantum key distribution system through a timing side channel. *Optics Express*, *15*, 9388.

[41] Yadav, S. P., Mahato, D. P., & Linh, N. T. D. (eds.). (2020). Distributed Artificial Intelligence: A Modern Approach. CRC Press.

[42] Hirota, O., Sohma, M., Fuse, M., & Kato, K. (2005). Quantum stream cipher by the Yuen 2000 protocol: Design and experiment by an intensity modulation scheme. *Physical Review A*, *72*, 022335-1–022335-8. quant-ph/0507043.

[43] Beaudry, N. J., Moroder, T., & Lütkenhaus, N. (2008). Squashing models for optical measurements in quantum communication. *Physical Review Letters*, *101*, 093601.

[44] Yuguang, Y., Some opinion on quantum key distribution protocol. *Communication Technology*, *4*, 2002, 1021–1024

[45] Vashisht, V., Kumar Pandey, A., & Prakash Yadav, S. (2021). Speech recognition using machine learning. *IEIE Transactions on Smart Processing & Computing*, *10*(3), 233–239.

Ayushi Prakash*, Sandhya Avasthi, Pushpa Kumari, Mukesh Rawat,
Puneet Garg

18 Modern healthcare system: unveiling the possibility of quantum computing in medical and biomedical zones

Abstract: The use of smart technologies such as Quantum Computing has become a transforming weapon in medical and bio medical applications. Quantum computing has proved itself useful in healthcare due to its transformatory and revolutionary ability. Quantum computing offers assurances to create new possibilities for faster, more agile, and mysterious efficiency improvements to all industries, and healthcare is no exception. The healthcare sector needs unprecedented speeds with the aid of quantum technology. Quantum computing will be yet another tool that can be employed to find solutions to diseases like Parkinson, cancer, and other ailments that affect so many lives every day. When we arrive at the more useful stage of quantum computing, one is quite certain that its utilization will be enabling the computers' ability to lead processes as well as analyze and offer remedies at super speed. Slow and extremely expensive trial procedures are a curse to the pharmaceutical and healthcare companies, affecting the development of new drugs and rollout of implementation timelines. Quantum computing has a lot of uses in healthcare because electronic medical records and ICT-based tools create so much of medical data. There are several reasons why health records need virtual environments where professionals will be able to analyze variables like body fluids, circulation, electrolytes, hormones, metabolism, and skin temperature.

*Corresponding author: Ayushi Prakash, Department of Computer Science and Engineering, ABES Engineering College, Ghaziabad, Uttar Pradesh, India, e-mail: ayushi5edu@gmail.com
Sandhya Avasthi, Department of Computer Science and Engineering, ABES Engineering College, Ghaziabad, Uttar Pradesh, India, e-mail: sandhya_avasthi@yahoo.com
Pushpa Kumari, Chemistry Department, Lok Maha Vidyalaya, Chapra, Bihar, India, e-mail: drpushpakumari5@gmail.com
Mukesh Rawat, Department of Computer Science and Engineering, Meerut Institute of Engineering & Technology, Meerut, Uttar Pradesh, India, e-mail: mukesh.rawat@miet.ac.in
Puneet Garg, Department of Computer Science and Engineering, ABES Engineering College, Ghaziabad, Uttar Pradesh, India, e-mail: puneetgarg.er@gmail.com

https://doi.org/10.1515/9783110798159-018

18.1 Introduction

Richard Feynman, in a now-famous talk given in 1982, proposed the concept of a quantum computer, which would follow the laws of quantum mechanics and act in a manner similar to that of quantum particles. This can be considered one of the earliest concepts of quantum computing [1]. He believed that quantum mechanical computer systems were necessary for accurately simulating natural phenomena. Quantum computers can achieve this by using quantum mechanical processes such as entanglement and superposition to provide the massive amount of computational power required to simulate complicated quantum systems. Massive commercial and academic interest in developing the world's first quantum machine stems from the possibility that quantum computing may provide processing capabilities that outperform today's supercomputers. Countless renowned organizations, such as IBM, Google, Microsoft, and Intel, as well as numerous ambitious start-ups, such as Rigetti and IonQ, are actively striving to create the world's first large-scale universal quantum computer. Quantum software and quantum algorithms have advanced at the same rate as quantum computing hardware.

Quantum computing derives from quantum mechanics. In quantum entanglement; physical quantum occurrences such as superposition state and quantum theory are used. A quantum computer can represent one bit in both "1" and "0", which is known as a quantum bit or even a qubit, thanks to a pioneering discovery in quantum physics. Using this concept, quantum computing creates powerful computer resources capable of handling large amounts of data at the same time. This entails allowing massive amounts of data to be computed in real-time. Researchers interested in quantum mechanics have recently expressed interest in taking computer processing capabilities to a higher level as humans progress beyond the Moore's law.

18.1.1 Quantum computing

In the beginning, quantum mechanics was the inspiration for quantum computing. Quantum superposition and entanglement are just two of the quantum physical phenomena used in quantum computing. It is possible for a single bit to stand in for both a "1" and a "0" in a quantum computer because of the use of a quantum bit, also known as a qubit, a rare observation from the field of quantum physics. Quantum computing takes advantage of this phenomenon to build a robust computer system that can analyze several data sources in parallel. This paves the way for the instantaneous processing of enormous data sets. With the end of the Moore's law era in sight, there has been a recent uptick in academic interest in quantum computing as a means to increase computing capacity.

It is now possible to operate, observe, and most crucially, isolate individual particles with their inherent quantum features, thanks to the decrease in the number of transistors, detectors, and access to extremely low temperatures (such as 273 degree centigrade). Due to the following characteristics, modern desktop and laptop computers stand out from quantum computers (see Figure 18.1). Theoretically known for more than a century, these characteristics have just lately been observed and confirmed for a variety of particles and systems. Although quantum mechanics may sound absurd, it has already significantly advanced a few fields of medicine (such as magnetic resonance imaging and laser surgery). The greatest potential technology for generating large improvements in processes that are currently beyond the scope of available computing power is quantum computing, should it be realized. Modern computers' processing power has mostly reached a plateau and is no longer increasing exponentially as it did in the previous century.

The location of a spinning electron at any one time cannot be precisely determined due to quantum superposition. Instead, it is modeled as a probability distribution in which the electron's chances of simultaneously existing everywhere and nowhere are equal but variable. A group of qubits can act as if they are one by using the superposition technique, which is used by quantum computers to carry out tasks quickly. The processing power of a q-bit quantum computer grows exponentially as $2q$, where q is the number of bits in the system and a qubit has one of the two possible states.

The paradoxical phenomenon, which Einstein referred to as "spooky activity at a distance," in which entangled electrons always spin in the opposite directions and affect one another over time and space, despite not being physically connected, is defined by the quantum entanglement feature. This innovation makes quantum algorithms significantly more efficient than conventional ones.

Last but not least, the quantum interference phenomenon describes how a single particle, like a photon (a particle of light), can obstruct its own path by slapping into it. Qubit production capabilities are developing quickly.

Even though the field has a lot of intellectual history and Richard Feynman came up with the term "quantum computing" in 1981, it is still in its early stages. Even so, the field is changing very quickly. Two important methods used today are superconducting circuits and the levitation of single atoms in electromagnetic fields. Quantum effects are hard to control, and stray heat or noise can flip 0s and 1s and mess with quantum phenomena like superposition. This is a big reason why quantum computing is not yet widely available. For this to happen, qubits need to be safe, and they also need to work in unusual situations, like when temperatures are very low, sometimes very close to absolute zero. Also, this makes people want to work on making quantum computers that can handle mistakes. Even though desktop or portable quantum computing processors are not yet commercially available, service providers have started selling specialized quantum computing equipment and offering quantum cloud computing services (e.g., Amazon Braket). Google's 54-qubit computer did something that was thought to take a traditional computer nearly 10,000 years to do. It did it in about 200 s. Due to how quickly quantum computing is changing, it is important to find ways to help existing healthcare systems. Quantum mechanics, category theory, and quantum algebraic geometry are just a few examples of the newly developed mathematical formalisms for algorithmic design that are paving the way for this promising new field in medicine and future surgical technology.

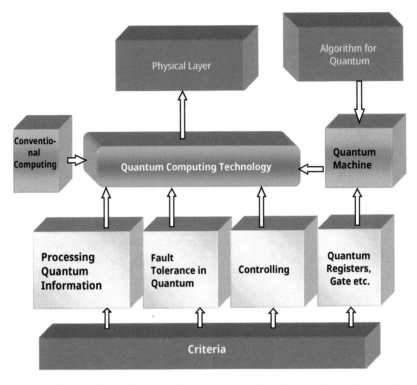

Figure 18.1: The conceptual diagram of quantum computing technology's transformation from traditional computing technology. Quantum computers have used the findings of quantum computing technologies.

18.1.2 Comparison of classical computing vs. quantum computing

The public health system relies on browsers exchanging data to improve process performance interconnection and reduce service provision. Smart healthcare uses the concept of interconnection between the virtual and real worlds to help in all areas. Given the preceding framework, the security of medical applications has become critical, even though facilities can be threatened in a variety of ways [1, 2], and [3]. The popularity of intelligent devices has grown dramatically in recent years, with the number of connected devices expected to exceed 75 billion by 2025 [4]. The massive expansion of smart devices necessitates the design of streamlined privacy, security procedures, and configurations, as well as assistance to the underlying IoT (Internet of Things) systems.

The advanced existence of the healthcare system also continues to pose security issues. The ability to provide improved security to web apps, e-mail systems, signals intelligence, and money transfers has all made public-key cryptography processes mandatory. Public-key cryptosystems like Rivest-Shamir Adleman (RSA), Diffie-Hellman, and

Elliptic Curve Cryptography (ECC) have become more popular in this setting. IoT systems and computer hardware use the Transportation Layer Security (TLS), which is based on these methods and other Internet standards. Nevertheless, advances in communication and processing technology have made it easier to carry out the modeling work required to breach specific security measures such as non-symmetric processes, paving the way for the minimum recommended key size to be increased indefinitely. Quantum computers had already emerged to solve problems.

18.1.3 Quantum computing for healthcare

The transition from parts to quantum states may open entirely new avenues for healthcare coverage. Quantum superposition's may enable supersonic drug design, in-silicon clinical trials with virtual humans simulated 'real – time,' full-speed entire genetic testing and predictive analysis, doctor's office cloud services, forecasting wellness, and healthcare data protection.

Attempting to develop pharma through long and expensive drug trials is certainly tough to pass: researchers and drug manufacturers began experimenting with alternative ways, including the use of AI technology, human organs-on-chips, or even in-silico trials, to accelerate the process and reduce the expense of drug development and discovery.

18.1.4 Supersonic drug design

Atomwise, for instance, utilizes powerful computers to retrieve treatments from a dataset of molecules. AtomNet, its profound convolutional neural network, monitors over 1 billion substances per day. Atomwise tried to launch a simulated quest in 2015 for established, secure medications that might be refitted to cure the Ebola virus. They found two drug targets in less than one day, cutting a month-long search in half. In another case, InSilico Medicine hit headlines when it announced that with the help of its smart algorithm, the process of creating a new drug took only 46 days. What would happen if such smart techniques were updated to record levels? The ability to run search queries on quantum computers could allow medical-intended tests to also be conducted in each potential model system or in silico body cells and systems in the shortest amount of time. This would open the door for discovering remedies to illnesses we had not ever thought before like for Alzheimer's, cancer etc.

18.1.5 Silicon clinical trials

In-silico clinical trials require no people, animal life, even a unicellular organism to test a new treatment or drug, but their own effect can be accurately documented. It refers to a customizable computer model utilized in the advancement or regulation assessment of a pharma, handset, or involvement.

It would also enable for 'live' clinical studies involving many hospitals provides as potential and elements customized based on the experts' preferences. It would not only radically reduce the amount of time for these kinds of trials, but it would also improve their quality and comprehensiveness.

18.1.6 Sequencing and analyzing DNA at full speed

Genetics and genomics have changed significantly over the past 20 years. It took over 15 years to decipher the living person DNA code: The Human Genome Project started in 1990, costing billions of dollars, and was expected to display its official outcome in 2006. In contrast, there are currently over 2,000 genetic markers for aspects of humanity. Such tests inform the patient regarding their genetic disease susceptibility as well as help healthcare providers in trying to diagnose illnesses.

18.1.7 Making patients truly the point of care

Quantum computers will be able to make sense of massive amounts of data, including individual pieces of health data. Furthermore, patient data from connected sensory systems may render traditional healthcare facilities obsolete, making patients the focal point of people's concern. Quantum computing may serve as the "front line" for such systems to function properly. Client mechanism decarbonization – another exciting prospect for this innovative industry linked to measurements is taking wellness forecasting to a whole new level. There have already been attempts to shift from precautionary to predictive health, but they are rare and in their initial stages. For example, there is an ophthalmology app that shows sick people how their eyesight will begin to change to cataract in five years if they do not use it.

18.1.8 Challenges in efficient healthcare services

The worldwide health situation offers a differing scenario. At one end, there are advanced medical equipment, medically qualified experts, and very well hospitals and clinics. On the other end, there are the increasing medical-care costs and older population unable to adjust to the present and a difficult future. Amid everything, there are people with aspirations who continue to struggle. They are entirely dependent on how successfully health insurers can overcome challenges and reduce the disparities in accessing healthcare, in order to provide better medical treatment.

18.1.9 Trying to take advantage

To understand fully the possibilities of health technologies to convert health systems and establish a connected health environment, healthcare leaders and healthcare professionals should develop stronger relationships with medical makers and software development firms. They can retrieve and share information [7–9], as well as create new business models and scenarios to improve the adoption of emerging health technologies.

18.1.10 Information and integrated health services

Health insurers can generate knowledge by using connected medical equipment and AI-integrated software. Physician health records, wireless device data, transcribed patient records, and patient survey data are all examples of data. Even the most prestigious healthcare systems, however, lack sophisticated architecture, and an information management system is a system that attempts to manage data from multiple sources. The value of the information they receive is not absolute because they will be using database systems that are incapable of effectively managing complex data collected from multiple sources. The shift from referential integrity to non-relational datasets may aid healthcare providers in managing substantial amounts of unstructured data.

18.1.11 Cyber security

The ability of quantum computers to breach the protection of regular tasks could have severe repercussions. Quantum vulnerability will increase the data breaches of delicate health and financial private information, put digital document integrity at danger, and burst certain crypto currency encryption.

18.1.12 Increasing medicine costs

The rise in pharmacy drug prescription prices is one of the most serious healthcare issues confronting both patients and physicians. "This could happen again because there is no verifiable proof, no individual to bring logic to having to decide drug prices," says Michael Rea, CEO of Rx Saving Solutions. To prevent or at least influence the price increase, a governing agency comprised of delegates from all stakeholders in the healthcare and pharmaceutical industry sectors could be established to oversee companies.

18.1.13 Payment processing and invoicing

Payment processing is a challenging aspect of any business world, but it is particularly difficult for healthcare providers. Privacy and security is a primary concern in a profession where patients should be protected both medically and personally. As a consequence, the healthcare online payment scheme that a practitioner selects must be given careful consideration and thought. One can safeguard payments along with personal data shared during these exchanges by doing so.

18.1.14 Pressure on pharmaceutical prices

The rise in drugstore prices is one of the most serious healthcare issues confronting both patients and doctors. "It can continue to happen because there is no business verification, no individual or organization to bring rationale to deciding drug prices," says Michael Rea, CEO of Rx Saving Solutions. To prevent or at least influence the price increase, a business regulatory body comprised of representatives from all interested parties in the pharmaceutical and healthcare industries could be established.

18.1.15 Disruption in the outside supply chain

Many external factors have decided to make shaky inroads into health coverage, which will certainly result in disruptive innovation. The increased use of mobile phones, as well as the rise of mobile applications and online marketplaces, has dramatically altered how business owners communicate with their customers. Clients in healthcare are no exception. They appear to be physically and emotionally vulnerable, necessitating good service quality.

18.1.16 Motivation

This study was inspired by an investigation into the complicated and critical requirements of today's modern medical systems, such as smart medications, ingestible devices, and health monitoring systems that rely on traditional computational models. Furthermore:

(i)   According to publications, most surveys involved smart healthcare technologies for remote monitoring of patients but they did not take into account all technological tools, such as wearables, body network connectivity, and electronic healthcare.

(ii) Previous research concentrated on monitoring patients using healthcare monitoring technologies such as IoT and cloud for smart healthcare, which are really susceptible to lag, serviceability, and different security threats. Beside that, no conversation or a study case of smart health technology assuring patients' online privacy has taken place.

(iii) As a result of this, we have presented a thorough questionnaire on smart health technology such as portable tech, body network connectivity, and electronic healthcare to observe patients' wellbeing in a secure, effective, and stable manner. We also looked at a case study that involved UAV-assisted safe healthcare coverage for the COVID-19 outbreak.

18.1.17 Contributions of this chapter

A few computer questionnaires have been published in the literature [5]. For example, debating the supercomputing limitations of traditional systems and the proposed linear combination and quantum entanglement-based solutions to address these issues. This chapter, on the other hand, covers complex quantum theory without delving into its social implications. The survey on IoT constraints proposes a questionnaire of cryptography-based IoT solutions [6].

18.2 Quantum computing healthcare applications

Whether as a result of disruptive technologies, unpredictability of health concerns, or the discovery of new diseases or medications, the healthcare business is frequently fraught with uncertainty. Prior study demonstrates that disruptive technologies cause obstacles and challenges for healthcare stakeholders. Few studies demonstrate how the increasing usage of telemedicine as an alternative to in-person visits indirectly affects pharmaceutical e-commerce platforms. Technology alters not just how system applications are utilized, but also how businesses operate, how projects are managed, how administrative duties are performed, how choices are made, etc.

The digital healthcare ecosystem is comprised of numerous forms of medical data and economic concepts. It also encompasses both personalized and broad healthcare information and services that are disseminated via various technologies. A practice-oriented healthcare ecosystem also discusses the significance of digitalization, viability, and connectivity [10]. The digital ecosystem enables the collection and real-time analysis of large data sets to examine healthcare trends, models, and predictive analytics.

It has resulted in the integration of industry 4.0 technology into the healthcare sector in order to deliver better, more precise, and individualized care. Since organizational processes rely around the flow of information, disruptive technological advances frequently produce uncertainty and ambiguity in the organization's information process [11, 12]. The author in [13] note that, according to the theory of information processing, the most crucial aspect of an organization's success is the direct relationship between the information, i.e., the resource, and how the information is managed. Specifically, the most significant component is an organization's capacity to process the proper amount and type of information. Unanticipated health concerns are typically a greater source of doubt and uncertainty, particularly in the healthcare industry. In addition, Covid-19 has placed a substantial burden on the healthcare industry [14]. For instance, the industry had to cope with and contain the pandemic, provide both diagnostic and preventive care, and rapidly develop and test new medications and vaccines against variations. Unanticipated events generate uncertainty and ambiguity, necessitating rapid knowledge transmission and technological solutions [15, 16]. In addition, these circumstances have the potential to generate vast amounts of big data, which could lead to improved data analytics. This comprises not only patient care data, but also data regarding virus types and gene mutations, ecological and geographical data, etc. that the technology and healthcare industries might utilize to generate forecasts and predictions [17, 18]. In order to apply quantum technology to address unpredicted health concerns, the healthcare industry will need to examine its current organizational structure to help people make better decisions and determine if this disruptive innovation can be combined with existing ones.

Countries are also investing heavily in healthcare technology, and other sectors have begun to invest in quantum technology research. This affords this innovative technology the opportunity to enter the most beneficial industry, namely healthcare. The pharmaceutical business seems to have a lot of potential for quantum computing. Existing corporations and start-ups are investigating how quantum technology could be used to develop new treatments, produce vaccinations, and do other tasks. When quantum technology is integrated with industry 4.0 technologies, it can accelerate innovation and discovery in any field of knowledge that is currently unattainable. It is anticipated that the quantum technology market would be valued at $1.9 billion by 2023 and $8 billion by 2027 [19, 20]. Quantum computing fits perfectly, and it may be used in six distinct ways to solve challenges in the healthcare industry that are typically large, complicated, unknown, and time-consuming to solve (see Figure 18.2). But the unpredictability, complexity, and volatility of disruptive technologies compel organizations to make trade-offs in how they allocate resources and design policies.

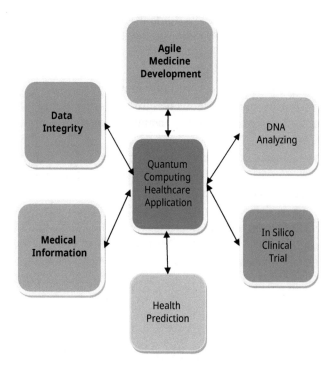

Figure 18.2: Quantum computing application in healthcare.

18.3 Security of quantum healthcare computing

Quantum computing is an emerging framework for attempting to solve computationally challenging issues [21]. Several businesses, such as IBM and D-Wave offer quantum computers over a cloud-based framework that includes several interesting properties, such as:

– Quantum hardware with various amounts of quantum bits as well as coupling charts at the virtualized end that give new computational power [22];
– Numerous equipment with exactly equal linkage map data that arise in the package;
– The linkage map of bigger hardware with a larger qubit can fit the coupling outline of many small equipment. In those other phases, the consumer needs to rely on the cloud company's dispatcher to allot resources to users' requests [23];
– Each piece of hardware has a distinct quality.
– The same user is not able to verify the beginnings of a results acquired from quantum equipment. In those other sentences, this same user needs to rely just on cloud company's dispatcher to allot the demanded equipment;

- The line of traffic of qubits programs at the cloud side is lengthy and the results of the process, which are really critical to decreasing expenses and aiding the science world in their exploration and discovery;

The mentioned factors inspire a new threat model for future prospects:
- In the long term, less-trustworthy quantum computers from external parties may allot poor quality equipment and save funds or encounter wrongfully qubit or quantum hardware requirements;
- The workload scheduling algorithm may contain a bug or malicious code segment that attempts to maximize throughput at the expense of allocating low-fidelity hardware. Such glitches are feasible for trustable suppliers;
- A disgruntled employee in a trusted hosting provider might attempt to undermine the company's public image by demeaning the consumer's calculation fidelity merely by trying to interfere with the scheduler or re-routing the software;
- A disgruntled employee could indeed steal data by rerouting initiatives to third party quantum equipment over which they have full control, if the hardware provided seems to be of inferior quality.

18.4 Open aspects and research challenges/future research opportunities

We gathered accessible security problems and research issues in smart healthcare technology in this section.

18.4.1 Safety

The data generated by different wearables and BANs may encounter different privacy and security concerns in the intelligent healthcare system even though patients' information might very well consist personal information that is exchanged between various medical staff before being sent to doctors. Moreover, data must be safeguarded from numerous wireless and sensor technologies that hackers can exploit to collect personal data. Therefore, counter-security metrics must be established to ensure safety and confidentiality inside the smart health service.

18.4.2 Data exchange

Data from IoT devices is decided to be shared with healthcare providers in intelligent healthcare systems, although there is no assurance about how one's data is handled or the number of individuals who are involved in the process before it is transmitted to the doctors. For example, if an hacker starts messing with data, patients could receive wrong medicine or no prescription from doctors. It may result in a delay in their diagnosis or be more harmful to their health. Consequently, there is a need to restrict data sharing or enforce a method to secure data transfer in the intelligent healthcare system.

18.4.3 Extensive data

Various wearables connected to bodies collect a large amount of data. Furthermore, as the patient's state changes, so does this data. It is difficult to manage such dynamic and enormous amount of data. Besides that, several types of information must be stored in different formats. For instance, an IoT detector may grasp the EEG of the brain in digital form in to run a machine learning model on it; the above data must be converted to CSV format. Therefore, there is a requirement for an efficient storage mechanism that directly converts files based on the needs of an application.

18.4.4 Excessive power consumption

Wearables are battery-powered equipment that constantly monitor and record the patient's health. In doing so, they consume a significant amount of battery power. As a result, the user should charge it many times. To solve this issue, the user must put their devices to sleep at periodic intervals when they are not monitoring their health status.

18.4.5 Inadequate standardization

In smart healthcare systems, devices are used to transmit health information. To communicate this data with medical staff, each device has its own set of procedures and configurations. Nevertheless, no centrally controlled consensus or consistency exists for IoT sensor information exchange, execution, and implementation in the health industry. Consequently, it is necessary to conduct research in this aspect because only then IoT systems with distinct protocols and specifications can converse voluntarily.

18.5 Conclusion

In this paper, we presented a comprehensive survey on the possibilities of Quantum Computing in healthcare technologies Quantum computing has transformed traditional algorithms by enabling previously unseen speed, effectiveness, and reliability. Health systems can profit from the huge amount of processing power provided by subatomic computer systems in an effective way. In this study, we looked at quantum information solutions from the point of view of healthcare systems. We started talking regarding new application areas where quantum physics can help with complicated math processing. We talked about the more essential areas of computational complexity implementations inside the healthcare paradigm. We established a categorization of existing quantum computer architectures for health systems. In addition, we debated quantum cryptography remedies for health systems. Finally, we debated current issues, their causes, and possible solutions. Research developments could greatly benefit from the application of quantum physics. We presented a taxonomy of numerous smart healthcare technologies, together with security problems based on this ground-breaking study, which highlights all the main topics. Future research will focus on a ground-breaking method that combines block chain technology with AI models to enhance the security and dependability of quantum computing healthcare solutions.

References

[1] Rafique, W., He, X., Liu, Z., Sun, Y., & Dou, W. (2019). CFADefense: A security solution to detect and mitigate crossfire attacks in software defined IoT-edge infrastructure. In: 2019 IEEE 21st International Conference on High Performance Computing and Communications; IEEE 17th International Conference on Smart City; IEEE 5th International Conference on Data Science and Systems (HPCC/SmartCity/DSS) (pp. 500–509). IEEE.

[2] Rafique, W., Khan, M., Sarwar, N., & Dou, W. (2019). A security framework to protect edge supported software defined Internet of Things infrastructure. In: International Conference on Collaborative Computing: Networking, Applications and Worksharing (pp. 71–88). Springer.

[3] Rafique, W., Khan, M., Zhao, X., Sarwar, N., & Dou, W. (2019). A blockchain based framework for information security in intelligent transportation systems. In: International Conference on Intelligent Technologies and Applications (pp. 53–66). Springer.

[4] Yunana, K., Alfa, A. A., Misra, S., Damasevicius, R., Maskeliunas, R., & Oluranti, J. (2021). Internet of Things: Applications, Adoptions and Components – A Conceptual Overview. In: Abraham, A., Hanne, T., Castillo, O., Gandhi, N., Nogueira Rios, T., Hong, T.-P. (eds). Hybrid Intelligent Systems (pp. 494–504). Springer International Publishing, Cham.

[5] Gyongyosi, L. & Imre, S. (2019). A survey on quantum computing technology. *Computer Science Review, 31*, 51–71.

[6] Fernandez-caramés, T. M. (2019). From pre-quantum to post-quantum IoT security: A survey on quantum-resistant cryptosystems for the internet of things. *IEEE Internet of Things Journal, 7*(7), 6457–6480.

[7] Prakash, A., Gupta, S., & Rawat, M. (2022). Design and Implementation of Novel Techniques for Content-Based Ranking of Web Documents, "Book Process Mining Techniques for Pattern Recognition" (pp. 11 eBook ISBN). Taylor & Francis Group, Imprint CRC Press, 1st, 9781003169550.

[8] Prakash, A., Gupta, S., & Rawat, M. (2022). Keyword based ranking of web pages by normalizing link score. *Published in Journal NeuroQuantology, 20*(6), 4725–4729, 10.14704/nq.2022.20.6. NQ22474.

[9] Prakash, A., Gupta, S., & Rawat, M. Content-Based Ranking of Web Documents by Normalizing Link Score. In: Lect. Notes in Networks, Syst., Vol. 479, Proceedings of Third Doctoral Symposium on Computational Intelligence 978-981-19-3147-5, 523483_1_En, DOI: 10.1007/978-981-19-3148-2.

[10] Stephanie, L. & Sharma, R. S. (2020). Digital health eco-systems: An epochal review of practice-oriented research. *International Journal of Information Management, 53*, 102032.

[11] Fixson, S. K., Khachatryan, D., & Lee, W. (2017). Technological uncertainty and firm boundaries: The moderating effect of knowledge modularity. *IEEE Transactions on Engineering Management, 64*(1), 16–28.

[12] Mikalef, P. & Pateli, A. (2017). Information technology-enabled dynamic capabilities and their indirect effect on competitive performance: Findings from PLS-SEM and fsQCA. *Journal of Business Research, 70*, 1–16.

[13] Fairbank, J. F., Labianca, G. J., Steensma, H. K., & Metters, R. (2006). Information processing design choices, strategy, and risk management performance. *Journal of Management Information Systems, 23*(1), 293–319.

[14] Cobianchi, L., Pugliese, L., Peloso, A., Dal Mas, F., & Angelos, P. (2020). To a new normal: Surgery and COVID-19 during the transition phase. *Annals of Surgery, 272*(2), e49.

[15] Massaro, M., Tamburro, P., La Torre, M., Dal Mas, F., Thomas, R., Cobianchi, L., & Barach, P. (2021). Non-pharmaceutical interventions and the infodemic on Twitter: Lessons learned from Italy during the Covid-19 Pandemic. *Journal of Medical Systems, 45*(4), 1–12.

[16] Avasthi, S., Chauhan, R., Tripathi, S. L., & Sanwal, T. (2022). COVID-19 Research: Open Data Resources and Challenges. In: Biomedical Engineering Applications for People with Disabilities and the Elderly in the COVID-19 Pandemic and Beyond (pp. 93–104). Academic Press.

[17] Avasthi, S., Chauhan, R., & Acharjya, D. P. (2021). Techniques, Applications, and Issues in Mining Large-scale Text Databases. In: Advances in Information Communication Technology and Computing (pp. 385–396). Springer, Singapore.

[18] Sousa, T., Soares, T., Pinson, P., Moret, F., Baroche, T., & Sorin, E. (2019). Peer-to-peer and community-based markets: A comprehensive review. *Renewable and Sustainable Energy Reviews, 104*, 367–378.

[19] Avasthi, S., Chauhan, R., & Acharjya, D. P. (2021). Processing large text corpus using N-gram language modeling and smoothing. In: Proceedings of the Second International Conference on Information Management and Machine Intelligence (pp. 21–32). Springer, Singapore.

[20] Orús, R., Mugel, S., & Lizaso, E. (2019). Quantum computing for finance: Overview and prospects. *Reviews in Physics, 4*, 100028.

[21] Nyári, N. (2021). The Impact of Quantum Computing on IT Security. *Biztonságtudományi Szemle, 3*(4), 25–37.

[22] Abd El-Latif, A. A., Abd-El-Atty, B., & Talha, M. (2017). Robust encryption of quantum medical images. *IEEE Access, 6*, 1073–1081.

[23] Saki, A. A., Alam, M., Phalak, K., Suresh, A., Topaloglu, R. O., & Ghosh, S. (2021). A survey and tutorial on security and resilience of quantum computing. In: 2021 IEEE European Test Symposium (ETS) (pp. 1–10). IEEE.

S. Karthik*, H. Summia Parveen, R. Sabitha, B. Anuradha

19 Quantum computing-assisted machine learning to improve the prediction of cardiovascular disease in healthcare system

Abstract: It has been determined that the presence of certain risk factors is one of the primary contributors to the development of coronary heart disease (CHD). A wide range of computational methods are utilized in the process of medical diagnosis of coronary heart disease symptoms – the diagnostic tools that can be utilized in the process of determining whether or not a patient has coronary heart disease. In this chapter, we develop a quantum backpropogation neural network model to classify the CHD disease. The model is designed with a preprocessing module and a classification module. A Python tool is used to validate the accuracy of the classification and the results of validation shows that the proposed QML has a higher rate of accuracy than other methods.

19.1 Introduction

It has been determined that the presence of certain risk factors, such as being overweight or obese, having high blood pressure, having high blood sugar levels, drinking excessively, etc., are primary contributors to the development of coronary heart disease (CHD) [1]. Other risk factors include smoking and not getting enough exercise. Despite the fact that some risk factors can be modified and that several metabolic symptoms can be used for predicting heart diseases, it is still difficult for doctors to provide a prompt and accurate diagnosis of cardiac disease, based solely on risk factors [2]. This is the case despite the fact that certain risk factors are modifiable and that several metabolic symptoms can be used [3].

The prognosis of a patient can be difficult to ascertain because the clinical symptoms of cardiovascular disorders are impacted by a diverse range of functional and

*Corresponding author: **S. Karthik**, Department of Computer Science and Engineering, SNS College of Technology, Coimbatore, Tamil Nadu, India, e-mail: profskarthik@gmail.com
H. Summia Parveen, Department of Computer Science & Engineering, SNS College of Technology, Coimbatore, Tamil Nadu, India, e-mail: summiaparveen@yahoo.in
R. Sabitha, Department of Computer Science and Engineering, SNS College of Technology, Coimbatore, Tamil Nadu, India, e-mail: dr.r.sabitha@gmail.com
B. Anuradha, Department of Computer Science and Design, SNS College of Engineering, Coimbatore, Tamil Nadu, India, e-mail: pskanu80@gmail.com

https://doi.org/10.1515/9783110798159-019

pathologic characteristics. In spite of the fact that early detection of CHD is famously challenging, it is of utmost importance to make this diagnosis as soon as possible because prompt treatment is contingent on it [4, 5].

Clinical decision-support systems have been the focus of a number of research initiatives that have been conducted in an effort to overcome these challenges through the application of novel methods such as data mining and machine learning [6]. These efforts to study have been ongoing for a considerable amount of time. A variety of data mining technologies have been created in recent years in order to improve the accuracy of medical diagnosis [7].

Some of these data mining technologies include neural networks, hybridized rough sets, and fuzzy learning vector quantization networks. In the field of medicine, some applications of these methodologies include principal component analysis, radial basis function neural networks, and association rules, to name just a few. These are just a few of the many different approaches that are now being utilized in the world [8].

When it comes to attempting to increase the precision of CHD predictions, machine learning (ML) is by far the most common type of technology that is used. When it comes to generalization in the context of CHD, ML is capable of doing well because it does not require any prior knowledge of the domain and can do so without any problems [9]. ML is also very good at analyzing complicated data, which paves the path for the discovery of one-of-a-kind pattern and information that is pertinent to CHD research [10].

On the other hand, in recent years, there has been a growth in the quantity of research that is focused on the difficulty of finding abnormalities in big datasets. This trend has been observed in a number of different fields. Because of this, it is critically required to construct a complex CHD forecast model for the goal of early-stage illness prediction that can be done at a reasonable cost [11]. In fact, by utilizing the data that is available, it is possible to forecast the incidence of these diseases by adopting machine learning algorithms that are equipped with a number of different classifiers and models. This can be done by making use of the data that is now available [12].

The automatic classification and diagnosis of CHD, based on deep learning, is an excellent answer to the issues that were previously described with traditional cardiovascular disease diagnoses, and the processing and analysis of data from wearable devices. This answer is based on the fact that assisted CHD can be automatically classified and diagnosed using deep learning [13].

As research make progress, a growing variety of cutting-edge open-source systems for the processing of streaming data in real time have emerged as a result. There has been recent progress in the field of medical diagnostics, which has led to an increase in the number of companies that are beginning to implement AI for the goal of performing diagnostics [14]. In recent years, deep neural networks have seen widespread usage in automatic ECG diagnosis [15]. This has primarily occurred as a means of satisfying the growing demand for ECG analysis that is both quick and accurate [16].

The processing of data with QML classifiers will play an important part in the identification of cardiac problems. In recent years, a number of research works that were targeted at achieving this goal have successfully concluded. The findings of each of these research works revealed that the application of computerized medical decision support systems is a prudent strategy that can assist medical professionals in arriving at precise and prompt diagnoses.

A method that is both effective and cost-efficient for making such predictions at an early stage in the progression of the disease is one of the primary goals that should be pursued in order to achieve this objective. In order to achieve this goal, new QML models should be examined using a wide variety of current information. Therefore, in order to provide a framework that justly supports the diagnostic approach, an attempt is made to construct a bridge between the specialized areas of knowledge that are held by various professionals.

19.2 Related works

A unique new quantum-inspired classifier for binary supervised learning was presented by Sergioli et al. [17] under the name Helstrom Quantum Centroid. Their investigation was predicated on density matrices as well as the formal aspects of quantum theory. The authors used fourteen distinct datasets in order to conduct an analysis in which they compared the effectiveness of their model to that of a range of more conventional methods.

Using decision theory, classical machine learning, and the idea of quantum detection, the authors [18] constructed a new quantum-inspired binary classifier (QIBC). They were able to accomplish this by utilizing one of the laws of quantum physics that is referred to as superposition. Compared to more traditional methods such as KNN and SVM, the newly developed classifier has the potential to achieve greater levels of precision, recall, and F-measure.

Ding et al. [19] presented a new technique that was inspired by quantum support vector machines and was able to tackle classification issues at an exponentially faster rate. Linear transformation that acts as the foundation of the algorithm is the primary idea of operation.

Dang et al. [20] developed an innovative model for the classification of images that makes use of both parallel computing and quantum KNN. Both the speed and accuracy of the classification process saw considerable improvements as a direct result of the model that they developed.

Quantum Nearest Mean Classifiers, commonly known as QNMCs, were first conceived of by Sergioli et al. [21] as a potential improvement to the conventional minimum distance classifier. They were introduced for the first time in their work. First, an encoding in which a theoretical quantum object is assigned to each pattern, which we will refer to as a density pattern; second, classification in which a quantum-inspired counterpart of a standard classification procedure is applied to a dataset of density operators rather than a dataset of real vectors. Third, there is a decoding step that decodes the classification process results in the domain of real vectors. Nevertheless, the only medical dataset in which it showed an improvement was the cancer dataset. The approach performed better than its traditional version (NMC) on a variety of different medical datasets; however, the cancer dataset was the only one in which it showed an improvement.

Chen, H. et al. [22] developed a novel Quantum K Nearest Neighbor (QKNN) algorithm that is based on one of the most well-known components of QC, which is known as superposition. This was accomplished through the utilization of strong parallel computing. Because of this, they were able to more swiftly locate their target.

On the basis of quantum SVM, the quantum Gaussian kernel and the quantum polynomial kernel [23] developed a novel model for the clustering of large amounts of data called Quantum Support Vector Clustering. This model is a one-of-a-kind approach to the clustering of large amounts of data. Lu, S. et al. [24], using a quantum form, created a decision tree classifier for their study. It is necessary to have both a measure of the fidelity of the quantum state as well as a measure of the entropy of the quantum state for the model to have any chance of being correct.

Yu et al. [25] reported the development of better quantum algorithms for ridge regression. Quantum K-fold cross-validation and quantum state encoding are the two main components that make up this methodology. A new framework for quantum clustering is presented in the study [26], and the Schrodinger equation is used as the theoretical underpinning for this framework.

19.3 Methods

Using QML [27–31], one may perform intelligent procedures on a number of datasets, which will result in outputs that can be acted upon. This can be done in order to get the desired outcome. QML is an appealing alternative for usage by decision-makers in fields such as medical diagnostics because of its efficacy in exploring, analyzing, and interpreting datasets. This is especially true in the light of the fact that QML is a declarative language.

QML appears to be an appropriate technique for addressing this issue in view of the fact that CHD diagnosis requires the training of a model through the utilization of a history dataset. In the light of this fact, QML appears to be an appropriate method for addressing this issue.

During the training phase, a classification model will be created, making use of a dependent variable (CHD class), in addition to a large number of independent factors. This will take place when the model is being trained (age, gender, medical history, symptoms, etc.). After that, a prediction is made regarding the value of the dependent variable using the model, based on the test dataset. The proposed model of QML is shown in Figure 19.1 below.

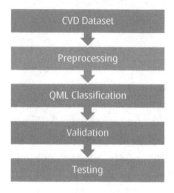

Figure 19.1: Proposed QML model.

19.3.1 Preprocessing

When it comes to resolving classification challenges during the preprocessing step, the structure of the dataset will be the determining factor in whether or not you are successful. Typically, falling prices do not have an effect on the outcome of the situation. As a result, as a primary order of business, we investigated the dataset to determine whether or not it had any values that were absent.

The study verified the missing values in a variety of different ways, including disregarding them entirely, substituting any number, substituting the longest period of time that most nearly fits that attribute, or restoring the value with the median value for that property.

In the CHSLB dataset that has been combined, there is not a single variable that is absent. The fact that the Cleveland dataset contains almost no gaps in its information is the icing on the cake. Preprocessing is the act of preparing data for analysis and is referred to by that very term.

It is vital before implementing techniques such as machine learning or data mining to authenticate the legitimacy of the information that will be utilized. This can be done through a number of different means. In spite of the fact that there are numerous approaches to data analysis, we choose to focus on the outlier detection strategy for the purpose of this inquiry.

On the other hand, one may make out a normal distribution in the CHSLB dataset, but this is not the case in the Cleveland dataset.

Utilizing interquartile range (IQR) method, we were able to identify statistical out-liers. In the event that the data being examined does not follow a normal distribution, this technique is the one that is applied. If the data that needs to be prepared is skewed, the IQR approach can assist you in preparing the data that needs to be prepared.

The study can calculate the interquartile range in four different ways: by sorting the data from smallest to largest, by locating the median, by determining the medians of the lower and upper halves of the data, and by calculating the IQR difference be-tween the upper and lower medians.

19.3.2 Classification in the presence of noise

In the context of a learning problem, noise can perform a number of potentially use-ful roles but the precise nature of these functions varies greatly, depending on the situation. It has been established that including noise in a typical environment can both improve generalization performance and reduce the incidence of local opti-mums. This was done through the use of simulations. When attempting to fit a model to data, these are two of the most prevalent issues that crop up. The former can bene-fit from gradient perturbation by jumping out of local optima, while the latter can be improved by making tweaks to the training inputs or outputs. Both can be improved. But in order to make one of these improvements, gradient perturbation is required.

In the field of quantum computing, a concept that piques the curiosity of a lot of people is the idea of making use of the benefits that come along with noise and mak-ing it work to your advantage. Because early quantum computers are expected to have too few qubits to implement full error correction, the community is actively seeking problems in which noise does not harm the computation, and can even play a positive role. This is because early quantum computers are projected to be released in the next few years and these will not have sufficient quantities of bits known as qubits.

Under some circumstances, the application of a technique that is founded on quantum physics to the study of issues that are associated with noisy learning can become highly fascinating. We are going to show that traditionally difficult problems in noisy learning may be efficiently solved by exploiting quantum resources, which is something that was not previously conceivable. This is something that we are going to demonstrate right now. Even though there has not been a lot of research done in this area just yet, it could lead to new examples of a divide-in-a-classroom situation be-tween the classical and quantum scenarios.

We think that by providing this section, we will be able to stimulate people's in-terest in the study of how quantum learners function in noisy circumstances, which will, in turn, pave the door for future in-depth research to be conducted in this area. In the first step of this project, we look into a variety of classical problems in order to acquaint quantum scientists with the potential benefits that noise could bring to ML. In the next part, we will provide a high-level overview of the common ways that ML professionals employ when modeling errors in quantum computing. In the concluding section of this article, we will talk about a few different scenarios in which the availability of quantum resources paves the way for the accomplishment of tasks that would be difficult for a mind that has been schooled in classical thinking and is used to approaching problems in a traditional way.

19.3.2.1 Noisy inputs

This work establishes the first causal relationship between Tikhonov regularization and the practice of introducing noise to training inputs (xi) ni = 1, and it does so by establishing the first causal association between the two. In this paper, we show that the optimization of a feed-forward neural network to reduce the squared error on noisy inputs is equivalent to the optimization of a feed-forward neural network to minimize the squared error using Tikhonov regularization on noiseless inputs. This is shown by comparing the results of the two. This can be seen by contrasting the two approaches using inputs with no background noise (up to the order of the noise variance).

This kind of regularization intuitively drives outputs from the surrounding inputs to be similar to one another by decreasing the gradient of the neural network function $f(x)$ with respect to the input x. This is accomplished by reducing the value of the input x. The neural network is responsible for achieving this goal.

Researchers have explored what happens to a neural network when noise is added to the inputs, outputs, weights, and weight updates of the network. They have established, on the basis of their findings, that adding noise to the inputs (and sometimes weights) can actually boost generalization performance in some instances. This was found to be the case in both cases.

19.3.2.2 Parameter updates

Recent empirical research has revealed that optimizing complex neural network models can be made easier by introducing annealed i.i.d. Gaussian noise to the gradients. This has been demonstrated to be effective in improving results. The application of the scientific process resulted in the discovery of this discovery. The practice of measuring the gradients of the objective function with respect to randomly chosen subsets of the training points is an additional source of stochasticity in the process of optimization (as in stochastic gradient descent). The two processes are easily comparable from an intuitive standpoint because the inherent uncertainty in these partial gradients can assist in the escape of local optima (and saddle points), and also because the (decreasing) gradient step size can be directly compared to the annealing temperature. Both of these factors contribute to the fact that the annealing temperature can be directly compared to the two processes.

It was also determined that the practice of including noise in the process of updating the parameters of models was an acceptable practice. There, random selections of training points are used to evaluate gradients throughout each iteration, and in addition to that, Gaussian noise is added to the parameter update. This ensures that the most accurate results are obtained. This occurs, following the completion of each stage (with variance equal to the decreasing step size). It has been demonstrated that after the initial phase of stochastic optimization, this method will begin generating samples from the posterior distribution over-model parameters if specific conditions are met. This was done in the context of a certain set of circumstances. Because of this, we are able to measure the uncertainty of the model and prevent it from being overfit without incurring any additional computational costs.

19.3.2.3 Noisy outputs

On the other hand, GP regression makes use of noise in the training outputs to help avoid inverting a possibly ill-conditioned kernel covariance matrix K. This is accomplished by the use of noise in the training outputs. This can be done by establishing (yi) ni = 1 in the equation. It is sufficient to invert a matrix of the form K + 2I in order to evaluate model predictions based on the premise that additive isotropic Gaussian noise is present. This is due to the fact that inverting matrices involves a vector space (with variance 2). On the other hand, GP regression makes use of noise in the training outputs to help avoid inverting a possibly ill-conditioned kernel covariance matrix K. This is accomplished by adding noise to the training outputs, such that (yi)ni = 1 in the equation. By assuming that additive isotropic Gaussian noise is present, it is sufficient to invert a matrix of the form K + 2I in order to evaluate model predictions. Inverting matrices involves a vector space with variance 2, which can be an advantage in the Hilbert space associated with the kernel covariance function. The kernel matrix becomes singular or ill-conditioned whenever training inputs are similar to one another or occur repeatedly, and this property can be exploited in GP regression. The connection that exists between these ideas makes this a potentially helpful point to bring up. This can be advantageous because the kernel matrix becomes singular or ill-conditioned whenever training inputs are similar to one another or occur repeatedly. The connection that exists between these two ideas makes this a potentially helpful point to bring up.

During the process of training generative adversarial networks, it was found that an overconfident discriminator, which is sometimes referred to as an evaluating node, can present a challenge. GANs are used to train generative models by trying to fool another model, which is referred to as the discriminator, into thinking that the generated images are a part of the actual data distribution (the generator). However, there is a possibility that there will be little overlap between the assistance supplied by the data distribution and the generator, particularly in the beginning of the training process. This is due to the fact that there is a likelihood that there will be little overlap between the two. This can result in the discriminator becoming overfit, which is a process that can improve the accuracy of label prediction.

Additionally, this can result in the discrimination choice having a modest dependency on the parameters of the generator, which is another factor that can increase accuracy. Fuzzing the labels, such as true and false, is the solution to the problem. The discriminator will make an estimate of the probabilities for each of the K labels for each training instance that it is given, with the probability of the actual label being equal to one plus one over the number of labels.

This is the same as the hypothesis that labels are chosen at random with a probability of K and that, in actuality, labels can be flipped at random, provided there is sufficient space for error. As a result of this, it is not in the best interest of the model to pin all of its expectations on locating the appropriate label, as doing so prevents it from being overconfident in its own forecasts. Label smoothing is a strategy that has been demonstrated to enhance classifier robustness against adversarial scenarios while also preserving the training signal for the generator. This is accomplished by minimizing the amount of noise introduced into the signal during the smoothing process. This has been demonstrated by the findings of a great deal of study carried out in a variety of settings.

19.3.3 QML classification

The developing discipline of quantum machine learning is working toward the goal of achieving these benefits, with the expectation that they will one day be included into more traditional machine learning approaches. We present a novel hybrid neural network that is built on a variational quantum classifier in order to examine the potential quantum advantage that could come along with quantum machine learning. This advantage could come about as a result of quantum machine learning. We are the ones that designed and built this network.

Comparisons between traditional neural network models and variational quantum classifier models can be made in a number of different ways. The model of a VQC classifier is more condensed than that of a traditional neural network, which is one of the ways in which it excels over the latter. A quantum-based analog of the traditional gradient descent technique has been incorporated into the model that has been proposed. Natural gradient descent on deep neural networks can frequently be computationally expensive because it requires inverting massive matrices. This is as a result of the requirement to understand intricate patterning. Despite this, we are still able to fine-tune our network by utilizing quantum gradient descent because of the benefits that the VQC provides in terms of model size.

Both classical and quantum gradient descent are applied in the process of maximizing the classical bias term and the quantum gate parameters of the model, respectively. Quantum gradient descent is utilized in the process of optimizing the model quantum gate parameters. An investigation toward locating the resonance was conducted, making use of this model. We compared these results to those that were achieved by a VQC that was optimized through the use of traditional gradient descent and by a neural network that rigorously adhered to classical principles.

The learning process was enhanced to its fullest potential by utilizing a hybrid instructional method. In terms of how rapidly new information can be learned, the hybrid strategy surpasses both the classically trained VQC as well as an analogous classical neural network. This is the case since the hybrid technique combines aspects of both these approaches.

Even when working with a relatively little amount of data, the hybrid VQC performance, in terms of accurate categorization, is unaffected. We feel that this method has the potential to be effective in data-driven classification situations that comprise a limited amount of data, despite the fact that our work was done with generated data in order to simulate real-world conditions.

When it becomes clear that the loss has hit a plateau while the model is being trained, the pace of learning for each model is slowed down. This happens as soon as it is discovered. In spite of this, it would appear that there is no impact on the efficiency with which the network is being trained even if the rate at which the network is learning is slowed down. Given how similar signal and noise are to one another, it should not come as a surprise that the network is not particularly good at differentiating between the two.

In order for researchers to engage in supervised learning, they developed an apparatus that is now known as a variational quantum classifier. The variational quantum classifier can be thought of as a type of quantum neural network. Constructing a quantum circuit that is capable of simulating the operation of conventional ML algorithms is necessary in order to realize this objective.

The algorithm for quantum machine learning makes use of a circuit whose parameters are educated to their optimal values in order to accomplish the goal of minimizing the value of a loss function. In order to do this, the parameters are learned to their optimal states through the use of a teaching circuit. The following is a definition of this trained circuit according to the operational properties that it possesses:

$$f(w, b, x) = y,$$

where f is network; y is output that estiamtes the loss function L; w, b are trainable parameter; and x is input data.

In the sense that the network in question is constructed out of discrete modular building pieces, the training processes that are utilized by classical neural networks and quantum circuits are comparable to one another and are used in both of these types of networks.

This classifier is analogous to a sophisticated and versatile system that determines the value of a loss function. The process of continuously modifying the parameters w and b, following the acquisition of y through a measurement, in order to continuously decrease the loss function L is directly related to the optimization of a network. This practice is done in order to maximize the amount of information that can be transmitted through the network.

The optimization of a quantum neural network is attainable in the same sense that the optimization of a traditional neural network is achievable. In either of these two sets of circumstances, a forward pass is executed on the model, and immediately following that, a loss function is computed. In order to do backpropagation on a network whose output varies as a function of a controllable parameter, $\theta = (w,b)$, we must first determine the gradient, f.

Only then can we proceed with backpropagation and the backpropagation will be performed, and applying the principles of parameter shifting enables one to perform the calculation necessary to determine the network output gradient of the quantum circuit. We are able to potentially train our variational quantum circuit, utilizing gradient descent methodologies, thanks to the computations of gradients for the outputs of quantum circuits. The method is exactly the same as the one that is utilized for the process of training and developing traditional neural networks.

19.4 Results and discussion

The method of estimate known as ten-fold cross-validation was utilized in the process of determining how well the machine learning algorithm performed on the dataset that was under evaluation.

We take the entire dataset and split it up into ten different portions, which we refer to as folds. The remaining one is the one that is put to use for testing after each iteration. Of these, nine are put to use for training machine learning models. Throughout the entirety of the process, a total of ten distinct counts of the error rate are obtained at various points. The ultimate error of the model is only the average of the errors that were made throughout the entirety of the calculation over ten iterations.

The amount of accuracy reached by machine learning-generated classification models can be evaluated with the use of the confusion matrix, which is used in the evaluation process. By consulting the confusion matrix, which is a contingency table displaying the number of cases allotted to each class, we are able to determine the classification accuracy, sensitivity, specificity, true positives (TP), true negatives (TN), false positives (FP), and false negatives. TP stands for true positive, TN stands for true negative, TP stands for false positive, and FP stands for false negative (FN). All of them are different ways of measuring diagnostic performance.

This recommends that traditional machine learning (Figures 19.2–19.5) employs a significant quantity of data, but has a weak feature extraction effect on data with more characteristics, which leads to subpar model generalization; the space under QML is equal, and its classification efficacy is strong. The ROC for all the models are presented in Figure 19.6.

Our proposed technique has the greatest ROC (Figure 19.7), which suggests that QML models are able to not only propose the characteristics of the dataset itself, but also accurately propose the time-domain features included within it. In other words, our method has the largest area.

Additionally, this illustrates that the deep learning model is able to efficiently extract the unilateral aspects of the data to a certain extent, which increases the

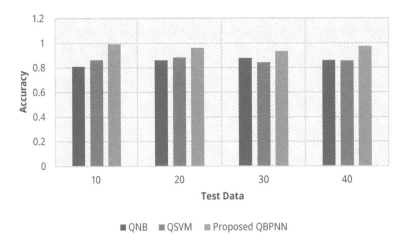

Figure 19.2: Accuracy.

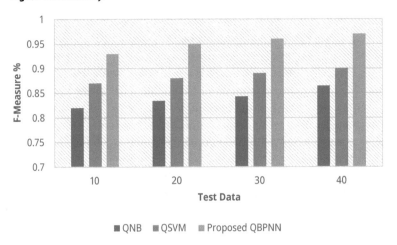

Figure 19.3: F-measure.

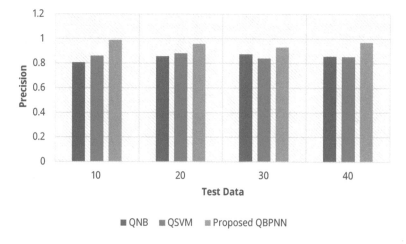

Figure 19.4: Precision.

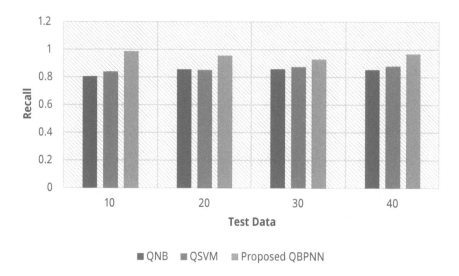

Figure 19.5: Recall.

network capacity to generalize. They have the potential to considerably increase the accuracy of the categorization if they are applied in conjunction with one another as described in the previous sentence. The importance of this element is one of the contributors to the great degree of generalizability that the model possesses as in Tables 19.1–19.3 for different datasets.

In this particular instance, we take into consideration the hybrid quantum-classical transfer learning architecture, which makes use of a classical model that has already been trained to extract features. Specifically, we make use of a model that has

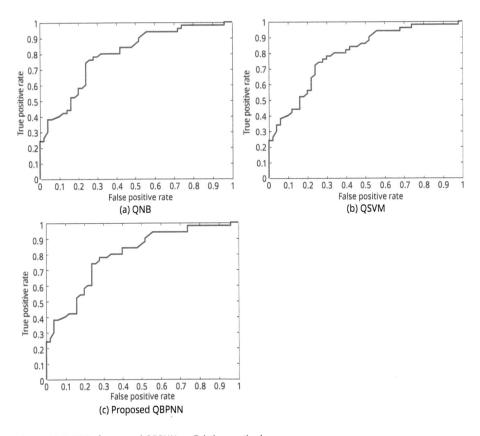

Figure 19.6: ROC of proposed QBPNN vs. Existing methods.

been taught to recognize faces. It is now only possible to employ a relatively small fraction of the qubits that are accessible in quantum computers and the simulation software that runs on them.

The transfer learning structure is one of the numerous potential applications that can be developed with the help of the recommended framework. In recent years, there has been the creation of a hybrid design that combines tensor networks and quantum circuits into a single operating system. This hybrid design was made possible by recent advancements in computer technology.

When compared to the pre-trained network that was utilized for this experiment, the performance of this hybrid architecture is much higher in terms of its capacity to generalize outcomes. It is necessary to conduct additional research in order to establish whether or not decentralized designs such as these are even possible. When larger-scale quantum simulators or genuine quantum computers become accessible, it will also be possible to do research on quantum machine learning.

The approach that has been suggested can not only be used to gain knowledge from the conventional data that has been utilized in this investigation, but it can also

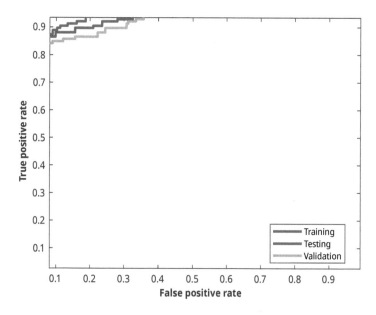

Figure 19.7: Comparison of modules in the proposed method.

Table 19.1: IEEE dataport dataset classification results.

Dataset	Training	Testing	Validation
10	82.05	84.55	89.14
20	82.42	76.69	88.20
30	77.14	80.24	88.01
40	72.97	83.14	84.01
50	71.08	79.18	75.27
60	79.80	81.41	87.98
70	59.01	62.67	82.44
80	82.67	82.09	90.04
90	81.72	85.30	89.02
100	82.25	81.46	87.21
110	82.59	87.15	90.92
120	83.25	84.83	89.51
130	84.26	85.69	89.52

be used to gain knowledge from a wide range of other sources. If this system is expanded, there is room for the study of quantum information, which is something that could be added into it.

The testing loss and accuracy will eventually converge to values that are on par with those reached by non-federal training, and this will happen regardless of the length of epochs that are spent in the local training. Also, the testing loss and accuracy will eventually converge to values that are on par with those reached by federal

Table 19.2: Kaggle dataset classification results.

Dataset	Training	Testing	Validation
10	88.05	85.46	88.32
20	88.37	80.86	87.31
30	81.08	81.59	86.27
40	77.37	86.84	83.56
50	74.99	80.79	75.74
60	83.61	85.23	87.29
70	66.87	65.79	82.16
80	85.19	82.44	91.79
90	87.74	85.29	88.04
100	88.23	85.28	86.42
110	86.09	87.79	88.86
120	86.68	84.87	91.31
130	90.08	86.49	88.49

Table 19.3: GitHub dataset classification results.

Dataset	Training	Testing	Validation
10	84.61	85.10	88.05
20	84.98	77.19	87.10
30	79.67	80.76	86.89
40	75.47	83.68	82.86
50	73.57	79.70	74.03
60	82.34	81.93	86.87
70	61.42	63.09	81.27
80	85.23	82.62	88.94
90	84.27	85.86	87.91
100	84.81	81.99	86.10
110	85.15	87.71	89.84
120	85.81	85.38	88.41
130	86.83	86.24	88.42

training. It would appear that a single session of local training is sufficient for the generation of a model with good performance. This is the most important conclusion that can be drawn from the research.

Local training is only carried out for a single epoch at a time, whereas federated training goes through multiple iterations, with each iteration using samples from five separate clients to drive changes to the model.

This difference is due to the fact that federated training is more efficient. According to these data, it would appear that QML models could benefit more from distributed training methods as opposed to traditional ones.

When training quantum models, it is best to use either a simulation platform with a high performance level or a set of small devices that have a moderate communication overhead. Either of these options is likely to produce the best possible results.

19.5 Conclusion

In this chapter, we developed a QML algorithm obtained from the CHD dataset. It is clear that additional investigation is necessary in order to improve the performance of the model, in particular with regard to increasing the rates of sensitivity and specificity. One of these endeavors involves conducting research to see whether or not the performance of the model predictions may be improved by making use of unsupervised learning procedures prior to generating a prediction. This is an example of an attempt that falls under this category. The research-based prediction model that was developed in this manner has the potential to be utilized in the development of a mobile application that assists in health monitoring and, ultimately, the early diagnosis of CHD. This possibility exists due to the fact that the research-based prediction model was developed in this manner.

References

[1]   Yu, C. H., Gao, F., & Wen, Q. Y. (2019). An improved quantum algorithm for ridge regression. *IEEE Transactions on Knowledge and Data Engineering*, *33*(3), 858–866.
[2]   Casaña-Eslava, R. V., Lisboa, P. J., Ortega-Martorell, S., Jarman, I. H., & Martín-Guerrero, J. D. (2019). A Probabilistic framework for Quantum Clustering. arXiv preprint arXiv:1902.05578.
[3]   Terashi, K., Kaneda, M., Kishimoto, T., Saito, M., Sawada, R., & Tanaka, J. (2021). Event classification with quantum machine learning in high-energy physics. *Computing and Software for Big Science*, *5*(1), 1–11.
[4]   Amin, J., Sharif, M., Gul, N., Kadry, S., & Chakraborty, C. (2022). Quantum machine learning architecture for COVID-19 classification based on synthetic data generation using conditional adversarial neural network. *Cognitive Computation*, *14*(5), 1677–1688.
[5]   Wu, S. L., & Yoo, S. (2022). Challenges and opportunities in quantum machine learning for high-energy physics. *Nature Reviews Physics*, *4*(3), 143–144.
[6]   Saravanan, V., Thirukumaran, S., Anitha, M., & Shanthana, S. (2013). Enabling self auditing for mobile clients in cloud computing. *International Journal of Advanced Computer Technology*, *2*, 53–60.
[7]   Yuvaraj, N., Raja, R. A., Karthikeyan, T., & Kousik, N. V. (2020). Improved Privacy Preservation Framework for Cloud-based Internet of Things. In: Internet of Things (pp. 165–174). CRC Press.
[8]   Ciliberto, C., Herbster, M., Ialongo, A. D., Pontil, M., Rocchetto, A., Severini, S., & Wossnig, L. (2018). Quantum machine learning: A classical perspective. *Proceedings of the Royal Society A: Mathematical, Physical and Engineering Sciences*, *474*(2209), 20170551.
[9]   Shukla, A., Kalnoor, G., Kumar, A., Yuvaraj, N., Manikandan, R., & Ramkumar, M. (2021). Improved Recognition Rate of Different Material Category Using Convolutional Neural Networks. Materials Today: Proceedings.
[10]   Houssein, E. H., Abohashima, Z., Elhoseny, M., & Mohamed, W. M. (2022). Machine learning in the quantum realm: The state-of-the-art, challenges, and future vision. *Expert Systems with Applications*, 116512.

[11] Schatzki, L., Arrasmith, A., Coles, P. J., & Cerezo, M. (2021). Entangled datasets for quantum machine learning. *arXiv preprint arXiv:2109.03400*.

[12] Schuld, M., Sinayskiy, I., & Petruccione, F. (2014). Quantum computing for pattern classification. In: Pacific Rim International Conference on Artificial Intelligence (pp. 208–220). Springer, Cham.

[13] Sheng, Y. B., & Zhou, L. (2017). Distributed secure quantum machine learning. *Science Bulletin*, *62*(14), 1025–1029.

[14] Adcock, J., Allen, E., Day, M., Frick, S., Hinchliff, J., Johnson, M., . . . & Stanisic, S. (2015). Advances in quantum machine learning. *arXiv preprint arXiv:1512.02900*.

[15] Banchi, L., Pereira, J., & Pirandola, S. (2021). Generalization in quantum machine learning: A quantum information standpoint. *PRX Quantum*, *2*(4), 040321.

[16] Yadav, S. P., Bhati, B. S., Mahato, D. P., Kumar, S. (eds). Federated Learning for IoT Applications. EAI/ Springer Innovations in Communication and Computing. Springer, Cham. https://doi.org/10.1007/ 978-3-030-85559-8

[17] Esposito, M., Uehara, G., & Spanias, A. (2022). Quantum machine learning for audio classification with applications to healthcare. In: 2022 13th International Conference on Information, Intelligence, Systems & Applications (IISA) (pp. 1–4). IEEE.

[18] Rani, P., Verma, S., Yadav, S. P., Rai, B. K., Naruka, M. S., & Kumar, D. (2022). Simulation of the lightweight blockchain technique based on privacy and security for healthcare data for the cloud system. *International Journal of E-Health and Medical Communications (IJEHMC)*, *13*(4), 1–15. http://doi. org/10.4018/IJEHMC.309436

[19] Tiwari, P., & Melucci, M. (2019). Towards a quantum-inspired binary classifier. *IEEE Access*, *7*, 42354–42372.

[20] Sergioli, G., Giuntini, R., & Freytes, H. (2019). A new quantum approach to binary classification. *PloS One*, *14*(5), e0216224.

[21] Ding, C., Bao, T. Y., & Huang, H. L. (2021). Quantum-inspired support vector machine. In: IEEE Transactions on Neural Networks and Learning Systems.

[22] Dang, Y., Jiang, N., Hu, H., Ji, Z., & Zhang, W. (2018). Image classification based on quantum K-nearest-neighbor algorithm. *Quantum Information Processing*, *17*(9), 1–18.

[23] Sergioli, G., Russo, G., Santucci, E., Stefano, A., Torrisi, S. E., Palmucci, S., . . . & Giuntini, R. (2018). Quantum-inspired minimum distance classification in a biomedical context. *International Journal of Quantum Information*, *16*(08), 1840011.

[24] Basheer, A., Afham, A., & Goyal, S. K. (2020). Quantum k-nearest neighbors algorithm. arXiv preprint arXiv:2003.09187.

[25] Bishwas, A. K., Mani, A., & Palade, V. (2018). Big data quantum support vector clustering. arXiv preprint arXiv:1804.10905.

[26] Lu, S., & Braunstein, S. L. (2014). Quantum decision tree classifier. *Quantum Information Processing*, *13*(3), 757–770.

[27] Sauceda, H. E., Gálvez-González, L. E., Chmiela, S., Paz-Borbón, L. O., Müller, K. R., & Tkatchenko, A. (2022). BIGDML – Towards accurate quantum machine learning force fields for materials. *Nature Communications*, *13*(1), 1–16.

[28] Schuld, M., & Killoran, N. (2022). Is quantum advantage the right goal for quantum machine learning? *arXiv preprint arXiv:2203.01340*.

[29] Wu, S. L., Sun, S., Guan, W., Zhou, C., Chan, J., Cheng, C. L., . . . & Wei, T. C. (2021). Application of quantum machine learning using the quantum kernel algorithm on high energy physics analysis at the LHC. *Physical Review Research*, *3*(3), 033221.

[30] Wu, S. L., Sun, S., Guan, W., Zhou, C., Chan, J., Cheng, C. L., . . . & Wei, T. C. (2021). Application of quantum machine learning using the quantum kernel algorithm on high energy physics analysis at the LHC. *Physical Review Research*, *3*(3), 033221.

[31] Gyongyosi, L., & Imre, S. (2020). Optimizing high-efficiency quantum memory with quantum machine learning for near-term quantum devices. *Scientific Reports*, *10*(1), 1–24.

M. S. Kavitha*, Ramachandra Rao G., K. Sangeetha, A. Kowshika

20 Mitigating the risk of quantum computing in cyber security era

Abstract: The existence of quantum computers poses a huge threat to the privacy and safety of information transmitted via the internet. Once large-scale, error-tolerant quantum physics is discovered, the methods of encryption that are currently employed by the majority of people will become outdated. Consequently, it is not only important but also opportune to take action in order to prevent this threat. This chapter presents the utilization of cyber security modeling using quantum algorithm. The model is designed using quantum CNN mechanism that enables better prediction of attacks from input datasets. Testing of the model shows a better prediction of the attacks than with other methods.

20.1 Introduction

The application of quantum computing has the potential to be of substantial use in a number of different fields, including the fields of artificial intelligence, healthcare, and weather forecasting, among others. Despite this, it presents a significant threat to the integrity of computer networks, which require modification to the way we approach the security of sensitive data [1, 2].

Even if the vast majority of currently used methods of encryption are susceptible to being decrypted by quantum computers, we still need to take precautions against such a possibility and work on developing solutions that are resistant to the effects of quantum computing. The implementation of quantum technology will also lead to an enhancement in the safety of communications that take place via the internet. They have the potential to be programmed to carry out the expansion of secret keys in an entirely secure manner, which is otherwise impossible with the technology available today [3–5]. There are many various ways that today quantum computing devices can be used to make a system more secure. These techniques have a number of advantages, one of which is that they may be used to make things more secure [6–8].

*Corresponding author: M. S. Kavitha, Department of Computer Science and Engineering, SNS College of Technology, Coimbatore, Tamil Nadu, India, e-mail: drmskavitha@yahoo.com
Ramachandra Rao G., Department of Computer Science and Engineering, SNS College of Technology, Coimbatore, Tamil Nadu, India, e-mail: grrsoft30@gmail.com
K. Sangeetha, Department of Computer Science and Engineering, SNS College of Technology, Coimbatore, Tamil Nadu, India, e-mail: sangithaprakash@gmail.com
A. Kowshika, Department of Information Technology, SNS College of Engineering, Coimbatore, Tamil Nadu, India, e-mail: shika2906@gmail.com

https://doi.org/10.1515/9783110798159-020

Quantum computers will be an essential part of our future communications and computation networks; we need to devise workable strategies for using them with the same security guarantees as those offered by secure (classical) computing. This is necessary because quantum computers will be an essential component of our future communications and computation networks. Quantum computers will play a significant role in the future of our species [9, 10].

Over the course of the last several years, there has been a significant expansion in the field of quantum computing. In quantum computing, the principles of quantum physics are applied to issues in order to find solutions to those issues that would otherwise be beyond the capability of standard digital computers. These issues include problems that would otherwise be unsolvable using traditional digital computers. Problems that are complex are defined by having a significant number of components that are linked.

It is difficult to develop a simulation that precisely portrays the behavior of individual molecules because of the intricate structure of the interactions between the many different kinds of electrons that are present [11]. This provides a challenge when attempting to create such a simulation. Quantum algorithms create multivariate spaces in which the relationships between various data points begin to take shape in order to tackle complex problems. These spaces can then be used to solve challenging problems. This allows the algorithms to work successfully with the data that they are given [12].

Both symmetric and asymmetric cryptography take advantage of quantum computing. It not only provides a method for the encryption of traditional symmetric safe key exchange ciphers [13], but it also holds the possibility of drastically modifying the process of cracking ordinary asymmetric ciphers (at least the ones in use at present).

Quantum cryptography utilizes the properties of quantum physics itself to encrypt and convey information in a way that cannot be intercepted. This allows information to be sent in a way that is secure from prying eyes. When data is encrypted and protected with the help of cryptography, access to that data is restricted to only those individuals who have been given authorization to do so [14].

In the not-too-distant future, quantum computing will have a significant impact on cyber security in a number of different domains, one of which is cryptography, which will be one of the first places where this impact will take place. While in transit via the internet or being saved in the cloud, nearly all of the vital conversations and data that are presently being transferred are encrypted using public key cryptography [15]. This ensures that they cannot be read by unauthorized parties. It has quickly become the strategy that is utilized by the vast majority of people. All modern browsers come equipped with public key encryption as a standard safety feature to safeguard the transmission of data between users while they are connected to the internet [19]. In addition, the vast majority of enterprises make use of public key encryption in order to safeguard sensitive information, communications, and user access to devices that are linked to a network.

The chapter presents the utilization of cyber security modeling using quantum algorithms. The model is designed using quantum CNN mechanism that enables better prediction of attacks from input datasets.

20.2 Related works

Data, software, and hardware are the three components that make up the internet, and all of them are vulnerable to attacks that could compromise its safety [7]. If these attacks are allowed to continue, there is a risk that sensitive data will be disclosed, in addition to the risk that they would cause harm or disruption if they are allowed to continue. It is difficult to imagine a scenario in which computers will not be absolutely necessary for all aspects of society and the economy. This is because of the exponential growth of technology [14].

Because of the widespread nature of criminal conduct and the attacks that take place online, cybersecurity is an absolute necessity. In order to ensure the safety of the traditional communications infrastructure, cyber quantum computing is currently implementing quantum encryption [15].

We explore the aspects that contribute to the fact that quantum computers have the potential to be of even greater aid as part of this research effort. To be more specific, we investigate the ways in which these computers could be used to improve system security in environments where scalability is not an issue, as well as avoid wastage of computing and communication resources. Specifically, we focus on environments in which scalability is not an issue [16].

Protection of sensitive information in cyberspace has emerged as an essential component of national security strategies across the globe [17]. The vast majority of encryption methods that are still in use today rely on algorithms that are either no longer relevant or can be broken with relative ease. This is one of the primary reasons why governments in all parts of the world are pouring huge sums of money into the research and development of quantum computing [18].

As a result of the randomness brought about by quantum optics in the form of behavior associated with superposition, quantum cryptography provides a one-of-a-kind form of security that ensures the privacy of communications. This is made possible by the fact that quantum cryptography offers a unique form of security [19].

In addition to the benefits of employing cryptographic techniques in space systems like satellites, which are a part of the telecommunications sector, quantum technology can be used to improve the security of a wide variety of different businesses [20].

20.3 Methods

In quantum computing, several quantum phenomena, such as superposition and entanglement, are utilized in order to represent classical data in a quantum context and modify it in such a way as to yield results that can be comprehended. This is accomplished through the usage of quantum computing. Quantum entanglement is the method that is used to achieve this goal.

Classical computers use bits to represent the state of the data being processed, but quantum computers utilize qubits, which can be in one of two conceivable ground states (0 or 1). Nevertheless, the state is a linear combination (superposition) of the basis states, each of which has a quantifiable probability while the computation is in operation. This means that the state can be thought of as a superposition of states. This state is the product of combining the basis states in a linear fashion.

By measuring the system, the superposition can be reduced to one of the basic states from which information regarding the status of a quantum computer can be extracted (QC). The QC reduces to just one of the basis states when the state is measured, which means that the computation that was performed only produces one of the possible outcomes. This indicates that a QC with n qubits has the capability of internally representing all n-bit integers and carrying out computations on all of them at the same time.

Quantum algorithms, on the other hand, try to amplify specific base states by making use of the underlying structure of the problem in order to home in on them. This can be done in a number of different ways. Because of this, the possibility of particular states is increased, which in turn, ensures that the result reached is both repeatable and definitive. When employed in some circumstances, quantum algorithms have the potential to produce a significantly improved runtime complexity in contrast to their conventional equivalents, which can result in a speedup as a direct consequence of this potential.

We hypothesize that the capability to participate in transaction hijacking is one of the distinctive properties of a rapid QCA. They make an effort to deduce the private key from the public key, which can be located in the input of a transaction that is broadcast to the network and is stored within the memory pools of individual nodes. This is done in order to be successful in accomplishing this goal. Therefore, in a manner comparable to a double-spending attack [19–22], this results in a conflicting transaction – spending the same amount of money (or the subset of money over which the QCA has gotten control), which ultimately leads to the theft of the victim's cash. This is accomplished in a manner analogous to a double-spending attack [23–41].

Timing is of the utmost importance in these types of attacks because not only does the attacker need to construct, sign, and broadcast the conflicting transaction, but they also need to run the Shor algorithm in order to gain access to the private key. This means that the attacker has a limited amount of time in which to complete all of these steps.

A sizeable portion of the probability that an attempt to hijack a transaction will be successful depends heavily on the quality control measures that are put into place. It is vital to bear in mind that the one who is responsible for this type of transaction hijacking is the recipient of the single benefit, as opposed to the person who was supposed to be the recipient of the first transaction. In contrast to the more common practice of spending twice as much, this entails spending only once.

Because the speedup that can be achieved is only quadratic and may be nullified by increasing the key size, we will not be discussing the concept of applying an algorithm to obtain the public key from an address in this piece. This is because the speedup that can be achieved is minimal and could be nullified by increasing the key size. Instead, we are going to talk about the possibility of utilizing a different way. In spite of this, a competitor may gain an unfair edge by using an algorithm while mining, which would make the situation even more unfair, in general.

Transaction hijacking, in conjunction with egocentric mining operations, is an extra approach that should be explored in addition to the strategies that have been detailed up to this point. These methods may be found in the previous section. Assuming that the QCA is also a miner, she might try to use her computing power to build up her own secret chain and then, once she is in the lead, selectively broadcast blocks in order to force a rearrangement of the public chain. This strategy is based on the assumption that the QCA is also a miner.

Because the attacker can now also carry out transaction hijacking, as was covered earlier, it is anticipated that the feasibility of such approaches will drastically increase when a QCA is present, in contrast to more traditional forms of selfish mining attacks. This is due to the fact that the attacker can now additionally execute transaction hijacking.

This takes into account not only block rewards and transaction fees but also the total sum of money that was used in the overwritten transactions. If the transactions had been recorded in a blockchain that was not quantum-resistant, this sum of money would not have been included in the blockchain's first iteration.

Our working hypothesis is that the Bitcoin community has already settled on a signature method that is resistant to quantum computing and has implemented this technique as an upgrade to the protocol. If this is the case, then our working hypothesis is correct. It is absolutely unreasonable to anticipate that all Bitcoin users will have transitioned to outputs that are resistant to quantum computing by the time the cryptocurrency reaches full adoption. Many Bitcoin users, if not the majority of them, will still have some or all of their currency units stored in non-quantum-resistant outputs, such as the most common P2PKH. This is because P2PKH was designed to be backwards-compatible with quantum computers. One example of this is the Bitcoin Private Key Hardware Wallet (P2PKH).

The protocol that is going to be discussed in the following parts will make it feasible for users to make a safe transition to quantum-resistant outputs, even if it is a gradual one. It implements a time-consuming security delay through a protocol known as commit-delay-reveal and can be added to Bitcoin through the use of a soft fork if the protocol is updated. Separate research is being conducted on particular facets of the Bitcoin implementation such as parametrization and the establishment of appropriate data structures.

It is important to keep in mind that once the protocol is live, the use of traditional ECDSA signatures will be prohibited, and clients will only be able to spend based on the quantum-resistant signature scheme or the transition scheme described in this work. Once the protocol is live, it is important to keep in mind that once the protocol is live, the use of traditional ECDSA signatures will be prohibited. It is essential to keep in mind that once the protocol is operational, the use of classic ECDSA signatures will no longer be permitted. This restriction will go into effect once the protocol is online. When a non-quantum-resistant public key is used to make a purchase with an outdated client, not only will the public key be revealed, but the transaction will also fail, resulting in the loss of the currency.

Although we are unable to provide a succinct description of the benefits or drawbacks of this quantum model in comparison to a classical one, we are able to highlight certain significant differences, which are as follows: You will acquire an activation that is directly comparable to a threshold if you run a classical model the way it was intended to be run. On the other hand, if you run a quantum model, you will acquire a binary output that you will need to iterate several times before you obtain a measure that is close to the theoretical value and comparable to the threshold. This will be the case if you want to get an accurate representation of the threshold.

If the nonlinearity function is satisfied, it is possible to comprehend the quantum measure in terms of the chosen category. This is because the binary structure of the quantum measure makes it possible for this to happen. This is a crucial point of differentiation. Last but not least, while feeding classical model patterns that have numerical qualities can be helpful, the majority of quantum models, including this one, restrict the input to only allow patterns that have binary qualities. This can be confusing because there are classical patterns that have numerical qualities. This is because classical models were created before binary attributes were discovered, which led to this result.

20.3.1 Proposed quantum CNN

A bit is referred to as a qubit in quantum computing, and it is implemented with the assistance of a two-level quantum system. In order to quantitatively characterize its state, it is possible to make use of a complex Hilbert space that consists of two dimensions. According to the quantum principle of state superposition, it is possible to express any arbitrary one-qubit state by using the equation $|\varphi> = \alpha|0> + \beta|1>$, First, an encoding in which a theoretical quantum object is assigned to each pattern, which we will refer to as a density pattern; second, classification in which a quantum-inspired counterpart of a standard classification procedure is applied to a dataset of density operators rather than a dataset of real vectors. Third, there is a decoding step that decodes the classification process results in the domain of real vectors. of the computational basis $|0>$ and $|1>$, respectively. This is done in accordance with the fact that it is possible to express any arbitrary one-qubit state. The α and β amplitudes are both complex numbers, and their validity is not affected by the condition that normalizes them, which is to say that it does not change them.

$$|\alpha|2 + |\beta|2 = 1.$$

Up to this point, the data formats and operations that are impacted by quantum mechanics have been broken down into finer depth. These might be exploited in the building of a standard model of a neuron, which is influenced by quantum mechanics and is illustrated in Fig. 1. In earlier research, it was presumed that each and every one of the UI weights is represented an actual integer. This was done in order to make it possible for the UI weights to be easily applied within the conventional framework for machine learning.

Each equation is made up of three parts: $f(x)$, which is a representation of the function; $\arg(x)$, which defines the argument of a complex number; and inputs $(x1, \ldots, xN)$, which are real values. $f(x)$ is a representation of the function that is specified by Equation (2). After running a number of computational simulations, we were able to prove beyond a shadow of a doubt that a fully linked network with complex-valued weights performs significantly better than an identical network with real-valued weights. The upgraded quantum-inspired neuron will be utilized by us in the process of constructing the convolutional neural networks.

20.3.2 Quantum-inspired convolutional operation

A convolutional neural network, also known as a CNN, is a specific type of artificial neural network that typically consists of two unique types of layers, namely convolutional layers and fully connected layers. A CNN is also known as the convolutional neural network. It feasible that neurons driven by quantum physics could one day be used to construct extraordinarily deep neural networks. In addition, the complex convolutional technique is capable of being executed in a manner that is comparable to the one that has been explained.

After the complex-space transition that is outlined has been carried out, the operation of multiplying the input pixel by the convolutional kernel is equivalent to carrying out a weighted summation. After the convolutional operation, which in this case is a rotational operation, a NOT operation is applied, just as it is in the quantum-inspired neurons. This is done in order to ensure that the output of the convolutional operation is the same as the output of the rotational operation.

We were able to build quantum-inspired convolutional neural networks by merging the quantum-inspired neutron model with the quantum-inspired convolutional operation model that we had already built. This allowed us to create quantum-inspired convolutional neural networks (QICNNs). The vast majority of the machine learning frameworks that are currently available are founded on real-valued representations and operations. As a result, we will first need to modify the complex-valued neutron and convolutional operations so that they can be easily implemented on the predominant frameworks.

$z = a + ib$ is the equation that represents a complex number. The real and imaginary components of a complex number are represented by the letters a and I, respectively. The basic purpose is to carry out complex arithmetic by carrying out just real-valued operations on both the real and imaginary parts of the equation. This is a challenge that must be overcome. Figure 20.1 illustrates the scenario in which m-channels that receive standard input data undergo the change from having channels with real values to having channels with complex values. This transition takes place during the course of the scenario. The initial m-channels are increased to 2 m after the real and imaginary components of the complicated features have been reconstructed. Real components are represented by the first m channels, whereas the imaginary components are shown by the second m channels.

Convolutional operations are performed on the complex values by utilizing the same line of reasoning as one would use when multiplying complex numbers. This is done so in order to execute these operations on the complex values. The complex filter matrix, which is denoted by the W, is defined as follows:

$$W = \text{wreal} + i\text{wimag}$$

where wreal and wimag are the real matrices that need to be learned; x is the data matrix; and xreal and ximag are the real matrices of the two channels.

The complex filter matrix is denoted by the letter W. There is another way to write this equation, and it is W = wreal + iwimag. Following that, the convolutional process is carried out in the manner that is described below:

20.3.3 QCNN architecture

We employ a conventional CNN as the foundation for the QICNNs so that we may more easily make comparisons between them. This model served as the basis for the standard template that CNN uses. The concept that would later become CNN originated with LeNet-5.

The Convolutional Neural Network (CNN) is made up of three convolution blocks and two completely linked layers. Inside of each convolution block are three layers: a convolutional layer, a ReLU layer, and a pooling layer. The fully connected linkages connect the entirely linked layers to one another so that they can work together.

Building QICNNs can be accomplished in the simplest way by employing a neuron that is influenced by quantum mechanics in the fully connected layers of a QICNN and a convolutional operation that is impacted by quantum mechanics in the convolutional layer.

In a quantum system, a layer that possesses the characteristics of a convolution layer is denoted by the name, the quantum convolution layer, which is the name of the layer. In the quantum convolution layer, a filter is applied to the input feature map in order to construct feature maps that incorporate newly obtained information. These feature maps are generated by the quantum convolution layer. The quantum convolution layer, in contrast to the convolution layer, is tasked with the responsibility of carrying out filter operations inside an environment that is governed by quantum computing.

Classical computers lack several capabilities that quantum computers do, including the ability to do superposition and parallel processing. Because of these properties, quantum computers are able to learn and assess information significantly more quickly than classical computers. However, the current generation of quantum computers can only deal with very simple quantum systems at this point in time.

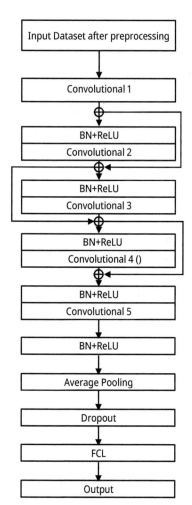

Figure 20.1: Proposed quantum CNN.

During the time that the picture map is being utilized for the quantum convolution layer, it is not immediately applied in its whole to the quantum system. Instead, data is processed in chunks that are no larger than the filter size, which enables even the most fundamental quantum computers to build it. This makes it possible for quantum cryptography to be used in practical applications.

The phase of encoding is required in order to complete the process of transforming classical data into quantum data. The most straightforward approach is to use a rotation gate on qubits in a manner that is synchronized with the information carried by a pixel. This is the simplest method. There is a wide range of encoding methods that may be used, and the one that is chosen not only has the potential to have an effect on the minimum quantity of qubits that is required but also on the efficiency with which the system learns. The method of decoding is established through the measurement of one or more quantum states.

Observing quantum states makes it feasible to acquire knowledge on the classical world. A single random quantum circuit can be constructed out of multiple gates by combining them in order to generate the number. It is possible to generate the number too by combining many gates into a single random quantum circuit.

Variable gates are used and the circuit is also able to optimize itself by employing the gradient descent approach. This is made possible by the fact that the method uses variable gates. The performance of this circuit, when it comes to learning, is quite variable and is greatly dependent on the design approach that was used.

20.4 Results and discussion

The dataset includes one million domains that Alexa considers to be the most popular as well as ten botnet DGAs. The entropy value measurements that are derived from Shannon function serve as the initial feature of the dataset.

Regarding the second point, the Kullback-Leibler divergence produces relative entropy (RE) values for the Alexa 1 M domain names. This divergence evaluates the distance (or similarity) of the domain name in relation to Alexa domain unigram distributions. Third, we analyzed each of the datasets from the botnets to see which one had the lowest value of the relative entropy of a domain name.

The Jensen-Shannon divergence function is used to produce the IRad value, which is the fourth characteristic, and measures the distance of a target domain name from each of the ten botnet datasets. This value is determined by the value of the fourth characteristic. Using the Jensen-Shannon divergence function, this value was determined. The length of the domain name is the second element that needs to be taken into consideration as in Tables 20.1 and 20.2.

In this section, we will concentrate on the use of performance evaluation to gain a better understanding of how well our QML framework trains on a variety of

Table 20.1: Classification results.

Class	QA	SSVM	Proposed model
10	83.59	83.29	85.59
20	83.92	83.51	85.81
30	82.9	82.51	84.93
40	83.74	82.7	85.27
50	82.54	81.18	85.35
60	83.69	83.1	85.83
70	81.56	82.61	84.21
80	83.16	83.11	85.08
90	80.94	82.46	85.21

Table 20.2: Error rate.

Class	QA	SSVM	Proposed model
10	16.26	14.42	15.63
20	15.94	14.2	15.42
30	16.94	15.07	16.4
40	16.11	14.74	16.22
50	17.3	14.65	17.72
60	16.17	14.18	15.82
70	18.27	15.78	16.31
80	16.69	14.92	15.81
90	18.89	14.79	16.46

datasets, as well as the effect of a probability amplitude regularizer. This will be done in order to gain a better understanding of how well our QML framework trains.

In order to determine how well it operates, we compare it to other methods, evaluate it in comparison to the present state of the art, and put it through training and testing without the regularizer. We do not choose classes nor do we attempt to interpolate the quantity of the data that is being received because our primary goal is to examine the scalability of QML.

Despite the fact that test accuracy has improved from 80% to 90%, there is still a 2.3% gap in domain size between the training set and the test set, as illustrated in Figures 20.2–21.4. The explanation for this can be found in the statement that came before this one. This shows the tremendous influence of the regularizer that was supplied in the QML framework, which we designed for multi-class classification possessed.

One epoch is measured from the time that the learner is exposed to the entirety of the training set; however, if the process is carried out in the traditional fashion, it can be repeated for an infinite number of epochs. Early training can be terminated if a specified threshold value has been reached in a metric whose maximum value we desire to achieve. Even though the entire process is simulated in order to obtain the

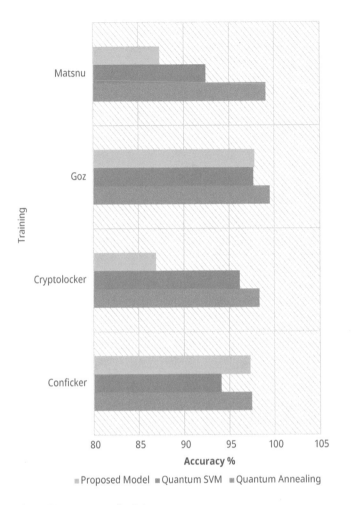

Figure 20.2: Accuracy of training.

best level of efficiency that is possibly attainable, it is perfectly suited to and ready to be carried out on a genuine quantum computer and has been prepared for this possibility. Further, the testing is conducted on various datasets and the results are presented in Tables 20.3–20.6.

20.5 Conclusion

In this chapter, we have highlighted how quantum CNN is susceptible to these types of threats. The dissemination of public keys has led to the introduction of this security flaw. We have suggested the implementation of a feature in Bitcoin known as

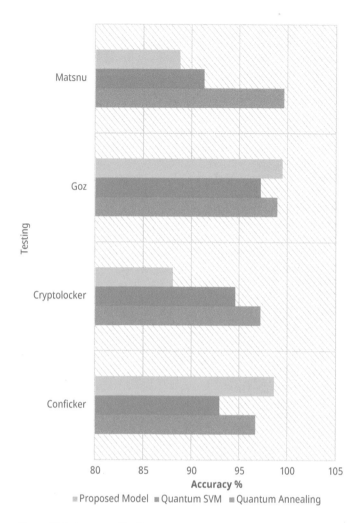

Figure 20.3: Accuracy of testing.

commit-delay-reveal in order to enable a risk-free upgrade to an address scheme that is resistant to quantum computing. This should be long enough for honest clients and miners to reach a consensus on rejecting manually any long-range forks that take place within that time period, and that consensus should be reached before the wait begins. We contend, however, that there must be a stretch of time during a chain rewind in which the community is unable to come to a decision on how to proceed because of the presence of a rival branch that was deliberately crafted by an adversary. In order for the chain rewind to be a success, it is necessary that this particular criterion be satisfied.

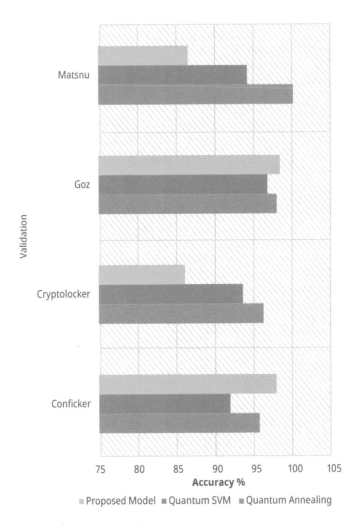

Figure 20.4: Accuracy of validation.

Table 20.3: Results of KDD cup 1999 data.

Features	Fuzzers	DoS	Backdoor	Reconnaissance
3	88.3	88.94	90.69	91.78
6	90.48	91.13	92.92	94.05
9	87.18	87.82	89.54	90.63
12	84.31	84.93	86.6	87.66
15	90.45	91.1	92.89	94.01
18	87.1	87.73	89.45	90.54
21	87.34	87.97	89.7	90.79

Table 20.3 (continued)

Features	Fuzzers	DoS	Backdoor	Reconnaissance
24	87.39	88.02	89.75	90.84
27	86.61	87.24	88.95	90.03
30	87.21	87.84	89.57	90.65
33	86.23	86.86	88.56	89.64
36	85.85	86.48	88.18	89.25
39	87.38	88.01	89.74	90.83
42	84.9	85.52	87.2	88.27
45	86.93	87.56	89.28	90.36
48	90.52	91.17	92.96	94.09

Table 20.4: Results of 2017-SUEE-dataset.

Features	Fuzzers	DoS	Backdoor	Reconnaissance
3	86.53	87.16	88.88	89.94
6	88.67	89.31	91.06	92.17
9	85.44	86.06	87.75	88.82
12	82.62	83.23	84.87	85.91
15	88.64	89.28	91.03	92.13
18	85.36	85.98	87.66	88.73
21	85.59	86.21	87.91	88.97
24	85.64	86.26	87.96	89.02
27	84.88	85.50	87.17	88.23
30	85.47	86.08	87.78	88.84
33	84.51	85.12	86.79	87.85
36	84.13	84.75	86.42	87.47
39	85.63	86.25	87.95	89.01
42	83.20	83.81	85.46	86.50
45	85.19	85.81	87.49	88.55
48	88.71	89.35	91.10	92.21

Table 20.5: Results of CTU-13 dataset.

Features	Fuzzers	DoS	Backdoor	Reconnaissance
3	85.15	85.77	87.45	88.51
6	87.25	87.88	89.60	90.69
9	84.07	84.69	86.35	87.40
12	81.30	81.90	83.51	84.53
15	87.22	87.85	89.58	90.66
18	83.99	84.60	86.26	87.31
21	84.22	84.83	86.50	87.55
24	84.27	84.88	86.55	87.60

Table 20.5 (continued)

Features	Fuzzers	DoS	Backdoor	Reconnaissance
27	83.52	84.13	85.78	86.82
30	84.10	84.71	86.37	87.42
33	83.15	83.76	85.40	86.44
36	82.79	83.39	85.03	86.07
39	84.26	84.87	86.54	87.59
42	81.87	82.47	84.09	85.12
45	83.83	84.44	86.09	87.14
48	87.29	87.92	89.64	90.73

Table 20.6: Results of IoT devices captures.

Features	Fuzzers	DoS	Backdoor	Reconnaissance
3	85.96	86.58	88.29	89.36
6	81.62	82.2	83.82	84.85
9	82.3	82.89	84.53	85.57
12	87.28	87.91	89.64	90.72
15	81.56	82.13	83.76	84.79
18	85.75	86.37	88.07	89.14
21	67.36	67.83	69.17	70.06
24	83.1	83.71	85.35	86.4
27	85.81	86.43	88.13	89.2
30	85.79	86.42	88.12	89.19
33	88.17	88.81	90.55	91.65
36	85.41	86.03	87.73	88.79
39	86.93	87.56	89.28	90.37

References

[1]   Austin, G. (2018). Cybersecurity in China: The Next Wave. Springer International Publishing.
[2]   Bova, F., Goldfarb, A., & Melko, R. G. (2021). Commercial applications of quantum computing. *EPJ Quantum Technology*, *8*(1), 2.
[3]   Raban, Y., & Hauptman, A. (2018). Foresight of cyber security threat drivers and affecting technologies. *Foresight*.
[4]   Thomasian, N. M., & Adashi, E. Y. (2021). Cybersecurity in the internet of medical things. *Health Policy and Technology*, *10*(3), 100549.
[5]   Rosch-Grace, D., & Straub, J. (2022). Analysis of the likelihood of quantum computing proliferation. *Technology in Society*, *68*, 101880.
[6]   Ali, A. (2021). A Pragmatic Analysis of Pre-and Post-Quantum Cyber Security Scenarios. In: 2021 International Bhurban Conference on Applied Sciences and Technologies (IBCAST) (pp. 686–692). IEEE.
[7]   Geluvaraj, B., Satwik, P. M., & Ashok Kumar, T. A. (2019). The future of cybersecurity: Major role of artificial intelligence, machine learning, and deep learning in cyberspace. In: International

Conference on Computer Networks and Communication Technologies (pp. 739–747). Springer, Singapore.

[8]   Cheung, K. F., Bell, M. G., & Bhattacharjya, J. (2021). Cybersecurity in logistics and supply chain management: An overview and future research directions. *Transportation Research Part E: Logistics and Transportation Review, 146*, 102217.

[9]   Yan, R., Wang, Y., Dai, J., Xu, Y., & Liu, A. Q. (2022). Quantum-key-distribution-based microgrid control for cybersecurity enhancement. *IEEE Transactions on Industry Applications, 58*(3), 3076–3086.

[10]   Ge, Z. M., & Yang, C. H. (2009). Chaos synchronization and chaotization of complex chaotic systems in series form by optimal control. *Chaos, Solitons & Fractals, 42*(2), 994–1002.

[11]   Jelčić Dubček, D. (2020). Quantum computers-an emerging cybersecurity threat. *Annals of Disaster Risk Sciences: ADRS, 3*(2), 0–0.

[12]   Yadav, S. P., Bhati, B. S., Mahato, D. P., Kumar, S. (eds) Federated Learning for IoT Applications. EAI/ Springer Innovations in Communication and Computing. Springer, Cham. https://doi.org/10.1007/ 978-3-030-85559-8

[13]   Dai, F., Shi, Y., Meng, N., Wei, L., & Ye, Z. (2017). From Bitcoin to cybersecurity: A comparative study of blockchain application and security issues. In: 2017 4th International Conference on Systems and Informatics (ICSAI) (pp. 975–979). IEEE.

[14]   Rani, P., Verma, S., Yadav, S. P., Rai, B. K., Naruka, M. S., & Kumar, D. (2022). Simulation of the lightweight blockchain technique based on privacy and security for healthcare data for the cloud system. *International Journal of E-Health and Medical Communications (IJEHMC), 13*(4), 1–15. http://doi. org/10.4018/IJEHMC.309436

[15]   Vadla, S., Parakh, A., Chundi, P., & Surbamaniam, M. (2019). Quasim: A multi-dimensional quantum cryptography game for cyber security. *Journal of the Colloquium for Information Systems Security Education, 6*(2), 19–19).

[16]   Saravanan, V., Thirukumaran, S., Anitha, M., & Shanthana, S. (2013). Enabling self auditing for mobile clients in cloud computing. *International Journal of Advanced Computer Technology, 2*, 53–60.

[17]   Raheman, F. (2022). The future of cybersecurity in the age of quantum computers. *Future Internet, 14*(11), 335.

[18]   Yuvaraj, N., Raja, R. A., Karthikeyan, T., & Kousik, N. V. (2020). Improved Privacy Preservation Framework for Cloud-based Internet of Things. In: Internet of Things (pp. 165–174). CRC Press.

[19]   Azvine, B., & Jones, A. (2019). Meeting the Future Challenges in Cyber Security. In: Industry 4.0 And Engineering for a Sustainable Future (pp. 137–152). Springer, Cham.

[20]   Sharma, N., & Ketti Ramachandran, R. (2021). The emerging trends of quantum computing towards data security and key management. *Archives of Computational Methods in Engineering, 28*(7), 5021–5034.

[21]   Cabaj, K., Domingos, D., Kotulski, Z., & Respício, A. (2018). Cybersecurity education: Evolution of the discipline and analysis of master programs. *Computers & Security, 75*, 24–35.

[22]   Schuld, M., & Killoran, N. (2022). Is quantum advantage the right goal for quantum machine learning? *arXiv preprint arXiv:2203.01340.*

[23]   Mailloux, L. O., Lewis II, C. D., Riggs, C., & Grimaila, M. R. (2016). Post-quantum cryptography: What advancements in quantum computing mean for it professionals. *IT Professional, 18*(5), 42–47.

[24]   Mahajan, R. P. (2011). Hybrid quantum inspired neural model for commodity price prediction. In: 13th International Conference on Advanced Communication Technology (ICACT2011) (pp. 1353–1357). IEEE.

[25]   Henderson, M., Shakya, S., Pradhan, S., & Cook, T. (2020). Quanvolutional neural networks: Powering image recognition with quantum circuits. *Quantum Machine Intelligence, 2*(1), 1–9.

[26]   Atchade-Adelomou, P., & Alonso-Linaje, G. (2022). Quantum-enhanced filter: QFilter. *Soft Computing,* 1–8.

[27]   Shi, S., Wang, Z., Cui, G., Wang, S., Shang, R., Li, W., . . . & Gu, Y. (2022). Quantum-inspired complex convolutional neural networks. *Applied Intelligence,* 1–10.

[28]   Ma, X., Tu, Z. C., & Ran, S. J. (2021). Deep learning quantum states for hamiltonian estimation. *Chinese Physics Letters*, *38*(11), 110301.

[29]   Ge, Z. M., & Yang, C. H. (2009). Hyperchaos of four state autonomous system with three positive Lyapunov exponents. *Physics Letters A*, *373*(3), 349–353.

[30]   Potok, T. E., Schuman, C., Young, S., Patton, R., Spedalieri, F., Liu, J., . . . & Chakma, G. (2018). A study of complex deep learning networks on high-performance, neuromorphic, and quantum computers. *ACM Journal on Emerging Technologies in Computing Systems (JETC)*, *14*(2), 1–21.

[31]   Huang, W., Mao, Y., Xie, C., & Huang, D. (2019). Quantum hacking of free-space continuous-variable quantum key distribution by using a machine-learning technique. *Physical Review A*, *100*(1), 012316.

[32]   Ge, Z. M., & Yang, C. H. (2007). Pragmatical generalized synchronization of chaotic systems with uncertain parameters by adaptive control. *Physica D: Nonlinear Phenomena*, *231*(2), 87–94.

[33]   Zokaee, F., & Jiang, L. (2021). SMART: A Heterogeneous Scratchpad Memory Architecture for Superconductor SFQ-based Systolic CNN Accelerators. In: MICRO-54: 54th Annual IEEE/ACM International Symposium on Microarchitecture (pp. 912–924).

[34]   Zokaee, F., & Jiang, L. (2021). SMART: A Heterogeneous Scratchpad Memory Architecture for Superconductor SFQ-based Systolic CNN Accelerators. In: MICRO-54: 54th Annual IEEE/ACM International Symposium on Microarchitecture (pp. 912–924).

[35]   Zaidenberg, D. A., Sebastianelli, A., Spiller, D., Le Saux, B., & Ullo, S. L. (2021). Advantages and bottlenecks of quantum machine learning for remote sensing. In: 2021 IEEE International Geoscience and Remote Sensing Symposium IGARSS (pp. 5680–5683). IEEE.

[36]   Chen, G., Chen, Q., Long, S., Zhu, W., Yuan, Z., & Wu, Y. (2022). Quantum convolutional neural network for image classification. *Pattern Analysis and Applications*, 1–13.

[37]   Kharkov, Y. A., Sotskov, V. E., Karazeev, A. A., Kiktenko, E. O., & Fedorov, A. K. (2020). Revealing quantum chaos with machine learning. *Physical Review B*, *101*(6), 064406.

[38]   Righero, M., Checco, P., Biey, M., & Kocarev, L. (2008). Network topology estimation through synchronization: A case study on quantum dot cnn. In: 2008 IEEE International Symposium on Circuits and Systems (pp. 101–104). IEEE.

[39]   Gao, X., & Hu, H. (2015). Adaptive–impulsive synchronization and parameters estimation of chaotic systems with unknown parameters by using discontinuous drive signals. *Applied Mathematical Modelling*, *39*(14), 3980–3989.

[40]   Yang, C. H. (2011). The chaos generalized synchronization of a quantum-CNN chaotic oscillator with a double duffing chaotic system by GYC partial region stability theory. *Journal of Computational and Theoretical Nanoscience*, *8*(11), 2255–2265.

[41]   Henderson, M., Gallina, J., & Brett, M. (2021). Methods for accelerating geospatial data processing using quantum computers. *Quantum Machine Intelligence*, *3*(1), 1–9.

J. Shanthini*, R. Sathya, K. Sri Hari, A. Christopher Paul

21 IoMT-based data aggregation using quantum learning

Abstract: In this chapter, quantum-assisted learning is introduced to aggregate data from the IoMT sensors for possible data processing and storage. The model is designed in such a way that it reduces redundant information and improves the flexibility of processing data. The entire modeling is conducted in a simulation environment to test the effectiveness of data aggregation from IoMT and its associated complexity. Experimental validation shows a reduced complex data aggregation task than with other methods.

21.1 Introduction

The term "Internet of Medical Things" (IoMT) was coined to describe the integration of Internet of Things (IoT) technology into the health technology industry, with the aim of enabling a more profitable future for this sector. The foundation of IoMT lies in connected and wireless medical devices, which facilitate the seamless flow of data and information. Leveraging advanced health technologies, these IoMT devices enhance the speed and accuracy of real-time diagnostics, ultimately benefiting the healthcare industry [1–4].

Several hospitals and clinics around the country are pouring financial resources towards the investigation and improvement of IoMT in order to better equip their clinical staff. Imaging, sensing, and diagnostics are all made possible in this new era of digitalization, thanks to the use of intelligent services, such as those supplied by the Internet of Things and smartphones [5]. The resolution of a mobile phone camera lens can be beneficial to real-time readouts of images such as optical microscopy, flow cytometry, and other imaging readouts. These readouts are carried out on the camera lens of a mobile device [6].

Using non-invasive mouth guard biosensors for salivary glucose, and fitness trackers equipped with Bluetooth low energy (BLE) technology, a data link of up to a

*Corresponding author: J. Shanthini, Department of Computer Science and Engineering, Dr. NGP Institute of Technology, Coimbatore, Tamil Nadu, India, e-mail: drjshanthini@gmail.com
R. Sathya, Department of Computer Science & Engineering, Dr. NGP Institute of Technology, Coimbatore, Tamil Nadu, India, e-mail: sathyagbsri@gmail.com
K. Sri Hari, Department of Computer Science and Engineering, SNS College of Technology, Coimbatore, Tamil Nadu, India, e-mail: harionto@gmail.com
A. Christopher Paul, Department of Information Technology, Karpagam Institute of Technology, Coimbatore, Tamil Nadu, India, e-mail: profachristo@gmail.com

https://doi.org/10.1515/9783110798159-021

few feet in distance has been shown [7]. This enables continuous monitoring of a patient's vital signs as well as their physical activity throughout the treatment process [8]. The development of smart fabrics that are capable of recording vital indications such as blood pressure, ECG, heart rate, and body temperature is the topic of research that is now being carried out.

It is possible to detect biomarkers of major diseases in non-invasive samples by using eDiagnostics devices; however, these devices are still in the research and development phase because the pathogenic levels of these biomarkers have not yet been identified. eDiagnostics devices can be used to detect biomarkers of major diseases [9]. It is possible that one method for eHealth systems to partially satisfy their diagnostic needs is for patients to wear a device that does electronic diagnosis. It is interesting to note that people with low and middle incomes are the primary adopters of cellphones, which supports the adoption of POCT with no additional expense. Cellphones also make it easier for people to communicate with one another. In addition to this, it will help the growth of low-cost medical services to rural communities and other sites further away [10].

In recent years, there has been a shift in emphasis toward decision-making that is informed by data analytics [11]. This shift came about as a result of an increased level of integration between point-of-contact (POC) systems and quantum learning (QL) algorithms, which are commonly referred to as artificial intelligence (AI).

Artificial intelligence (AI) offers experts in the medical field an additional tool with which they may personalize patient care and track their development. It is now possible for AI systems to provide assistance to medical practitioners in the field of determining whether or not a patient is at risk for illnesses such as cardiovascular disease, cancer, or trauma [12–14]. The multistep experiment is initially carried out by AI sensors with the support of a portable analyzer, and then the biomarker concentrations are automatically digitized after the experiment is complete. QL enables the prediction of a wide variety of diseases by employing a number of different methodologies (such as classification, clustering, pattern recognition, and features of diseases) that influence therapeutic options [15–16]. These play an important role in personalized medicine.

In this chapter, a quantum-assisted learning is introduced to aggregate data from IoMT sensors for possible data processing and storage.

21.2 Related works

Regarding the internal security vulnerabilities that are offered by diverse IoMT devices, Habib et al. [17] highlighted medical data protection access control as an alternative to privacy-based medical data protection (MDPAC). Protection of information and knowledge is a duty that is crucial to a society but also presents a significant challenge because it is embedded in every facet of the society. Because of the enormous stakes involved in matters relating to a person's life and health, this is especially true in the area of medicine. The new model ensures that patients and medical professionals can connect in a way that is not only safe and discreet but also helpful to both parties.

The Internet of Medical Things Security Assessment Framework is the name of a proposal for a framework that has been developed by Alsubaei et al. [18]. Abuse of security and privacy in IoMT is quite unlikely, particularly in comparison to the large variety of cloud-based applications that wirelessly communicate sensitive medical data. It is impossible to organize, administer, monitor, and account for protection if it has not been first computed. Early adopters of IoMT, on the other hand, have reported experiencing challenges throughout the safety testing process, in particular when it comes to identifying acceptable and robust security behavior. They developed an IoMT-SAF by employing a web-based method in order to give security estimations in IoMT solutions, in accordance with a novel ontological scenario. This was carried out so that we could assess the level of security and disruption offered by IoMT solutions. Because of its size, its ability to be scaled up or down, and its flexibility to satisfy both newly acquired customers and the ever-evolving technological and medical standards, IoMT-SAF performs a very specific function for the industry. This is made possible by its combination of these three characteristics.

For the goal of controlling blockchain-based medical devices, Malamas et al. [19] conducted research on the forensics-by-design paradigm. Relationships with doctors, patients, hospital staff, and product vendors, all of whom have various but overlapping concerns about patient confidentiality, are potential sources for obtaining this sensitive information. In order to restrict access to IoMT devices and the medical data that is associated with them, they have built an innovative framework for fine-grained authorization (FGAF). When it comes to the creation of brand-new systems, two of their primary concerns are the forensic design of the system and the granularity of the access it provides. Validation of the privately owned blockchain ecosystem is accomplished by the utilization of a proof-of-medical consensus technique, which was designed specifically for medical applications.

The presentation that Manogaran and Lopez [20] gave offered an overview of the current machine learning approaches that are utilized for managing vast volumes of data in applications such as the healthcare industry. The goal of this research was to provide an application-oriented design for large data systems and it was effective in achieving that goal. Analyzing big data architectures that already existed for a range of different use cases was the method that was used to achieve this goal.

Alabdulatif et al. [21] provide the privacy-preserving edge of things (EoT) framework, also known as the PPEOTF, with the purpose of providing a secure IoT edge and smart healthcare monitoring. This will be of assistance in achieving the goal that was specified earlier. Problems with data management that are caused by the billions of linked devices that are part of the Internet of Things present a significant barrier for the cloud of things. Edge computing provides a practical answer since it functions as a go-between between the devices that make up the Internet of Things and the cloud storage facilities that house their data. They developed a system for the intelligent monitoring of healthcare that makes use of the Internet of Things (IoT) and protects user privacy at the network edge. As a consequence of this, in order to provide an explanation of the conceptual framework, they investigate a case study that makes use of data derived from a patient's biosignals. In addition to accelerating the pace of research and improving its overall performance, the framework ensures high levels of methodological precision and data safety.

21.3 Methods

It is possible to determine the likelihood of homogeneous IoMT devices participating in mutual authentication by utilizing the equation that is presented in eq. (21.1).

$$Qyx(yj, xj) = Qy(yi)Qx(xi) \tag{21.1}$$

We are able to perform a likelihood analysis on devices that have a homogenous IoMT by using eq. (21.1). This analysis can be done on devices. Because it enables clinicians to have a better understanding of their patient histories, dynamics, complications, and current situations, as well as the likely reactions that they will have, the precision of the data contained in medical devices can be beneficial to both inpatient and outpatient clinics.

Patients stand to benefit from a treatment strategy that is in the same proportions, both time and labor efficient as well as successful. The decisions that are made with homogenous IoMT probability theory are heavily dependent upon a range of sectors, including the academic world, the medical profession, the insurance and financial industries, and other fields as well. In order to provide an explanation for the exposures and the health risks that are associated with them, epidemiology makes use of probability theory.

Students who are participating in medical research projects are given guidance by researchers as they plan experiments, determine the kind of data they will need to collect, analyze the data, interpret the results, and collaborate with one another to write up the findings of their studies. Due to the fact that the data and the documents in question are consistent with one another, it is possible to rely on the documents.

The information quality management and governance system relies heavily on the accuracy of the data that is collected; this acts as the major support structure. In a nutshell, data integrity refers to the process of inspecting information for errors and modifications that are not authorized by the owner. Incorrect information can be the root cause of many problems, including fraud, aggressiveness, lack of data, and poor or inadequate care for patients. Each of these problems presents considerable hazards to the health of patients. It is possible that measures that are beneficial to sales will prove to be more effective when they are supported by data that is accurate and has been cleaned. If one aspires to raise levels of customer satisfaction while simultaneously reducing levels of resource waste, possessing data that is correct and up-to-date is an imperative must. One example of this would be squandering both time and money by sending mails to addresses that have been deactivated or are otherwise obsolete. The proposed model is shown in Figure 21.1.

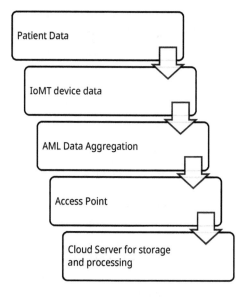

Figure 21.1: Proposed method.

21.3.1 Data aggregation

Before data can be saved on the cloud, it must first pass through a variety of intermediaries. This is a prerequisite for cloud storage. Gateways and fog servers are two examples of the forms that these intermediaries can take. Patients' smartphones serve as the gateways via which their caregivers are able to monitor the patient's circumstances. This allows the caregivers to better serve their patients. On the other hand, fog servers make it possible to instantiate the system at healthcare establishments.

When they reach their destination, these servers are able to function as local hospital information systems (HIS), which simplifies the process of viewing and maintaining electronic medical records. Technologies that are based on big data processing, machine learning, and web analytics process the aggregated, anonymized data that is kept on the cloud for the purposes of knowledge extraction and statistical analysis.

Cloud services that let the sharing of data have the additional benefit of making it possible to make the information accessible to applications that are not attached to one another. This is an advantage that is not offered by services that do not permit the sharing of data.

21.3.2 Architecture

The platform's three-tiered design is made of architecture layers for the purposes of integrating devices, integrating data, as well as extracting and visualizing information. This information may be accessed through the platform.

Data consumers are not technically regarded to be a component of the platform because they are often end-users or third-party applications. For example, doctors fall into this category. Its purpose is to make it clearer how the platform may be exploited, not just by apps within the firm but also by clients who are not affiliated with the company.

21.3.3 Devices integration layer

This layer is responsible for administration, and its major duty is to integrate and combine the various clinical data sources and sensors (i.e., other EHRs or non-standardized HIS).

When we were deciding what course of action to take, we took into account the following three categories of data: The IoMT is comprised of three distinct types of medical devices, which are as follows: i) IoMT devices that comply with the OneM2M standard and send sensed data to a OneM2M gateway; (ii) IoMT devices that do not comply with the OneM2M standard and do not belong to an IoMT platform; and (iii) an IoMT platform data source entity, which is a representation of Internet of Medical Things platforms that works with various types of healthcare data (EHRs available in the HIS of healthcare institutions or other healthcare repositories).

The ability to connect the latter two categories is made feasible by data adapters, which are third-party applications that perform data collection and transformation on OpenEHR behalf. The capacity to connect the last two categories was previously impossible. Every data source requires its own adaptor, which can be stored in the cloud or at the edge of the network (in an IoMT fog server or gateway), depending on which option is more convenient (following an infrastructure and platform as a service in the IN-CSE).

21.3.4 Data integration layer

The data integration layer is accountable for ensuring that the data are consistent, have their integrity preserved during processing, and can be accessed by users. The CSE is a component of OneM2M that offers a variety of services for aggregating the data that is generated by Internet of Things devices that are part of OneM2M. However, now that adapters are available, it is possible to deliver data that was compiled using information obtained from a wide variety of other sources.

It is the job of the data coordinator to guarantee that both the OpenEHR reposi-
tory and the OpenEHR storage data warehouse are kept up-to-date, and the two entities work together to accomplish their respective goals. The OpenEHR record is then
mapped to FHIR resources so that information can be transferred using the FHIR Application Programming Interface. The data marts on the OLAP server are updated
with the new record, (ii) the data wrangling entity prepares the data for use by the
data mining tools, and (iii) data mining tools use the data.

This tier is comprised entirely of items that are web-based services that are
hosted on the cloud. Gateways and fog servers still have the capacity to construct instances of adapters, notwithstanding this fact.

21.3.5 Data visualization layer

This layer offers capabilities not only for the viewing of data but also for the extraction of insights. It is the responsibility of the organization in charge of data visualization to provide graphical user interfaces for dealing with OLAP.

This makes it possible to conduct an analysis of the data. Because of this, medical
practitioners now have the ability to easily apply analytical processing to the huge
volumes of data that have been collected by a variety of institutions and IoMT systems. This has been made possible as a direct result of the aforementioned scenario.

Software that specializes in data mining and machine learning makes it possible to
use Hadoop Map Reduce and other methods of processing big data, as well as the capability to train a wide variety of machine learning models (including, but not limited to,
decision trees, neural networks, clusters, and linear and non-linear regressions). This
software also makes it possible to train a wide variety of machine learning models.

This company offers a programming interface in order to enable individuals to
communicate with one another regarding the freshly gained knowledge regarding
models. Last but not least, the FHIR Application Programming Interface (API) provides
the REST endpoints that allow third-party applications to harvest the electronic health
records (EHRs) that are described by the FHIR standard available. This is an important function of the API.

21.3.6 Implementation

The most essential features and capabilities of the platform are described here. In this
section, a condensed overview of the most important technologies as well as the progress that has been achieved toward the proof-of-concept have been described.

The research offer a development framework that is penned in the object-oriented paradigm of C++ as a means of simplifying the process of developing AE and
binding protocols because IoMT devices are required to comply with the OneM2M

specification. This is done so because of the fact that IoMT devices are required to communicate with one another (BPs).

Extending the IoMTSensor abstract class to represent the physical sensors necessitates implementing methods to obtain the sensor ID (which is obtained in the gateway and fog server following a registration process), read an observation value, retrieve the unit of measure associated with the observations, and obtain a friendly measure name.

In addition, the IoMTSensor abstract class must be extended to include a method to obtain a friendly measure name (such as temperature, blood pressure, among other names). Other ways involve reading a value from an observation, receiving the unit of measure that is linked with the observations, and obtaining a measure name that is user-friendly (such as temperature or blood pressure, among others).

In order to define unique or personalized OneM2M binding protocols, it is necessary to extend the BindingProtocol abstract class. The SendValue, Connect, and Set Communication Devices methods will need to be reinterpreted according to these protocols.

By expanding the capabilities of their current methods, this development framework has already provided these classes with the ability to support MQTT, CoAP, and REST BPs. There is no way to access a network remotely unless the essential communication is established and the framework supports implementing Wi-Fi, GSM, and Ethernet modules. If the essential communication is not implemented, then there is no way to access the network remotely; it is impossible to do anything else.

The ApplicationEntity class is the one that oversees managing the monitoring procedure, and it provides features such as time tracking via the Universal Coordinated Time format and the Network Time Protocol (NTP) services, in addition to the conversion of sensor observations into the data format known as SenML (Sensor Markup Language). The ApplicationEntity class offers the user access to these functions so they can make use of them.

21.3.7 Quantum learning

Since the introduction of quantum algorithms [22–29], the field of algorithm development has been the focus of a significant amount of attention and investigation. The question of how to incorporate the benefits of quantum computing, which includes increased capacity for both storage and computation, into the algorithms that are currently in use has received a lot of attention and focus recently [30–35].

Given that the development of intelligent algorithms has been a primary focus for a substantial amount of time, it is only natural to support the utilization of quantum theory with intelligent computers. The inadequacies of the intelligent algorithm will be properly compensated for with the assistance of the possibilities offered by quantum parallel computing.

The Quantum Evolutionary Algorithm (QEA) is a novel evolutionary algorithm that employs a technique that is developed from quantum computing. Combining quantum computing with evolutionary computing became a theoretical possibility after the introduction of the concept of quantum genetic algorithms, which opened the door to the potential of doing so.

Using the one-of-a-kind features of quantum computing enables already sophisticated optimization algorithms to attain the same level of intelligence as quantum computing. This is a significant step forward in the development of artificial intelligence. The term quantum optimization refers to an approach to optimization that makes use of the benefits of quantum computing while maintaining the powerful global search capabilities and extraordinary robustness of intelligent algorithms.

Quantum optimization is also known as quantum computing optimization. One technique to dramatically raise the effectiveness of intelligent optimization is by making use of a quantum mechanism's capacity for parallel computing, to increase the population diversity and the pace at which it searches. Increasing the extent of the search space is one way in which this objective might be met.

The Quantum Evolutionary Algorithm, commonly known as QEA, is a novel form of evolutionary algorithm that makes use of the basics of quantum computing. This form of evolutionary algorithm is also known as QEA. A genetic algorithm with the fundamentals of quantum physics was able to successfully complete a task that was a first in its field.

The study of quantum genetic algorithms and the convergence of evolutionary computation and quantum computation are now open topics of discussion as a direct outcome of this action. In comparison to traditional methods, which are lacking in these areas, QEA excels in a number of areas, including rich population variety, large global search capacity, rapid convergence, and simple integration with other algorithms. These are just some of the areas in which traditional methods fall short. In the most recent few decades, QEA has been the focus of a considerable amount of interest and has produced successful results as a result of this attention.

The application of QEA makes it possible for a quantum chromosome to represent a superposition of several states, which ultimately results in greater population variability than is attainable through the use of conventional evolutionary approaches. Even though the total number of members in the QEA population is very low, the population genetic variation may be maintained with just a single member because to the one-of-a-kind encoding mechanism that the population uses. In addition to this, it is more suited to the use of parallel architecture, which boosts the efficiency of the searches. This is a significant advantage.

It is conceivable to encode each and every unique member of the population with quantum bits by making use of QEA, which is founded on the concept of quantum rotation gates. The notation $Q(t)$ is used to refer to quantum populations, where t stands for the iteration that is currently being performed and n is the total population size. The notation that follows can be used to accurately represent the jth member.

If you change each bit so that it reads zero, the amplitude will be zero, but if you change it so that it reads one, the amplitude will be one. Changing each bit so that it reads zero will result in an amplitude of zero. In addition, the equation $\alpha^2 + \beta^2 = 1$ is valid for each of the columns when applied to themselves. This encoding strategy makes it possible for a quantum chromosome to express 2 m probabilistic amplitudes, which indicates that the information storage capacity of chromosomes in evolutionary algorithms can be improved as a direct result of applying this strategy. As the quantum chromosome gets closer to either 0 or 1, it will finally settle on a solution that is determined by chance alone.

The QEA that is based on quantum gates makes use of quantum coding and updates that are produced by quantum gates in order to generate iterations that are more likely, while still improving upon previous iterations. Because quantum chromosomes have been incorporated into QEA, the robustness of the algorithm as well as its ability to perform parallel processing has been significantly enhanced. Due to the high degree of parallelism inherent in the methodology as well as the restricted communication that takes place between quantum chromosomes, QEA is positioned to be a potentially helpful instrument for the management of huge datasets.

21.4 Results and discussion

Using Tiny OS, we are going to construct an approximation of a performance projection for the methodology that was described in this part. The experimental setup that was provided for the method investigates the energy consumption model in terms of discrete power. The MICA2 mote and the small operating system, which were designed especially for low-power wireless devices, work together to make this possible. Within an area that is one hundred meters by one hundred meters, we have modeled anything from fifty to one hundred nodes, and the radio range of each sensor node was set to fifty meters.

Utilizing important performance parameters such as the ratio of delivered packets, the ratio of dropped packets, the lifetime of the network, and the energy usage is how the performance analysis of the offered method is displayed.

It is possible that the mechanism that is now being utilized to manage the cluster head will become inefficient if the number of nodes that are part of the cluster continues to grow. The findings of the simulation indicate that putting into practice the method that was suggested results in both an increase in the accuracy of the estimates and a decrease in the degree to which they are subject to variation.

It has led to a decrease in both the amount of energy that is consumed and the costs that are incurred to run the business. Even if the upgrade brings everything up to the next level, there is still work to be done on the system to guarantee that the best outcomes possible are being given. This is true even if the upgrade gets everything up to the next level as shown in Figures 21.2 and 21.3.

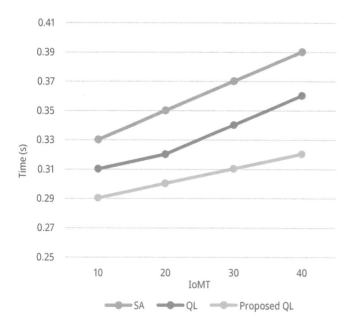

Figure 21.2: Computational complexity.

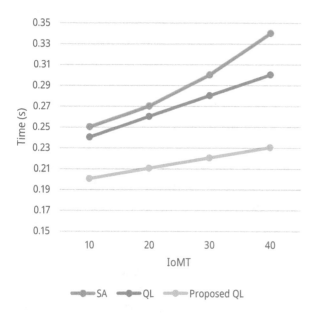

Figure 21.3: Communication complexity.

In addition, the SDA-PCA methodology is implemented so that secure data aggregation can be carried out. Using this strategy throughout the entire procedure protects not only the privacy of the data but also its completeness and accuracy. When it comes to the protection of sensitive information, the use of suitable analysis ultimately leads to the achievement of a result that is more satisfactory.

The experimental result that was obtained reveals that the proposed method provides superior performance to the existing methodologies in terms of packet delivery ratio, packet dropping ratio, residual energy, network lifetime, and energy consumption. This is observable from the fact that the results of the experiment were obtained as in Figures 21.4 and 21.5.

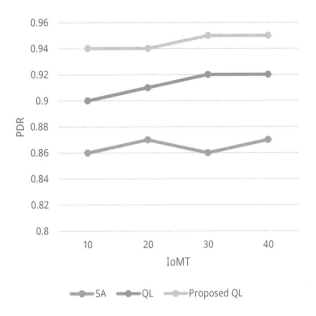

Figure 21.4: PDR.

Figures 21.6–21.7 shows the results of the confusion matrix of SA. Figure 21.8 shows the results of the confusion matrix of QL. Figure 21.5 shows the results of the confusion matrix of the proposed QL and Figure 21.9 shows the results of the classified results of the proposed QL with 50 IoMT devices. From the results, it is found that the proposed method achieves a higher rate of classification accuracy than the other methods.

The idea of latency was analyzed at the application layer, which is an extremely important aspect to take into consideration as part of this research. A number of factors come into play, including the amount of work done by the IoMT device, the fog server, and the cloud infrastructure.

Once a message has been processed, there is a possibility that the latency will lengthen as a result of delays in queuing and processing. Another issue that may have

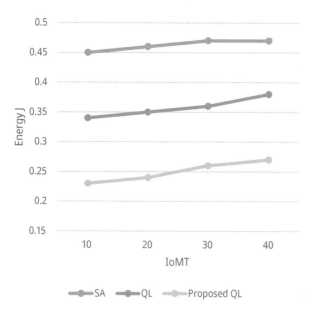

Figure 21.5: Energy consumption.

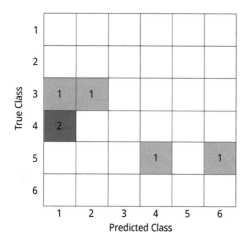

Figure 21.6: Confusion matrix of SA.

an effect on the findings is the amount of processing work involved in converting SenML signals into prototype OpenEHR observations.

When it comes to the delivery of predetermined payloads in an autonomous environment, free of interference from other actors, the findings of several earlier studies have confirmed the performance of the CoAP, MQTT, and REST protocols, despite the

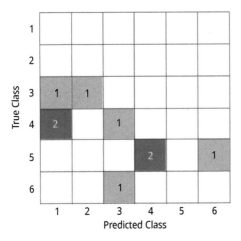

Figure 21.7: Confusion matrix of QL.

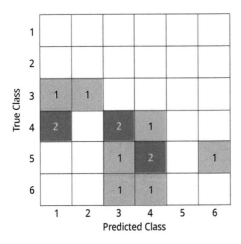

Figure 21.8: Confusion matrix of the proposed QL.

fact that those findings differ from those found in this work. However, the conclusions of those earlier studies have been confirmed by the findings of this work.

We would want to see the suggested platform validated in a real-world situation where performance is affected by considerations such as those described in the previous sentence. This is our preference. As a direct consequence of this, more accurate criteria for evaluating the performance of the platform are able to be established.

It would be advantageous to evaluate our proposal in light of the current state-of-the-art technology by carrying out a performance comparison with platforms that are equivalent to one another. In other words, it would be beneficial to analyze our idea in light of the current state-of-the-art technology. Because of the disparities in platform

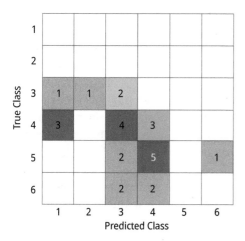

Figure 21.9: Classified results of the proposed QL with 50 IoMT devices.

goals, network architectures, and topologies, to name just a few of the variables that contribute to this issue, it is difficult, if not impossible, to create a direct comparison.

In addition, over the course of this investigation, open-source healthcare platforms were unable to be located. As a consequence of this, in order to carry out an analysis that can be relied upon, it would be necessary to get started on the process of developing alternative platforms.

It was discovered that many healthcare platforms have a propensity to concentrate on the treatment of a particular illness, and that they frequently use proprietary data formats and protocols, both of which are incompatible with our proposal. Another finding was that many healthcare platforms have a tendency to focus on the prevention of illness.

Through adhering to generally accepted standards, supporting semantic interoperability, and taking into account an approach that is based on big data, our platform intends to cover the entirety of the healthcare business. This aim will be accomplished by facilitating semantic interoperability.

The findings could potentially have some influence on applications that have tight criteria for very low latency. The CoAP BP protocol produced the greatest results in terms of latency, but it is not adequate for telesurgery or other applications that require extremely low latency. As a result of the facts presented here, we are able to draw the conclusion that systems make it possible for BPs to utilize unconventional communication protocols.

In any event, the platform that was suggested to be used is not designed to be utilized in such a manner, and the preliminary findings from the testing on the standardization, processing, and exchange of healthcare data have been positive. The solution is capable of satisfying the latency requirements for remote omnipresent monitoring as well as the needs for data aggregation from wearable IoMT sensors.

21.5 Conclusion

In this chapter, the benefits of utilizing an evolutionary approach to provide quality assurance data are broken down and explained in further detail. In the beginning, the best nodes in the network are chosen based on a variety of characteristics, such as mobility, node degree, energy level, and the quality of sensor nodes. In addition, the best nodes are selected. During this time, we are focusing our efforts on locating and expelling any hostile actor that could be active within the network. The procedure for clustering begins with the node that possesses the most desirable qualities. In this particular situation, the clustering process is carried out by the proposed QL algorithm in order to lower the quantity of power that is consumed by the network and to increase the network lifespan. These two goals are mutually supportive and work together to achieve the intended effect.

References

[1]   S. Rubí, J. N., & L. Gondim, P. R. (2019). IoMT platform for pervasive healthcare data aggregation, processing, and sharing based on OneM2M and OpenEHR. *Sensors, 19*(19), 4283.

[2]   Azeem, M., Ullah, A., Ashraf, H., Jhanjhi, N. Z., Humayun, M., Aljahdali, S., & Tabbakh, T. A. (2021). FoG-oriented secure and lightweight data aggregation in IoMT. *IEEE Access, 9*, 111072–111082.

[3]   Usman, M., Jan, M. A., He, X., & Chen, J. (2019). P2DCA: A privacy-preserving-based data collection and analysis framework for IoMT applications. *IEEE Journal on Selected Areas in Communications, 37*(6), 1222–1230.

[4]   Ullah, A., Azeem, M., Ashraf, H., Alaboudi, A. A., Humayun, M., & Jhanjhi, N. Z. (2021). Secure healthcare data aggregation and transmission in IoT – A survey. *IEEE Access, 9*, 16849–16865.

[5]   Arul, R., Al-Otaibi, Y. D., Alnumay, W. S., Tariq, U., Shoaib, U., & Piran, M. D. (2021). Multi-modal Secure Healthcare Data Dissemination Framework Using Blockchain in IoMT. In: Personal and Ubiquitous Computing, 1–13.

[6]   Yadav, S.P. (2022). Blockchain Security. In: Baalamurugan, K., Kumar, S.R., Kumar, A., Kumar, V., Padmanaban, S. (eds) Blockchain Security in Cloud Computing. EAI/Springer Innovations in Communication and Computing. Springer, Cham. https://doi.org/10.1007/978-3-030-70501-5_1

[7]   Khosravi, M. R. (2021). ACI: A bar chart index for non-linear visualization of data embedding and aggregation capacity in IoMT multi-source compression. *Wireless Networks*, 1–9.

[8]   Yadav, S. P., Bhati, B. S., Mahato, D. P., Kumar, S. (eds). Federated Learning for IoT Applications. EAI/ Springer Innovations in Communication and Computing. Springer, Cham. https://doi.org/10.1007/978-3-030-85559-8

[9]   Yuan, X., Zhang, Z., Feng, C., Cui, Y., Garg, S., Kaddoum, G., & Yu, K. (2022). A DQN-based frame aggregation and task offloading approach for edge-enabled IoMT. *IEEE Transactions on Network Science and Engineering*.

[10] Gobinathan, B., Mukunthan, M. A., Surendran, S., Somasundaram, K., Moeed, S. A., Niranjan, P., . . . & Sundramurthy, V. P. (2021). A Novel Method to Solve Real Time Security Issues in Software Industry Using Advanced Cryptographic Techniques. Scientific Programming, 2021

[11] Xiong, H., Jin, C., Alazab, M., Yeh, K. H., Wang, H., Gadekallu, T. R., . . . & Su, C. (2021). On the design of blockchain-based ECDSA with fault-tolerant batch verification protocol for blockchain-enabled IoMT. *IEEE Journal of Biomedical and Health Informatics, 26*(5), 1977–1986.

[12] Saravanan, V., Rajeshwari, S., & Jayashree, P. (2013). Security issues in protecting computers and maintenance. *Journal of Global Research in Computer Science, 4*(1),55–58.

[13] Nikolaidou, M., Kotronis, C., Routis, I., Politi, E., Dimitrakopoulos, G., Anagnostopoulos, D., . . . & Bensaali, F. (2021). Incorporating patient concerns into design requirements for IoMT-based systems: The fall detection case study. *Health Informatics Journal, 27*(1), 1460458220982640.

[14] Yan, H., Bilal, M., Xu, X., & Vimal, S. (2022). Edge server deployment for health monitoring with reinforcement learning in internet of medical things. *IEEE Transactions on Computational Social Systems.*

[15] Kumar, A., Sharma, K., & Sharma, A. (2021). Genetically optimized Fuzzy C-means data clustering of IoMT-based biomarkers for fast affective state recognition in intelligent edge analytics. *Applied Soft Computing, 109*, 107525.

[16] Begum, B. A., & Nandury, S. V. (2022). A survey of data aggregation protocols for energy conservation in WSN and IoT. *Wireless Communications and Mobile Computing, 2022.*

[17] Habib, M. A., Faisal, C. N., Sarwar, S., Latif, M. A., Aadil, F., Ahmad, M., . . . & Maqsood, M. (2019). Privacy-based medical data protection against internal security threats in heterogeneous internet of medical things. *International Journal of Distributed Sensor Networks, 15*(9), 1550147719875653.

[18] Alsubaei, F., Abuhussein, A., Shandilya, V., & Shiva, S. (2019). IoMT-SAF: Internet of medical things security assessment framework. *Internet of Things, 8*, 100123.

[19] Malamas, V., Dasaklis, T., Kotzanikolaou, P., Burmester, M., & Katsikas, S. (2019). A Forensics-by-design Management Framework for Medical Devices Based on Blockchain. In: 2019 IEEE World Congress on Services (SERVICES) (Vol. 2642, pp. 35–40). IEEE.

[20] Manogaran, G., & Lopez, D. (2017). A survey of big data architectures and machine learning algorithms in healthcare. *International Journal of Biomedical Engineering and Technology, 25*(2-4), 182–211.

[21] Alabdulatif, A., Khalil, I., Yi, X., & Guizani, M. (2019). Secure edge of things for smart healthcare surveillance framework. *IEEE Access, 7*, 31010–31021.

[22] Li, G., Song, Z., & Wang, X. (2021). VSQL: Variational Shadow Quantum Learning for Classification. In: Proceedings of the AAAI Conference on Artificial Intelligence (Vol. 35, No. 9, pp. 8357–8365).

[23] Zhu, E. Y., Johri, S., Bacon, D., Esencan, M., Kim, J., Muir, M., . . . & Wright, K. (2022). Generative quantum learning of joint probability distribution functions. *Physical Review Research, 4*(4), 043092.

[24] Pritscher, C. P. (2021). *Quantum Learning: Beyond Duality*. Brill.

[25] Tran, Q. H., & Nakajima, K. (2021). Learning temporal quantum tomography. *Physical Review Letters, 127*(26), 260401.

[26] Liu, J., Tacchino, F., Glick, J. R., Jiang, L., & Mezzacapo, A. (2022). Representation learning via quantum neural tangent kernels. *PRX Quantum, 3*(3), 030323.

[27] Mangini, S., Tacchino, F., Gerace, D., Bajoni, D., & Macchiavello, C. (2021). Quantum computing models for artificial neural networks. *Europhysics Letters, 134*(1), 10002.

[28] Jerbi, S., Gyurik, C., Marshall, S., Briegel, H. J., & Dunjko, V. (2021). Variational quantum policies for reinforcement learning. *ArXiv Preprint arXiv:2103.05577.*

[29] Arunachalam, S., Grilo, A. B., & Sundaram, A. (2021). Quantum hardness of learning shallow classical circuits. *SIAM Journal on Computing, 50*(3), 972–1013.

[30] Adil, M., Khan, M. K., Jadoon, M. M., Attique, M., Song, H., & Farouk, A. (2022). An AI-enabled hybrid lightweight authentication scheme for intelligent IoMT based cyber-physical systems. *IEEE Transactions on Network Science and Engineering.*

[31] Rehman, A., Abbas, S., Khan, M. A., Ghazal, T. M., Adnan, K. M., & Mosavi, A. (2022). A secure healthcare 5.0 system based on blockchain technology entangled with federated learning technique. *Computers in Biology and Medicine*, *150*, 106019.

[32] Hermawan, D., Putri, N. M. D. K., & Kartanto, L. (2022). Cyber physical system based smart healthcare system with federated deep learning architectures with data analytics. *International Journal of Communication Networks and Information Security*, *14*(2), 222–233.

[33] Kavitha, D., Vidhya, A., Prema, V., Priyadharshini, M., Kumaresan, G., & Sangeetha, G. (2022). An efficient IoMT based health monitoring using complex valued deep CNN and political optimizer. *Transactions on Emerging Telecommunications Technologies*, e4610.

[34] Sadhu, P. K., Yanambaka, V. P., Abdelgawad, A., & Yelamarthi, K. (2022). Prospect of internet of medical things: A review on security requirements and solutions. *Sensors*, *22*(15), 5517.

[35] Muneeswari, G., Hegde, R., & Prasanth, A. (2022). Self-diagnosis platform via IOT-based privacy preserving medical data. *Measurement: Sensors*, 100636.

Index

https://doi.org/10.1515/9783110798159-022

Quantum computing (QC)

Already published in the series

Pethuru Raj, Abhishek Kumar, Ashutosh Kumar Dubey, Surbhi Bhatia and Oswalt Manoj S (Eds.)
Quantum Computing and Artificial Intelligence
ISBN 978-3-11-079125-9, e-ISBN (PDF) 978-3-11-079140-2,
e-ISBN (EPUB) 978-3-11-079147-1